The Liberal Proj[Human Rights

The 'Liberal Project' aims to transform society in accordance with liberal values and practices. This volume argues that the United Nations regime on human rights is an attempt to realize this project on an international level. The authors provide an engaging theoretical and historical context for this argument, defining the concept of liberalism, its origins and evolution, and identify it as a universal value that constitutes the very essence of the international human rights regime. The book explores the possibility of a cross-cultural consensus on the issue being reached, but problems of sovereignty and nationalism are also discussed as potential obstacles to the liberal project's completion. This penetrating and insightful work will appeal to a wide range of scholars and students interested in liberalism and human rights from the fields of international relations, law, political theory and political philosophy.

JOHN CHARVET is Emeritus Professor of Political Science at the London School of Economics.

ELISA KACZYNSKA-NAY is a lawyer and researcher in economic development and international law.

The Liberal Project and Human Rights

The Theory and Practice of
a New World Order

JOHN CHARVET AND ELISA KACZYNSKA-NAY

CAMBRIDGE
UNIVERSITY PRESS

CAMBRIDGE UNIVERSITY PRESS
Cambridge, New York, Melbourne, Madrid, Cape Town, Singapore, São Paulo, Delhi

Cambridge University Press
The Edinburgh Building, Cambridge CB2 8RU, UK

Published in the United States of America by Cambridge University Press, New York

www.cambridge.org
Information on this title: www.cambridge.org/9780521883146

© John Charvet and Elisa Kaczynska-Nay 2008

First published 2008

Printed in the United Kingdom at the University Press, Cambridge

A catalogue record for this publication is available from the British Library

Library of Congress Cataloguing in Publication data
Charvet, John.
The liberal project and human rights : the theory and practice of a new world order /
John Charvet, Elisa Kaczynska-Nay.
p. cm.
Includes bibliographical references and index.
ISBN 978-0-521-88314-6 (hardback) – ISBN 978-0-521-70959-0 (pbk.)
1. Liberalism. 2. Human rights. I. Kaczynska-Nay, Elisa. II. Title.
JC574.C4853 2008
320.51'3–dc22
2008038191

ISBN 978-0-521-88314-6 hardback
ISBN 978-0-521-70959-0 paperback

*For our children and grandchildren
Emma and Rosa, Vera and Oliver and
in memory of Guy*

Contents

Abbreviations

ACHPR	African Charter on Human and Peoples' Rights
ACtHPR	African Court on Human and Peoples' Rights
ACHR	American Convention on Human Rights
ADF	African Development Fund
BLIHR	Business Leaders Initiative on Human Rights
CAR	Central African Republic
CCA	Common Country Assessment
CDF	Comprehensive Development Framework
CEDAW	Convention on the Elimination of All Forms of Discrimination Against Women
CERD	Convention on the Elimination of All Forms of Racial Discrimination
CESCR	Committee on Economic, Social and Cultural Rights
CHR	Commission on Human Rights
CIS	Commonwealth of Independent States
CMCOE	Committee of Ministers of the Council of Europe
COE	Council of Europe
CP	Cultural and Political
DAC	Development Assistance Committee
DAF	Development Assistance Framework
DPI	Department of Public Information
DRC	Democratic Republic of Congo
E7	Seven largest emerging market economies (China, India, Brazil, Russia, Indonesia, Mexico and Turkey)
ECHR	European Convention on Human Rights
ECOSOC	Economic and Social Council
ECOWAS	Economic Community of West African States
ESC	Economic, Social and Cultural
FDI	Foreign Direct Investment
FRY	Federal Republic of Yugoslavia
G7	US, Japan, Germany, UK, France, Italy and Canada

GA	General Assembly
GATT	General Agreement on Trade and Tariffs
GDP	Gross Domestic Product
GNP	Gross National Product
HAP-I	Humanitarian Partnership Accountability International
HCHR	High Commissioner for Human Rights
HDI	Human Development Index
HIPC	Heavily Indebted Poor Countries
HRC	Human Rights Council
HRDR	Human Rights Development Report
HRIA	Human Rights Impact Assessment
IACHR	Inter-American Commission on Human Rights
IBRD	International Bank for Reconstruction and Development
ICC	International Criminal Court
ICCPR	International Covenant on Civil and Political Rights
ICESCR	International Covenant on Economic, Social and Cultural Rights
ICISS	International Commission on Intervention and State Sovereignty
ICJ	International Court of Justice
ICTR	International Criminal Tribunal for Rwanda
ICTY	International Criminal Tribunal for Yugoslavia
IDA	International Development Association
IFC	International Finance Corporation
IFRC	International Federation of Red Cross and Red Cross Societies
IGOs	International Governmental Organizations
ILO	International Labour Organization
IMF	International Monetary Fund
INGOs	International Non-Governmental Organizations
LRA	Lord's Resistance Army
MDGs	Millennium Development Goals
MDRI	Multilateral Debt Relief Initiative
MICs	Middle-Income Countries
MIGA	Multilateral International Guarantee Agency
NAM	Non-Aligned Movement
NATO	North Atlantic Treaty Organization
NGO	Non-Governmental Organizations
NIEO	New International Economic Order

OAS	Organization of American States
OAU	Organization of African Unity
ODA	Official Development Assistance
OECD	Organisation for Economic Co-operation and Development
OEWG	Open-Ended Working Group
OHCHR	Office of the High Commissioner for Human Rights
PDD	Presidential Decision Directive
PRSPs	Poverty Reduction Strategy Papers
R2P	Responsibility to Protect
RTD	Right to Development
SC	Security Council
SPIRI	Stockholm International Peace Research Institute
TNCs	Transnational Corporations
UDHR	Universal Declaration of Human Rights
UN	United Nations
UNCCAs	UN Common Country Assessments
UNCF	UN Children's Fund
UNCTAD	UN Conference on Trade and Development
UNDP	UN Development Programme
UNESCO	UN Educational, Scientific and Cultural Organization
UNGA	UN General Assembly
UNHRC	UN Human Rights Committee
WDR	World Development Report
WHO	World Health Organization
WTO	World Trade Organization
WWF	World Wildlife Fund
WWI	World War I
WWII	World War II

Preface

Our concern in this book is with rights-based liberalism as a way for human beings to live together in peace and justice at both the domestic and international levels. Our aim is to explain its theory and practice but also to defend and commend it as a better way than alternative schemes of human association.

The heart of what we call the liberal project for world order has now become the United Nations human rights regime, the discussion and evaluation of which constitutes the centre of this study. Many books have been written on this regime on the one hand and on liberalism on the other. A few combine the two: the best of which being J. Donnelly's *Universal Human Rights in Theory and Practice*. There is also an excellent book on the evolution of international human rights in Lauren's work of that title. However, what is distinctive about our book is that it situates the UN human rights regime in the context of an evolving international society of sovereign states, the character of which we see as shot through with liberal assumptions. We show this by exhibiting the nature of liberalism as a theory and by revealing the affinities between liberal theory and the developing practice of state sovereignty both domestically and internationally.

After an introduction in which we explain what we understand liberalism to be, Part I is a study of the historical context from the seventeenth century, covering both early rights-based liberal theory and state practice in which the UN commitment to a strong human rights programme came to be made. Part II is devoted to an account of the UN regime, understood in a broad sense to include the international human rights activities of regional organizations, liberal states and international non-governmental organizations whose influence is significantly dependent on the existence of the UN regime. While we examine in some detail the content and implementation of the main rights, a major concern of ours is how they relate to and form part of the liberal scheme.

Part III is a theoretical defence of liberal human rights against liberalism's critics. Chapter 9 examines the principal attacks on liberalism in the Western intellectual tradition. Chapter 10 discusses the conflict between liberal human rights and some major non-Western ethical cultures and explores the resources in these cultures for accommodating the liberal ethic and, consequently, for arriving at an international consensus on liberal values from different cultural perspectives. Finally, Chapter 11 draws together the main points made against liberalism's critics and attempts to get to the root of ethico-political hostility to liberalism.

While both authors endorse the general approach and line of argument of each part of the work, John Charvet, as a political theorist, has been responsible for the introduction, Parts I and III and the more theoretical sections of Part II, and Elisa Kaczynska-Nay, as an economist and international lawyer, has written most of Part II.

Many colleagues, students and authors have over the years contributed substantially to the development of our ideas on the issues covered in this book. This includes the students on the course we both taught at the LSE summer school on the theory and practice of international human rights. To name them all would be impossible but without such a background and inspiration this work could not have been written. However, we are particularly indebted for reading and commenting on parts or the whole of versions of this work to John Braithwaite, Anne Charvet, Po-chung Chow, Sheila Fitzgerald, David-Lloyd Thomas and Axel Seemann. They have kindly attempted to save us from error and cannot be held responsible for the many that undoubtedly remain.

Introduction: what is liberalism?

Liberalism and free individual choice

We take a wide rather than a narrow view of what liberalism is. As we see it, liberalism is a disputatious family of doctrines, which nevertheless share some core principles. These principles are by now – at least in the West – hardly new. But they constitute a radically different way of understanding and organizing the best scheme of human association from the many other understandings that have been produced in the course of human history in Western and other civilizations. While liberal doctrines and practices are at present well established in the West, it should not be forgotten how recently they were threatened with extinction in their heartlands. They are still constantly under attack and are often not well understood, in part because of the tendency to identify liberalism with one or other member of the family only – a tendency that in America makes liberalism out to be a politically leftist doctrine of state welfare and state intervention, while in contemporary France it has become associated with the supposedly *laissez-faire* policies of recent Anglo-Saxon governments. Part of what we mean by the liberal project, then, is that from a broad historical perspective liberalism is a fairly new and certainly radically different conception of social and political order from its predecessors and subsequent rivals. But the main significance of our idea of liberalism as a project for a new world order refers to the application of liberal ideas and practices to the organization of international relations principally through the human rights documents and instruments produced by, or under the patronage of, the United Nations after World War Two (WWII). The attempt to promote the general acceptance of these declarations and covenants on human rights constitutes a project for a new order both for the internal organization of the many states of the world and for the way these states relate to each other internationally.

In order to understand the idea of human rights in these documents as the expression of liberal principles, we need first to get a grasp of what liberalism is about. Liberalism in both theory and practice is concerned to promote social outcomes that are, as far as possible, the result of free individual choices. However, the choice of one person that does not respect the equal freedom and rights of others is invalid. Thus, economic liberalism in the economic sphere upholds the rights of individuals to make any choices they please in the exercise of their labour and the use of their wealth and income so long as they respect the liberty, property and contractual rights of others. Social liberalism, in general, extends this idea to all aspects of life except the political and requires freedom of thought and expression, of religion, of movement and association, of sexual orientation and ways of life,[1] all subject to the condition that the exercise of any particular freedom is to be respected only insofar as it does not violate the equal freedom of others. Equal freedom could mean, of course, everyone's unrestricted freedom to do as he or she pleases, including the 'right' to kill or injure another. However, the result would be a freedom that was constantly open to the invasion of others. The freedom of everyone can, then, be increased by the mutual acceptance of equal limits on what anyone is entitled to do. The basic content of these limits is the exclusion of force and fraud, so that interactions among human beings can take place with the free consent of each party. Coercion is justified only against someone who violates those limits.

Political liberalism cannot be understood in quite the same way, since decisions in the political sphere must, *ex hypothesi*, be collective and binding on all members of the polity. However, its foundations in respect for individual liberty remain the same. Political liberalism affirms the rights of individuals to choose their governors in periodic elections through the exercise of individual and equal votes, the right to stand for election and to associate politically as they please in order to promote the policies and parties of their choice. Political liberalism also involves the design of institutions that will provide some guarantee of government accountability to the people and will limit the government's power to attack or erode individual liberty. The standard devices for this purpose have been the institutions of representative government and the separation of the legislative, executive and judicial powers.

Liberalism and human rights

Liberalism, then, consists in the structuring of individual interactions in society on the basis of a set of rights that require human beings to respect each other's liberty and equality. These rights do not have to be expressed as natural or human rights. There are liberal theories that defend the adoption of such rights on the grounds that societies so organized will achieve a greater sum of utility or happiness than any alternative social scheme. British thinkers, such as Jeremy Bentham and John Stuart Mill in the eighteenth and nineteenth centuries, have been very influential liberal theorists in the utilitarian tradition. The other major source of theoretical support for the liberal organization of society has been the belief in natural rights as developed by innovative theorists of the seventeenth century, such as Hugo Grotius in the Netherlands, Samuel Pufendorf in Germany and Thomas Hobbes and John Locke in England. Human beings, on this view, have a fundamental natural right to liberty consisting in the right to do whatever they think fit to preserve themselves, provided they do not violate the equal liberty of others unless their own preservation is threatened. This tradition may be said to have been transformed and rationalized by the immensely influential liberal theory of Immanuel Kant at the end of the eighteenth and beginning of the nineteenth centuries.

Nevertheless, the theories that came to dominate the nineteenth century were utilitarian and historicist. The weaknesses of these theories in upholding basic liberal rights together with a developing scepticism in the twentieth century as to the feasibility of adequately grounding justificatory theories of ethics and politics at all, led to the situation that liberal societies have faced since the rise in the 1930s of various forms of totalitarian terror. There was a strongly felt need to reaffirm the overriding importance of basic liberal rights and indeed to develop legal instruments whereby these rights could be given special protection. At the same time there was little agreement on how or even whether the belief in such rights could be theoretically justified. The result has been the flowering of a theoretically ungrounded language and practice of human rights since the end of WWII. Talk about such rights has become the dominant form of liberal practice in Western societies and the United Nations has committed itself to the attempt to spread this practice around the world.

These rights are believed, like natural rights, to be the inherent rights of human beings. This means that individuals are entitled to enjoy such rights by virtue of their nature and dignity as human beings. Thus, the 1948 United Nations Universal Declaration of Human Rights, which has acquired iconic status for the contemporary Human Rights movement, affirms in its Article 1 that 'All human beings are born free and equal in dignity and rights. They are endowed with reason and conscience and should act towards one another in the spirit of brotherhood.'[2] In this sense, human beings possess these rights whether or not the rights are recognized in the politico-legal system of which they are members and to which they are subject. A politico-legal system that does not respect such rights is in violation of fundamental ethical requirements.

A standard criticism of the natural/human rights view of inherent rights that a human being is born with consists in asking where these rights come from if they are not recognized in any actual legal system. The traditional answer of natural rights theorists was that they are aspects of a natural law that is binding on all human beings everywhere. There are two crucial features of this answer. The first involves the claim that there are universally applicable general rules or principles of conduct for human beings and the second that such rules or principles have overriding moral authority. They command human beings to respect the rights arising from these rules in all their practices and associations. With regard to the first, we will have much to say in due course but the fundamental rule is one of equal liberty, the rationality and utility of which each human being can grasp for him or herself. In respect of the second, the answer given by the natural rights theorists was that the rules' authority came ultimately from being commanded by God.

As we have already indicated, contemporary supporters of the human rights regimes of the United Nations, the European Convention, and so on, tend to put aside the question of ethical justification and appeal to the fact that these rights have been recognized by the international community and are embedded in international legal instruments. Thus, they are said to be grounded in actual practices.[3] However, the consensus presupposed is to some degree illusory. While all states pay lip service to human rights, some engage in massive violations of them without compunction and others claim to interpret the human rights in the light of their own prior ethical or religious commitments, such as Islamic Law or so-called Asian values. This has the effect of severely constraining the liberal force of the UN programme by subordinating the principle of maximal equal liberty to the hierarchical values of traditional Islam and Asian Community. Furthermore, even if there existed at the present time a genuine consensus on the liberal meaning of human rights, the absence of any ethical justification of the practice leaves it vulnerable to shifts in opinion. Such shifts have occurred in the recent past in Western societies with near catastrophic consequences and the spirit of anti-liberalism continues to exist as a strong undercurrent in them. It is for this reason that an essential part of our object in this work is to defend as well as explain the liberal character of the human rights regimes.

The liberal project, as we understand it then, has as its aim the transformation of the basic structure of the separate modern societies and of the international society they together constitute, so that they all come to express liberal values. It should be stressed from the outset that this is not to say that the goal is to be achieved by any means, including military ones, nor is it to say that the substantive character of the different societies is to be made the same. We will raise the question of the appropriate policies for promoting the general acceptance of liberal values in due course, and also the issue of humanitarian intervention, but we do not think that a policy of getting peoples to accept liberal-democracy by bombing them into submission is justifiable from either an ethical or a pragmatic point of view. With regard to the question of the uniformity of the different societies, there is no reason why the general acceptance of a liberal basic structure should prevent some societies being predominantly Muslim, others Christian, Buddhist, secular or whatever, so long as the adherents of these different ways of believing and living accept the fundamental principles of liberalism by treating their own members as well as outsiders as entitled to an equal liberty.

The range of liberal rights and values

The principle of equal liberty promotes social outcomes that are, as far as possible, the result of individual choice under circumstances in which all individuals can respect each other as equals. This principle makes no sense without the supporting belief that every normal adult human being has the capacity to decide for herself how she can best live her life and ought to have the right so to decide without being subject to the coercive authority of others. This belief is perfectly compatible with the recognition that some people are more intelligent than others and may make wiser or better informed choices. It is, however, to claim that such inequalities are irrelevant to the fundamental equality that all enjoy, which is to possess the capacity for self-direction to a sufficient degree that it would be wrong to coerce them to live their lives contrary to their own wishes.

We have been putting the stress, in the above remarks, on an equal liberty as the core value of liberalism. However, both the older natural rights theories and even more so the contemporary human rights documents affirm other rights besides liberty rights. For John Locke, the basic rights were to life, liberty, health and possessions, while our stress on liberty seems to leave out the whole category of welfare, or social and economic, rights that are generally considered now to be an integral part of an adequate understanding of human rights. Of direct relevance to this issue is a widely made distinction between classical liberalism and revisionist or new liberalism. On this distinction, classical liberalism upheld the *laissez-faire* economy and the night watchman state, while the new liberalism became concerned with ensuring that everyone enjoyed a sufficient level of social and economic rights in order to be able to exercise their liberty effectively as an equal member of society. In effect, the assumption the new liberalism makes is that the adequate development in each person of their capacity for self-direction standardly requires a certain level of educational opportunity and social welfare, so that access to such levels constitutes a crucial aspect of their rights to be recognized as an equally valuable self-directing being.

In this way, the fundamental values of the new liberalism remained the same as those of classical liberalism: namely liberty and equality. Hence, we can still affirm the foundation of liberalism in an equal freedom while embracing welfare rights as the necessary condition of their adequate realization. What about the Lockean conception of basic rights as those of life, health and possessions as well as liberty? This suggests that life, health and possessions are to be treated as valuable in themselves independently of their relation to liberty. Nevertheless, we think that it is clear enough in Locke's scheme that it is not just life and health as such that are valuable in themselves but the life and health of human beings who are understood as rational, self-directing beings and hence entitled to an equal liberty. Otherwise, animal life and health would be seen as equally valuable as human life and health. Furthermore, the right to possessions is justified explicitly by Locke in terms of the right to self-preservation and is to be exercised through acts of individual liberty in appropriating parts of the earth's surface. In other words, rights to life, liberty, health and possessions can all be seen as implications of the fundamental value of humans as rational, self-directing beings. This shows, we believe, that the primary liberal values in the classical liberalism of Locke, at least, were indeed liberty and equality, where liberty is to be understood both in positive terms as the realized capacity for self-government and in negative terms as not being prevented by other human beings from doing what one chooses; but that there was space, also, even in the thought of classical liberalism for considerations of welfare.

One can, nevertheless, identify a very broad family of liberal doctrines that ranges from an anarchical libertarianism at one extreme through *laissez-faire* and the minimal state to the big bureaucratic state of welfare liberalism and on to the other extreme of liberal socialism. The first departs from more mainstream liberal theories by rejecting the standard argument for the state, namely that it is necessary to elaborate and effectively enforce through a legal order a coherent system of rights based on natural rights. The liberal anarchist believes that such state functions are better left to voluntary agencies or self-help. The socialist form of liberalism, at the other extreme, rejects the economic liberalism of market society altogether on the grounds of its incompatibility with equality but otherwise affirms liberal values regarding opinion, religion, movement, association, sexual orientation, and so on. Both extremes can reasonably claim to be versions of liberalism since even their deviations from more mainstream positions are based on appeals to the core liberal values. The view we shall argue for is a form of liberalism that recognizes the necessity of the state on the one hand, and the need for a substantial degree of economic liberty together with social and economic rights on the other.

The distinctiveness and originality of liberalism

Liberalism is a theory and set of practices regarding what is a just social and political order. As such, it is concerned with the right to coerce persons to act in accordance with the requirements of just order. The mainstream liberal believes that this right is possessed by the state. A crucial function of the just state is to guarantee to the citizens that, if they act justly by complying with the rules of the just state, they will not expose themselves without reasonable protection to exploitation by the unjust. The liberal anarchist believes that the right to coerce the unjust is possessed by each individual and that to transfer that right to the state is to put oneself foolishly into the hands of a potential monster. Most liberals, however, believe that they have found a method of taming the monster and making it serve the liberal idea.

The distinctiveness and originality of liberalism, then, can be understood as an attempt to restrict the area of human life that is subject to justified state coercion to a much greater extent than alternative conceptions of the just state. This is expressed in the liberal idea of maximal equal liberty. It allows individuals to decide for themselves or in voluntary association with others, to the greatest extent possible, how they will live compatibly with everyone else enjoying an equal right. The most obvious way in which the liberal and the variety of anti-liberals are opposed is in the sphere of freedom of religion and of thought and expression more generally. The liberal holds that the belief in and practice of one religion is perfectly compatible with the freedom of all others, provided that none requires its adherents to forcibly convert, subordinate or kill the followers of other religions. Such requirements clearly violate the principle of equal freedom and cannot be permitted within a liberal scheme.

The partisan of the aggressive religion will, naturally, seek to act on what he believes is part of the true religion and hence to coerce non-believers. But even without such explicitly domineering elements in a religion, its illiberal practitioners may believe that it should be enforced on others as the common faith of a political community. This may be because it is held to be the true faith and because it is believed that it is wrong to allow people the liberty to live in error. As the early Christian philosopher, St Augustine, said: 'There is no worse death for the soul than the liberty to err.'[4] An alternative justification for coercion in matters of religion is that agreement on religious values and practices is essential to the unity and identity of a political community. This view doesn't involve the belief that the religion is true but that it is the necessary cement to hold people together in a common political life without which they would not form a coherent body at all. In addition, such an enforced scheme provides a hierarchy of values and authorities through which the members of the community can learn to subordinate their selfish interests to the good of the whole.

The liberal rejects these claims. Truth in these matters is too uncertain to justify coercing others and in any case the unbeliever is not as such harming the faithful unless unity of religious belief and practice is essential to a community's existence. However, the liberal denies that political unity depends on the maintenance of a consensus on such disputed issues. It is not that the liberal believes that consensus is altogether unnecessary, but rather that a consensus on liberal values is possible and that this consensus allows everyone to practice their religion within the limits of an equal liberty.

What is true of religious disagreement applies also for the liberal to disagreement over other substantive values and ways of life. The liberal demands agreement on certain higher order or 'thin' values, namely the scheme of equal liberty, but this permits disagreement on substantive values such as different conceptions of the religious life, of non-religious or secular lives directed at pleasure or achievement, art or play, self-assertion or serving others, knowledge or wealth. The liberal is a pluralist in respect of such values. There are many different human goods and ways of life and there is no objectively determined hierarchy of values that subordinates some to others. So, it is wrong to base the state's coercive order on the superiority of one of these substantive conceptions of the good life for human beings. Liberalism is the idea that people should be free to choose what values to pursue in their lives provided that they pursue them within the limits of an equal liberty.

On this view, there will always be a bedrock of liberal values in a liberal community that underlies and constrains the choices that its individual members make. These are liberty and equality and the fundamental respect for human beings as autonomous choosers that grounds their entitlement to an equal freedom. This agreement on a scheme of co-operation that permits people to live together in peace while disagreeing over substantive questions of religion and other values is indeed the essential point of liberalism as a distinctive form of social and political order. Liberalism holds, first, that human beings do not need to construct the necessary socio-political consensus for community on such divisive bases as religion. This leads to devastating conflicts and unnecessarily high levels of coercion and suffering.

Liberalism holds, second, that it is in any case wrong to coerce people in these matters because such coercion does not respect their nature as free choosers. The value of each as a free chooser is an integral part of whatever value is chosen insofar as what is chosen is due respect.

Liberalism and the subjectivity of value

It may look as though liberalism, as we have been presenting it, involves a subjectivist conception of value. What is valuable is whatever is chosen by individuals in the exercise of their lawful freedom. This apparent subjectivism may be repugnant to some people. However, in the first place, what is chosen in violation of lawful freedom is not valuable. Liberals should hence not think that their own fundamental principles are a matter of subjective choice. They should believe in the objective superiority of their conception of the realm of higher order or 'thin' values on which legitimate political coercion is based. If they did not believe this, they could not justify liberal coercion with a good conscience. They could at most say that, as liberalism is the dominant belief in our community and community has to be based on some kind of coercive order, then we can impose it on everyone. But, this provides no ground for defending liberalism should the community move towards anti-liberalism or even should the anti-liberal minority seek to win power and impose its conception of order. For the appeal to the majority is only an invocation of superior power, unless backed by some set of reasons, that the minority could prove wrong.

In the second place, liberals should not be subjectivists even in respect of substantive values. What they should be is pluralists in respect of values. A pluralist believes that there exists a range of objective or natural goods for human beings. These are the goods through the enjoyment of which human beings can lead flourishing lives. This enables us to be confident in asserting, for instance, the worthlessness of a life of compulsive gambling. Nevertheless, there are many different valuable lives that human beings can lead and there is no unique ranking or combination of values that individuals must choose if they are to live well. On the contrary, it is up to the individual to choose which of the range of human goods to pursue or to what extent to pursue them. The list of such goods standardly includes love, beauty, art, friendship, family, knowledge, play, pleasure, achievement, wealth, health, and so on. Liberty, equality and autonomy are the higher order values, essential to liberalism, that are not subject to choice on the same basis, since they structure the way in which the other values may legitimately be pursued. The cultivation of art, love, friendship, and so on do not justify one in violating the basic rights of others.

Equal liberty in the economic sphere

The idea of an equal liberty in respect of religion and belief more generally is that of individuals adopting ways of believing that do not limit the liberty of others. Each way of thinking is independent of the others in the sense that the practice of one does not restrict the practice of the others. Such independence does not mean that each has no interest in or interaction with the other ways. They may, quite to the contrary, be engaged in intense discussions and debate but only on the basis of free co-operation and exchange. Yet such a model of equal liberty cannot apply to economic liberty, understood as liberty of access to and control over economic resources. Since these resources will standardly be limited at any one time relative to the number of human beings seeking to control them and to their level of technology, equal liberty cannot mean that each individual can appropriate as much as he wants, provided he does not use force or fraud, without limiting the access of others. There must be more elaborate rules for determining what is to count as equal liberty in this sphere. The original natural rights theorists who thought about this subject, in particular John Locke, conceived equal economic liberty as beginning with individual appropriation of unowned nature. Locke makes such appropriation subject to the condition that enough and as good of the resource appropriated was left for others and that no resources were allowed to rot or go to waste. This would appear to restrict individual accumulation of property holdings severely, but Locke argued that the voluntary agreement to introduce money values into exchange permitted large and unequal individual accumulations that satisfied the no waste condition and also made it possible through gains in labour productivity resulting from capital accumulation for everyone to be better off than they were in the original pre-monetary situation. Thus, inequality of control over resources is justified, partly on grounds that it was the consequence of actual voluntary agreement to introduce money as a medium of exchange and store of value and partly on grounds that no one could reasonably object to the improvement in his standard of living that it creates.[5]

If we express this view in more general terms, we can say that it conceives economic liberty in terms that permit indefinite individual accumulation provided that no one falls below a level of welfare that they could have enjoyed in a primitive initial situation in which each appropriates some unowned resources and there is enough to go round. Provided all subsequent economic transactions are just on the basis of these principles and inheritance is allowed, the existing holdings of property will be just. However, since the history of property acquisition and transfer does not correspond to this story at all closely, to say the least, but has proceeded through high levels of violence and massacre, the present distribution of holdings cannot possibly be justified by these arguments.

There are various other possibilities of conceiving equal liberty in this sphere: (i) economic liberty based on existing holdings with inheritance allowed but with a degree of equality of opportunity and a welfare state (this is more or less the position adopted in contemporary liberal states); (ii) economic liberty with no inheritance but based on initially equal holdings for all members of each generation; (iii) equality of outcome or welfare. The latter will involve minimal liberty in production, since collective control over resources will be necessary to secure equality of outcome. This is in effect economic socialism. No doubt any of these general programmes can be carried out in different ways, in different combinations and to different degrees. It is also the case that the range of disagreement in this sphere is due to the fact that liberty and equality are in serious conflict within it, arising from the scarcity of resources together with the possibility of making gains from trade. Given any initial distribution of resources, the freedom to trade will tend to make some better off even if no one is worse off. Even if one starts off with an equality of holdings, economic liberty will quickly disrupt it. Hence to maintain equality, liberty must be restricted.[6]

The political resolution of liberal disagreement

What is to count as an equal liberty in respect of the economic sphere is, then, a highly contested issue and a major part of liberal politics. Other presently contested areas within liberalism include the rights of minority groups who may be disadvantaged relative to the majority not by their poverty but by their culture. Some of the problems of minorities can be surmounted through considerations of economic equality. But if their internal culture is illiberal, equality of treatment for them as minorities will perpetuate what are injustices from a liberal point of view. In such cases, the liberty of the group to follow its traditional culture conflicts with the entitlement of its members to be treated as free and equal individuals in a liberal community. This is a problem that is not only internal to liberal states but also one for the international society of states insofar as it is seeking to promote respect for liberal human rights throughout the world.

Thus, when we spoke of a necessary consensus on liberal principles as the basis for a viable political community, we did not suppose that there are not substantial and long-standing disagreements within the liberal point of view. Nevertheless, the standard liberal method for containing and resolving such conflicts by peaceful means is through constitutional arrangements which guarantee basic rights to freedom of association, movement, thought and expression, to political representation and periodic elections, while allowing disputed areas to be settled by majority voting. There is, then, a consensus on the basic rights and procedures within which disagreements over the best interpretation of the fundamental liberal principles can be debated and resolved peacefully.

The equal worth of human beings and the value of individuality

Liberalism, as we have said, is, in its standard non-anarchist form, a type of coercive political order that justifies itself as minimally restricting people's choices under conditions of treating each other as equally worthy autonomous beings. Still, many around the world see the values of liberty, equality and autonomy that liberalism commits itself to as highly contentious. Apart from the objections raised above regarding the possession of the true doctrine and the need for unity, some people do not like the idea that human beings should be as free as possible to govern their own lives because they do not believe that most of them are capable of making responsible choices and hence they reject the idea that human beings are equally worthy through their possession of the capacity for autonomy. They believe that most human beings need to be subject to those wiser than themselves and that the best scheme is one in which society seeks to develop the capacities of the superior sort of person to make judgements about the good and to guide and rule the others on that basis. This was the view of Plato and is the practice of those Islamic states that give a special place in their constitution to the most renowned Islamic scholars.[7]

Liberals should accept that autonomy is a matter of degree and that some people possess a higher degree of autonomy than others. They can even agree with Plato that the highest degree of autonomy involves philosophical reflection on and understanding of the grounds of ethical life. However, they must reject the Platonic conclusion that therefore the philosopher should rule. Instead, they believe that every normal adult person possesses the capacity for autonomy to a sufficient degree to count as an equal member of society enjoying the same basic civil and political rights. What is required by this sufficient degree of autonomy is the capacity to take responsibility for one's life in its various aspects by making the choices that govern it. Thus, one needs to be able to make responsible decisions regarding one's employment, one's sexual life, one's religious and other associations and the political party one supports. No doubt, people make mistakes and everyone needs advice. But the issue is whether these central issues in a person's life should be ultimately in the hands of an authority such as parents or religious, philosophical or political guardians of some traditional 'true way', or indeed of some new 'truth', rather than up to each individual to decide for himself. The liberal believes that, even allowing for the propensity to make mistakes, it is both better and right that each person possess this responsibility. It is better because, thereby, persons have to develop their inherent capacity to take responsibility for their lives. They are, as it were, thrown into the world and have to learn how to swim in it with the help of their family, friends, schools and other associations.

Yet, the decisive point is that it is right that everyone should have to face this responsibility because they are ultimately a value in themselves. A person is born into some family, resident in some society and is standardly deemed to have some rights and duties arising from membership of these groups. But the liberal rejects the view that individuals exist solely as group members to fulfil the ends and maintain the values of the group. Individuals are in their own separate reflective lives necessarily ends for themselves. They have individual destinies that constitute their unique place in the world. Even if one believes that human beings are the creation of God and responsible to God for how they live their lives and that there is an after-life in which this accountability is made actual, the individual's unique destiny is only, thereby, extended to a future place. As possessors of unique destinies that are, from the individual's point of view, not determined in advance and are therefore ones for which they must believe themselves to be responsible, their existence serves no end external to it. It has its value in itself. This is the meaning of individuality. It is not to be conceived as a selfish, self-centred view of human life. It should be seen rather as realized through individuals' enjoyment of some combination of the natural goods through the possession of which humans flourish. Their pursuit of these will necessarily bind them directly or indirectly to others, while their liberal commitments will require them to respect and promote others' individuality.

Individuality is not incompatible with a religious point of view either. From that perspective, individuality is a central feature of the human being as it has been created by God, and in creating it, God must have wanted us to realize it in our lives. We do realize it by taking responsibility for them. In that sense, liberalism as the social and political form through which individuality is best realized is a better expression of a religious conception of human life than earlier and illiberal views.

It may be thought that this understanding of the value of an individual life is incompatible with that form of liberal justificatory theory that has been particularly prominent in British thought – namely utilitarianism. On a crude utilitarian view, the value of an individual life consists in its contribution to the general utility. However, liberal utilitarians believe that the best way to promote the general utility is through the establishment of the standard liberal rights. These rights make no sense unless individuals have the capacity to take responsibility for the main aspects of their lives, and it is better for them on the whole and thus for the total utility if they are required to develop that capacity in order to flourish. The rights and associated capacities enshrine the value of individuality, as J. S. Mill fully realized in his book *On Liberty*.[8] For, taking responsibility for one's life under the aspect of liberal rights is to treat one's life as a value in itself, however much that value may be realized in service to others or the general good. In effect, the utilitarian justification of liberal rights requires that the general utility be pursued indirectly through the organization of society on the basis of respect for individuality. The worry that the utilitarian theory still presents is whether that respect for individuality and its rights can be made adequately secure against being trumped by the general utility.[9]

PART I

Liberal beginnings

1 | The contextual origin of liberal thought and practice

The relative and universal value of liberalism

What we have so far said about the nature of liberalism suggests that we are committed to a simple liberal universalism: it would be better for human societies to organize themselves through liberal forms at all times and places. But such a claim looks fairly implausible. It is not at all clear that liberalism has much relevance to small-scale and face-to-face societies such as tribal or peasant forms of life. It seems much more sensible to say that liberal ideas and practices arose in a certain context and that they are primarily relevant to and realizable in contexts of the same type. Its original context was the series of events occurring in Europe, in the first place, from the sixteenth century and associated with the rise of the modern sovereign state, the development of market economies and the emergence of devastating and unresolved religious conflict. Liberalism is undoubtedly a European product but it is a product of European developments that have spread throughout the world and hence, even on the contextualist view, have made liberalism relevant, and in our view justifiable, on a universal basis. Every society now enjoys or seeks to acquire the institutions and rights of sovereign statehood and a dynamic economy and is also marked by some degree of ethno-cultural or religious diversity.

It is true that liberalism involves a mode of thinking that can be crudely called individualist. It requires its adherents to be able to think of themselves 'abstractly', as having interests and worth as undifferentiated individual human beings in relation to other such individuals as well as 'thickly' characterized in terms of their place and function in society or their religious affiliation or ethno-cultural identity.[1] We say 'crudely called individualist' because we believe that the liberal individual's abstract and general self-understanding as undifferentiated individual human being, in order to have ethical content, necessitates the idea of a community of such beings based on their mutual respect

19

as equals. Nevertheless, insofar as this form of thinking is inherent in liberalism as a successful practice, it may be held that it is a peculiarly European response to the political and economic developments of the early modern age based on its own intellectual traditions and as such is not assimilable by other 'non-individualist' cultures.

We do not believe this.

We believe that the ideas of liberalism are better ways of thinking about the fundamentals of human nature and human relations than alternatives and hence that they are in principle universal 'truths'[2] that are capable of being understood and endorsed by sufficiently reflective persons in non-Western cultures. The emergence of these ideas in seventeenth-century Europe involved a substantial transformation of Western intellectual traditions and just such a transformation is required in non-Western culture for the full domestication of liberalism in them. We do not think that there is any reason to suppose such changes are not possible, even if it must be admitted that the transition to the new mode was facilitated in Europe by its being a purely indigenous creation and also by certain 'individualist' ideas developed in Renaissance and Protestant thought.[3]

We want to say, then, both that liberalism expresses universal 'truths' and that it is to be understood as primarily relevant to certain political and socio-economic conditions that are characteristic of the modern age. How can we affirm both? The universal 'truths' are that human beings are fundamentally free and equal and that a society that does full justice to their nature must be based on the mutual respect of its members as free and equal. Such freedom and equality underlies the thicker social identities through which human beings in all types of society perceive and express their ethical relations to others. But in small-scale, tribal face-to-face societies the political, economic and social conditions do not exist for their members to be able to grasp in their ordinary experience of social relations the relevance of the liberal ideas. The conditions under which such representation of liberal ideas in practice can be most readily achieved are the ones we have mentioned above: the modern sovereign state, the market economy and religious or ethno-cultural diversity. The crucial relevance of the sovereign state is that it subjects all individuals equally to its sovereign rule, even if it allows unequal ranks for utilitarian purposes. The market economy is itself economic liberalism in practice: namely, the determination of economic outcomes by the free exchange of goods and services by persons with fundamentally equal rights (although not to equal things). Religious toleration also is (at any rate potentially) an expression of the liberal idea of equal freedom. In small-scale societies, the political and economic relations contain no such abstract institutional elements in which the ideas of freedom and equality can be perceived to be embodied. Ideas of justice and right are directly realized in the age, gender and family roles that constitute the social structure. The abstract 'truth' of human beings' free and equal nature has and could have no effective resonance in such a society's organization, although it can be represented to them in religious terms as the equality of all human beings in God's eyes and their individual responsibility for the salvation of their souls, as in the Christian and Islamic traditions.

Attempts to incorporate such small-scale societies within liberal structures of the rule of law and individual rights are likely to be disastrous, as we have seen in the experience of aboriginal societies in modern liberal states.[4] This line of argument against the universal relevance of liberalism, however, does not apply to large-scale modern societies organized through sovereign states and industrial economies, even if their intellectual traditions are illiberal. The problem for them in adopting liberal practices is not solely institutional but also intellectual. They have to reform their modes of thinking – whether Islamic, Confucian, Hindu or whatever – in order to create liberal forms of these traditions. We discuss some of the difficulties in attempts to do this in Chapter 10.

The point of this chapter and the rest of Part I is to provide some degree of historical and theoretical depth and understanding to the study of the UN regime of human rights in Part II. More particularly, the aim is to show the special relevance of liberal ideas to the new forms of domestic and international society that arose in Europe in the course of the sixteenth and seventeenth centuries. We believe that rights-based liberalism has an exceptional ethical affinity with the form of the modern sovereign state and that the international form of sovereign statehood is a direct expression of the liberal idea as applied to states as individual units. The attention we give to early liberal natural rights theory both at domestic and international levels, then, reflects our belief in the importance of theory in understanding the normative implications of these regimes. The present chapter focuses on the domestic dimension of the sovereign state; Chapter 2 gives a historical sketch of the emergence and evolution of the so-called Westphalian society of sovereign states up to the UN, while Chapter 3 is concerned with the liberal universalist foundations of that society and the developing liberal universalist practices in it, which we see as coming to a kind of fullness in the contemporary UN regime.

The rise of the modern sovereign state

The modern state is a politically independent, self-governing society that concentrates the major regulatory and enforcement powers over a definite territory and its population in a central institutional structure. These powers came to be identified in the course of the seventeenth and eighteenth centuries as the legislative, executive and judicial powers of the state. The institutional structure through which the powers are exercised is conceived as an impersonal public power that is independent of the magistrates who wield it at any one time. Of course, the institutions have to be run by persons assigned to the appropriate offices but the offices exist as a structure of government prior to the appointment of the magistrates. The state is the whole independent society as organized and governed in this way and the governing officials are its servants. This state claims to be the guarantor of law and order in its territory and for its people. Without the state there is only anarchy. It is sovereign or supreme power, since it alone is the creator and source of legitimate order within its realm. Other bodies may exercise powers only through its authorization or consent. Thus, although the state may create distinctions between subjects and bestow privileges on some, all subjects are, nevertheless, fundamentally equal individuals before the state's authority. As sole source of political authority within its territory, the state is also necessarily externally sovereign. This does not mean that it must claim superiority over all external bodies, but rather that it can acknowledge no superior to itself with regard to its own territory and policies and thus cannot permit any external power to intervene in its control of these.[5]

The sovereign state clearly needs some person or body of persons to exercise this sovereignty, set the state in motion and determine its direction: the king, the people or some elite section of the people or, as in the version that evolved in England, the king in Parliament. In this sense, the king or the people or the king in parliament can be said to be sovereign. Whoever is sovereign is the ultimate political legal authority in a territory. But this sovereign must exercise authority through the impersonal structures of sovereign government and not as a personal possession.

States understood in this way emerged in Europe, first of all to some degree in Renaissance Italy, but more clearly in western and northern Europe, in such places as Spain, France, England, Sweden and the Netherlands, in the course of the sixteenth and seventeenth centuries.[6] The process by which these states came into existence involved the elimination of the autonomous judicial, fiscal, military and police powers, both of feudal lords and self-governing towns, and the subjection of all to national courts, national economic and taxation policies and a nationally organized military force. The impetus in this process was the desire and need of kings to acquire greater fiscal and military power both *vis-à-vis* internal challenges to their authority but especially with regard to external threats to their power from other sovereigns. The towns were more sympathetic to the royal power than to the feudal lords and on the whole were willing to support it in its struggle to impose order on the feudal anarchy in the interests of trade, even though at the same time they sought to resist the encroachment of the centralizing monarchs on their own traditional self-governing rights. This three-way struggle led to a significant transformation of the feudal regime throughout Europe as a stage in the development of a more orderly and sovereign state through the co-option of the feudal aristocracy and the representatives of the towns in national assemblies, parliaments or diets.[7]

The system of rule by estates was hardly a stable one since it produced two power centres in king and parliament. The estates wished to preserve the privileges of their towns and fiefs while the king sought to establish a uniform system of justice and administration and to pursue economic policies that promoted the wealth of the country as a whole at the cost of abolishing local rights and powers. This struggle between kings and parliaments was resolved in most countries in favour of the monarch as the sovereign state consolidated itself in monarchical form. There were, of course, exceptions: the most notable being the English Parliament at one end of the continent and the Polish *Sejm* at the other. The success of these two assemblies in maintaining or expanding their power had completely opposite consequences for their respective states; in the former case, Parliament took over and completed the task of creating a modern sovereign state that rose to extraordinary prosperity and power in the course of the eighteenth and nineteenth centuries, while in the latter the Polish nobility succeeded only in weakening the kingdom relative to its competitors, leading to its temporary disappearance at the end of the eighteenth century.[8]

The centralizing drive of the monarchies, however, would have had little effect had not the economies of the late middle ages become increasingly prosperous, thus making it possible for the monarchs to boost their tax revenue and at the same time producing a larger body of entrepreneurs, particularly in England and the Netherlands, whose interests also lay in the destruction of the trade-restricting powers of the self-governing towns.

What made it particularly important and convenient for the king to acquire more resources were major military developments that occurred in Europe in the sixteenth century. These developments consisted, on the one hand, in the invention of the musket and pike and of greatly improved artillery, and, on the other hand, in the changes in tactics and organization necessary to make effective use of these devices. The combined use of musket and pike annihilated the heavy cavalry of the feudal knights while the new artillery destroyed their castles. These changes also required systematically trained professional armies and military bureaucracies for their organization. Such armies could be afforded by rulers only if they could increase their resources substantially. However, once acquired, they dramatically altered the balance of power between the king and the other estates.[9]

Furthermore, once this process had gone some distance in one country, thereby increasing the ruler's power and independence relative both to other rulers and to nominal overlords such as the Holy Roman Emperor, strong pressure was placed on other rulers to embark on the same process of expanding and consolidating their domestic power. Only thus would they be able to protect their dynastic interests against their external competitors. The internal and external processes clearly fed off each other in a way that led to the emergence of a set of vertically divided independent sovereign states, replacing a horizontally divided European-wide society of different ranks with the various kingdoms, principalities, self-governing cities and endless fiefdoms constituting so many administrative divisions under the overlordship of Pope and Emperor.[10]

The centralized modern state was not inherently liberal in its social or political form. Politically, the dominant regime was that of a monarchy conceived as more or less absolute in its powers. Socially, the modern state was generally mercantilist in economic policy rather than liberal and few such states showed much interest in religious toleration: the precursor of a more general social liberalism. Nevertheless, by concentrating power in central government and destroying the autonomy of rival bodies, the modern state did bring about the socio-political conditions under which liberalism could flourish. This is because a liberal society is one whose members are understood to be free and equal persons interacting in the pursuit of their natural interests through voluntary associations, and non-voluntarily subject only to the coercion of the state. It is, thus, essential for such a society that there should be no persons or groups, other than the state itself, with the power to subject others to their will without their consent. By eliminating the power of the feudal nobility and the domination of the self-governing towns, the modern state freed individuals for membership in a relatively undifferentiated national society.

Furthermore, insofar as an essential attribute of the modern state is conceived to be that of sovereignty, one can see an affinity between liberal modes of thinking and the modern sovereign state. The doctrine of internal sovereignty, as developed by Bodin in the sixteenth century and Hobbes in the seventeenth, held that, for a state to exist, there must be a final authority within a territory and over its population from which the legitimacy of the laws and institutions of the society derive. The final authority is necessarily absolute since, were it to be subject to certain conditions of which it was not itself the final judge, there would be no means of authoritatively resolving a dispute between it and its subjects over whether those conditions had been satisfied.[11] There would be a void in the structure of lawful authority that would sooner or later bring the edifice down. As a consequence of this view, subjects necessarily face the sovereign as a collection of equal and undifferentiated individuals. Although the sovereign can through its legislative will establish hierarchies and distribute privileges (with a view to the common good) which differentiate citizens among themselves, there are no natural ranks or privileged bodies whose inherent rights the lawgiver must respect. The pre-legislative position of the subjects, so to speak, is that of an undifferentiated equality.

This conception of political society as comprised of a collection of equal individuals held together by their common subjection to a sovereign authority was also how the proto-liberal seventeenth-century natural rights theorists conceived the state, although they understood much more by the notion of equal individuals than was presupposed by the doctrine of sovereignty. This is not to say that either the doctrine of sovereignty or that of natural rights swept the board. Various combinations were possible, including that of sovereignty and the divine right of kings: a compound popular among absolutizing monarchs.[12] In England where the struggle for control over the new centralized state did not lead to royal absolutism but, after much conflict, to a shared sovereignty between king and Parliament, the theory of mixed government received much support. This latter theory could be combined with a natural rights doctrine, as in John Locke's thought, but it was also a central theme of a republican doctrine, refurbished by Machiavelli, and tracing its ancestry back to the ideas of the republican city-states of the ancient world and in particular to Rome.[13]

The development of market economies

A pure market economy is one in which owners of land, labour and capital are free to enter into whatever agreements they please, subject only to the requirement to respect the person, property and contractual rights of others. A completely free market in these factors of production would not allow state-imposed restrictions based on concern for the health, safety and well-being of producers and consumers. It would leave it up to free individuals to make whatever arrangement they liked. However, the market economies we now inhabit are hedged around with legal constraints and protections regarding such matters and many of these are no doubt well-justified from a liberal point of view that embraces the social and economic rights of persons.

Prior to the rise of market economies, medieval Europe possessed an agricultural economy in which land could not be freely bought and sold and labour was owned by the feudal lord and tied to the land, and a manufacturing regime in the self-governing towns, in which terms of entry into and exercise of a trade or industry were controlled by monopolistically inclined guilds of producers concerned with protecting their own local interests.[14] The connection between market economies and liberal thinking is self-evident. Market economies directly express liberal values in the economic sphere: free and equal individuals interact in pursuit of their economic interests on the basis of voluntary arrangements. So, it is reasonable to suppose that the growth of free labour, land and capital in Europe in the period from the fifteenth to the seventeenth centuries contributed substantially to the emergence in the seventeenth century in the theorists of natural rights of a more generalized liberal way of thinking about human affairs.

The growth of a national market economy from the fifteenth century was particularly marked in England and above all in the Netherlands, whose extraordinary economic and political success in the late sixteenth and seventeenth centuries made it the envy of, and model for, its neighbours.[15] Indeed, these two countries became the main sources of the new liberal thinking. The modern state was also promoting economic development as a by-product of its hostility to the autonomous powers of towns and nobles. So, the freedom-seeking capitalists were often happy to ally themselves with the royal power in its drive to eliminate its rivals. Nevertheless, the policies pursued by the new states were more mercantilist than liberal. The state's aim was, indeed, the promotion of national prosperity by encouraging free trade and industry domestically for the most part, but its central focus was on boosting export trade, restricting imports and capturing foreign markets in the belief that this would secure full employment at home and hence maximize national output. To this end, it was willing to grant monopolies to favoured capitalists.[16] The classical liberal economic theory, in which free trade internationally as well as domestically is seen as the best means of advancing national prosperity and power, only makes its appearance in the eighteenth century in the famous work of Adam Smith.

Religious diversity and religious conflict

In 1517, Martin Luther pinned his famous ninety-five theses attacking Catholic practices and beliefs to a church door in Wittenberg, thereby starting the process that led to the massive split in the Christian Church in the West known as the Reformation. The new Protestant version of Christianity achieved widespread popularity in most of northern Europe and was willingly embraced by rulers anxious to affirm their complete independence of the religious and political overlordships of Pope and Emperor.

The medieval Catholic Church had never recognized the liberty of the religious conscience. It had regularly persecuted heretical beliefs through the coercive arm of the state, not so much in order to compel belief but rather to stop the propagation of false doctrine and the corruption of weak minds.[17] It now sought to suppress Protestantism through the medium of sympathetic rulers, in particular in France and in the Spanish Netherlands. In the Netherlands, the Protestants rose in revolt and after an eighty-year war succeeded in being recognized as an independent state at the Peace of Westphalia in 1648. In the meanwhile, many horrendous massacres of Protestants by Catholics and of Catholics by Protestants had taken place. In France, after the massacre on St Bartholomew's Day in 1572 of many Protestant notables lured to Paris for the celebration of the marriage of their leader Henry of Gascony into the royal family, they too rebelled and there followed a series of merciless butcheries by both parties. The hostilities between Catholic and Protestant powers culminated in 1618 in the Thirty Years War fought on German territory but involving also the Catholic and Protestant states of the Holy Roman Empire of the German Nation, Denmark, Sweden, Spain and France. The normal losses of warfare to the German people through thirty years of more or less continuous fighting were compounded by the atrocities regularly perpetrated by both sides, leaving Germany devastated and exhausted.

It has to be said that the Protestants were not simply reacting to persecution by the Catholics. The main reformed churches, the Lutheran, Calvinist and Anglican, were as ardent persecutors of those who did not accept the 'true' faith as the Catholics. Calvin, in particular, instituted in Geneva an exceptionally intolerant system of religious and moral regimentation. Nevertheless, the Reformation did have a profound effect on the development of religious toleration both indirectly and directly.[18] Religious toleration can be understood as the template for liberal social freedom generally. Its principles require that strongly opposed parties of believers agree to live together on terms which abstract from the content of their disagreements, so that each party allows the other to live freely in accordance with its beliefs.

The indirect influence of the Reformation on the movement for religious toleration came about because of the widespread revulsion at the huge and continuing scale of the religiously inspired carnage. Several parties were formed aimed at bringing about a reconciliation and mutual toleration between the churches on the basis of their common adherence to a minimum set of Christian dogmas, either by appealing to the simplicity of original Christian faith or simply as a pragmatic measure. The former were the humanists, the most important of whom was Erasmus of Rotterdam, while the latter were the Politiques, especially influential in France in securing the Edict of Nantes in 1598, which established a measure of toleration for the French Protestants, but also in the Germany of the Peace of Westphalia and in England in promoting the Toleration Act of 1689 which recognized the right of public worship of non-conformist (non-Anglican) Protestants.[19]

The direct influence of the Reformation on support for toleration came from the radical Protestant sects such as the Anabaptists and Baptists, Socinians and Unitarians. These interpreted Luther's individualist principle of the priesthood of all believers literally, conceiving the churches either as voluntary associations of believers or as a broad organization inclusive of all Christian opinion. Luther's principle affirms the crucial importance of each person's direct relation to God unmediated by a special priestly class. It looked as though it should undermine the authority of organized religion and lead to the acceptance of diversity of belief. The radical sects were persecuted by both Catholic and the main Protestant Churches, but nevertheless acquired many adherents in England and America in the course of the seventeenth century.[20]

The main natural rights theorists were directly involved in these concerns. A central plank of their argument was the naturalness of radical disagreement between human beings over religion and their idea of natural law was that it constituted common ground in abstraction from areas of disagreement. Thus, they supported a minimalist view of Christian dogma and both Pufendorf and Locke wrote widely read works specifically on toleration using an argument from natural liberty.[21] On Locke's view in his famous and influential 'Letter Concerning Toleration' of 1689, the state is concerned with the external acts of human beings and not with the care of their souls and hence has no right to restrict individuals' liberty in matters of faith. Churches are to be understood as voluntary societies for the public worship of God. Their members do not surrender their natural liberty in matters of religion to their church and so the church has no right to coerce its members beyond that of expelling them for appropriate reasons.[22] Furthermore, our knowledge of the truth in religious matters is too uncertain and incomplete to justify us in holding that we are right and the others wrong. Human beings sincerely differ about these issues and only toleration of the differences will bring public peace and reflect true Christian charity. Nevertheless, Locke does not accord tolerance to atheists, since they would not be bound by their promises, or to religions that owe allegiance to a foreign prince (Catholics, Muslims), since that would be incompatible with the right of their own sovereign, or to sects that are subversive of the social order.[23]

Seventeenth-century natural rights theories and their liberal character

We shall now embark on an account of the development of natural rights theorizing in the seventeenth century, with a view to bringing out what we take to be its inherently liberal character. However, we should not suppose that liberalism emerges in a fully developed form in these theorists. For one thing, they are not democrats, and while there are good reasons for distinguishing liberalism as a conception of the organization of social and economic life from democracy as a view of the organization of politics, the fundamental egalitarianism of liberalism would seem to find its natural political expression in democracy. So, the undemocratic character of the seventeenth-century natural rights thinkers must surely count as a limitation on their liberalism. Furthermore, while they developed the fundamental approach of a rights-based liberalism to liberal practices such as the freedoms of belief and private property, they do not by any means understand these freedoms to have the same extent as later, generally accepted doctrines of liberal toleration and economic liberalism.

The major theorists of natural rights in the seventeenth century were all northern European Protestants: Hugo Grotius of the Netherlands, Thomas Hobbes and John Locke of England and Samuel Pufendorf of Germany. They developed a new understanding of the idea of a natural law that was to serve as the foundation of a legitimate social and political order. The new interpretation contained the elements and basic strategies that have come to be called liberalism.

What the seventeenth-century theorists invented was an **individualist** doctrine of natural rights. The language of natural rights they did not invent. The original Latin term translated into English as natural right was *jus naturale*. This term was first used by Roman political and legal theorists such as Cicero and became a central part of the moral and political theory of medieval Christianity.[24] The traditional view of natural right was a non-individualist one that we shall call holist. On a holist view of rights, persons possess rights only insofar as they are fulfilling a function in a larger whole. An example of a holist conception is the right of a judge to sentence persons convicted of a crime to certain punishments. This is a rightful power that the judge has, not as an individual human being, but by virtue of his occupying a role in the legal system. Of course, the judge's right is not a natural or human right but one arising from the organization of a particular legal order.

Pre-modern moral and political theorists of natural law have a holist conception of natural right. An enormously influential medieval Christian expression of such a view was that of St Thomas Aquinas. Aquinas' account of natural law is contained within a vision of a hierarchically ordered universe consisting of many different kinds of being. This is the Great Chain of Being, stretching from God at the apex through the angels, human beings and down to the varieties of animal, vegetable and inanimate being. God created all things to work harmoniously together and this is expressed in his eternal law by which the nature and essential activity of every kind of being is established. Everything happens according to his will and since God is the greatest good, he created all things to be good and to seek the good in conformity with its natural goal as established in his eternal law. Law, for Aquinas, is a rule of reason directed at the common good by the being that has the care of the community. Thus, eternal law is God's rule of reason for the common good of the universe. All beings participate in this law in their distinctive way. Human beings' place in the universal order is that of rational animal. As rational beings, they can acquire knowledge of their own nature and its essential activity and hence of God's rule of reason for them. They can direct themselves with self-conscious will to their natural ends. As animal beings, they naturally seek to preserve themselves and to propagate their species through families. But as rational beings, they can know this end and can guide themselves to its fulfilment in more rational ways than animals can. Human beings also have specific ends arising from their rational nature. These are, Aquinas says, to live in society and to seek knowledge of God. The ultimate goal of the human being is union with God in eternal life. This fully realizes human potential and brings eternal happiness. To achieve this end, human beings need God's freely given grace. Their natural reason enables them to know and obey God's natural law and thereby attain a righteous will and earthly happiness. This prepares them to receive God's grace and to arrive at the state of blessedness in eternal life.

For Aquinas, all human beings can know the basic principles of natural law – seek good and avoid harm – and know that this involves not murdering people, not stealing what is another's and other such simple laws. But he believes that there is great inequality in human beings' capacity to elaborate these principles in more precise laws and to apply them to particular circumstances and cases. This is because first, our sinful nature inherited from Adam leads all of us to reason with bias towards our own interests but to different degrees; and second, because only the educated and wise can master the complexity of reasoning involved in applying the basic principles to particular circumstances. Thus, although all human beings have a moral conscience implanted by God which enables them to know the difference between good and evil, the mass of them need guidance by priests and rulers as to how to live their lives in order to attain earthly happiness and eternal life.[25]

On the individualist view of natural rights that we are attributing to the seventeenth-century theorists, the rights are held by individuals independently of their fitting into, and fulfilling a function within, a God-ordered purposive whole based on the good. However, this does not mean that the seventeenth-century theorists were essentially secular and anti-religious writers. They were Christians with a minimalist view of necessary Christian doctrine and a minimalist view of what could be known about God. With regard to the latter, they believed that the world must have a creator whom human beings called God. As the creator of the world and all the beings in it, God made human beings with the specific nature they have: that of rational animal. Although God must have had some purpose in creating the world and in doing so with the specific beings to be found in it, they denied that human beings could know anything about that purpose, other than that God must have intended that each being live in accordance with its created nature; and, hence, that human beings should live consonantly with their rational powers and natural interests. Yet, as we have no direct access through the exercise of our rational powers to God's intentions and laws, we can only use our reason to work out on the basis of experience and observation the rules we should follow in living together in peace. In this way, we can know that such rules for peaceful association are how God wants us to live and hence we can treat them as laws commanded by God for us to follow.

The significant point in distinguishing the modern version of natural law from the medieval is that in the former rights are ascribed to individuals independently of a comprehensive vision of how human beings and their rights fit into God's purpose for the world. We work out what rights they should have and what rules they should obey by considering them as independent beings capable of governing themselves by their own reason in pursuit of their natural interests. Their primary interest is that of self-preservation. However, as Locke puts it, that includes not only an interest in life but also interests in liberty, health and possessions. If God made us with such natural interests, he must want us to act to preserve ourselves and hence we must have a natural right to do so. Furthermore, since we are created as rational beings capable of directing ourselves to our natural ends, our natural right must be to decide for ourselves how best to achieve self-preservation. Of course, since everyone has the same rights, the basic principle of natural law must be to respect one another's rights.

Human beings on this conception are naturally free and equal. Liberty enters in a two-fold way: first, in negative form as the natural interest in not being subject to the control of another without our consent; and second, given our rational nature, the positive side of that negativity is to be our own master by directing ourselves to our natural ends. Equality arises from the assumption, given the minimalist nature of this ethical view, that all human beings have the same basic capacity to follow the natural law and hence must have equal basic rights.

The seventeenth-century thinkers sought an understanding of natural law and natural right that was accessible to the rational capacities of each human being and was not susceptible to the controversies that arise from more complex theories of the good life. One obvious source of this minimalist project was the widespread revulsion at the horrors perpetrated in the course of the religious wars between Protestants and Catholics. Many thinkers, including the natural rights theorists, were seeking to promote an understanding of Christianity that all parties could accept.

The natural rights theorists were also responding to the ethical scepticism of thinkers such as Montaigne, who were themselves reacting to the intractability of religious controversy in this period.[26] These sceptics denied the possibility of arriving by the exercise of reason at universal rules of moral and political order. Since they were neither irreligious nor anarchist, they concluded that one should follow the rules and beliefs of one's own society and hence advocated a conservative quietism. The natural rights theorists did believe that reason could establish universally valid rules for social living and they thought that they could do this by constructing a set of minimally necessary rules for peaceful association grounded in human beings' most basic interests rather than in the idea of the best and most complete life for them. These rules would allow persons whose conceptions of the best life were in conflict nevertheless to live together in peace by respecting each other's freedom.

Hugo Grotius

The founder of modern natural law and natural rights doctrine is widely agreed to be Hugo Grotius (1583–1645). Grotius was a lawyer and politician in the Dutch Republic, which had established a *de facto* independence from Spain, and later diplomat in the service of Sweden. He published his major work in this field, *De Jure Belli ac Pacis* (Of the Rights of War and Peace), in 1625.[27] Much of this work covers what was then known as the law of nations and is now called international law, which we will discuss in the next chapter. However, in order to arrive at the law governing the relation between states, he begins with the idea of the natural law that regulates the interactions of individual human beings. It is what Grotius has to say about this natural law that is so influential on subsequent thinkers.

Fundamental to Grotius' new vision is the reduction of necessary religious belief to a minimum: God is one and is the all-powerful and providential creator of the world. Since he created human beings with the natural inclinations we have, we can work out through our own reason and experience how such beings can best live together and these will be natural laws. But we know nothing about why God created us in this way or why he created anything at all. So, we can have no conception of any ultimate end or purpose either for human beings or for the world more generally.[28]

Given that we have no direct access to God's mind, we have no reason to suppose that God created the world as a harmony from which human beings have fallen away through sin. What we know from our own nature is that we are naturally inclined to conflict and quarrel. We come into conflict over our natural interests in preserving ourselves and in acquiring the possessions to enable us to do so, and we are naturally inclined to get into disputes about religious and ethical doctrine. The Grotian problematic then becomes how such naturally quarrelsome creatures can live together in peace. This formulation is quite different from the medieval conception of an original natural harmony, albeit disrupted by sin.[29]

The Grotian solution to this problematic rests on the claim that human beings are naturally sociable as well as naturally quarrelsome. We have contrary inclinations: to interact peacefully but also to fight each other. Natural sociability, for Grotius, is not an enlightened extension of self-interest. It is not because peace is in each person's self-interest that we seek and can live by rules of peaceful interaction. That is standardly taken to be the view of Thomas Hobbes. For Grotius, we have a quite separate natural inclination to enjoy each other's company. Hence, we naturally desire to live in society.[30]

The laws of nature are, then, empirically discoverable directives or rules that solve the problem of how such anti-social yet sociable beings can live together in peace. The solution involves a new view of natural rights. We seek naturally to preserve ourselves and to do so by taking from nature what we need. Natural right is the right to do this. The rights to life and possessions are attributes of individuals who exist on their own in a state of nature and quite apart from an overall vision of human beings' place in the grand scheme of things. However, the right is seen as a moral quality that makes it lawful for individuals to do the acts in respect of which they have the right to preserve themselves, to acquire a property in things and to enter into binding agreements with others concerning property.[31]

With regard to the acquisition of property rights, Grotius says that God gave men generally a right to things of a lower nature. Since these things were not given to human beings individually but to them generally, everything was common. But he immediately goes on to say that, because they were common, each man could take for his use what he would and the use of the thing would establish a property right in it in the sense that others may not dispute it. Yet, such a use-right is not a full property right, since he adds that men departed from this community of things when they invented agriculture and pasture and agreed to divide possessions, either expressly or by tacit consent, by recognizing occupation as the basis of ownership. In other words, full property rights in land get established on the basis of conventions that are justified by their necessity for the support of the new practices of agriculture. (Note that he also attributes the conventions to the vice of ambition.)

Nevertheless, Grotius maintains that the original right of each person to preserve himself or herself by taking from the common property cannot be extinguished by this new convention regarding property rights in land, so that the destitute retain a residual right to take from the superfluities of the rich. This provision can be seen as a primitive form of recognizing welfare rights.[32]

The laws of nature, for Grotius, require human beings to respect one another's rights. The rights appear to inhere in each person and the natural law to be derived from the independent existence of the rights. Many critics of the natural rights theorists take them to hold such a view. But if they do, it is very obscure as to how human beings come to have these rights in the first place and how the rights could be compatible with any moral or legal order. Each person's right would be constituted independently of a relation to the rights of others and would appear to be absolute and unlimited. In fact, as stated above, the natural rights theorists hold that the rules regarding rights can be worked out by human beings through the exercise of their reason on the basis of the observation of their own nature, interests and capacities. This enquiry yields the conclusion that the right way for human beings to live at peace with one another is through mutual respect for rights.

Unfortunately, this formula may still leave the impression that rights are the primary moral entities and it is difficult to see how they can be without the absurdity of treating them as absolute and unlimited. There are, however, two possible interpretations of the formula that avoid this unreasonableness. One is to hold that the rule requiring mutual acknowledgement of rights is derived from considerations of the general utility. The other is to say that following the rule is in the interest of each person. While Thomas Hobbes certainly argues at times for the latter view, it is by no means clear how the others' conception of the rationality of the rule is to be understood. What Grotius says is that the tendency of human nature to the conservation of society, in agreement with human intellect, is the source of natural law, and that, in a wider sense, natural law is the judgement, rightly framed, of what is advantageous and disadvantageous for the present and the future.[33] But he also says that natural law is the dictate of right reason, indicating that any act from its agreement or disagreement with the rational nature of man has moral turpitude or moral necessity (and hence is forbidden or commanded by God).[34] Provided the judgements of right reason regarding what conforms or does not conform to the rational nature of man take into account his interest in society, then Grotius can be taken to be appealing in some way to the general utility. However, whether rational moral judgements are formed by reference to the general, or to each individual's, utility, it will still be the case that the individual's rights are not self-standing moral entities but an aspect of the best rule for human beings' association. Hence, each person's right will form part of a system of mutually limiting equal rights.

One problem with the rational version of the rule respecting rights is that it does not allow for a strong sense of moral obligation. That the rule is in my interest or in the general interest doesn't create that special recognition of bindingness that ensures that one must obey the rule whether it is in one's own or the general interest or not. The solution adopted by all the major natural rights theorists is to appeal to God in an indirect way. Since God made the world and all things in it, he made human beings with the nature, interest and capacities we have and so must want us to live in accordance with that nature. This tells us to follow the rules we can establish through our reason as the best rules for beings with that nature. These rules, then, are the commands of God. We are morally obliged to obey them because we are morally obliged to do what God commands us.[35]

If the foundation of rights is God's commands to us to preserve ourselves and, in John Locke's formulation, to preserve others also by respecting their rights,[36] then rights are no more the primary moral entities than under the rational constructions mentioned above. What is fundamental is God's law to preserve ourselves and others and respect for rights are the rules through which God's wishes are to be realized. Hence, individual rights are part of God's system of rule for human beings. This system consists of a set of mutually limiting equal rights.

Under this limited and derivative view of the natural rights ascribed to human beings by the seventeenth-century theorists, the individualism of the theory appears to be more muted than was at first suggested. We contrasted the modern view of natural rights with an older tradition that we called holist because rights on the latter conception were held by persons in respect of their fulfilling a function in a larger whole. On the seventeenth-century view, we do not know what the larger whole is other than as the society of human beings who are bound to interact on the basis of mutual respect for rights. Individuals possess rights only as part of the general system of rights that constitutes the basic rules of the natural society of humankind.

While the ground of rights is the law binding humans to mutual respect, the general scheme can be said to have substantial individualistic elements in the following senses. First, what the law commands is for each to look after himself and to look after others only by not interfering with their looking after themselves, although this includes ensuring, if possible, that no one is deprived of access to the means to preserve himself. The society of humankind does not exactly have strong communal bonds; nevertheless, the bonds have to be strong enough to prevent people preying on each other and excluding others from the wherewithal to live. It should be noted, also, that there is nothing in this conception of the basic rules of natural human society that prevents individuals from entering into voluntary co-operative arrangements with each other. Such agreements would be valid insofar as they did not violate anyone's rights.

Second, the society is an anarchic one. Although the members are bound by a common law, there are no common institutions for interpreting and enforcing the law. Natural human society is a state of nature in which each person has to interpret and enforce the law himself or herself. Each is an independent sovereign, naturally subject to no other, and hence the equal of everyone. Freedom and equality are the fundamental values of the society; freedom in the negative sense of not being interfered with by others but also in the positive sense of being one's own master,[37] and equality because all have the same basic moral status and enjoy the same rights.

It follows from this understanding of natural human society and its law that political authority is not natural but conventional. Political authority, as the right of making and enforcing laws for the common good, must be based on an agreement or contract between naturally free and equal persons to accept some person or body of persons as their sovereign. Why naturally independent persons should enter such a contract is for the sake of utility. Only by creating such a power can humans effectively oblige themselves, Grotius says. By this, we take him to mean that the sovereign power, by enforcing our rights, provides us with the security that we cannot find in the state of nature.[38]

Grotius takes it for granted that many such political societies will come into being through explicit or tacit contracts and this assumption provides him with the substance of the main concern of his major work, namely the laws of war and peace of the society of states, which we will be discussing in Chapter 3. Since political authority for Grotius derives from the wills of those subject to it, the latter are in a position to decide who shall wield the sovereign power. It does not, however, necessarily belong to the people. Grotius holds that just as a man may alienate his natural freedom by selling himself into slavery, so may a people exercise their freedom by bestowing absolute power on a king. Nevertheless, whoever possesses sovereign power is not subject to the control of another and his or its acts cannot be rendered void by anyone. The state necessarily has a superior right over the subjects since this is the condition of securing public tranquillity. It follows that there is not ordinarily a right of resistance by subjects against the sovereign. However, Grotius allows that in extreme cases such resistance may be legitimate as in the case of the Dutch themselves towards their murderous Catholic overlord, the King of Spain.[39]

We see, thus, that although the fundamental values of the theory are human beings' natural freedom and equality, their exercise, for Grotius, does not lead necessarily, or in the case of politics even often, to individual self-government and popular sovereignty. Whether such outcomes are warranted by the theory, we will consider later.

Grotius' seventeenth-century followers: Hobbes, Locke and Pufendorf

Grotius' main seventeenth-century followers were Thomas Hobbes (1588–1679) and John Locke (1652–1703) in England and Samuel Pufendorf (1632–1694) in Germany. They can be said to be Grotius' followers because they all accept the Grotian problematic and their work constitutes variations on, or developments of, his main themes.

Thus Hobbes's crucial variation is to remove the motivational force of natural sociability and hence to turn the state of nature into a totally insecure state of war of all against all in which no one can enjoy any rights.[40] Fear of descent into such anarchy leads Hobbes to emphasize the unconditional nature of absolute sovereignty much more strongly than Grotius. Nevertheless, the rules that the sovereign has most reason to follow in governing are ones that promote a large degree of toleration among Christians and maximal equal liberty among subjects.[41]

Pufendorf and Locke both seek to distance themselves from Hobbes. Both reaffirm natural sociability and hence the belief that the natural state is marked by a degree of peace and the existence of a natural moral order, although the peace is weak and the enjoyment of natural rights insecure, so that the creation of political society and sovereignty become necessary.[42]

Locke has come to be regarded as the foremost rights-based liberal thinker of the seventeenth century. However, the main lines of his thought are clearly not original, but derived from Grotius. What is distinctive in Locke is a much more developed theory of the natural right to property, which, while grounding the right in self-preservation and limiting it by the need to accommodate everyone, aims to show that huge inequalities in property can subsequently be justified on the grounds that all can be made better off by allowing such accumulations.[43] His other significant departure from other Grotians is to hold that sovereignty inheres in the whole political community as determined by the majority will and not in the holders of legislative or executive office. But this does not lead him to abandon the theory of the necessary absoluteness of this sovereignty on the standard grounds that any limitation would involve the dissolution of society and the return to the state of nature.[44]

Conclusion

We see from the above account that a theory that is recognizably liberal in its foundations developed in northwestern Europe in the seventeenth century and that the societies of this region were beginning to acquire features that were either conducive to the emergence of liberal practices or were already forms of liberalism. In regard to the latter, we discussed the rise and nature of the modern state, the development of market economies and the existence of deep-seated religious conflict. Of these, the market economy is itself the practice of liberalism in the economic sphere and its increasing influence in social life and theorization by economists was bound to have a powerful effect on the spread of liberal attitudes more generally. Deep-seated religious conflict is of significance for us insofar as it led to the growth of religious toleration in practice and to the theorization of toleration in terms that express the fundamental liberal idea of mutual respect for each other's liberty.

The modern state, on the other hand, was not in itself a liberal form but could be said to have affinities with liberalism, since it provided the socio-political structure within which individuals could come to think of each other as free and equal voluntary co-operators, subject only to a sovereign state. The sovereignty of the modern state consists in its claim to be the supreme regulatory authority for the affairs of the people inhabiting its territory, so that no one else has regulatory power without the state's permission and all inhabitants are equally subject to its law. This is not to say that there are no sources of power besides state power within these societies. Obviously, there are economic and ideological sources that are not immediately subject to the state's will. But these sources cannot establish legislative authority for their power. To do so, they have to work through the state. Liberalism as an ideology has to do likewise. It does so by getting the state to build into the basic structure of society the liberty and welfare rights that are fundamental to its conception of just human association. Liberalism may be said to be particularly appropriate to the modern state because, while it endorses the modern state's view of subjects as bound together politically only by a common subjection to a sovereign state, it also provides individuals with basic rights that should protect them, not only against oppression by each other, but also by the potentially very powerful and tyrannical modern state itself.

2 | *The Westphalian society of sovereign states*

The Peace of Westphalia

The Westphalian international system or, more grandly, society of sovereign states, is the term widely used to describe the system of relations that existed between European states roughly from the time of the Peace of Westphalia in 1648 at least to the foundation of the League of Nations after World War One (WWI) and, after the failure of the League, to the revised attempt to create a new system through the United Nations after WWII, 300 years later. From the nineteenth century the system began to be extended to non-European states. It is so called, of course, because of its supposed origin in the Westphalian treaties. These treaties put an end to the Thirty Years War in Germany and the eighty-year Dutch war of independence against their Spanish overlords.

These wars had a substantial religious content. In Germany, it was largely a war between the Protestant princes and principalities of the German Empire together with the independent Protestant states of Denmark and Sweden against the Catholic powers led by the Hapsburg Emperor and supported by his Spanish Hapsburg cousins. In the Netherlands, it was a war of the Protestant provinces against their Catholic rulers for the freedom of their religion as well as for their political independence. The Catholic Hapsburg rulers of Spain and the German Empire sought to recover ground that had been lost to Protestantism since the Reformation of the previous century and to re-establish through the counter-reformation movement the lost Catholic unity of Europe.

However, the war in Germany was also about the attempt of the Emperor to carry out in Germany an expansion and consolidation of the royal power in its own territory that had been taking place already in other states, and that is known as the rise of the modern sovereign state. The war was, then, a war for the traditional freedoms of the

German princes and other autonomous units of the Empire against the encroachment on them of their Hapsburg overlord, the Holy Roman Emperor. It is in respect of this aspect of the war that we can understand how it was that Catholic France intervened on the Protestant side in both the Dutch and German wars by at first subsidising the Protestant combatants and subsequently, when the Hapsburgs looked like winning the war, by direct military action. France's concern was above all with the possibility of an almost complete encirclement by hostile Hapsburg power, which threatened to stretch from its Spanish border through northern Italy along its frontier with the German Empire and into the Netherlands. The Peace of Westphalia forced the Emperor to give up both his religious and political aspirations for Germany and forced the King of Spain to recognize the independence of the Dutch Republic. It preserved the freedom of the German princes and the Protestant religion and ensured for over 200 years the weakness of the German Empire in relation to its neighbour France. It thereby also preserved all the states of Europe from the threatening hegemonic rule of the House of Hapsburg.

It is evident from this sketch that the Peace of Westphalia did not bring the sovereign state into being in 1648. The process by which the medieval society of Europe was transformed from a multi-layered hierarchy under the supreme authority of the Pope in matters of religion and the Holy Roman Emperor in civil affairs into a set of independent sovereign states that recognized no superior had begun well before that date. The process involved domestically, as we have seen, the strengthening of the royal power over the power of the estates. At the level of European society as a whole, it involved the loss of the unifying authority of Pope and Emperor. Evidently, the Pope ceased to have religious authority for the Protestant states, while the Emperor's authority had been steadily eroded by the growing power of the centralizing states and the diminution of the threat to Europe as a whole of the Muslim Empire of the Ottoman Turks.

Europe before Westphalia, then, was already divided into *de facto* independent states; and what Westphalia can be said to have achieved was the consolidation of an emerging system of states and an appreciation of some of the principles and practices by which this system could be managed. Above all, it recognized states to be autonomous entities responsible for their own domestic and foreign affairs, not subject to any overlord, except in certain largely formal respects in the case of the states of the German Empire, and with a dominant interest in preventing the rise of a hegemonic power.[1]

The parties to the settlement were all the German states and the Holy Roman Emperor, Spain, France, the Netherlands, Sweden, Denmark, Poland, Portugal and the Venetian Republic. All parties were to be recognized as autonomous, self-governing units. In the case of the German states, this autonomy was qualified by their recognition of overall allegiance to the Holy Roman Emperor. Nevertheless, the German states were acknowledged to have the right to manage their internal affairs without interference by the Emperor, to conduct their foreign relations as they pleased, short of declaring war without the Emperor's consent, while the Emperor was compelled to accept the traditional rights and institutions of the German realm, down to the smallest principality and free city. In matters of religion within Germany, three religions were recognized, Catholicism, Lutheranism and Calvinism, and subjects had the right to practise any of these faiths whatever the official religion of their state.

For the state parties as a whole, no allegiance was acknowledged to Pope or Emperor. A sense of community was expressed in the self-designation of the Congress as the Senate of the Christian World and this did indeed signify that the contracting parties saw themselves as engaged in the business of collectively regulating the affairs of Europe. The common principles accepted, however, were limited, first, to the reaffirmation of the customary rights of rulers over their territories, involving the rejection of the Swedish and French claims to parts of the German lands in the north and west on the basis of a right of conquest. The kings of Sweden and France did, indeed, retain control of these lands but only by acknowledging the overlordship of the Emperor in respect of them. Second, and in the long run of most significance, was the mutual recognition of the parties as autonomous units. This meant that each accepted the entitlement of the others to manage their domestic affairs and foreign alliances as they pleased except insofar as the treaty itself limited this right, as it did notably in respect of the officially recognized religions of the German Empire by giving member states of the Empire a legitimate interest in the treatment of their co-religionists by other states.

The autonomy principle implied, of course, the fundamental equality of the autonomous units. Some states were clearly larger and more powerful than others, but each enjoyed the same status in the system, since there was no authority to interpret and enforce the rules other than the states themselves through their mutual agreements. The question as to who was a member of this system of autonomous units and hence entitled to its rights was simply determined by historical contingency. Whatever units had established themselves as independent at the time were recognized to have the right to such independence. These units were overwhelmingly monarchical in character, but included the newly recognized Dutch Republic, the Venetian Republic and the Swiss Confederation.[2]

The evolution of Westphalian society

This system evolved into a much more self-conscious one, with more elaborate and formal rules and procedures, in part as a result of the attempts by the French, first under Louis XIV and then under Napoleon, to establish their own hegemonic rule in Europe. A central theme of the management of the system now became the balance of power.[3] The states developed also the practice of maintaining permanent ambassadors in each other's capitals, around which important conventions evolved facilitating diplomatic exchanges. Of major significance, however, were the congresses of the greater and lesser powers that met from time to time, in the first instance to achieve a peace settlement after a major war, such as the Peace of Westphalia itself, and subsequently the Treaty of Utrecht of 1714 that marked the end of the first French bid for hegemony, and the Congress of Vienna a hundred years later that marked the end of the second. These congresses can be seen as the parliaments of the European Commonwealth, along the lines of the self-understanding of the congress of Westphalia, although in secular terms. With the Congress of Vienna, the arrangements came to be dominated by the Great Powers – Britain, France, Prussia, Austria and Russia – who assumed responsibility for the running of the system and undertook for that purpose to meet more frequently.

It has to be accepted that an essential part of the management of the balance of power by which the security and autonomy of the members was to be maintained was the waging of war. These could be major and long-lasting conflagrations fought to defeat a bid for a general or regional supremacy, such as the War of the Spanish Succession of 1701–14 and the Great Northern War of 1700–21 which ended

Sweden's drive for complete control of the Baltic Sea, or they could be limited and moderate affairs. Most wars in the seventeenth and early eighteenth century were fought, officially, on the basis of dynastic claims to a territory. Even if the obvious aim was the expansion of the dynast's power and the achievement of glory, the justification for initiating hostilities had to incorporate a hereditary claim. In that sense wars had to have a just cause. But in the course of the eighteenth century, dynasts became increasingly ready to exchange territory with a view to consolidating their power in more compact, territorially contiguous units without regard to hereditary right.[4] As a result, the justification for war came to be expressed in terms of the state's interest, which each state as an autonomous entity was entitled to judge for itself. So, during the eighteenth century, the issue of whether a war was for a just cause ceased to be of importance and attention turned more towards the question of *jus in bello* or justice in the conduct of war.[5]

The acceptance of state interest as the determining principle in matters of war made explicit what was, in effect, essential to the operation of Westphalian society understood as a society of autonomous, self-governing states. Since that society was dedicated, at least formally, to preserving the independence of its members by being ready to form alliances sufficiently strong to defeat the hegemonial ambitions of any single power, its members had to be capable of assessing the international situation in terms of state interest rather than of dynastic right. However, the principle of state interest could also be used to justify actions that were detrimental to the independence of some members. The most notorious example of this were the successive treaties between Russia, Austria and Prussia at the end of the eighteenth century carving up the territory of Poland and leading to the complete disappearance of that state from Westphalian society. This action was justified by the parties on the grounds that it was necessary to preserve the balance between them, when the fears of Austria and Prussia were that, if they did nothing, Russia would swallow the whole of Poland. Another egregious act of unprincipled state power was the seizure by Frederick the Great of Prussia of the province of Silesia from Austria. We see in these examples that the principle of state interest, while necessary for Westphalian society, could easily come into conflict with the principle of autonomy and regularly rode roughshod over the principle of territorial integrity that came to be understood as a corollary of sovereignty and implicit in the idea of an autonomous unit that is master in its own house.

There continued to be no principle of legitimacy for membership of this society, other than the historically contingent one of recognizing as members those units that succeeded in establishing their independent status as international actors,[6] of which the most significant new unit in the eighteenth century was the United States of America. However, a major principled alternative did appear on the scene at the end of the eighteenth century with the American and French Revolutions. These affirmed the right of a people to choose its own rulers. In the case of France and the British colonies in America, the question of who constituted a people was relatively uncontroversial. But the principle threatened not only the legitimacy of most rulers in Europe but also the existing distribution of territories between rulers, since the inhabitants of territorial but not sovereign units, such as Ireland, Poland, all the German and Italian states, could come to think of themselves as a people and appeal to this new principle to establish their political independence. Yet, the major disturbance to the traditional order of Europe was wrought, not by the success of the populist and nationalist principles, but by Napoleon who proceeded to conquer most of continental Europe and reorganize it in new monarchical units ruled by his protégés.

After the defeat of Napoleon by the allied powers, principally Great Britain, Russia, Prussia and Austria, the Congress of Vienna of 1814 set about restoring the old order, but in fact changed its operation substantially. In the first place, the four main victors, later joined by a France that had not been punished other than by being returned to its pre-war boundaries and royal dynasty, determined the peace terms, which were then passed on to the lesser powers to accept, and collectively assumed responsibility for managing the peace through regular congresses: an arrangement that came to be known as the Concert of Europe or the Concert of the Great Powers. In the second place, the Great Powers could not just accept the existing authorities appointed by Napoleon in the various territories outside France that he controlled. They affirmed instead a principle of dynastic legitimacy. The rightful ruler was heir of the dynasty that ruled the territory prior to the Revolutionary and Napoleonic wars. However, the Great Powers were not of one mind on the dynastic principle. Except for Great Britain, they wanted to guarantee monarchical authority against revolutionary populism through joint action to suppress revolts. The British wanted to guarantee the territorial settlements established at Vienna rather than the type of government. The British idea eventually replaced that of the Holy Alliance; but in either case, the Concert was an attempt to maintain the peace of Europe through a coalition of the Great Powers by which each undertook not to seek gains for itself without the consent of the others.[7] Its relative success in avoiding any war between the Great Powers for forty years was due to a sense of collective interest in the existence of a balance of power in Europe. It broke down over Russian conquests of Ottoman territory in the Crimea when France and Great Britain defended the Ottomans against Russian aggression. However, this was only a temporary breakdown and led at the subsequent peace treaty to the incorporation of Turkey in the public law of Europe with its accompanying territorial guarantee.

The Concert of Europe was more seriously tested by the nationalist transformations that led to the creation of the unified German and Italian states and to the emergence of new states in the former Turkish territories in the Balkans. Yet, these new states did not immediately upset the balance of power in Europe and it was not until Germany had become the richest, and militarily the most powerful, state by the early twentieth century and began to pursue a hegemonic role in Europe that the Concert was undermined and the Great Powers took refuge in a system of separate alliances that were soon called into action in the devastating destruction and loss of life of WWI.[8] This event came to be widely perceived as revealing the bankruptcy of Westphalian society and requiring radical departures such as were undertaken with the creation of the League of Nations in 1919.

The expansion of the European system

As an eventual consequence of the European colonial expansion over the rest of the world from the sixteenth century onwards, the Westphalian states system came to be enlarged by incorporation of non-European states. The first to be acknowledged were the new states of America that acquired their independence from Britain, Spain and Portugal through revolt against imperial rule at the end of the eighteenth and beginning of the nineteenth centuries. Although the new states were recognized as sovereign states, they had no interest in getting involved in European affairs and played no part in its problems until the USA, which by the end of the nineteenth century had become a substantial economic and military power, began participating in the management of conflicts of interest in Asia and was eventually drawn into the struggle for power in Europe by entering WWI in order to defeat the German bid for supremacy.

Then there was the Ottoman Empire. This had conquered substantial territories in South-Eastern Europe and had been a significant presence in the European balance of power since the sixteenth century. But it had not become an accepted member of the European society of states and did not participate in the great congresses by which that society managed its affairs, namely those of Westphalia, Utrecht and Vienna. The regulatory arrangements established between the European states and the Ottomans, and subsequently extended to Asian states, were different from those the European states followed among themselves. Of major significance was the system of capitulations by which European consulates exercised jurisdiction over their own nationals in Ottoman territory. These were, in the first instance, privileges granted by the Ottoman ruler at his discretion, and only subsequently, with the decline of Ottoman power, came to be seen as impositions by the European powers limiting the sovereignty of the states that were subject to them. Despite this transition to a limited sovereignty the Ottoman Empire was drawn into the operation of the European system in the course of the nineteenth century. It was represented at the peace conference of 1856 that settled the Crimean War and recognized to be part of the European system of public law.[9] It was present at the Hague Peace Conferences of 1899 and 1907 as were the USA, Mexico, Japan, Persia and Siam. The second also included sixteen Central and South American states.

The standard view of the emergence of a universal international society in the twentieth century is that it consisted in the extension of the rules of the European club to non-European states. Candidates for recognition were states that met European standards of domestic state sovereignty and were willing to accept the rules of the European system. Even so, while non-European states were being recognized as participants in the running of the international society of states before WWI, they were, with the exception of the American states, still not given full recognition as equal members of the family of nations but were liable to the discrimination of regimes of unequal treaties, extraterritorial jurisdiction and the denial of racial equality. It was not

until the advent of the United Nations in 1945 that an international
society based formally on full equality and reciprocity of all states was
established.[10]

The principles of international law

The practices of the European society of states, as they had developed
since the Treaties of Westphalia, began to be codified in substantial
legal treatises in the course of the nineteenth century and what we
now know as international law is a modification of the rules of that
society. The rules were understood as the positive or actual law that
the European states recognized as governing their relations. The states
were held to be the creators of the law or its legislators as well as
being the subjects of the law. Of course, the nearest thing to an actual
legislative assembly in this society was the international congresses
that, in the first instance, met to establish peace settlements after major
wars but subsequently, in the course of the nineteenth century, were
convened more frequently and with a view to forestalling conflict.
Apart from what was expressly agreed to in such multilateral treaties,
the law was understood in these legal treatises to consist in the customary practices of states that were held to be binding by them as
revealed in a succession of bilateral treaties, agreements, official
statements and diplomatic acts.[11]

   The states that were the makers and subjects of the law were to be
understood as independent entities. Independence meant that a state
was not subject to the authority of any other state. However, the
independent states were bound by their common law and might be
said to constitute a society, albeit an anarchical one. The independent
states were held to be autonomous in the sense that they were deemed
to have the capacity to control their own people and resources and
hence act as responsible agents in relation to other states by entering
into treaties with them and by complying with their international legal
obligations. International law defined a state as an entity that had a
definite population and territory, a government that was in control of
both and had the capacity to enter into relations with other states.
Such an entity was a candidate for membership of the international
society of sovereign states.[12] What membership involved was recognition as an equal sovereign with the full rights and duties of a member.[13]
However, one could be such an entity without being recognized by

other states as a member or as a full and equal one. This was the fate of many non-European states prior to the Charter of the United Nations and has more recently been true of Israel in respect of Arab states and Taiwan in respect of most members of the international community.

A further principle held that states and only states possessed inter-national legal personality: that is to say, the capacity of an entity to be a bearer of rights and duties under international law, to enter into binding treaties and make legal claims against others. Individual human beings and associations of human beings other than states had no status in international law.[14] They were held to belong to the state of which they were subjects and were, in a sense, that state's property. Only a state that 'owned' them could make claims against other states regarding their treatment. Individuals had no rights.

States were supposed to enjoy the right of territorial integrity. Acc-ording to this principle, the state had exclusive authority within its own territory and other states were not permitted to intervene in this domestic jurisdiction. What was to count as an illegal intervention is the subject of some dispute.[15] But it is clear that a state could not use military force or its threat to make another state's policies comply with its wishes. Territorial integrity did not mean that territories could not legally be transferred from one state to another: a practice widely engaged in under the Westphalian system. Such transfers occurred largely through the medium of peace settlements at the end of a war, such as the transfer of Alsace to France at Westphalia, back again to the new German Empire after the Franco-Prussian war, and back again to France at the Treaty of Versailles after WWI. Apart from the preservation of the form of a legal transfer and in the first transac-tion the maintenance of the formal overlordship of the Holy Roman Emperor, there is little to suggest that these transfers and many others were secured other than by the 'right' of conquest.

Sources of international law

States were the sole source of the authority of law in the system. But they could create international institutions and delegate authority to them, as was the case with the treaties establishing the League of Nations in 1919 and the United Nations in 1945; and with other bodies possessing powers to make binding rules for members, such as the World Trade Organization. In this sense, the creation of the

United Nations and other international institutions has not altered
the constitutional foundations of international society as a society of
states.

International law arises in two principal ways. First, it comes about
through treaties. Here a distinction is made between law-making
treaties and treaty contracts. The former specify rules of conduct
that are intended to be universal, such as the treaties establishing the
League of Nations or the United Nations. It is intended that every
state be a party to the agreement, although no state is bound by the
rules unless it has ratified the relevant treaty (or the rules of the treaty
have become customary international law, which we discuss below).
Treaty contracts have no such universal intent. They are bilateral agreements covering trade, military alliances, and so on that are intended
only to cover the parties to them.[16]

Second, international law emerges through the customary practices
of states. The idea here is that customary practice is evidence of a
general practice accepted by states as law. A general practice accepted
as law is composed of two elements: (i) the material facts regarding
the actual behaviour of states; and (ii) the subjective beliefs of states
that such behaviour is legally required or binding on them. The latter
is the crucial element called *opinio juris*.

Evidence that something is state practice having the force of law is
to be found in official statements of states as to what they believe to be
lawful and unlawful, diplomatic acts regarding the conduct of other
states, and so on. While, for something to be regarded as a binding
customary practice, the practice must be generally and consistently
followed by states, it is obviously not necessary that there should be
no instances of illegal behaviour. However, since there is no police
force or courts of law to punish violations,[17] it is necessary that ille-
galities should be condemned by other states if the customary practice
is to be maintained as law. Otherwise, the danger is that increasing
numbers of states cease to follow the practice and its status as their
general practice disappears.

Both treaty-based international law and customary international
law are held to get their authority as law from the consent of states.
As sovereigns, and hence subject to no one, they can be bound only
by their own will. However, it is doubtful whether this claim is sustainable other than on the basis of a theory of implicit, rather than
actual, consent. No one thinks that a state can withdraw from all its

international legal obligations simply by asserting that it no longer holds itself, or never did hold itself, to be bound by them. For one thing, it will be held to be bound by the treaties it enters into according to the fundamental principle of international law, *pacta sunt servanda* (treaties are to be kept). This principle cannot be justified as the product of explicit consent by the parties, since that would lead immediately to an infinite regress. If the bindingness of the principle *pacta sunt servanda* is grounded in the consent of the parties to it, what is that consent grounded in? Another act of consent? And so on *ad infinitum*. At most one can argue that consent to the bindingness of treaties is implicit in the very act of entering into one, for otherwise, the act would be a lie which could not be revealed to the other party.

Furthermore, a state that purports to withdraw from the bonds of international law does not thereby become a *res nullius* or unowned territory that can be seized by other states as they please, nor does it become legally free to ride roughshod over any state in its power. The best example of such a rogue state is Nazi Germany. It treated international law with contempt and violated its rules with enthusiasm as it conquered and murdered its way through the rest of Europe. But its leaders were held responsible under international law and the state itself, as distinct from the regime, was not considered to be without rights. This suggests that the idea of an international society of states held together by law presupposes that all actual states are subject to principles or laws that are obligatory for them whether or not they have consented to them. The idea would be that, merely by interacting with other states on a regular basis, a state implicitly or rationally consents to accept certain fundamental principles as binding on it. These would be the peremptory norms of international law such as the principle *pacta sunt servanda*. If a state were to persist in rejecting these norms, it is surely implausible that the other states could continue to accept it as a partner.

The problem here is that the positivist character of the treatises on international law that were compiled in the nineteenth and twentieth centuries meant that the lawyers were hostile to natural law principles and so sought to derive all international law from the consent of the parties. They did allow as a source of international law, in addition to treaties and custom, what they called general principles of law recognized by civilized nations. Under this heading were included basic rule-of-law principles. Perhaps, one could say that the positivist character of this provision was contained in the treatment of the principles as the customary principles of law adopted by civilized states. Yet, the point of the term 'civilized' was to contrast the European states who were setting these standards with the 'less civilized' states of Asia and the 'primitive' states of Africa. In this case, it is difficult to see how such a hierarchy can be justified unless there is an implicit appeal to objectively valid or rational standards.[18]

The content of the laws

International law covered, of course, the subjects touched upon in the above discussion of its principles. In an influential compilation by Vattel in the eighteenth century the following topics are also listed: the conduct of trade, navigation, fisheries, embassies, truces, neutrality in war and treaty-making. In a standard contemporary textbook on international law we find the following topics discussed: law of treaties, personality, statehood and recognition, jurisdiction and sovereignty, immunities from national jurisdiction, law of the sea, state responsibility, peaceful settlement of disputes, the use of force, human rights.[19] All these topics would occur in pre-1945 treatises except for human rights, which, under this heading, is entirely a product of the UN programme on human rights. Most of the other topics, however, have undergone significant development or modification in the new UN era.

One of these is the law of war. The medieval Catholic Church held that war was permissible only if it were a just war and only if carried on justly. This was the distinction between *jus ad bellum* and *jus in bello*. In the seventeenth century, as we have seen, the practice of states was to justify their military enterprises in terms of the hereditary rights of their rulers, and influential commentators such as Hugo Grotius continued to stress *jus ad bellum*, although for him what was important was the belief of the parties that their cause was just. But in the course of the eighteenth century, state practice came to be formulated purely in terms of *jus in bello* and the right of states to make war as an instrument of national policy came to be accepted.[20]

The right to make war as an instrument of national policy may be thought of as another corollary of the sovereignty of the state. If sovereignty means that a state is subject to no higher authority, it would seem that it must have the right to decide for itself what is necessary to protect and promote its national interests subject to the requirement that it recognize the equal right of all other states to a similar self-determination. In an anarchical world, where there is no impartial judge and executor of the laws, each must be its own judge and must have a right to use force against other states if it deems this to be necessary to preserve its own vital interests.

Westphalian international relations as society or system?

Hedley Bull in his much discussed book, *The Anarchical Society*, distinguishes between an international system and a society of states. The latter exists when 'a group of states, conscious of certain common interests and common values, form a society in the sense that they conceive themselves to be bound by a common set of rules in their relations with one another and share in the working of common institutions'.[21] The sort of rules he has in mind are ones governing respect for state sovereignty, honouring agreements, co-operating in international institutions and procedures and observing limits on the use of force. An international system exists when two or more states interact systematically, so as to make it necessary for each to take account of the intentions and actions of the other states in the calculation of its own interests, but without any sense of common interests and while being motivated solely by self-interest.[22]

The conception of international relations as an international system expresses a realist view of the world, which has been the dominant understanding in Western academies since WWII, at least until recently.[23] The realist view does not preclude a limited degree of international co-operation through laws and institutions insofar as each from the standpoint of its own separate self-interest perceives such co-operation to be rational. The realist, obviously, recognizes the importance of creating and maintaining a balance of power and accepts the unavoidability of war or at least its threat. What the realist cannot allow is the existence of the capacity of states in an anarchical world to act 'socially', that is to subordinate their pursuit of their separate self-interest to their common interests as members of the whole society of states. Separate self-interest will always trump the common interest, so that a genuine society of states is inconceivable.[24]

The dispute between adherents of system and society corresponds, to a certain degree, with the different conceptions of the individual state of nature in early modern natural law theory discussed in the last chapter. Hobbes, in effect, adopts the realist point of view and believes that the state of nature will be a war of every man against every man. Grotius, on the other hand, held that human beings are naturally sociable as well as competitive and conflicting and hence were capable of acting from a conception of common interests. Yet, all these thinkers concluded that the state of nature was an intolerably insecure and threatening condition and that the only solution lay in the creation of a sovereign state. The Grotian believes that human beings can act from the social point of view if the conditions are in place for them to do so, namely a sovereign state. But Hobbes's view is little different. In the sovereign state, an individual's self-interest is systematically aligned with that of the sovereign and all other individuals, so that a stable and peaceful world is possible, although each acts only with regard to his own interest. The problematic feature common to both Hobbesian and Grotian individual states of nature is that each unit has a basic natural right to preserve itself and is unavoidably its own judge of whatever is necessary to achieve that aim. Hence, in a world in which at least some units do not act, or are suspected of not acting, with self-restraint and, consequently, one in which mutual distrust is rife, insecurity and fear would be rampant and the potentiality for Grotian solidarity would count for nothing.

Is there any reason to believe that the international state of nature is different from the individual one? Hobbes certainly thought so. He believed that because states were relatively independent of each other and could create areas of peace and prosperity in their territories, insecurity at the international level would be much less than at the individual one and states could live in reasonable peace with each other without being subject to a sovereign superior.[25] If that were indeed so, then it would, surely, also be possible for Grotian solidarity between states to be a significant contributory motive for them to exercise self-restraint and adhere to the norms of a society of states.

Hedley Bull thought that societies of states were possible and that Westphalian international relations constituted an example. However, he also believed that such societies depended for their relative success on the possession of common values and a common culture.[26] It is, certainly, true that members of the Westphalian settlement saw themselves as a society and that reflective European thinkers depicted it as such. This is evident in the Westphalian treaties themselves in which the parties describe themselves as the Senate of the Christian

World, while the conception of Europe as a society of Christian princes and like-minded republics is maintained down to the French Revolution and the nineteenth century when it gets replaced by the idea of Europe as a society of states based on the rule of law and setting the standard of civilization for the world. Besides the theorists from Grotius to Vattel, whom we will discuss shortly, Voltaire characterized Europe as 'a kind of society ... a sort of great republic divided into several states', while Edmund Burke similarly believed that the states of Europe formed one great republic under a common system of laws and customs and Kant believed that what he called the assembly of States General at the Hague in the first half of the eighteenth century 'thought of all Europe as a single federated state'.[27]

However, even if we accept this self-understanding of Westphalian states as constituting a society governed by norms and sharing a common culture, it has to be admitted that the rules were very ineffective in preventing states from seeking to expand their territories and power at the expense of others contrary to the principles of Westphalian sovereignty. The major aggressors were, in the first place, Sweden and France in the late seventeenth and early eighteenth centuries in their attempts to achieve dominance in Northern and continental Europe respectively. But most states were in the same business. Prussia and Russia made substantial gains in the course of the eighteenth century, while Napoleon appeared by far the most successful of these seekers of power and glory until his downfall led to the first serious attempt to control the incessant conflict through co-operation between the Great Powers.[28] That this eventually broke down through the renewal of hegemonic ambition by Germany was widely held to reveal the bankruptcy of the traditional states system, now worldwide, and led to the experiment of the League of Nations.

The League was an attempt to create a permanent association of all independent states in running international society that guaranteed the security of each state by the association as a whole. Its dismal failure was standardly attributed to the refusal of the United States, by then a great power, to join from the beginning and the subsequent rise of overtly hostile and rabidly militaristic regimes in Germany, Italy and Japan and, to a lesser extent, the Soviet Union. It is clear that collective security cannot work except through the co-operation of the Great Powers. Hence, the League probably had no chance of succeeding in the circumstances but it was not helped by the constitution of an executive council with insufficient authority[29] and a world society lacking any commitment to common values and refusing to accept even a basic principle of racial equality. After the world had undergone the further extraordinary sufferings of WWII, another attempt at institutionalized international co-operation was made, this time with a more powerful Great Power-dominated Security Council and, most significantly for our purposes, on the basis of common values provided by everyone's endorsement of universal human rights.

3 | The growth of liberal universalism

Liberal pluralism and liberal universalism

Just as there is no inherent connection between the internal organization of the modern sovereign state and liberalism, so also is there no inherent connection between the external organization of the sovereign state in Westphalian society and liberalism in practice or theory. One might think that the affinities between liberalism and the modern state in its domestic form that we referred to in Chapter 1 will be even weaker at the international level. The sovereign state is a form that can be filled both in respect of its internal practices and its theoretical self-understandings in different ways. However, at the international level the Westphalian system, in its official ideology at least, is organized around the relations between states as independent and autonomous units: that is to say, in respect of their form as sovereign states and hence irrespective of their practical and theoretical substance. All such states have equal rights of self-government and so can decide for themselves how they will arrange their domestic affairs. Westphalian society, thus, seems committed to not having any connection with a particular conception of a just social and political order such as liberalism.

However, there is a sense in which Westphalian society does embody a liberal conception of international relations. Insofar as we conceive the society to be constituted by independent and autonomous entities that are individual states rather than individual human beings, then we can think of it as organized on the basis of a rights-based liberalism that applies directly to states and not to their subjects. It is states that enjoy the natural right to freedom and that are entitled to pursue their good as they see fit so long as they do not violate the equal freedom of other states by imposing some harm on them. Since the internal affairs of each state comprise that state's own area of negative freedom, it will be an illegitimate interference in its domestic jurisdiction to require it to pursue liberal policies in regard to its own subjects. Yet, this requirement would seem to be imposed on all member states of the United Nations through that organization's human rights programme. The contrast between these ideas of an international society of states is characterized by Gerry Simpson as one between liberal pluralism and liberal non-pluralism.[1] We prefer to call the latter liberal universalism. Liberal pluralism recognizes the diversity of states' internal values and practices while liberal universalism seeks to turn all states into liberal ones. The full liberal project for world order, as we understand it, is liberal universalism.[2]

The problem with liberal pluralism, or liberalism at the international level only, is that it cannot ground the values of international society on anything more than a *modus vivendi*. It would be an international society bereft of any substantive moral doctrine regarding how human beings should live, which could explain and justify why states should recognize each other's independence and autonomy other than as a pragmatic measure that would be inherently vulnerable to the fears and ambitions of its members. As we have seen, international law and hence the duty to respect the sovereignty of other states came to be seen in the course of the nineteenth century as the positive law of the European society of states, subsequently extended to the rest of the world, and grounded in the agreement of the members. Yet, such an account cannot avoid the implicit appeal to the moral law that agreements should be kept which itself presupposes a conception of the self-binding agents as independent and autonomous entities deserving of respect. But why should a powerful state respect the sovereignty of less powerful ones if international legal pluralism has no moral foundations?

A justificatory doctrine for international principles would seem to be required. Furthermore, whatever justificatory doctrine is adopted to explain states' rights and duties at the international level must be the same as, or at least coherent with, the doctrine that is taken to apply to the internal organization of the state. The two main candidates in the seventeenth century were the theory of the Divine Right of Kings and the Natural Rights/Social Contract theory, both of which endorsed the idea of sovereign statehood. Of these, the doctrine of the Divine Right of Kings would have had the disadvantage of imposing a monarchical orthodoxy on Westphalian society that would have been incompatible with its implicit pluralism in regard to domestic regimes.

The Natural Rights/Social Contract theory fitted much better. It both explained the moral duties states have towards each other through its understanding of natural law governing both individuals and their political associations, and allowed for a pluralism of regimes through its idea of the creation of sovereign power by the contractual designation of a person or a body of persons as sovereign by the subjects. Thus, we find that the main early modern theorists of international society in the seventeenth and eighteenth century, Grotius, Pufendorf, Wolff and Vattel, whose ideas on international ideas we will discuss in the next section, are all adherents of this tradition. The trouble with this doctrine, as we have seen, is that it permits illiberal outcomes because of its commitment to the absolute nature of sovereignty. This lack of coherence between its foundations and political conclusions enabled it to endorse liberal pluralism at the international level and absolute monarchy at the domestic level. But from a theoretical point of view, at least, it cannot be considered a satisfactory combination. John Locke dodged this problem in a sense by making the government responsible to the sovereign community acting through its majority, although in the end that merely displaces the potential source of illiberalism onto the majority. The only adequate solution would be to conceive the will of the sovereign community as an ideal general will in the manner of Rousseau and to reject its identification with any constitutionally defined decision maker.[3] In this way, the constitutional actors are always responsible to the whole community but only in its character as a liberal community pledged to liberal principles. Be that as it may, liberalism in practice evolved in the course of the eighteenth century, under the influence of Locke and Montesquieu, into a doctrine of constitutional constraints on government through the rule of law, the separation of powers and representative institutions and eventually became closely identified with democracy.[4] As a result, it became less suitable as a justificatory theory for an international society committed to a pluralism of domestic regimes. Indeed, as already mentioned, the nineteenth century saw the rise of the international lawyers' conception of international society in positivist terms and the eclipse of the natural law tradition. But, insofar as liberalism with its increasing identification with democracy remained a growing force in European society, its influence at the international level took the form of pressure to incorporate liberal values into international law and organization and hence move that society in the direction of liberal universalism. This pressure took a huge step forward with the UN programme on universal human rights. If this programme were successful, it would provide the common values and moral foundations that were never very strong in Westphalian society and had almost entirely disappeared in the first half of the twentieth century.

The rest of this chapter, then, is concerned first with the theoretical basis of liberal universalism in international society and, subsequently, with the expression of the universalist spirit in its practical life.

International political theory from Grotius to Kant

As we have just indicated, the major theorists of the new and developing international relations of the modern state were adherents of the Natural Rights/Social Contract model of political morality, the application of whose views to international relations we touched on at the end of the last chapter. The point of giving these theorists so much attention is because they originated an essentially liberal strategy for theorizing the problems of political association and because we believe that this liberal theory is the most plausible moral foundation for an international society of sovereign states. The theory explains why state sovereignty is a morally compelling view of the nature of the unity of an international realm in the modern world and explains, at the same time, when properly conceived, the limits to that sovereignty arising from their subjects' human rights. The ultimate aim of the theorizing of the writers to be discussed in this section was to explain the nature of relations between states. But the liberal character of the foundations got dissipated because of their adoption of the theory of absolute sovereignty and the liberalism of their premises gets carried through to the international level only if we think of the individual beneficiaries of the liberal freedoms to be the states and not their subjects.

Grotius

Hugo Grotius, whom we have already met as the widely acknowledged founder of modern natural law theory, is also generally accepted as the originator of the modern theory of international law. His major book of 1625, *Of the Laws of War and Peace*, has, indeed, the international law of war and peace as its main focus, and has been so influential in the development of domestic political theory because his theory of international law is grounded in the law of nature, which is also the ground of the domestic theory. So, for Grotius, and subsequent writers on international law in this tradition, there is one overarching theory of natural law within which we can distinguish domestic and international applications.

However, Grotius accepts a traditional distinction that arose in Roman and medieval thought between the law of nature and the law of nations. The former is a set of rationally necessary principles of human interaction, while the latter consists of those rules and practices that states themselves have come to accept as authoritative.[5] The latter are the product of human contingent will and may change over time. Although the law of nations looks as if it should contain only practices common to all states, Grotius allows that its contents may be accepted by a majority only and even that different groups of states may follow different rules; for instance, Christian states do not accept the legitimacy of enslaving captured Christian soldiers or populations, although this is standard practice among other states.[6]

The law of nature's first law is that of self-preservation for beings who also have a need for and seek to enjoy the society of their fellows. The basic rules of this law, it will be recalled, are the abstention from taking what belongs to another, the restitution of possessions taken and reparation for damage done, the fulfilment of promises and the punishment of violators of the law. States arise, and derive their authority, from a contract made by human beings in a state of nature who, in accordance with the natural law, seek thereby to improve their own security and the enjoyment of each other's society. States, established by contract, constitute among themselves another society whose contingently willed rules are the laws of nations. The latter are based on the same combination of self-interest and the general advantage of society as the civil laws of particular states, only that society is now the society of states. Grotius takes issue with the claim that great states do not need justice in the way that individual human beings do because no individual is strong enough on his own to do without the help of others, while powerful states are in such a position. Grotius holds, to the contrary, that no state is so strong that it may not need the assistance of the combined force of many nations.[7] He believes, of course, that self-interest is not the sole source of the need for law but that the desire for society and its common good is also present. However, without the spur of the former, the latter alone may not be enough.

The rules of natural law apply directly to the relations between states. States have rights and duties derived from the natural rights and duties of their members. Thus, states have duties to abstain from taking the property of others, to return possessions seized and to provide reparation for damage done. They have a duty to keep their compacts and a liability to punishment for the violation of the natural laws. Through the agreements, both tacit and express, that they enter into, they create the rules of the law of nations from which further rights and duties arise. Thus, the authority of the law of nations is derived from the law of nature with regard to contracts, just as the civil laws of particular states acquire their authority from the contractual basis of sovereign power.

International law for Grotius is essentially the law of war and peace and this involves determining what is a just war (*jus ad bellum*) and what is justice in war (*jus in bello*). The legitimacy of war is grounded in the right of self-preservation or the right to defend oneself if attacked. The justice of wars, then, depends on whether they can be justified as a defence of one's rights.[8] This condition applies to individuals making 'private war' against other individuals and to states making public war against other states. Private wars may be legitimate if they are in defence of one's rights, as they clearly may be in a state of nature. Otherwise, force is prohibited. Hence, wars engaged in for the sake of empire or wealth are unjust. Also unjust for Grotius are wars undertaken as pre-emptive strikes against a rising power that may threaten one's security at some time in the future. There has to be clear evidence of a present hostile intention on the part of the rising power for an attack on it to be justified.[9] Grotius outlaws as well wars embarked on for the reason that the nation attacked is a nation of brainless savages or natural slaves or is Godless or lacking in virtue. Even if these claims are true, no state has a right to impose its rule on another nation on such grounds.[10]

However, Grotius does allow that states have a right to punish violations of the natural law even when they are not themselves the immediate victim. This right is derived from the right of each individual in the state of nature to punish violators of the rights of others as well as of oneself.[11] This is because, according to Grotius, nature dictates that evil-doing should be punished. The individual's right is transferred to the state by the contract that brings sovereignty into being and thereby creates the right of the state to treat the fundamental interests and rights of its members as its own. Nevertheless, Grotius is wary of the use of such a justification and believes that wars so vindicated are suspect unless the crimes to be punished are very great. These crimes include the destruction of religious sentiment (since belief in God is necessary for human society), cannibalism, euthanasia, piracy, the killing of settlers on waste land (such as the European settlers on unfarmed land in America), and the cruel treatment of his subjects by an oppressive tyrant.[12]

Grotius' emphasis on the need for wars to be just and his condemnation both of wars of aggrandizement and of pre-emption ties him to the medieval tradition that accepted the legitimacy of war only if it were for a just cause and carried on with a just intention. It appears to be far from the understanding of war, which came to prevail in Westphalian society, as an essential aspect of the members carrying on their society's affairs by looking after their national self-interest and maintaining a balance of power in the society as a whole. In that understanding the issue of the justice of the war was played down and attention was concentrated on *jus in bello*. However, Grotius does allow that there may be justice on both sides in a conflict in the sense that both parties believe in good faith that their cause is just. Since most wars are carried on by states believing in the justice of their cause, one can see that this line of thought could end in the downgrading of issues of *jus ad bellum*.[13]

In regard to *jus in bello*, the general principle that Grotius puts forward is that what is lawful is what is necessary to achieve a lawful end. Thus an individual may use any means necessary to preserve his life.[14] But what that means for a state defending a just cause is not clear. For he distinguishes at this point between what is permitted by the law of nations, what is accepted by Christian nations as governing their relations and what should be the constraints of *jus in bello* arising from considerations of morality and religion. Thus, in regard to slavery, Grotius says, firstly, that by the law of nature no one is a slave. However, he goes on to say that slavery is possible by an individual's own act; one may enter into a contract with another by which one sells one's labour for the rest of one's life in return for sustenance. Such slavery does not entitle the master to kill his slave and extreme cruelty justifies the slave in escaping. Secondly, he acknowledges that slavery is permitted by the law of nations. Originally, the law of nations entitled the victor to put his captives to death, so that the introduction of enslavement as an alternative was an advance. Yet, Christian states had long accepted that prisoners of war should not be enslaved and both morality and religion require us to spare the lives of our enemies, and to avoid harm to women, children and other non-combatants.[15]

Again, he distinguishes between the permission under the law of nations to seize and retain enemy territory and to acquire empire over a conquered population in a just war on the one hand and what justice enjoins on the other. Under the latter, we should return what we have seized (unless it is in payment for damages or debt incurred in an unjust war), and restore a conquered population to its sovereign independence under those who had rightful authority over it. Clearly, Grotius believes that state practice would be improved if it were brought into line with the law of nature. But he does not unequivocally say that a state ought not to follow existing state practice if it does not accord with the law of nature.

Since Grotian international theory is simply the extension to the international realm of the rationally necessary principles that apply universally and in the first instance to the domestic realm, the liberal-individualist character of the fundamental principles ought to be manifest throughout their application. The domestic political theory is grounded in the rights of individuals to life, liberty and possessions together with the right to be one's own master and subject to no one without one's consent. These rights are transferred through consent to one's sovereign state.[16] The state, thus, concentrates in itself all the rights and duties of its subjects and in acting as their agent is thereby obliged in its relation to others states and individuals to follow the natural law principles governing life, liberty, possessions, consent and punishment.

However, Grotius does not make fully explicit this relation between individual rights and the rights of states – a task fulfilled above all by Pufendorf. Furthermore, the liberal character of the theory is partially concealed by what Grotius takes to be permissible through the exercise by an individual of his liberty of contracting. The issue is essentially that of the legitimacy of slavery. An individual, for Grotius, may by his own free act sell himself into slavery. Likewise, a whole people may contract together to subject themselves to an absolute monarch.[17] In both cases, the contract is held to be binding, unless the slave/ subject is exposed to extreme maltreatment, because he entered into the contract freely and with a view to his own good, namely sustenance or security.[18] As a consequence of this justification, states, both at the domestic and international levels, may pay little attention to the need to respect individual rights so long as they do not engage in extremes of oppression.

To avoid these illiberal interpretations of the natural rights to liberty and contract, we must think of the binding contracts that individuals may enter into as those that people would reasonably agree to from an initially fair situation.[19] No one would freely and reasonably enter into a contract of slavery unless in their situation this were the only means available to them of preserving themselves. But according to the theory of natural rights itself, everyone has the natural right to preserve themselves by taking what they need from nature as the common property of mankind and this right cannot be overridden by the private property claims of others. Hence, no one is entitled to an exclusive private property that condemns others to the alternatives of slavery or starvation. Similarly, no one would reasonably enter into a political contract establishing a sovereign power that did not implicitly or explicitly limit the sovereign's right by the principles of natural law themselves as these are necessarily present in the rational collective will of the members to create and maintain a political society in their own interests and to preserve their own rights. Once binding contracts are understood in terms of these inherent limitations, the foundations of the theory in individual rights can manifest themselves with greater transparency and less incoherence at the level of the national state and international society.

Just as, at the domestic level, subsequent writers in the modern natural law tradition developed the implications of the Grotian problematic in different ways, this, we will now show, is true of the international level also.

Grotius' successors in international theory

The great English exponents of the modern natural law doctrine, Hobbes and Locke, had little to say on international relations. Unlike Grotius and Pufendorf, the English theorists' focus is almost entirely on the implications of the Grotian view of natural law for the domestic order. Nevertheless, Hobbes in particular has some remarks about relations between states that make him, together with Machiavelli, an early hero of the realist school. For Hobbes, states face each other in an international state of nature governed by the same rules that apply to individuals in such a state, namely to seek the peace but if one cannot obtain it, one may use all the means and stratagems of war. However, Hobbes does not believe that the international state of nature will lead to the establishment of a world sovereign. This is because states succeed in creating a degree of security and prosperity within their own territories and are relatively independent of each other. So, while the logic of the state of nature drives states to arm themselves to the teeth and permits them to engage in war on the basis of their own judgement of their state interest, the insecurity of inter-national anarchy will not be as pressing as at the individual level.[20]

As in his domestic theory, Pufendorf is rhetorically closer to Grotius than to Hobbes. He develops the doctrine, implicit in Grotius, that the state is a moral individual constituted by the transfer of rights from its subjects and hence is a bearer of rights and duties in international society in its own person.[21] He thus supports the solidarist conception of international society. However, he differs from Grotius in several respects. He denies the natural right of individuals or states to punish violators of the natural rights of others. Punishment is an attribute of sovereign authority and a function of the state in relation to its sub-jects.[22] Only when a people is subject to intolerable suffering is the use of force to help them legitimate.[23] He also rejects the Grotian view (supported by Locke) that it is permissible for European people to settle uncultivated land in America that comprises the traditional hunting grounds of native societies. Such territory belongs to the local society which had a right to dispose of it as it chose without giving any outsider a right to settle.[24]

Pufendorf's international theory greatly influenced the work of two noted eighteenth-century writers on international society, the German Christian Wolff (1679–1754) and the Swiss Emerich de Vattel (1714–67). Wolff develops Pufendorf's ideas regarding individual and state duties of mutual aid towards the conception of a global entity which he calls the supreme state and which embodies the common good of humanity.[25] The supreme state is composed of the separate but equal nations, which should act by majority decision to promote the common security and welfare.[26] But the supreme state does not have any institutional content and the states remain independent entities in charge of the forces of coercion.[27]

The very influential Emerich de Vattel also adopts the general Grotian-Pufendorfian-Wolffian conception of independent states forming a great society[28] and specifically refers to the European states as a Republic with a common interest in its self-preservation as a society composed of sovereign states.[29] But he recognizes that each state retains the right to judge for itself what its obligations are and whether they are superseded by its right to give precedence to its own self-preservation.[30] He also recognizes that the preservation of the society as a whole, as distinct from the preservation of every individual member, requires the operation of a balance of power and a willingness to undertake anti-hegemonic wars.[31]

The Grotian position on international relations is now referred to in the specialist literature as solidarist and is opposed to the realist view of Hobbes.[32] It holds that states form a society with a common good and binding law consisting of the law of nature and the law of nations. This law prescribes duties of mutual aid as well as duties to respect the rights and sovereignties of each other. It is a decentred or anarchical society in which each state retains the right to decide for itself what its duties are under the law and how they are to be assessed relative to its fundamental right to preserve itself. Each state, likewise, has the right to make war to defend itself and other states against a perceived violation of its own or others' rights. There is some disagreement among members of this tradition as to when a state may intervene in the domestic affairs of other states in order to uphold natural law and protect subjects of other states from oppression but most recognize that there will be circumstances when this is permissible.

One may wonder how far apart the Grotians and Hobbesians are in regard to the practical effects of their doctrines. They are, of course, far apart in their general rhetoric. But both recognize the anarchical nature of the international realm and the right of states to act to preserve themselves, if necessary by waging war, and that each must be judge for itself in that matter. The Grotians emphasize that the international realm is governed by law and that the right of states is only to exercise their judgement within the bounds of the law. Yet, Hobbes can say as much. For him, the law of nature commands us to seek peace and to follow the rules of peace in order to obtain it.

However, the law itself says that if we have no hope of attaining it, we may take any steps we deem necessary to preserve ourselves. It is not clear that the Grotians could say anything different. Insofar as they differ, it would seem to be over the degree of insecurity to be expected in the international realm. Yet even Hobbes believes that the situation of states in the international state of nature is vastly better than that of individuals in their state of nature. Given states' relative independence of each other, there seems scope for them to affirm solidarist principles and entertain solidarist sentiments. That Hobbes does not recognize them is ultimately because he believes that one cannot rely on such motivations in the case of the vast majority of mankind and hence that one cannot trust others to abide by rules unless they are subject to a sovereign power that can punish them for their infractions.

Immanuel Kant

That the Grotians are not so different from the Hobbesians is the view of Immanuel Kant (1724–1804). He calls them 'sorry comforters' because they promote the idea of a society of states ruled by law, but in fact accept that it will be regulated by a balance of power and the rule of war.[33] Kant is the last of the great Natural Right/Social Contract theorists. We did not discuss his work in Chapter 1, because he grounds his political theory in a radically new and complex theory of the foundations of right in an autonomous, self-legislating rational will, rather than in God's will as expressed through individuals' natural rights, which leads some commentators to deny that he is part of that tradition at all. His international theory, however, is simple to describe and offers a possible way out of the dissatisfactions of Westphalian society understood as containing elements both of Hobbesian realism and Grotian solidarism.

Kant endorses the standard modern natural law view of an equal natural right to liberty and possessions that cannot be adequately realized in a state of nature and therefore requires a state to secure the benefits of the rule of law. Furthermore, there must be a plurality of such states, since a world state would be too large and its citizens too diverse in language and religion for such a state to be able to realize the value of the civil condition of a lawful peace. But Kant rejects the Grotians' acceptance of the need for a balance of power and of the normality of war as regulatory mechanisms for the society of states. This defeats humanity's goal of regulating the interactions of its members by rational law.[34]

The alternative that Kant proposes is that republican states – that is to say, those states that domestically are governed by natural law principles, which at the political level include the sovereignty of the general will, the representation of the people and the division of powers[35] – should enter into what he variously calls a federal union, a federative associate partnership, a confederation or a permanent congress of states. Kant dithers over exactly what the federal union would involve, but we are interested in the following version. The union is limited to republican states only.[36] This ensures that decisions to go to war must be endorsed by the people who will be reluctant to do so. The union guarantees the freedom of each state, abolishes standing armies and outlaws the settlement of disputes between members by war. The success of the union will attract new members until it covers the whole world.[37]

Kant's political theory, in both its domestic and international aspects, is clearly liberal in its basic form. A just state is one that is organized internally in accordance with the fundamental natural law principle of equal freedom and this must be expressed in the political realm through republican institutions. At the international level, he demands a form of life that effectively ensures that all human interactions are governed by the same natural law principle of equal freedom. This, he thinks, will be possible through the creation of an association of free (i.e. republican) states that gradually draws the rest of the world into its flourishing orbit. In this sense, Kant is internationally a liberal universalist who seeks to arrive at the goal of a universal liberal international society through the progressive but voluntary expansion of the republican core.

It cannot be said that Kant's conception of a federation of free states had any practical effect on the evolution of Westphalian society in the nineteenth century, although it contributed to that body of dissatisfied opinion which after the disaster of WWI led to the attempt to transform that society by the creation of the League of Nations.

In fact, the nineteenth century saw the abandonment of the natural law tradition of political theorizing both at the domestic and international level. The dominant theories became the utilitarian and historicist. Neither was necessarily opposed to liberal principles and practice. Indeed, most forms of utilitarianism powerfully supported liberal practice. But such support was not grounded in the inherent rights of human beings and allowed for their actual rights to be overridden by considerations of the general utility. The major theorists of the historical development of society were either, like Hegel, and the British idealists influenced by him, also generally supportive of liberal-individual rights or, in the case of Marx, unqualifiedly hostile to them. Furthermore, as we have already mentioned, international legal writing took off in the course of the nineteenth century in a strongly positivist direction which concentrated on the actual practices of the states regarding what they understood to be binding on them in their interactions. This law was the law of Westphalian society as recognized by the European states and subsequently by the non-colonial, independent states of the rest of the world that were drawn into the system.

The growth of liberal universalist practices in international society

What we have in mind in this section is not so much the development of an international market economy, although that was certainly an important and inherently liberal feature of international relations in the nineteenth century. It is rather the increase in humanitarian concerns at the international level regarding the conditions and treatment of individual persons or categories of persons and the success in turning such concerns into binding international agreements.

Humanitarian preoccupations do not necessarily reflect a liberal philosophy, let alone one based on natural or human rights. However, in this context the concerns were with the relief of human suffering deemed to be caused by the wrongful actions or inactions of other human beings. Hence, they presuppose, in some sense of rights, that the sufferers have rights to the relief of their wrongful suffering. Thus, it is clear that in the case of the movement to abolish slavery and the slave trade, the fundamental belief in operation was the inherent wrongness of such radical deprivations of individual liberty. Other humanitarian concerns that changed the international law of Westphalian society, such as the so-called humanitarian laws of war, manifested at least a belief in the importance of individuals and the desirability of preventing their unnecessary suffering. The significance of such developments is that they require a modification of the traditional view of the nature of international law that emerged in the course of the nineteenth century and that we discussed in Chapter 2 above, namely that states were its sole subjects and objects. It is part of the traditional view that the international human rights law of the United Nations transformed the laws of Westphalian society by giving a prominent place in them to the rights of individuals and hence by making states responsible to each other for how they treated their subjects. The developments mentioned in this chapter point to areas of international law where Westphalian society was already paying attention to the interests of individuals, even if it did not explicitly recognize their rights. In this sense, we can think of the developments as facilitating or indeed preparing the way for the United Nations' transformations. What follows is intended only as a brief sketch of these changes designed to give some substance to the above claims.

The abolition of slavery and the slave trade

The anti-slavery movement was directed at first towards the trade in slaves from Africa to the Americas, which was largely organized by European merchants and out of which vast profits were made at a huge cost in human life and suffering. The movement to abolish this trade began among the Protestant sect of Quakers in Britain and North America as early as the seventeenth century and became increasingly organized, influential and international towards the end of the eighteenth century. The trade was made illegal in Denmark in 1802, in Britain in 1807, in the United States in 1808 and in France in 1815. The trade was condemned in the Treaty of Vienna in 1815, although no steps were taken to stamp it out. The British played an active role in suppressing the trade internationally in the course of the nineteenth century through a series of bilateral agreements allowing the British navy to seize slaving ships on the high seas. By 1870, the Atlantic trade had been effectively suppressed; by 1890, the East African trade with the Middle East followed the same path. The international conferences of Berlin in 1885 and Brussels in 1889 bound all participants to co-operate in the suppression of the trade; and the former conference in the suppression of slavery also.

Slavery itself was abolished in the British dominions in 1833. Other European and American states followed suit in the course of the nineteenth century, culminating in the International Convention on

Slavery of 1922 held under the auspices of the League of Nations, acceded to by fifty-two states (most of the states then existing) and binding them to abolish slavery. Freedom from slavery was recognized as a fundamental human right in the United Nations' 1948 Universal Declaration of Human Rights. However, while slavery is now universally condemned in law, this does not mean that there are not in actuality very many workers bound by slave-like conditions.[38]

The humanitarian laws of war

These laws cover the treatment of prisoners of war and the wounded as well as civilians. They developed as customary rules prior to their codification in the Geneva Convention of 1864 and the Hague Conventions of 1899 and 1907.

The *jus in bello* rules forbade the killing or enslavement of prisoners of war, laid down standards of care for the wounded and outlawed the direct military targeting of civilians. However, the double-effect rule held that it was permissible to bring about civilian loss as an unintended side effect of the pursuit of legitimate military objectives, provided that the amount of force used was not disproportionate to the threat posed by the enemy.

The humanitarian laws of war should protect the interests of soldiers and civilians in life, liberty and property from being ignored by states in their pursuit of military advantage. Nevertheless, these rules were treated by international lawyers, not as protecting the rights of individual human beings, but as imposing obligations on states towards other states. Only states, and not individuals, were recognized as being entitled to make a complaint against another state regarding the conduct of its armies under the rules. This made the rules conform to the dominant view of international society as purely a society of states that were the sole subjects and objects of international law.[39]

The treatment of aliens, the rule of law and the standard of civilization

With the rise to world dominance of the European states in the course of the eighteenth and nineteenth centuries, the Europeans began to distinguish an international society composed of what they initially identified as Christian states from a larger society of states which included ones that, although independent of the European powers, were not seen as equal sovereign members of the European family of nations. The distinction Christian/non-Christian mutated in the course of the nineteenth century into one between civilized and uncivilized states and the basis for the distinction came to be understood in good part in terms of a state's treatment of its resident aliens. The civilized states of Europe had come to treat such aliens as having the same basic civil rights regarding the freedom of their person and property as their own citizens. Uncivilized non-European states were ones that did not recognize such rights either in regard to European traders and missionaries or their own subjects. The failure to meet such a standard was then used by the European states as justification for imposing so-called unequal treaties or capitulations by which Europeans were exempted from subjection to local law and regulated instead by the laws of their own country which were applied by their consular officials, as mentioned in the previous chapter.[40]

The standard of civilization used by the European powers to justify unequal treatment, or indeed outright conquest and imperial rule in Africa, contained liberal elements and was another example of liberal universalism as opposed to liberal pluralism. The liberal element did not simply consist in the rule of law understood as the just application of given laws under fair procedures that included the independence of the judiciary. That version of the rule of law is compatible with very illiberal laws. It was the rule of law understood as including respect for individual rights regarding freedom of property and contract and, in some degree, freedom of religion, association and movement. This liberal standard had come to be seen as central to European civilization in the nineteenth century and as in part establishing the superiority of that civilization over others.[41] Furthermore, the Europeans used this standard as the criterion for full and equal membership of their international society. To the extent that states fell below the standard, they had to be content with an inferior status. Thus, there was strong pressure on them to adopt European liberal practices in their internal affairs. There was, however, undoubtedly, an element of racism in the Europeans' attitude. This became clear at the Versailles Peace Conference when, despite the Japanese participation on the Western allies' side in the war and despite their adoption of Western domestic legal standards, the Western powers refused to endorse their proposal to include in the League of Nations Covenant an affirmation of racial equality.[42]

The protection of the rights of minorities

As we have seen, the Peace of Westphalia recognized the rights of Lutherans, Calvinists and Catholics in the territories of the Holy Roman Empire to practise their religion even if it was not the official religion of their state. Other treaties in the seventeenth century contained such provisions. These treaties established a limited degree of religious liberty, supposedly guaranteed by treaty law. They also established a right of intervention of the treaty powers on behalf of their co-religionists in the case of violations of the treaty provisions. However, no procedures for monitoring compliance were created and since criticisms tended to produce international incidents, the treaty guarantees were of little practical effect.

The liberation of the Balkan provinces of the Ottoman Empire in the second half of the nineteenth century was the occasion for an attempt to give an international guarantee of more generously conceived rights. The Congress of Berlin of 1878 recognized the statehoods of Montenegro, Serbia and Romania and the autonomous principality of Bulgaria. The treaty guaranteed equal civil and political rights for the adherents of all religions and hence full religious liberty in these territories. But once again arrangements for the implementation of the guarantees were lacking. Intervention had to be by a state party to the treaty and was seen as an encouragement to a minority of separatist aspirations and an excuse for further maltreatment.

There was also international pressure on the Ottomans with regard to their treatment of the Armenians in the years 1894–7 which was based on the Treaty of Berlin's guarantee of Armenian safety to be supervised by the Great Powers. The massacres of Armenians by the Turks, which reached a new level during WWI, led to an Allied Declaration of 1915 condemning the massacres as crimes against civilization and humanity and undertaking to hold the perpetrators personally responsible for their crimes – an undertaking that was not pursued.[43]

A major effort was made to give effective protection for the rights of minority populations in the new states that came into being in Eastern Europe at the end of WWI as a result of the collapse of the Austro-Hungarian, Ottoman and Tsarist Empires. The American delegation to the Versailles Peace Conference under President Wilson wanted to incorporate a general provision regarding the protection of the rights of minorities in the treaty establishing the League of Nations but the other victors of the war, having potential minority problems of their own, opted for the traditional form of a guarantee incorporated in separate treaties with each of the new states. That there was a serious problem of minorities in Eastern Europe was a result of the attempt to base the new states on the nationality principle. Because national populations were so commingled, it was impossible to allocate a territory to one nationality without incorporating other nationalities within it.

In these treaties the minorities were granted full protection for life and liberty and equal civil and political rights with the majority population. They also had special minority rights regarding the use of their own language both in private and in the public courts, the control of their own educational, religious and social institutions and an equitable share of public money. While the state parties to the treaties guaranteeing the rights were the allied powers, the rights were also placed under the special protection of the League of Nations.

On the face of it, this was a clear attempt to limit some states' domestic sovereignty through treaty-based law requiring those states to respect the individual rights of some of their members. It might be thought that these were rights of groups rather than of individuals, but this view would be mistaken. The rights were individual rights to life, liberty, religion, language, and so on; however, only the members of minorities were guaranteed protection for the enjoyment of them. Yet, what created the most resentment was the discriminatory nature of the scheme. The restrictions on domestic sovereignty applied to the new states of Eastern Europe but not to old states, many of which had minorities of their own, not to speak of the vast empires of subordinated peoples that some of the allied powers possessed.

In general, the scheme cannot be considered a success. It was resisted by those states on which it was imposed. It was never wholeheartedly endorsed by League members concerned about its implications for the right of non-interference in a state's domestic jurisdiction and by many who believed in the eventual assimilation of minorities to the majority culture. It was exploited by the Nazis to stir up trouble among the many German minorities and finally disintegrated in the face of the fascist and authoritarian regimes' complete contempt for rights.[44]

Besides these legal changes, there was an enormous increase, in the period before WWI, in the number and activity of organizations

concerned with equal rights for women and the coloured races, with
the prevention of exploitation and oppression of colonial and aboriginal peoples, as well as with the rights of workers. In 1901 the
French-based Ligue des droits de l'Homme, originally formed in
relation to the anti-Semitic Dreyfus affair, committed itself to campaign for human rights anywhere in the world. Similar ideas and
movements could be found not just in Western countries but also in
modernizing China and Japan and among Muslim peoples.

After the war, Woodrow Wilson's statements in support of human
rights and the formation of the League of Nations itself raised great
expectations and the inter-war period saw not only the rise to power
of regimes that were utterly opposed to and contemptuous of human
rights but also the multiplication of organizations and individuals
dedicated to the worldwide protection and promotion of human
rights. Among these was the Institut de Droit International which
adopted in 1929 an influential Declaration of the International Rights
of Man. These rights included those to life, liberty and property without distinction of nationality, race, sex, language or religion. Even
Latin American governments participated in the movement of opinion
and aspiration, producing in 1938 the Lima Declaration in Favour
of Women's Rights and another declaration in Defence of Human
Rights.[45]

Thus, when the discussions on the creation of a new world organization to replace the defunct League were taking place, there existed
a substantial body of international opinion pressing for the inclusion
of a commitment to international human rights based on the non-
discrimination principle.[46] We believe that this movement in opinion
and practice towards the recognition of international human rights
has brought to the surface what was implicit in the liberal moral
foundations of Westphalian sovereignty, once acceptance of the formal and absolutist understanding of that sovereignty was undermined
by the horrendous course of events. This is not to say that the older
view has not continued to have powerful attractions for illiberal-
minded rulers. It is only to say that the obvious moral justification for
the notion of the sovereign state in the modern world is that it combines and expresses the wills of its autonomous members and that
when so understood, sovereignty contains an inherent constraint
arising from those members' rights.

PART II

The UN regime on human rights

To change people's mentality, that cannot be done in one generation, it takes many generations and you have to start in the cradle and work your way up through the kindergarten. The trouble is we all think in terms of one human life. One human life is too short a term. I'm now past 85 and I've worked on this problem 60 years. It's a long time but I'm just beginning to scratch the surface. I've seen great progress during my lifetime but you can't expect to change the way people think in one generation. (Nuremberg prosecutor, Ben Ferencz.)

4 | The UN and regional declarations and covenants on human rights

In Part I we have provided a sketch of the emergence of the liberal project in Europe from the seventeenth century as both a body of ideas about the bases of legitimate political association, domestically and internationally, and as a set of corresponding practices. At the international level, liberalism evolved in two conflicting forms: on the one hand, the initially dominant liberal pluralism, which emphasizes the autonomy and liberty rights of sovereign states and, on the other hand, the growing concern for what we have called liberal universalism, which seeks to curb state sovereignty through protecting the liberties and rights of states' subjects.

At the same time, the development of liberalism was accompanied by the rise and spread of nationalism. While a nationalist spirit is needed by the liberal polity in a sense to be explained in the next chapter on the right of peoples to self-determination, the forces of nationalism have no inherent respect for liberal rights. In their most extreme form, in the fascist states of the first half of the twentieth century, they all but overwhelmed the liberal constraints of European civilization. They thereby helped to produce, together with the supposed excesses of liberal pluralist sovereignty in the two devastating world wars, the reaction contained in the UN Charter's commitment to restrict state sovereignty both in regard to states' war-making rights and in regard to the rights of their subjects. The UN regime is a striking expression of liberal universalism. Its character and problems are the subject of Part II.

UN agreements

UN Charter

In August 1941, President Roosevelt of the United States and Prime Minister Churchill of the United Kingdom proposed in a joint declaration a set of principles for international collaboration in maintaining peace and security. This declaration came to be known as the Atlantic Charter declaration; and it was signed one month later by the USSR and the nine governments of occupied Europe: Belgium, Czechoslovakia, Greece, Luxembourg, the Netherlands, Norway, Poland, Yugoslavia and by the representatives of General de Gaulle of France.[1] In October 1944, the United States, the United Kingdom, the USSR and China reached an agreement at Dumbarton Oaks on the aims, structure and functioning of the proposed world organization. This agreement served as a basis for the subsequent United Nations Charter, drawn up and signed in San Francisco by representatives of fifty countries on 26 June 1945. These were basically all the then existing states of the world except for the defeated powers of WWII, Switzerland and the Vatican, as well as Poland who could not attend the conference but was left a space to sign the Charter later (15 October 1945).[2] On 24 October 1945, after the Charter had been ratified by the required number of signatories, the UN came officially into existence.

As with the League, the Charter states that the basic purpose of the UN is to secure and maintain peace. The Charter forbids states to use, or to threaten to use, force against another state,[3] except in self-defence (individual or collective) against an armed attack,[4] or as authorized by the Security Council acting under its Chapter VII powers when in its judgement international peace and security have been threatened (as in the case of the Gulf War of 1990). Enforcement measures can then be undertaken either by the Security Council itself, by a coalition of forces authorized by the Security Council or by a single member acting with Security Council authorization.

The Charter thus removes the right of states to wage war as an instrument of national policy, insofar as that had not already been abandoned in the Briand-Kellogg Pact of 1928.[5] In this respect the UN Charter endorses also the precedent set by the International Military Tribunal in Nuremberg which tried, convicted and executed Nazi leaders for, among others, crimes against peace or waging aggressive war.

The UN Charter declares further that among its fundamental goals is that of encouraging respect for human rights and promoting their observance; and the members pledge themselves to take action for the achievement of these human rights objectives.

As a matter of fact, the Charter refers to human rights seven times: in the preamble, and in articles 1, 13, 55, 62, 68 and 76. However, while referring to human rights and fundamental freedoms, it does not tell us what they are. The responsibility for that was given immediately by the UN to one of its organs, the Commission on Human Rights.[6] This was the genesis of probably one of the most important documents of our time, the Universal Declaration of Human Rights (UDHR).

Universal Declaration of Human Rights

Among a number of other recommendations in our report we suggested that the first work to be undertaken was the writing of a Bill of Human Rights. Many of us thought that lack of standards for human rights the world over was one of the greatest causes of friction among the nations, and that recognition of human rights might become one of the cornerstones on which peace could eventually be based.[7]

The Commission on Human Rights, appointed in 1946, was composed of eighteen member states and was charged with producing an international bill of rights. The Commission set up a drafting committee composed of representatives from Australia, Chile, China, France, Lebanon, the USSR, the United Kingdom and the United States of America and chaired by Mrs Eleanor Roosevelt. The United Nations Secretariat produced the basic working paper of the committee.[8]

There had been little or no disagreement among the Western allies, in the aftermath of the atrocities of WWII, about the need to incorporate the promotion of respect for human rights among the central purposes of the UN. Disagreements developed in the Commission, however, over the form that the document specifying the rights should take: that of a declaration of rights only or of a binding covenant? The content of these rights was also disputed. Ultimately, the Commission settled on a declaration rather than a treaty; and on the inclusion of economic, social and cultural rights as well as civil and political. It was felt – particularly by the US representative – that a declaration, carrying a moral but not legal weight, would be more practical at this stage; and could then become the foundation for a future legally binding international bill of human rights. This proved to be a wise decision, for the self-standing Declaration has acquired a remarkable status as the most authoritative document of the international human rights movement.

The title of the declaration, the Universal Declaration of Human Rights, emphasized that it was to be seen as a standard of rights for all people everywhere without regard to race, sex, colour, political persuasion or ethnic background. Article 1 reflects this emphasis by stating that:

All human beings are born free and equal in dignity and rights. They are endowed with reason and conscience and should act towards one another in a spirit of brotherhood.

Clearly, the belief expressed is that the rights in the Declaration are inherent in human beings and not bestowed on them by states or even by the United Nations. The Declaration merely affirms that these rights already exist and that all individuals and societies are obliged to promote respect for them. The following statement that human beings are endowed with reason and conscience could be taken to mean that it is in virtue of being rational and moral beings that they have these rights. Others interpret it to mean only that it is through our reason and conscience that we can recognize that they exist and act upon them. This vagueness reflects the fact that the members of the drafting committee were more interested in affirming the existence of basic rights than in reaching agreement on their philosophical foundations.

The rest of the Declaration is a masterly compilation of rights that are subsequently divided into two separate types that were made the subject of separate covenants: civil and political on the one hand and economic and social on the other. In particular, Article 3 ensures general civil and political rights:

Everyone has the right to life, liberty and security of person.

Article 25 ensures general economic and social rights:

Everyone has the right to a standard of living adequate for the health and well-being of himself and his family, including food, clothing, housing and medical care and necessary social services, and the right to security in the event of unemployment, sickness, disability, widowhood, old age or other lack of livelihood in circumstances beyond his control.

There is also a general limitation clause. Article 29(2) states that:

In the exercise of his rights and freedoms, everyone shall be subject only to such limitations as are determined by law solely for the purpose of securing due recognition and respect for the rights and freedoms of others and of meeting the just requirements of morality, public order and the general welfare in a democratic society.[9]

Importantly, Article 29(1) specifies that:

Everyone has duties to the **community** in which alone the free and full development of his personality is possible.[10]

The Declaration was presented to the General Assembly of the UN in December 1948. The General Assembly endorsed the text of the Declaration without amendment. There were no dissenting votes, but the Soviet Union and its satellites, as well as Saudi Arabia and South Africa, abstained.

Unlike with the drafting committee – whose members had been drawn from all parts of the globe and from different cultural traditions – the General Assembly members represented mainly the 'Judeo-Christian' tradition. There were thirty-seven members from Christian countries, as opposed to eleven Islamic members, six Marxist, four Buddhist and one Hindu.[11] Yet, there appears to have been little or no sense that the Universal Declaration on Human Rights was imposed on the rest of the world by Western states.

Indeed, the General Assembly, in adopting what they called a Universal Declaration, intended that it be understood as a document adopted by all nations – since none opposed it – and applying to all. The abstentions did not necessarily indicate opposition. The Soviets' official reason for abstaining was that in the USSR there was no conflict between the individual and the state. In reality, however, they abstained only because they wanted to include a clause that permitted the restriction of human rights when they conflicted with the interests of the state. Once the proposal was overwhelmingly rejected, they continued to participate vigorously in the drafting commission and in general supported the idea of human rights. However, the Saudi Arabians abstained because they would not accept Article 16 on equal marriage rights or Article 18 on the right to change one's religion, and no doubt others regarding non-discrimination clauses. South Africa abstained officially because it rejected the idea of social and economic rights; but, in fact, they did not like the racial discrimination clause.

As a result of the long delay in ratifying the International Covenant on Civil and Political Rights and the International Covenant on Economic,

Social and Cultural Rights (see below), the Universal Declaration of Human Rights, as the only broadly based human rights instrument available, achieved major significance in the movement for human rights and was constantly invoked. Nevertheless, its international law status is generally taken to be hortatory or aspirational rather than binding. There are, however, some who hold that, since the UN Charter is binding on its members as a multilateral treaty in international law and the Charter commits the members to respect and promote human rights – which the Declaration specifies – the Declaration can be held to be binding in international law also.

Regardless of its binding nature, we would like to conclude our discussion of the Declaration by sharing with Eleanor Roosevelt the following sentiment:

> It seems to me most important that the Declaration be accepted by all member nations, not because they will immediately live up to all of its provisions, but because they ought to support the standards toward which the nations must henceforward aim ... The work of the Commission has been of outstanding value in setting before men's eyes the ideals which they must strive to reach. Men cannot live by bread alone.[12]

International Covenant on Civil and Political Rights (ICCPR) 1966 (entry into force 1976)

The civil and political (CP) rights are standardly called first-generation human rights as compared with second-generation rights of the economic, social and cultural (ESC) rights type, and something called third-generation rights, an extremely broad spectrum of rights that have not yet been formally adopted in a UN covenant but include the right to development and environmental rights.

CP rights are called first-generation rights because, so it is claimed, in the tradition of thinking about natural or human rights beginning in the seventeenth century these rights were the only ones identified. However, as we have shown in our discussion of that tradition in Chapter 2, this view is incorrect. What is true is that the liberal and partially democratic states of Europe of the eighteenth and nineteenth centuries were primarily concerned with CP rights, and ESC rights only came to political prominence in the course of the nineteenth and twentieth centuries with the rise of socialism and the labour movement. The idea of 'third generation' rights is much more recent and has been adopted predominantly by developing states.

The preamble to the Convention makes clear that the CP rights derive from the inherent dignity of every individual and that they accord with the spirit of the Universal Declaration of Human Rights. It also refers to the indivisibility of the two sets of rights by stressing that:

The ideal of free human beings enjoying civil and political freedom and freedom from fear and want can only be achieved if conditions are created whereby everyone may enjoy his civil and political rights, as well as his economic, social and cultural rights.

Article 2(1) of the ICCPR imposes immediate obligations on the state party to respect, protect and ensure CP rights to all persons without discrimination. State parties are to take immediate steps, including legislation, to give effect to the rights and provide all persons with effective remedies. This involves a duty to protect individuals' rights from interference by non-state actors.[13]

The CP rights themselves may be classified as follows:

- protection of an individual's physical integrity; for example, freedom from torture, arbitrary arrest and deprivation of life;
- procedural fairness, provisions on arrest, trial and imprisonment;
- equal protection norms;
- freedoms of belief, speech, association, movement; and
- political participation.

The CP rights may be seen therefore mainly as aimed at protecting the individual from an abuse of power by the state. There are, however, also some 'oddities', such as Article 23(2), the right to found a family (more of a social right?); Article 1, the right of peoples to self-determination (group right?); Article 27, the right of minorities to their own language and culture (social and cultural and group right?); and Article 47, the right to natural wealth and resources (economic right?).

The ICCPR has a general derogation clause.[14] Article 4 specifies that in time of public emergency that threatens the life of the nation, state parties may derogate from their obligations under the Convention.[15] However, the Convention also provides that some rights cannot be derogated from in this way. Article 4(2) states that no derogation may be made from the right not to be arbitrarily deprived of life

(Article 6), prohibitions on torture (Article 7) and slavery (Article 8, paragraphs 1 and 2), the right not to be imprisoned merely on the ground of inability to fulfil a contractual obligation (Article 11), the right not to be held guilty of any criminal offence for an act which did not constitute a criminal offence at the time it was committed (Article 15), the right to be recognized everywhere as a person before the law (Article 16) and the right to freedom of thought, conscience and religion (Article 18).

Besides the general derogation clause of Article 4, there are also specific limitations on some rights, which can be restricted (i) in accordance with the law; and (ii) if necessary in a democratic society in the interests of national security or public safety, public order, protection of public health or morals, or protection of the rights and freedoms of others. These limitations can be found in Article 12 (freedom of movement), Article 18 (freedom of religion and belief), Article 19 (freedom of expression), Article 21 (right of peaceful assembly) and Article 22 (freedom of association).

Furthermore, the Covenant contains some general non-discrimination articles. Articles 2 and 26 forbid discrimination on grounds of race, colour, sex, language, religion, political or other opinion, national or social origin, property, birth or other status. Article 3 ensures equal rights of men and women.

Some of the CP rights have been the subject of more specific conventions such as the Genocide Convention 1948 (right to life); Convention on Elimination of all Forms of Racial Discrimination 1965 (equality), Convention against Torture 1984; Convention on Elimination of Discrimination against Women 1979 (which is the subject of Chapter 7 in this book). These more specific conventions attempt to spell out in more detail what the content of these rights are.

Another important issue is that of the jurisdiction of state parties to the Convention. While Article 2 refers to persons 'within [a State party's] territory and subject to its jurisdiction', the Human Rights Committee that monitors the implementation of the Covenant has clarified that 'a State party must ensure and respect the rights laid down in the Covenant to anyone within the power or effective control of that State party, even if not situated within the territory of that State party'.[16] Similarly, the International Court of Justice in its *Advisory Opinion on the Legal Consequences of the Construction of a Wall in the Occupied Palestinian Territories* recognized that the jurisdiction of states is primarily territorial, but concluded that ICCPR extends to 'acts done by a State in the exercise of its jurisdiction outside of its own territory'.[17]

International Covenant on Economic, Social and Cultural Rights (ICESCR) 1966 (entry into force 1976)

While the first-generation rights dealt mainly with liberty, the second-generation rights deal mainly with equality considerations.

The covenant begins, like the ICCPR, with the right of peoples to self-determination. We discuss this right in detail in the next chapter. We shall therefore say nothing more about it now other than to remark that its presence at the forefront of both the ICCPR and the ICESCR is to be explained in terms of the importance this right had for the forces of decolonization of the European empires.

The other rights affirmed are the following:

• economic rights: such as the right to work (Article 6), to form and join trade unions (Article 8), to social security (Article 9), to an adequate standard of living (Article 11);
• social rights: such as the right to the highest attainable standard of physical and mental health (Article 12), to education (Article 13); and
• cultural rights: such as the right to participate in the cultural life of the community and enjoy the benefits of scientific progress and its applications (Article 15).

Even with good will, these economic, social and cultural rights could not always be immediately implemented by states because of scarcity of resources. As we saw, this is not the case with many CP rights: in principle (and as expected under Article 2), they could be implemented immediately by stopping torturing, enslaving, arbitrarily imprisoning and detaining people. In fact, of course, if these practices are deeply embedded in a particular regime, it is not possible to drop them overnight. Still, stopping them is not a matter of a major commitment of wealth so much as of will to root out abuse of power and oppressive practices (although a well-functioning democratic voting system, for example, will also require a major expenditure). A very poor country, on the other hand, cannot afford to give all its members an education or high standards of health, guarantee the right to work, social security, and so on. This is indeed recognized in the ICESCR which imposes different obligations on state parties under Article 2 than the equivalent obligation under Article 2 of the ICCPR.

State parties' obligations under Article 2 of the ICESCR are recognized thus as being subject to available resources; and, accordingly, to constitute an obligation of progressive realization only.[18] However, as the Committee on Economic, Social and Cultural Rights states in its *General Comment No 3*, Article 2(1) does impose immediate obligations which include the undertaking to guarantee ESC rights without discrimination[19] and to take positive steps towards the realization of all ICESCR rights.[20] Furthermore, Article 2 imposes a core obligation to satisfy minimum essential levels of basic rights: in other words, states are duty-bound to develop programmes to guarantee minimum levels of economic, social and cultural well-being.[21] In case of developing states, resource constraints and global economic conditions are also relevant in considering their obligations; especially in respect of non-nationals.[22]

Article 22 of the Covenant establishes a mechanism by which the Economic and Social Council may bring to the attention of relevant United Nations' bodies any matters arising out of reports submitted under the Covenant 'which may assist such bodies in deciding, each within its field of competence, on the advisability of international measures likely to contribute to the effective progressive implementation of the ... Covenant'.[23]

As with the Universal Declaration of Human Rights and the ICCPR, there is a general limitation clause in Article 4 (as you may remember, Art. 4 ICCPR is properly speaking a derogation clause, but we are treating the two as the same here). The test is restricted in this case to the purpose of promoting the general welfare in a democratic society.[24]

There is another way in which Article 2 of the ICESCR is different from Article 2 of the ICCPR besides the timing of the obligations (i.e. immediate versus progressive realization of the rights): the extent of jurisdiction is different. We saw that Article 2 of the ICCPR restricts the obligation of states to respect and guarantee civil and political rights 'to all individuals within its territory and subject to its jurisdiction'. Article 2 of the ICESCR does not contain such restriction; and otherwise states that each state party 'undertakes to take steps, individually and *through international assistance and cooperation*' (emphasis added). Hence, while the primary duty to promote the welfare of all individuals subject to their jurisdiction must clearly lie in each state, the question arises as to whether all states have a duty to promote economic and social welfare throughout the world.

A positive answer to that question can be supported by a number of other articles in the Convention: in particular, Article 11 which recognizes everyone's right to be free from hunger and which, like Article 2, imposes a duty on states to take, individually or through international co-operation, a number of measures to achieve that objective more effectively;[25] while Article 23 provides for a number of methods for international action to achieve the Convention's rights.[26] More generally, given the UN Charter commitment of all states to promote the achievement of human rights throughout the world and given the binding nature of the Charter, it would seem to be part of the international law requirement on each state to assist other states in realizing the goals of ESCR.

However, there is no consensus among states on that matter. A report on a session of the UN working group on the Optional Protocol to the ICESCR states, for example, that, 'during the session, there was a division as to whether international cooperation and assistance is a moral or a legal obligation. The African group, as well as Ecuador, Indonesia and Iran made it very clear that they considered it a legal obligation that must be included in the Optional Protocol. On the other hand, Canada felt it is a moral obligation'.[27] We will discuss this question further in Chapter 6.

Finally, the question of duty bearers: in general, it is recognized that the prime duty bearers in respect of both CP and ESC rights are states. However, the preamble to both covenants states that:

the individual, having duties to other individuals and to the community to which he belongs, is under responsibility to strive for the promotion and observance of the rights recognized in the present covenant.

Similarly, the preamble to the Universal Declaration on Human Rights holds that:

every individual and every organ of society, keeping this Declaration constantly in mind, shall strive by teaching and education to promote respect for these rights and freedoms ... both among the peoples of Member States themselves and among the peoples of territories under their jurisdiction.

It is thus for each one of us to strive to promote the rights enumerated in the Declaration and the covenants.

Why have two covenants, rather than only one (as with the Universal Declaration)?

There are two main reasons for this development. First, the powerful conservative element in the United States Senate had become suspicious of the human rights movement as a whole but was especially hostile to the notion of economic and social rights. The Soviet Union and its allies, on the other hand, had strong reservations over CP rights. It was thus felt that one covenant combining both sets of rights ran the danger of being rejected outright, while two offered states the option of supporting one and not the other. In the end, of course, both covenants have received the endorsement of the great majority of states.

Second, it was also felt that, because of the different nature of the two types of rights, it would be impossible to develop a single system of implementation. Most CP rights could be enacted immediately by states, while the ESC rights required long-term programmes. A further connected reason was that it was believed that one could have an international tribunal for the CP rights but not the ESC ones. Indeed, decades later the UN set up two special International Criminal Tribunals to deal with international crimes committed in the former Yugoslavia and in Rwanda, and a permanent International Criminal Court for crimes committed against humanity, such as torture, genocide, and so on. We look at these courts in Chapter 8.

Regional systems

It was always intended that the UN programme on human rights should be supported by regional conventions around the world. A number of these have indeed been created. These are the European, the American, the African and the Convention of the Commonwealth of Independent States of the former Soviet Union. The first two conventions were closely modelled on the Universal Declaration on Human Rights.

The European Convention on Human Rights, ratified by forty-seven states, including Russia (as of November 2007), dates from 1950. It covers primarily CP rights. ESC rights are contained in a separate document called the Social Charter and in fact take the form not of rights but of long-term social objectives.

The American Convention on Human Rights of 1978, ratified by twenty-four states, but not by the US or Canada, also covers mainly

CP rights. ESC rights are dealt with in a protocol to the Convention known as the Protocol of San Salvador of 1999 that has been ratified by twelve states.

The African Charter on Human and Peoples' Rights (Banjul Charter) of 1986 covers not only CP and ESC rights but also third-generation rights, including the rights of peoples to development and to a satisfactory environment. This Charter also contains a list of duties of individuals to their state, their society and their family, such as a duty to preserve and strengthen social and national solidarity and independence.

The Commonwealth of Independent States (CIS) Convention of 1995 was signed by seven of the eleven CIS member states and came into effect in 1998 when ratified by three (Russia, Tajikistan and Belarus). The Convention covers both CP and ESC rights.

We discuss all of these conventions in more detail in Chapter 8.

Liberal character of the human rights documents

While all the rights in these documents are necessary to the full realization of a liberal society and polity, some of them could be implemented in regimes that were thoroughly hierarchical and illiberal. For instance, the articles forbidding slavery and torture could be respected in strongly authoritarian regimes in which all had rights but these were unequal and based on rank. Slavery was abolished in Saudi Arabia in 1962 without there being any danger in mistaking that country for a liberal one. The general point is true also of rule-of-law rights such as the articles concerning arbitrary deprivation of life or liberty, retroactive punishment, presumption of innocence, and so on. While all these rights are of great importance to the secure enjoyment of liberal freedoms, they could be recognized in stable hierarchical societies in which the rights to be enforced were not equal and did not include the fundamental liberal freedoms of movement, association, thought and expression, and religion.

The latter, then, are quintessentially liberal rights. However, to retain their liberal character, they must not be qualified by reference to the interests of a non-liberal social order. Thus, suppose that the Nazi government of Hitler had issued a Nazi Declaration of Human Rights which proclaimed everyone's right to freedom of movement, association, and so on, subject to the interests of the Aryan people, which meant that the freedom of Jews and other 'undesirables' was limited to their sleeping quarters in the concentration camps, we would consider the declaration to be the height of cynical absurdity. Yet, the Soviet government of Stalin proclaimed a constitution guaranteeing such apparently liberal rights subject to the interests of the toiling masses, and this meant in effect that the freedoms did not extend to anyone who disagreed with the Soviet government. Similarly, there are much more recent Islamic declarations of human rights and constitutions affirming standard liberal freedoms but qualifying them by reference to the requirements of Islamic Law, which in its traditional form discriminates between men and women, Muslim and non-Muslim and does not permit apostasy.

The only qualifications to individual rights that are compatible with the maintenance of their liberal character are, as we saw, (i) the general limitation/derogation qualifications such as the ones mentioned in Article 29(2) of the Universal Declaration on Human Rights,[28] Article 4 of the ICESCR,[29] and Article 4 of the ICCPR;[30] and (ii) specific limitations on some ICCPR rights, which can be restricted in accordance with law or if necessary in a democratic society in the interests of national security or public safety, public order, protection of public health or morals, or protection of the rights and freedoms of others. The latter are found in articles on freedom of movement, freedom of religion and belief, freedom of expression, right of peaceful assembly and freedom of association.

Of course, how the latter qualifications are to be interpreted is a crucial issue that we will discuss shortly.

The consideration that effectively guarantees the liberal character of the civil and political freedoms in these documents is the non-discrimination requirement, as in Article 2 of the Universal Declaration of Human Rights which forbids discrimination on grounds of race, colour, sex, language, religion, political or other opinion, property, birth or other status; as also in Articles 2, 3 and 26 of the ICCPR.[31] The articles we have characterized as essentially liberal affirm the equal freedoms of all persons subject only to what is necessary to ensure the existence and operation of a legal and political system that will give effect to these rights, and to considerations of public morality and decency.

With regard to the political rights that give the documents a democratic character, the relevant articles are Article 21 in the Universal

Declaration on Human Rights and Article 25 in the ICCPR: these affirm the right of everyone to take part in the government of their country directly or through the election of representatives on the basis of a universal and equal suffrage. However, without the liberal freedoms of association, assembly, and expression, a polity can be democratic while being far from liberal.

We have identified the liberal elements in the documents solely in terms of CP rights only and without regard to ESC rights. This is because, on our view of liberalism, they constitute the primary core of liberal beliefs while social and economic rights are justified relative to this core as comprising the conditions necessary for everyone to be able to exercise the former rights effectively.

The economic and social rights on their own are perfectly compatible with an illiberal organization of society, such as that of Soviet communism, which provided substantial welfare benefits to its citizens but denied them all liberal freedoms and even rule-of-law rights. Hence, economic and social rights form part of a liberal scheme only insofar as they are conceived in the above way as conditions for the fair enjoyment of the equal liberal freedoms.[32]

The standard view of the UN bills of rights is that the rights are held by individuals against their state rather than against other individuals. But this should not be seen as a problem for our conception of the liberal core as a set of equal rights. For on our liberal understanding of rights, the state is just the organ through which an ideal system of rights held by individuals against each other is to be realized.

It is, indeed, the case that, in these documents, the primary duty to promote respect for human rights falls on each state in relation to its citizens. But, since respect for the liberal core of human rights by the state can mean only respect for a system of equal rights in which the rights are held by individuals against each other, the apparent primacy of the state's duty is misleading. From an ideal ethical standpoint, from which the idea of the system of rights is derived, the primary duties are those of individuals to each other. The primacy of the state's duty is a pragmatic one. The state is the organ that gives reality to the scheme and thereby activates the, so to speak, dormant duties of individuals. It is true that the rule-of-law rights can be held only against something like a state but these rights, as we have argued, are not part of the liberal core.

Interdependency thesis

The official UN position on the relative standing of the two sets of rights dates back to the Universal Declaration on Human Rights and was reaffirmed at the 1993 Vienna Conference on Human Rights: the two covenants and sets are of equal status, universal, indivisible, interdependent and interrelated.[33] They are all necessary for human dignity, on the same footing and with the same emphasis.[34]

But what does indivisible, interdependent and interrelated mean? It cannot mean literally that one cannot enjoy one of these rights without enjoying all the others. For, it is obvious (and has actually been the case) that it is possible for the civil rights to be respected in a polity without being accompanied by political or economic and social rights, and conversely the economic and social rights can be recognized without any respect for CP rights. As mentioned above, one can even have political rights without civil or economic and social rights.

Perhaps, what is meant is that one could not **securely** enjoy the one category without enjoying all the others. Thus, one's exercise of one's CP rights could be undermined by lack of access to health care or unemployment relief, while one's welfare rights would be insecure without possessing the CP rights that would enable one to ensure their protection. However, security is a matter of degree and there can be no absolute security in these matters, since respect for rights depends ultimately on the will of governments and their peoples to uphold the scheme and this will can disappear.

Hence, we believe that the only justifiable claim regarding the interdependency thesis is that together the rights constitute the social-structural conditions of a full human life of freedom and dignity. If one enjoys all these rights, then one is in possession of the best social-structural conditions for flourishing as a self-determining human being responsible for one's own individual life and for participating in the direction of the collective life. As particular rights are withdrawn, these conditions become less and less favourable. Of course, to flourish a person needs also other goods, such as the love and friendship of others, but these cannot be provided for by a system of rights. That system governs only the basic structure of individuals' associational life.

This understanding of the interdependency thesis is obviously compatible with the acceptance of the need on occasion to prioritize some, or indeed whole categories of, human rights over others. The UN's official view appears to involve the belief that the interdependency thesis requires the rejection of all prioritization. But it clearly does not. It may, of course, be unnecessary to prioritize. However, this must be a matter of pragmatic judgement. We will consider these matters in Chapter 6.

Are ESC rights really human rights?

In your discussions about social and economic rights, you will need to consider this argument, that the inclusion of such rights broadens the framework of rights so far as to blur the focus of rights protections. What I would suggest in fact is that it does the opposite. With emerging jurisprudence it is becoming clear that the inclusion of economic and social rights actually refines the focus of constitutional rights so that the issues of the most disadvantaged groups are not lost, so those who most need the protection of the constitution are not ignored, so the claims that are actually at the heart of these fundamental values of dignity and equality are validated and made central to the ongoing process of rights claiming. (Bruce Porter)[35]

As we saw, the adoption of two rather than one encompassing covenant on human rights arose from the belief that some states were opposed to one or the other and if combined the whole thing might be rejected. That the communists and other illiberal states should be opposed to CP rights is readily understandable. But what were the reasons why some liberally inclined states – above all the USA – have objected to the inclusion of ESC rights in their legal systems or constitutions?

The objections of the liberal states can all be grouped under a main claim: that it is simply inappropriate to treat ESC goods as objects of rights. They may be desirable social goals but to treat them as rights is to confuse rights and goals and threaten the whole rights discourse, including the civil and political rights, with disintegration. As we have seen, the European welfare states may also be said to have taken this view, at least in part, when separating off the welfare 'rights' in a Social Charter (whose non-binding content is not subject to the jurisdiction of the European Court of Human Rights, unlike the rights recognized in the European Convention).

A widely discussed attack on ESC goods as rights is that of Maurice Cranston.[36] His claim is that for something to be a human right it must satisfy three criteria:

1. Practicability: if someone has a right, there must be another person with a duty to satisfy the right claimed and such a person cannot be under a duty if he is unable to perform. Thus some poor countries are unable to fulfil the right claims to ESC goods of their members. So they cannot be under a duty to do what they cannot do. Furthermore, if no one is under a duty, no one can have a right.
2. Universality: if someone has a human right, it must be a right of a human being as such against all other human beings. But some ESC rights are not of this kind, e.g. the right of workers to holidays with pay. According to Cranston, this can be a right only of employees against their employers and cannot therefore be a human right. In general, ESC 'rights' are held against one's own society, while CP rights are held against all other persons.
3. Paramount importance: holidays with pay (ICESC, Art.7(d)) may be desirable but they are hardly essential to a life of human dignity.

On the basis of these criteria, Cranston concludes that only CP rights can be genuine rights and ESC 'rights' must be understood as goals.

We strongly disagree with this, as we believe that ESC rights can also be 'genuine human rights'. To explain why, let us begin with the question whether an ESC type of good can ever be the appropriate object of rights. We mean by this that we should forget for the moment that we are concerned with human rights and ask whether you can have within your society a system of legal rights the object of which are ESC-type goods. In other words, could the legal system incorporate rights such as the right to education, to social security, to holidays with pay, and so on?

There is little difficulty in this, as we know. Domestic legal systems incorporate ESC rights. Even those systems which do not explicitly recognize ESC rights guarantee their residents rights which are in reality ESC rights. The claim cannot be, then, that ESC-type goods are incapable of being the appropriate object of rights. It must be rather that they cannot, for some reason, be the appropriate object of **human** rights. Is that claim correct? Let us answer by looking in turn at Cranston's three objections mentioned above.

Practicability issues

This is the claim that since, under some circumstances, when the supposed right cannot be enforced, no one is under a duty in respect of it, there cannot be a **human** right to ESC goods.

The first trouble with this argument is that, in some circumstances, even CP rights may be unenforceable because the conditions are such that it is unreasonable to hold anyone to be under a duty, for example in circumstances bordering a Hobbesian state of war (i.e. anarchy). In such circumstances, one could not hold a state to the obligation of ensuring CP rights such as due process, no arbitrary violence, no torture, and so on, since the state would have collapsed. And yet, Cranston does not say that in such cases states are under no duty to implement CP rights and hence that there cannot be any **human** CP rights.

Second, is it really correct to hold that if the supposed rights cannot be enforced then they cannot be human rights? Surely, if true, this argument would in effect undermine the idea of human rights altogether. It leads to a view that the only rights people can have are legal rights or the rights recognized by and enforced in some social system. So people can have rights to CP liberties if they are fortunately members of some liberal regime. But if they are the subject of some barbarous and murderous regime, they have no rights.

This indeed is a standard argument against the very idea of human rights of the utilitarian school, which we will discuss later. However, Cranston is not a utilitarian and is not objecting to the idea of human rights but to holding that there can be ESC human rights.

Our response to his argument is that one should think of human rights as **an ideal basic legal structure for human associations**. In other words, all human associations ought to conform to this ideal structure of rights. The ideal as such is neither enforceable nor unenforceable. It exists as an idea. But as a normative idea, it requires those who recognize it to seek to translate it into the world of actuality. Understood in this way, there is no reason why it cannot cover both CP and ESC rights. The UN, in proclaiming this ideal in the Universal Declaration of Human Rights, commits its members to act to realize it in their territories; and in including it in its human rights covenants, imposes a legally binding obligation on the state parties to engage in such an action.

Justiciability

The real question raised by the practicality problem is hence how best to provide for the realization of human rights; and who should be the arbiter of how to do it. This brings us to the problem of the justiciability of ESC rights: that is, to the problem of how to translate a human right into a reasonably definitive law which can serve as a basis for a judicial procedure in which rights can be upheld and corresponding duties enforced.[37]

Indeed, for a right to be able to be realized (not just to remain a pious aspiration), the judges must be able to decide what the right implies in practice, what constitutes a violation of that right, and what the remedy for that violation should be. Were I to complain that my right to adequate housing has been violated, for example, a judge should be able to decide what that right implied to start with (a tent with access to basic facilities, a one-room flat, a mansion?), whether the state violated that right and why, and what my remedy should be.

Traditionally, the view of many Western practitioners and scholars has been that (i) ESC human rights are too vague to be given this translation from an abstract right into a specific law; and (ii) even if they were not too vague, judges should not get involved in this translation. This is because, unlike civil servants advising the government, the judges have no expertise in determining social or economic policy. The government alone ought to decide what to provide and how; and it should only do so when it thinks it appropriate and not because it is obliged to do so by mostly ignorant judges.

This problem does not arise with CP rights because, it is argued, CP rights are *negative* rights. They require state officials *not to do* certain things: not to engage in torture, arbitrary rule, invasions of individual freedom, and so on. ESC rights, on the other hand, are *positive* rights: they require states *to do something*, to provide benefits to individuals (housing, money, work, etc). State officials have therefore to continuously make judgements as to the appropriate level of these benefits. Were ESC rights justiciable, judges would have to make these judgements instead: and yet, they have no special training to do so. That lack of training does not matter with CP rights, it is said, as judges do not have to make resource allocation judgements with negative rights.

Attack on individual freedom

There is another reason for which there has been hostility to the idea of ESC rights, besides the question of justiciability. It is that positive rights are generally taken to be potentially dangerous for individual freedom, as they demand a greater state involvement in a range of activities. The outcome may be an excessive curtailing of personal liberties, disincentives to wealth creation, and the like.[38] If anything, the state should be restrained in its provision of ESC-type goods rather than allowed to commit itself to their growth through legislating for ESC human rights. To be sure, people have ESC interests. However, the ESC interests of people should not be termed rights, as to do so would contaminate the whole idea of a set of human rights to be used as a standard for claims regarding the moral acceptability of a system of legislation. These interests should best be satisfied by people's individual efforts to acquire wealth, not by state meddling with private property and individual choices.

Evaluation of Cranston's practicability criterion

We believe both the above arguments are very weak.

First, as to the distinction between negative and positive rights, it has been frequently pointed out that a sharp distinction is hopeless, since the effective enjoyment of secure CP rights requires an expensive and well-trained judicial, police and penal apparatus that the state is supposed to provide; while in regard to some ESC rights the state has to act negatively by, for instance, protecting workers' rights to form and join trade unions, to go on strike, and so on. Furthermore, special training could be provided to judges with respect to ESC rights and questions of resource allocation; and special courts established with judges with particular expertise in relevant ESC rights.

Second, the issue regarding the state's curtailment of individual freedom as a result of its involvement with positive rights is easily resolvable, in principle at least. On the liberal view we defend, welfare rights in general are justified to ensure that everyone has a fair opportunity to develop and exercise their capacities for freedom. A prohibition on welfare rights would enlarge the freedom of some at the expense of others. On that view, ESC rights do not threaten the liberal model: on the contrary, they reinforce it.

If we are right, however, and these arguments against the ESC rights do not hold, why is it that European practice, for instance – the most developed system of human rights adjudication in the world – nevertheless treats these rights as non-justiciable?

The answer may lie in the relativity of the appropriate standard of welfare to each state, which seems to conflict with the very idea of human rights as a universal standard for all societies everywhere. Of course, we have taken the view that the liberal conception, although implicitly universal, applies specifically to modern and modernizing societies. But that view would still seem to demand that a justiciable ESC human rights convention constitutes the same standard for all those societies. The existing covenants and charters clearly do not do this; and could not, in view of the different stages of development of the societies to which they have to be applied.

However, this is not a reason for not writing provisions concerning citizens' entitlement to a minimum level of welfare into the constitution of particular states, as has been done in the South African and Indian constitutions and for their courts not to get involved in the question of appropriate interpretations of these rights.[39] For, the question of appropriateness here is relative to a particular society rather than to all. Above all, it is not a reason for denying that there are ESC human rights. The affirmation of human rights is, as we have continuously stressed, the affirmation of an ideal structure of rights; and if, in the case of ESC rights, these have to be progressively realized in the course of a society's social and economic development, this does not affect their nature as the relevant ideal.

In any case, exactly the same problem arises with CP rights, since a fully developed liberal system of such rights is not something that can be introduced at the drop of a hat into a society that possesses no cultural affinity with, or state experience of, liberalism.

Universality

The second Cranston argument was that for something to be a human right it must be universal. It must be held by each person against all persons; and since some ESC rights are held only by a certain category of person, for example only workers can have rights to holidays with pay, then they cannot be human rights.

We disagree with this argument on two grounds:

1. Some CP rights are universal but some are not. Civil rights may be held against everyone. Political rights, however, are not so. They are held against other members of one's society.
2. Some ESC rights could be universal, for instance the right to subsistence. Others, at first sight, would appear not to be, such as the right

to holidays with pay. But this right is clearly a gloss on the more universal right to decent and reasonable conditions of work. Perhaps, the point is that the rich do not have to work, so not everyone is a worker. Yet, this point is easily dealt with. One need only say that every human being, should she be a worker, has the right to decent and reasonable conditions of work. The same formula, in fact, applies to some civil rights also. Not everyone is accused of a crime. But every human being, should she be accused of a crime, has a right to a fair trial.

Cranston could still hold that such conditional rights are not truly universal and hence not truly human rights. But, on our account of human rights, they are to be understood as constituting the fair basic terms of associational human life under modern conditions. Hence, they must cover the standard contingencies that could unfairly destroy a person's opportunities to participate in that life, such as being accused of a crime, ill-health, unemployment, and so on. So, some of the terms will be conditional on a person's falling into a category that not everyone could occupy or is likely to occupy at the same time. Nevertheless, all together compose the necessary conditions for a life of human freedom and dignity.

Paramountcy

Paramountcy is the idea that the relevant need on which the right claim is based must be of paramount importance. In other words, the general idea of a human right is that it must relate to what are essential interests of human beings or fundamental human goods. Cranston's claim is that many so-called ESC rights do not satisfy this criterion. His favourite example is holidays with pay.

Certainly, we agree with Cranston that a human right must be of paramount importance, and that not all our needs can be seen as such. For example, to function effectively as academics we need access to a research library and time to do research. But it is not an essential human interest to be an academic; nor is it a standard contingency undermining one's fair opportunities that everyone under modern conditions is liable to experience. Access to a research library cannot therefore be a human right. But ESC rights are essential and universal human interests, we believe, and hence of similar importance to the CP rights in creating an ideal basic legal structure for human association.

We would like to conclude our discussion of the relative importance of ESC and CP rights with an apocryphal anecdote from the eighteenth century:

A thief accused of stealing a loaf of bread comes before a French judge. 'Your Honour' he says 'I steal because I need to survive'. The judge replies: 'I do not see the necessity'.

Unlike the eighteenth-century judge, we follow Locke in believing that all human beings 'need' to survive; and that, in today's world, this necessity demands (at least) a full set of human rights as promulgated in the Universal Declaration of Human Rights of 1948, and the ICCPR and ICESCR.

Nonetheless, one cannot deny that there is a hierarchy of rights in that some rights are of such an importance that they can never be interfered with, while some others can be limited or derogated from in specific circumstances.

The limitation clauses and the margin of appreciation

The most basic utilitarian critique of human rights lies in the assertion that resources are scarce in any society ... This scarcity inevitably leads to utilitarian calculations to allocate those resources in a way that will maximize the greatest good. In the end, it is argued, all the benefits listed as human rights, even life itself, are subject to the promotion of the greatest good in a society. As such an individual's benefits claimed as a human right may be compromised, diluted, or even completely denied in specific situations where that right has to be weighed against the claim of another individual or of society as a whole. (Andrew Heard)[40]

We have seen how, besides a general derogation clause in the ICCPR, several of the rights affirmed in the ICCPR have limitation clauses attached to them; and the ICESCR and the Universal Declaration of Human Rights have a general limitation clause (allowing limitation of rights on grounds of morality, public order and the general welfare in a democratic society).

The European Convention on Human Rights contains specific limitation clauses similar to the ICCPR. The limitation clauses state the legitimate ends by reference to which some rights (for example freedom of movement, religion or expression) may be limited. For the most part, these refer to the rights and freedoms of others, national security, public safety, public order and public health or morals. A standard qualification to the limitations in the ECHR, as also in Articles 21 and 22 of the ICCPR, is that the means adopted to achieve the legitimate ends must be 'necessary in a democratic society'. Some rights in both the European Convention and the ICCPR are, however, unqualified and said to be absolute rights because they do not allow derogation from them on any grounds. In the main, these are the right to life (not to be deprived of one's life arbitrarily), freedom from torture and slavery, and some rule-of-law rights.

We shall concentrate in this section on the interpretation of limitation clauses by the European Court of Human Rights, since the practice of the court contains the main (if not only) substantial jurisprudential evidence on the working of such limitations. However, we will first raise some general issues about their very existence in bills of human rights.

As suggested by our initial quotation to this section, the idea that the human rights of individuals can be trumped in some way by reference to the general interests of the community seems to express the utilitarian notion that what rights human beings should have should be determined by the general welfare. Indeed, the European Convention on Human Rights is often interpreted as having as its main goal in the cases of qualified rights the striking of a fair balance between the individual interests and the general interest.[41]

In our view, this understanding of the limitation clauses is misleading. It is true that ends such as national security, public order and public health appeal to the general interest. But the general interest in these cases should be conceived as the interest of rights-bearing individuals in the general conditions under which they can effectively exercise their rights. Without any national security, public order or public health, no one can enjoy any rights. Thus, it is in the interest of each person to co-operate with the others in bringing about and maintaining the conditions under which exercise of their rights can be real. The aim is hence to strike a balance between each individual's interest in their own rights and each individual's interest as a rights-bearer in the general conditions for the enjoyment of rights. It is not to impose an extraneous conception of the general welfare, such as the greatest happiness of the greatest number, on individual rights but to elicit the general interest from each person's interest in relating to others through a secure system of rights.

The same applies to the protection of the rights and freedoms of others, another legitimate aim by reference to which rights may be limited: it is the obvious corollary of the fact that all the rights affirmed are held equally by each person. Hence, one person's right must be in principle limitable by whatever is necessary to ensure the equal entitlement of others to their rights. Such limitations will not always be necessary. Thus, in regard to the so-called absolute rights, it is not necessary to limit the rights of others in order to secure one person's right not to be enslaved. However, it clearly is necessary to limit the freedom of the press in order to protect the right to privacy.

The question of morals as a legitimate limiting end presents more serious problems. Since nothing is said in the documents as to what is covered by the notion of public morals, what prevents a state claiming that any of the following are necessary to preserve public morals: religious belief and practice, the banning of alcohol, dancing and music, the strict censorship of the media, the criminalization of extra-marital sex and homosexuality, the restriction of women in public along the lines of puritanical Islam, and so on?

It is unclear, in our view, why there should be any reference to morals at all among the legitimate ends. Do individual rights-holders have a general interest in a standard of public morals? The answer must be that, if a standard of public morals is necessary for the flourishing and reproduction of a liberal society of mutually respecting rights-holders, then each right-holder would have an individual interest in the maintenance of such morals. There obviously are moral standards that are necessary for the flourishing of any society, let alone a liberal one. These are such virtues as honesty, truthfulness, justice, charity and public-spiritedness. It does not follow, of course, that their corresponding vices should be criminalized – only that society should seek to promote such virtues in its members.

Are there any specifically liberal virtues? Fundamental to a liberal society is the toleration of difference and respect for each other's liberty. The difference to be tolerated must not, naturally, involve the violation of the rights of others or undermine the general interest. Thus a liberal society should tolerate differences of belief and opinion where these do not involve conspiracies to destroy liberal society, and differences of conduct where these do not threaten others' rights or general interests. An example of the latter conduct that has been widely criminalized in the past but is not now in most liberal societies is homosexuality. Similarly, a substantial area of heterosexual conduct that has been subject to public, even if not criminal, sanctions in the past is now widely tolerated. Individual rights-holders in a liberal society, then, have a fundamental interest in the promotion of the virtue of toleration among its members besides the more traditional social virtues.

Is there a general interest of rights-bearers in a liberal society in any public regulation of sexual conduct? If there is, it has to do with the interests of individuals in the flourishing of the family and with public decency. The ICCPR declares in Article 23 that the family is the natural and fundamental group unit in society and specifies certain individual rights connected with this valuation, such as the right to marry. Assuming that the family is of fundamental importance to society's self-reproduction, then the morals that are necessary to sustain this institution are of public concern and should be promoted. Would this line of argument allow, in principle, the justification of all the above-mentioned puritanical constraints on individual freedom? Probably not, as any proposal for constraint would have to meet the criterion that it is necessary in a liberal society and it is very unlikely that such claims could be substantiated.

At this point, we need to refer to the practice of the European Court of Human Rights in interpreting the requirement that any limitation of individual human rights must be necessary in a democratic society. The Court has, in effect, redefined democratic to mean liberal-democratic. The Court holds that the hallmarks of a democratic society are pluralism, toleration and broad-mindedness and on this basis has struck down legislation criminalizing homosexual conduct in Northern Ireland (*Dudgeon*).[42] As a society can be democratic without being liberal, the crucial jurisprudential requirement is the liberal component of liberal-democracy, not the democratic. The significance of this reading of the democratic condition by the Court is that any appeal to one of the legitimate ends in constraining individual rights must satisfy the demand that it be necessary having regard to the general interest of liberal right-holders. This is not a qualification of liberal rights by the interests of the majority or some other non-liberal principle such as a religious conception of the good, but only the qualification of a rights-holder's individual interest in their rights by the same rights-holder's general interest in the conditions of exercising their rights.

The European Court has, more specifically, adopted the following criteria for a restriction to count as necessary in a democratic society:

- that it involves a pressing social need;
- that it is proportionate to the legitimate aim pursued; and
- that the reasons given are relevant and sufficient.[43]

The last so-called proportionality principle is widely regarded as of central importance.[44] It involves being able to demonstrate that (i) there are relevant and sufficient reasons for the proposed restriction; (ii) there is no less-restrictive alternative; (iii) the proposal involves procedural fairness; (iv) it is subject to safeguards against abuse; (v) it does not extinguish the very essence of the right; and (vi) the harm or burden to the individual is not excessive compared to the importance of the social need.[45]

The European Court, in interpreting the limitations on the Convention rights, has adopted another doctrine that has received widespread attention and much commendation for its supposed accommodation of national and cultural diversity with the universality of human rights. This doctrine is called *the margin of appreciation*. According to it, each national state is initially responsible for making the decision as to what is a fair balance between individual interests and the general interest. This decision is then subject to a supervisory review by the Court. The margin of appreciation arises in this process because the Court holds that the domestic authorities are in a better position to judge what is a necessary restriction in their democratic society taking into account the local conditions and traditions than an international judge. Nevertheless, the domestic authorities are not given a *carte blanche* to decide how they please but are subject to overruling by the Court if they go beyond a certain limit and clearly strike an unfair balance. The margin of appreciation is supposed to consist in the discretion allowed to different domestic authorities to decide issues in different ways subject to a minimum standard applied by the Court. However, the margin is said to vary according to context. The Court allows a wide margin in regard to subjective matters such as questions of morals or national security or economic policy but allows only a narrow margin where the rights involved are held to be of major importance, for example freedom of speech and the right to privacy, or where there exists a general European consensus on how to treat an issue.[46]

Many commentators believe that the doctrine is obscure and uncertain and only a sloppy way of dealing with the central issue of proportionality.[47] One trouble with the doctrine is that it claims to apply a different margin according to whether there exists a general consensus on attitudes to an issue or not. But this does not offer a principled basis for restricting the discretion of the domestic authorities when a consensus exists. If all states but one are agreed on where a fair balance lies, why should the majority view be imposed on the minority? In such cases, the Court applies a minimal discretion rather than a minimal standard of fairness and is thus not exercising its own judgement as to what is an acceptable interpretation of proportionality. It is simply adopting the view of the majority. With regard to rights deemed to be of central importance to individuals, the case cited is that of the right to an intimate sexual life as part of the right to privacy as a ground for overriding any public morals' interest in banning homosexuality. This is a bad piece of reasoning. The Court should have held that there is no public morals' interest in banning homosexuality.

Whatever the Court's lack of clarity in applying the doctrine of the margin of appreciation, the notion itself does seem an important one for any system of adjudication by an international court of human rights issues. This is because the human rights and the limitation clauses of the international covenants and conventions are unavoidably expressed in very broad and open-textured terms, so that the idea of a fair balance between different rights and between individual and general interests can be developed and elaborated in detailed legislation in different ways.

We believe that any international scheme for promoting, or indeed applying, liberal human rights should adopt a wide version of the doctrine of the margin of appreciation and allow domestic authorities considerable discretion in determining what is a fair balance throughout the scheme of rights. What an international court should apply in pursuit of this wide version is a test of what is a reasonable restriction of individual rights having regard to the public needs of a liberal-democratic society. To be able to do this, it must be much more forthcoming about what the minimum standard of reasonableness is and this requires that it develop a clearer notion of the kinds of restrictions that are not acceptable in a liberal-democratic order.

5 | The right of peoples to self-determination

Who possesses this right?

We have not yet discussed a right that is given great prominence as Article 1 in both the ICCPR and the ICESCR. The article expresses the right thus: 'All peoples have the right of self-determination. By virtue of that right they freely determine their political status and freely pursue their economic, social and cultural development.' Such a right is not mentioned in the Universal Declaration of Human Rights. However, Chapter I Article 2 of the UN Charter states that one of the purposes of the UN is 'to develop friendly relations among nations based on respect for the principle of equal rights and self-determination of peoples'. Article 55 reiterates this language. Yet, it is doubtful whether the authors of the charter intended the right to be understood with quite the same meaning that it had acquired by the time it was given pride of place in the UN's two main human rights covenants.[1]

This meaning was effectively defined by the 1960 UN General Assembly Declaration 1514 On the Granting of Independence to Colonial Countries and Peoples.[2] The Declaration was the first to use the formula quoted above and by doing so specifically in the context of the decolonization process gave it the implications that have subsequently been attached to it. The Declaration was adopted by eighty-nine votes with *nem con*, although the European colonial powers and the United States abstained. While the Declaration as a UN General Assembly resolution was not in itself legally binding on the members, the principle it affirmed is now recognized to have acquired that status by virtue of being endorsed by all subsequent UN declarations and resolutions dealing with the subject and by the ICCPR and ICESCR. Furthermore, the International Court of Justice has accepted the Declaration as establishing the legal basis for the process of decolonization.[3] Hence, it is now generally acknowledged that there is a right of peoples to self-determination in international law that is binding on all states, while some commentators hold that the principle is part of *jus cogens*, that is to say, a peremptory norm of international law admitting of no derogation.[4]

The right applies to colonial people and people under foreign military occupation.[5] Most commentators would deny that it applies to national minorities, such as the Basques, the Kurds, the Tamils, the Kosovo Albanians, and so on.[6] The minority view is expressed in a frequently quoted judgement by the Supreme Court of Canada in *re Secession of Quebec*:

[a] number of commentators have further asserted that the right to self-determination may ground a right to unilateral secession in a[nother] circumstance ... the underlying proposition is that, when a people is blocked from the meaningful exercise of its right to self-determination internally [i.e. when it is denied meaningful access to government to pursue their political, economic, social and cultural development], it is entitled, as a last resort, to exercise it by secession. [However], it remains unclear whether this ... proposition actually reflects an established international law standard.[7]

The standard view is, then, that the right does not apply to minorities, including minorities in the colonial territory entitled to independence. The right has to be exercised collectively by all its inhabitants. This is because, in the words of Higgins:

peoples is to be understood in the sense of all the peoples of a given territory. Of course, all members of distinct minority groups are part of the peoples of the territory. In that sense they too, as individuals, are the holders of the right of self-determination. But minorities as such do not have a right of self-determination. That means that they have no right to secession, to independence, or to join with comparable groups in other states.[8]

This understanding of a people with the right to self-determination is what we call a statist one applied to the colonial situation. A people in the relevant sense is that collection of persons who are the subjects or citizens of an independent state or, in the case of a colony, are the subjects of a separately administered dependent territory. Why the Turkish (or Iraqi or Iranian) control of Kurdish lands is not a colonial situation is because the Kurds are supposed to be full and equal members of the Turkish (or Iraqi or Iranian) state. They are self-determining citizens of Turkey (and so on), not the inhabitants of a dependent territory. Thus India in ratifying the ICCPR entered a reservation to Article 1 stating that it takes the article to apply only to peoples living under foreign rule.[9] Since all the inhabitants of Indian territory are full and equal members of the Indian state, even though some of them may believe that they are ruled by a foreign power, the right to self-determination does not apply to them.

Returning to the prominence given to the right in the two main covenants, we can understand this, not as a reflection of a belief in the permanent primacy of this right over other human rights but as a reflection of the concerns of the growing number of newly independent states at the UN to hasten the demise of the colonial empires and destroy the white racist regimes of southern Africa. These latter, although self-governing, did not qualify for the right because of their exclusion of the great majority of their populations from its exercise.

The history of the principle in international society and international law prior to the UN

It is generally accepted that international society through its customary and treaty-based law did not recognize any right of peoples to self-determination at least until the Versailles Conference and Treaty of 1919.[10] Even though the principle of popular sovereignty had become more and more widely acknowledged as the underlying principle of legitimacy for states and had led to the creation of the independent states of the New World in North and South America at the end of the eighteenth and beginning of the nineteenth centuries, from international society's point of view the people were that collection of persons organized in an existing state (or colonial territory).

At the same time, the forces of nationalism promoting a very different understanding of the people entitled to exercise political self-determination – namely particular ethno-cultural groups such as the Germans, the Italians, the Irish, the Serbs, the Greeks, and so on – grew ever stronger in Europe and beyond. These forces brought about the new states of Germany and Italy, which transformed the balance of power within Europe with fateful consequences, and carved other states out of the decaying Ottoman Empire. These states, once established, came to be recognized and incorporated in the international community. But such recognition in no way implied a right of secession or political independence for ethno-cultural, or any other, groups. International society was merely giving legal recognition to the fact of new states.[11]

The Versailles Conference of 1919 appeared to change this situation radically. President Woodrow Wilson's famous Fourteen Points outlining the war aims of the allied powers stated that the principle of justice to all peoples and nationalities was fundamental to their programme and subsequently declared that national self-determination was an imperative principle of action for the Allied leaders at Versailles.[12] Wilson accepted that the principle was not to apply to the European states' colonial peoples but only to those 'nations' emerging from the break-up of the Austro-Hungarian, Tsarist and Ottoman Empires, such as the Poles, Hungarians, Croats, Czechs, and so on. The aim was to use the principle to redraw the map of Eastern Europe so that states' territories corresponded as much as possible with distinct ethno-cultural populations. The plebiscite, another feature of the principle of self-determination, was also used to resolve border disputes in certain areas.

We have already discussed above how the Treaty was signally unsuccessful in fulfilling the aim of aligning borders with nations, leaving many millions of people as national minorities in alien nation states. This was above all true for the Germans whose size and power would have substantially increased had the principle of national self-determination in the ethno-cultural sense been more consistently followed. The Allied leaders in the end seemed more intent on hemming in a potentially resurgent Germany by a ring of medium-size states than on being true to the principle of national self-determination. Furthermore, in a well-known ruling of 1921 on the political status of the Aaland Islands, the League of Nations special committee set up to examine the claims of the islanders held that the principle of national self-determination was not a legal rule under international law.[13] The Aaland Islands were inhabited by people of Swedish origin, language and culture but had been ceded by Sweden to Russia together with the territory of Finland at the conclusion of an unsuccessful war in the early nineteenth century. The Islands had then been integrated by the Russians into their Duchy of Finland and had remained attached to Finland until Finland achieved independence at the time of the Russian Revolution of 1917. The Aalanders then wished to be returned to Sweden. But the League took the view that, conditionally on the Finns respecting the cultural and linguistic rights of the Swedes, the Islands must remain part of Finland.

This decision may appear difficult to understand, given that the case fell within the category of the break-up of the Tsarist empire and seemed to be an uncontroversial instance of a people wishing to exercise national self-determination. However, it can be seen as reflecting the League's fear that, if the Aalanders were allowed to transfer, all the other national minorities that had been created under the Versailles Treaty would demand similar transfers. Yet, the League's representatives also held: (i) that the Aalanders had not been oppressed by Finland and, thus, a possible *political* reason for secession – a case when minority protection could not be regarded as sufficient – did not apply. Indeed, as the Commission of Rapporteurs, appointed by the League to recommend a programme of action stated: 'The separation of a minority from the State of which it forms a part and its incorporation in another State can only be considered as an *altogether exceptional solution*, a *last resort* when the State lacks either the will or the power to enact and apply just and effective guarantees';[14] and (ii) that the meaning of 'peoples' should be that of a nation as a whole, not a small fraction of a people. As Borgen points out: 'the Swedes on the Aaland Islands, who were only a small fraction of the totality of the Swedish "people" did not have a strong claim for secession in comparison to, for example, Finland, which, when it broke away from Russian rule, contained the near totality of the Finnish people'.[15]

The present scope of the right to self-determination in international law

We see from the above account of the principle of self-determination in the UN regime that the attempt of the Versailles Conference and Treaty to accommodate the claims of nationalist movements within international law has been effectively abandoned and international society's traditional understanding of popular sovereignty, together with the non-acceptance of any right of part of a state to secede from it, has been reaffirmed. The statist conception of a people has triumphed.

Nevertheless, there have been some notable secessions since WWII, above all that of Pakistan from India and Bangladesh from Pakistan; and most recently of Kosovo from Serbia. They also include Rwanda and Burundi and the North Cameroons. Separations agreed by the parties include Slovakia from the Czech Republic and Singapore from Malaysia. The new states that have come into existence through such a process have also been on the whole recognized by the international community and joined the United Nations without the acceptance of any right of such entities to secede.[16] The recognition has been given to established facts, not to pre-existing rights. The new states that emerged from the break-up of the Yugoslav and USSR federations should probably not be seen as instances of successful secession. What happened was that the federation split into its separate territorial units, which then became independent states. Given that the violent attempt in parts of the former Yugoslavia to redraw those boundaries to correspond with ethno-cultural divisions has been stubbornly and so far successfully resisted by the international community, the situation should be understood rather as instances of statist-defined peoples exercising their right to self-determination with the disappearance of the federal union.

There have, however, been some anomalous cases where the statist understanding of the right as described above has not been followed. Thus some colonial territories whose people should have had a right to self-determination under the established understanding have been forcibly incorporated into a neighbouring state. Goa was seized by India, West Irian and East Timor by Indonesia and the Spanish Sahara by Morocco.[17] In the first two cases the international community accepted the seizures, but in the latter two, because of the dissatisfaction of the respective peoples, it has in the end insisted on a referendum allowing the people to decide. However, while the East Timorese have subsequently achieved independence, the Spanish Saharans have not yet been able to vote. The parties to the dispute have been unable to agree on who exactly is entitled to exercise the vote, since so much of the original population has fled the territory as a result of the fighting.

In the case of the Falkland Islands and Gibraltar, still colonial territories of the UK, where the overwhelming proportion of the populations wish to retain that political status, the UN does not accept that the right to self-determination has been exercised, although they would seem to be clear enough instances of a statist-defined people freely determining their political status.[18] A somewhat different situation was presented by Algeria. This territory was incorporated fully into the state of France and its inhabitants were formally full and equal citizens of the French state. Hence on the statist definition of a people, the Algerians were already exercising their right to self-determination.

Nevertheless, Algeria was treated as a colonial situation unlike Turkey's control of the Kurds.

Most of these anomalies can be understood as the expression of a strong bias against the former or actual European colonial power and its people.

Is this right a group human right and is it compatible with liberal-individual rights?

If the main point of asserting this right with such prominence was to hasten the demise of colonial and racist regimes, why not simply proclaim the wrongness of racist and colonial regimes? Because the principle that established their wrongness was that of popular sovereignty and that indeed is the axiom underlying the right of statist-defined peoples to self-determination. The legitimacy of a political regime, including that of a colonial territory, depends on its government being the expression of the will of the people, that is, the subjects of the regime.

It is no wonder, then, that the UN Charter blithely affirms the right of peoples to self-determination. For the sovereignty of the people has become the unchallenged principle of legitimacy for the modern state. Even communist and fascist dictatorships claim legitimacy on the basis of being the true expression of the people's will. The principle first came to prominence in the American and French Revolutions and in the course of the nineteenth century overcame the rival dynastic principle through most of Europe and America with the exception of the Tsarist, Austro-Hungarian and Ottoman Empires, while the colonial powers claimed legitimacy for their conquests and general dominance on the basis of their civilizing mission. The first world war swept away the autocratic empires and the second and its aftermath put paid effectively to the colonial powers, leaving popular sovereignty in uncontested control of the field.

The principle of popular sovereignty is perfectly compatible with liberal-individual rights. Indeed, it is surely the best interpretation of the dominant rights-based contract theory of sovereignty of the seventeenth and eighteenth centuries. As we have seen, according to that theory the only way for human beings to enjoy their rights securely is to enter into a political association that creates an authority with the essential political powers of giving determinacy to the basic principles in a system of laws and of enforcing the laws against violators. Hence, the authority of the political power, even in the monarchical theories of Grotius and Pufendorf, derives from the will of the associating people. Indeed, it can be argued that Hobbes's attempt to avoid this conclusion by denying that the people can possess any unity except in the unified will of the sovereign that their contract brings into being is incoherent. On this view, the underlying and subsequently explicit (in Locke and Rousseau) sovereignty of the people is the political form through which the system of equal liberal rights is to be made effective in the world.

It is assumed for the most part by these writers, although sometimes openly argued, that human beings will have to create a plurality of such political associations. This assumption raises the issue of which collections of human beings are entitled to their own state. The liberal contract theory, in effect, developed as though it did not much matter very much how states were distributed among human beings, provided that all states performed their functions properly in promoting respect for human rights. In practice, the principle was applied in France and America (North and South) in a statist way to the people organized in an existing sovereign state or colonial territory. But the turmoil created in Europe by the French Revolutionary and subsequent Napoleonic wars and conquests stirred up everywhere a sense of being a people possessing a claim to associate as a single political unit. This feeling had especially profound consequences among German- and Italian-speaking peoples, as already mentioned. Even before these events, Rousseau had raised the question as to what makes a people fit for self-government and had given an ethno-cultural answer. He had also defended the right of the Poles and the Corsicans, who were the subjects of 'foreign' powers, to their own states. Hence, although popular sovereignty was becoming the dominant legitimizing principle for the modern state, the principle had left entirely open the issue of how a people possessing the right to self-government was to be identified.

Nevertheless, let us assume for the moment that we can identify a people possessing the valid claim to self-determination in statist, or contract theory, terms and ask whether such a right would be a group human right. It would seem plausible enough to construe it as an individual human right, since an obvious expression of it is the right of individuals to participate in the government of their country directly or through freely chosen representatives (Article 21 Universal Declaration of Human Rights). Of course, individuals can only enjoy and make use of this right through membership of a group: namely the group of persons organized as a distinct polity. But this is no different, as Donnelly points out, from the right of workers to form trade unions or the right to a fair trial.[19] All these rights presuppose organized groups of persons through which alone they can be enjoyed by individuals. Indeed, the contract theory holds that **none** of these human rights can be effectively enjoyed outside the association of individuals in organized polities. They are, nevertheless, individual rights. They rest on the claim of individuals on other individuals that living together as members of organized groups is fair only if the association is based on the recognition of these (human) rights as the equal rights of all participants.

However, it is possible to read the right of peoples to self-determination as a group right in a strong sense which calls in question its compatibility with liberal-individual rights: namely by identifying a people in ethno-cultural terms and by understanding the relation between individual and ethno-cultural group in what we call communitarian terms (after the contemporary communitarian philosophy which we discuss in Chapter 9). On the communitarian view, the individual's identity is constituted by his relation to his cultural group. This means that, although he is a human being, this identity is a very thin one consisting in his being a language-speaking, reason-giving being, the substance of which is provided by his membership of a particular cultural community, such as the German or French, and its language, culture, beliefs and values. Apart from such a cultural substance, the individual is nothing. The ground for holding such a view is that individuals do not and cannot develop their human capacities of reason-giving and language-using beings as independent individuals but only through being born into and formed by a distinct cultural group.

We do not believe that this obvious sociological truth entails the normative implications about identity that the communitarians, and before them some ethno-cultural nationalists, seek and have sought to draw. These implications are that because individuals are embedded in the cultural communities in which they have been formed, they cannot step outside the system of thought and action that these cultures constitute and so cannot develop the mode of thinking about oneself and one's interests expressed in liberal-individualist philosophy. They cannot abstract themselves in thought from their identity as members of this or that group and think of their basic interests as human beings and construct on that basis the conception of conditions of association that would be fairest for human beings as such and hence for themselves as Germans or Frenchmen.

Nevertheless, if it were true that individuals are irredeemably embedded in their ethno-cultural group, then the right of such a group to its self-determination through the possession of sovereign statehood would indeed be a group right that was not reducible to the rights of its members as individual human beings to take part in the government of their country. For on the ethno-cultural view, individuals could have rights only as these were determined within the cultural tradition of his group. If these were illiberal, then the individual could have no access to liberalism. Insofar as the idea of liberal-individual rights is arrived at through a process of abstraction and universalization of individual identities, it would seem extremely implausible that the rights determined within a non-universalizing tradition could ever take a liberal form. However, one way out, which we will discuss at length in Part III, would be to treat the tradition as universalizing but relativist. Thus, there could be a liberal tradition that was expressed in formally universalist terms but whose validity was constituted only for liberals. Whether this is a coherent view, we will be considering later. At any rate, in such a relativist view, there are absolutely no grounds on which to stand to criticize meaningfully an illiberal ethno-cultural tradition either from within the tradition or from without.

Would such a group right also be correctly described as a **human** right? Probably. Insofar as what it is to be a human being is to be irredeemably a member of an ethno-cultural group, then the right of the group would be the human right *par excellence*. There would in fact be no other human rights, since the group identity constitutes the essence of the human identity and establishes no other universality than its claim to self-determination. We can see, then, that both the statist and the liberal elements in international society combine to exclude as far as possible the extreme communitarian version of the ethno-cultural group in the understanding of a people's right to self-determination. But can it be excluded altogether?

The weakness of the statist and strength of the ethno-cultural version of a people

Just as we argued in Part I that there is an affinity between the modern state and liberalism in the sense that liberalism is the most plausible normative theory legitimizing the basic structure of that state, so we hold also that there is an affinity between rights-based liberalism and nationalism. The connection between them runs through the notion of popular sovereignty. We have seen how the principle of popular sovereignty is at first implicit and subsequently becomes explicit in the rights-based contract theories of the seventeenth and eighteenth centuries, issuing in the American and French Revolutions.

On this view, the unity of the state depends on the unified will of the people to pursue their good together as members of the same state. The people constitute a homogeneous body from a political point of view and this body possesses sovereignty. How is such a unified will possible? The original contract theorists said nothing about this matter. They wrote as though any collection of people had sufficiently strong common interests of a universal nature in co-operating politi-cally, in order to give determinacy and effective enforcement to their rights, that the issue was not important, since their common interests would outweigh any conflicting interests that might emerge. In this sense, their writings assumed a statist account of the people.

This was a fairly naïve position. For, while the theory was no doubt correct in positing strong common interests as the basis of the state, it was recognized, nevertheless, that the general principles had to be given determinacy in a concrete system of laws. Although the laws had to be general and bestow equal fundamental rights, there seemed to be no awareness that such laws were compatible with the systematic promotion of the interests of one cultural group to the detriment of others in matters of language, education, religion and history. There was, indeed, little serious acceptance, until Rousseau came along, that such laws were compatible also with major class conflicts.

Rousseau was also the first major writer in this tradition to raise the cultural issue. His idea of an appropriate system of laws is one that first satisfies the universal principles of freedom and equality, but in the second place, it must be suited to the position and interests of a particular people. So, he asks the question, 'which people, then, is fit to receive laws?', and answers 'a people, which, finding itself bound together by some union of origin, interest or convention, has not yet borne the yoke of law [the state] ... one which combines the cohesion of an ancient people with the malleability of a new one'.[20] Clearly, Rousseau is supposing that the basis of the state should, if possible, be a popular will that is itself formed out of a pre-political unity. In that same chapter he predicts that the Corsicans (in revolt against their overlord, the city of Genoa) will come to exist as an independent state that will astound Europe – a prediction that led the Corsicans to seek and obtain from him a legislative scheme for an independent Corsican state. More famously, he provided the subjugated Poles with ideas for their self-government that emphasized in particular the promotion of a unified cultural self-consciousness as the basis of a Polish state.[21]

Later, J. S. Mill argued explicitly, in a much-quoted passage, for the connection between the principle of popular sovereignty and that of national self-determination in the ethno-cultural sense. He says, 'It is in general a necessary condition of free institutions that the boundaries of government should coincide in the main with those of nationality.'[22] This is because, Mill says:

where the sentiment of nationality exists in any force, there is a prima facie case for uniting all the members of the nationality under the same government, and a government to themselves apart. This is merely saying that the question of government ought to be decided by the governed. One hardly knows what any division of the human race should be free to do, if not to determine with which of the various collective bodies of human beings they choose to associate themselves.[23]

In this passage, Mill clearly supposes that there are natural or historically given divisions of the human race called nationalities. His argument, then, is that, since the question of government ought to be decided by the governed, and a nation constitutes a non-arbitrary collection of individuals and hence has a pre-political unity, then such collections ought to have the right to decide. The line of reasoning here is similar to that of Rousseau: since legitimate government rests on the unified will of a people and a nation is already a 'natural' unity, the best government will be one that coincides with the nation.

Mill's argument for single-nation states has another somewhat more pragmatic character. He says, 'free institutions are next to impossible in a country made up of different nationalities'.[24] Here the idea would seem to be, not that a nation, as a people in its own right, must be entitled to decide how it shall be governed, but that the competition for dominance in the state by several nationalities will result in the loss of free institutions and the subjection of the losers. The contemporary liberal political philosopher of single-nation states, David Miller, has a similar pragmatic argument. His claim is that without the fellow-feeling arising from the consciousness of belonging to the same nation, the citizens of a modern democratic state will not support the kind or level of redistributive welfare that is necessary to achieve liberal justice for all under modern conditions. He points to the poverty of the welfare state in multi-national America and the marked lack of enthusiasm for redistributive welfare at the international level compared with the high provision of welfare rights in the old nation states of Europe as evidence of his thesis.[25]

While these contentions suppose that there are 'natural' or historically given and relatively stable nationalities or nations, neither Mill nor Miller is committed to a strong communitarian view of the group that makes it difficult to combine with liberalism. Liberal justice is the fundamental criterion for both writers, and single-nation states are the best way to achieve liberal justice. Mill, indeed, holds that the successful blending of several nations to form a common union 'is a benefit to the human race ... The united people, like a crossed breed of animals ... inherits the special aptitudes and excellencies of its progenitors'.[26] But this process still requires the production of a united people and what Mill doubts is that the blending process can be successful under free institutions. Nevertheless, neither Mill nor Miller believes that strong ethno-cultural group identities preclude the development in their members of a universal consciousness as human beings and an apprehension of universal values that limit the acceptability of their purely national values.

Given, then, the need of liberalism for the formation of strong common wills as the basis of effective and legitimate states, should we accept the claims of Mill and Miller and seek to make state boundaries coincide as far as possible with the geographical distribution of 'nationalities'? This would mean abandoning the present UN and international law commitment to a statist view of a people and would require us to seek to accommodate such apparently clear divisions of the human race as the Basques, the Kurds, the Tamils, and so on, not to speak of the many thousands of tribes of Africa. It would help in such a task if we had a lucid view of what one of these 'natural' human groups is. Let us now examine this problem.

What is a nation?

On an extreme communitarian view of the nation, it is a natural division of the human race that has its own unique cultural character and language and is quite distinct from and independent of others. Each pure and uncorrupted nation possesses inherent worth and its members achieve the fulfilment of their own natures by living spontaneously in accordance with their national life and through contributing to its ends. This is a view of the nation to be found in the historical and cultural writings of Herder.[27] Some nations become corrupted by adopting essentially foreign customs and even language, such as his contemporary Germans were in danger of doing as a consequence of the cultural and more recently the military and political domination of German peoples by France. To be themselves and live as they were meant to, they must 'spew out the ugly slime of the Seine and speak German, O you German!' Herder believed that each pure nation should have its own state but was not very exercised by the political details. This is the concern of Fichte in his Addresses to the German Nation of 1807–8 in which he makes use of the Herderian idea of the nation to rouse the Germans to unite politically to throw out the Napoleonic French and establish their own state out of the multiplicity of German-speaking kingdoms, principalities and cities.[28]

This conception of the nation is not acceptable either from a sociological point of view or from that of a liberal political morality. There are very few, if any, nations that would qualify as such under the Herderian criterion and very few states that could be called genuine nation states. Morally, the communitarian philosophy is deeply illiberal as we show in Chapter 9 below. Nevertheless, contemporary academic discourse about the nation tends to preserve something of the nationalist force of the Herderian-Fichtean view: that nations ought to be independent and self-governing – while making the identity of the nation into a much more subjectively constituted entity.[29]

Thus, a fairly widely held contemporary view is that a nation is composed of some objective features, such as common ancestry, language, religion, culture, history and territory together with a subjective element that is treated as of crucial importance in the constitution of that nation.[30] This is the psychological-normative bond by which the members identify themselves as a nation and thereby acknowledge the appropriateness of strong feelings of mutual sympathy and moral commitment. In other words, the belief that they are a nation is the belief that the nation constitutes for them the primary focus of their socio-political moral rights and duties. It is a moral community rooted in a distinctive ethno-culture and territory that has *ipso facto* a claim to political self-government.

The significance of their stress on the subjective factor is that it allows the presence of the objective elements of ethno-culture to be downgraded. It is not necessary for all these elements to be present to establish the ethno-cultural ground. Thus an entity like the Swiss nation has no common ancestry, language, religion or culture but survives on a common history and territory and a large dose of subjective identification. However, the greater the emphasis on the subjective element, the less plausible becomes the nationalist force of the notion of a nation: the idea that a nation as a person's most significant moral community has thereby a claim to self-government. Why should a largely subjectively constituted grouping think that as a nation it has any claim to pressure others into giving them special treatment? Without such claims, few people would bother much with the notion of a nation.

We believe that the answer to this lies in the affinities we have already pointed to between the modern state and the liberal legitimizing principle of the will of the people, together with an affinity between the liberal grounding principle and nationalism. The modern state is not, of course, inherently nationalist any more than it is inherently liberal. In itself, it expresses nothing more than the will of a ruler to establish supreme control in a territory by subordinating all other groups equally to his unifying command. However, in subordinating all interests to that of the state, including the interest of the ruler himself, as in Frederick the Great of Prussia's self-designation as the first servant of the state,[31] it appeals to an entity that has no definite substance. The state of Prussia, insofar as it is not the state of the Hohenzollern dynasty or the state of the Prussian people, but they rather are its servants, has no definite content. It has no legitimizing boundaries or limits. It has no legitimizing principle at all other than the effective power it exercises in a certain territory. Hence, to appeal to the allegiance of the subjects of a given state is just to call upon them to obey a superior power. Should another state seize its territory and population, the new sovereign would have a better right to the inhabitants' allegiance than the old. This exactly expresses the philosophy of sovereignty of Thomas Hobbes.

Obviously, what the modern state needed was some independent legitimizing principle. This requirement was initially satisfied in practice, and to a certain degree only, by the dynastic principle, but not completely since republican states, such as the Venetian, the Dutch and the Swiss, were accepted as legitimate sovereigns in Westphalian society, not to speak of all the independent cities and bishoprics of the Holy Roman Empire of the German Nation. As we claimed in Chapter 2 above, Westphalian society operated at first without a formal principle of legitimacy and on a basis of *de facto* sovereignty that facilitated the power struggle between states inherent in the pure notion of state sovereignty. Nevertheless, there is an affinity between the modern state and liberalism. This arises from the denial by the modern state of any legislative authority to any entity in a collection of individuals other than itself. All individuals are fundamentally treated as equal atoms within the state. The state may well establish different ranks and privileges in society but they exist only at the state's will and in its interests. Since rights-based liberalism starts with free and equal individuals and justifies the state's sovereign authority in terms of what they need for the secure enjoyment of rights, it offers a legitimizing principle well attuned to the modern theory of state sovereignty. This principle is that the state expresses the rational will and interest of the people.

The move from the will and interest of the people to that of the nation, understood not in statist terms but ethno-cultural ones, comes about because the people need to have, and to understand themselves to have, a certain unity and common interest if the state is to be justified as the expression of their will. But the state itself, as we have seen, has no specific boundaries and the people of a state, being just the collection of individuals organized in a state, will have no substantive content either. A people, on this view, will be just any collection of individuals thrown together in a state. The nation, however, as an ethno-cultural group, has by definition a degree of pre-political and substantive unity that once the state is identified as the expression of its will can give the state a dynamic force. We believe, then, that it is no accident that the modern states that came to great prominence in the early modern period have the best claim to be called nation states, where nation is to be understood in ethno-cultural terms. These were the Dutch, the English, the French and the Swedes. The fact that these states emerged as powerful nation states was not, however, due to the claims of the English, French, Swedish or Dutch nations to their own state, but rather to the contingent fact that these states already had, no doubt to different degrees, relatively homogeneous populations from an ethno-cultural point of view, so that they could, easily enough, come to think of their state as defending and promoting the nation's interests. Furthermore, the success of these nation states in the struggle for power provided very strong incentives to other states to build their own national consciousness and to other nations, not already organized in their own state, such as the Germans and Italians, the Irish and the Poles, to acquire one. Especially significant in encouraging the conversion of national sentiment into a political principle was the effect of the French armies under Napoleon trampling on and reorganizing most of the old states of Europe. The defeat of Napoleon and the attempt to reconstruct European society on a resurrected dynastic principle delayed the spread of nationalism for a while, but by the end of the nineteenth century, it had effectively triumphed.

Our point in raising the question as to what a nation is was to put ourselves in a better position to say whether it is desirable for international law to recognize ethno-cultural nations as the true possessors of the right of peoples to self-determination, rather than to stick with the statist view of a people. We believe that in accepting the fairly loose connection permitted in the contemporary literature between ethno-cultural group and nation, we should at the same time accept that the term nation is fairly imprecise, that it can be multi-layered in the sense that an ethno-cultural group can be part of a larger group, which itself can be incorporated in a larger national entity, and so on. There is no one level that is **the** nation in the political sense of being entitled to self-determination. We will, then, have to recognize that the level we identify ourselves with as the appropriate set of people to claim political independence may well be a matter of choice. We must also allow that the political form of national consciousness can be affected by the promotional activities of states or of unofficial nationalist entrepreneurs. A clear example of this was the deliberate promotion of the idea of British nationality consequent upon the political union of England and Scotland in 1707. The choice as to whether to identify oneself politically as primarily Scottish or English rather than British is still there for many people. But British nationality does not necessarily exclude Scottish nationality. The former can perfectly well incorporate the latter as indeed could both be incorporated in a European nationality.

Our conclusion from such considerations is that, while a self-determining people must have some thick ethno-cultural content to hold it together – although the ethnic part may become very thin and almost entirely disappear, as in the USA and to a lesser degree in other immigrant states such as Canada and Australia and even conceivably Great Britain – it is not the case that any nation has *ipso facto* a *prima facie* right to political independence. To accept such a right of all so-called nations would be a recipe for widespread anarchy and violence as groups tried to carve out territories for themselves. Hence, we believe that an ethno-cultural group that finds itself inhabiting a state with whose existing national identity it is not happy, is not thereby entitled to its independence. It must provide good reasons why it should be given special treatment.[32]

Here is a list of possible reasons:

1. Substantial and persistent injustice towards members of the group (the Irish, the Jews, the Palestinians);
2. Fear of the loss of the group's distinct identity (the Quebecois);
3. Increase in the group's power and status in the world through uniting the members in one state (the Germans, the Italians, the Kurds);
4. Economic advantage.

Of these reasons, the last is clearly not a good reason unless it falls also under the category of substantial and persistent injustice, such as discriminatory taxation or other economic handicaps, uncompensated exploitation of natural resources, and so on. To seek independence just because, although fairly treated, one could be better off having got rid of the poorer regions of one's state, is clearly unjustifiable. It is probably the motivation of the North Italian nationalists, who wish to dump the poor South and is also probably present to some extent in Scottish nationalism, and was in Biafran claims in respect to 'their' oil.

With regard to the third category, it is difficult to see what reason one could have to try and prevent a group such as the Germans or

Italians from uniting in this way, except as a self-interested concern to profit from its political disunity. Insofar as they are subjects only of different German or Italian states and so long as injustices are not perpetrated in the achievement of the goal, it must be accepted as a good reason. However, should the unification of the group involve the loss of territory to other states, whose populations are not members of the unifying group, as would be the case with the political unity of the Kurds, we may get a direct conflict between two nationalisms over the possession of a certain territory, as in the case of Northern Ireland, Kosovo and Palestine/Israel. We do not think that there is any obvious solution to some of these problems. But if the group seeking independence has a historically well-grounded claim to the territory it occupies, and is not satisfied with reasonable alternatives, as described in the next section, to which it has given a fair trial, it should be allowed to secede, as a pragmatic measure and not as a right. The pragmatic nature of the acceptance of the secession indicates that it is not worth fighting to retain a people who through free votes clearly express their will to leave.

The second category does not seem to us to constitute a good reason. The situation may be altered by the granting of a degree of regional autonomy but the reason for doing this should not be to try and preserve a disappearing ethno-cultural identity. If an ethno-culture is losing its distinctness despite just treatment for its members, then there should be no duty on others or on the state to try and preserve it. We will, however, have more to say on this matter in the next section.

An obviously good reason for forming a national will for secession is that members of the group are substantially and systematically unjustly treated in one way or another, giving rise to the belief that the oppression can be ended only by the group's acquisition of their own state. This was no doubt a powerful element in the formation of a national will among the Irish, the Jews and the Palestinians. This type of case is the one that presents the greatest challenge to existing international norms. To accept it as a good reason would be to allow a right of secession in such cases and, as we have shown above, few commentators believe that there exists a right of secession in international law. However, we will discuss international society's response to the problem of injustice to minorities in the next section.

The protection of minorities in current international law

Because of the failure of the minorities regime established by the Versailles Treaty in Eastern Europe and discussed above, the UN Charter and the Universal Declaration on Human Rights and subsequent international covenants did not return to the problem. The hope was that insofar as states could be brought to respect individual rights to civil freedom and cultural rights to language, religion and culture, the problems of minorities would disappear. Thus, Article 27 of the ICCPR states that persons belonging to 'ethnic, religious or linguistic minorities ... shall not be denied the right, in community with the other members of their group, to enjoy their own culture, to profess and practice their own religion or to use their own language'.

In 1992 after the end of the Cold War and the re-emergence of ethnic conflicts and nationalist claims within Europe as well as elsewhere, the UN produced a General Assembly Resolution 47/135 on The Rights of Persons Belonging to National or Ethnic or Religious or Linguistic Minorities. This resolution states that it is inspired by the provisions of Article 27 of the ICCPR and aims to elaborate its content. However, it nowhere defines 'a minority' any more than the famous UN covenants and resolutions regarding the rights of peoples ever defined 'a people'. Standardly, minorities' experts take a minority to be a non-dominant minority of a population possessing distinctive characteristics, such as race, religion, or language. At the same time, members of the group must have a sense of belonging to the group and a desire for the group's identity to be preserved over time.[33]

The Resolution states in Article 1 that the basic duty of states is to protect the identity of such minorities but also positively to encourage the conditions for its promotion. This is taken to mean that persons belonging to minorities have the right to enjoy their own culture, as specified in article 27 of the ICCPR but also to participate effectively in cultural, religious, social, economic and public life. In particular, they have the right to 'participate effectively in decisions on national and where appropriate regional level concerning the minority to which they belong'. Article 4 elaborates on the positive measures the state should take to support its minorities. They should ensure that members of minorities have adequate opportunities to learn their mother tongue or have instruction in it, to encourage in society generally knowledge of the history, traditions, language and culture of minorities in their territory. However, Article 8 specifies that the exercise of these rights shall not prejudice the enjoyment by all persons of universally recognized human rights and fundamental freedoms and that nothing in the Declaration allows activity contrary to the purposes and principles of the UN, including the sovereign equality, territorial integrity and political independence of states. This discourages secessionist movements and interference by other states inhabited by members of the same group as the minority.

The Declaration does not tell us how to distinguish between national and other minorities. National minorities, however, are standardly understood to inhabit their own territories, such as the Welsh, the Scots, the Quebecois, the Basques, etc., while other minorities such as religious or immigrant groups have no historical connection to a particular region of the country. Yet, the basis of this distinction, as it is made emphatically by the influential contemporary writer on minorities, Will Kymlicka, is not simply one of territorial location. It is also that the national minority is supposed to possess a national culture. By this he means 'an intergenerational community, more or less complete institutionally, occupying a given territory and sharing a distinct language and history'.[34] The trouble with this account of a national minority as distinct from immigrant minorities is that apart from territorial location the criteria are fairly vague and do not clearly distinguish the two types. Even territory may be an unsatisfactory criterion, since immigrant populations may take over large parts, or the whole, of certain cities or even the countryside. They are intergenerational communities, may be more or less complete institutionally and share a distinct language and history. Furthermore, some national minorities, such as Kymlicka's fellow citizens, the Quebecois, whom he has most in mind, are immigrants also, while others do not have a distinct language or history and may not be complete institutionally. We are thinking, for instance, of the Israeli Arabs. Still, we surely have an intuitive grasp of the distinction and understand the typical national minority to be a group that has inhabited a particular region for hundreds of years and has maintained its distinct identity as a people into the present. It is a nation in the first sense given above and may form a political will in the sense at least to the extent of seeking a degree of self-government within the wider political body. The point of the distinction is, indeed, precisely to justify a policy of regional self-government or autonomy as one way of dealing with the claims of cultural minorities.

The basic right of a cultural minority, according to the 1992 UN General Assembly (UNGA) Declaration, is to receive the protection and enjoy the opportunities that will enable it to preserve its distinct identity in the larger whole, while its members possess the equal rights accorded every citizen. However, on our view, the whole must also accommodate the minorities, not simply by protecting their cultural and citizen rights, but by giving them some recognition in the overall national identity. Thus, British identity is supposed to be one that unifies English, Scots and Welsh (not to speak of the Irish), not by obliterating their separate characters but by cultivating multi-layered identities in each, so that there is no problem in thinking oneself both Scots and British at the same time. Whether British identity is flexible enough to accommodate substantial immigrant minorities of very different cultures, religions and language is still an open question (although it certainly seems to have managed to accommodate smaller minorities: German Jews and Ugandan Asians, for example). But the aim must surely be to develop an overarching identity while allowing the parts to maintain their distinctness, at least to a meaningful degree, if they so wish.

However, the 1992 UNGA Declaration is not content to require states to protect and accommodate their minorities, it also imposes on them the positive duty to promote their language and culture by ensuring that their members have adequate opportunities for instruction in their mother tongue and that there is a general awareness in society of their history, traditions, language and culture. In our view, the duty of the state is to promote whatever is necessary for the protection and development of the common good of its members. This includes the promotion of a common sense of identity as free and equal citizens of a particular state. It includes also the provision of adequate opportunities for all members to cultivate their capacities for autonomy so as to be able to take responsibility for their own personal choices as well as to participate in the making of collective choices. Minorities may be entitled to special help under these requirements. Personal choices, on the other hand, are for each individual to decide for himself, so long as they do not violate the rights of others. It is not for the state to promote any particular personal choice, but only those values that are of importance to the common good, such as education in general, scientific research, and so on. The choice of members of a minority to preserve their distinct language and cultural identity constitutes a series of personal choices, which the state has a duty to protect but none to promote, any more than it has a duty to promote religion or mountaineering or sailing. Indeed, for the state to encourage and promote separate cultural identity, especially when these are many and very diverse and when the members of minorities already experience difficulties in integrating in the national whole, is not only not required but seems foolhardy and self-defeating.

Our main concern in this chapter, however, is not with non-national immigrant minorities, but with peoples or nations occupying a region of a larger state, some proportion of whose members have formed a political will and seek self-determination. This type of case, exemplified by the Kurds, the Tamils, the Basques, etc., should not be lumped together with the problem of other minorities. For an acceptable option, short of outright secession, exists in this case that is not readily available or desirable in the case of immigrant minorities. This is the option of granting the national minority some degree of self-government within its national territory, as has been occurring recently in Britain and other states of Europe. Of course, the danger here is that the secessionist element in the national minority will feel encouraged by this concession to press even harder for complete separation, even if other 'nationalists' are satisfied with the compromise. Nevertheless, regional autonomy within the original sovereign state is an obvious alternative to the murderous nationalist struggles for independence that have raged, or are still raging, in many parts of the world. But this measure is not likely to be successful, if the minority is still not treated fairly as free and equal citizens in the larger state. Furthermore, should the national minority still want its independence, despite enjoying regional autonomy and just treatment, and would be capable of sustaining itself on its own, then our belief is that it should be allowed its political freedom on the pragmatic grounds mentioned in the last section.

The rights of indigenous peoples

Indigenous peoples could be seen as a national minority, but they obviously constitute a special case of some kind as has come to be recognized by the international community. The problem they present is that their identities and cultures are inhospitable to the fundamental categories of the modern state and in particular to liberalism. As a consequence, it is extremely difficult for their members to integrate successfully into the surrounding state structures within which they have been formally incorporated. At the same time, to protect and promote these indigenous cultures and practices is for the state to commit itself to protect and promote forms of life that violate the basic rights and fundamental freedoms of some of their citizens. The UN's declarations and conventions regarding minorities always make respect for everyone's human rights the condition for the recognition of minority cultures. But this cannot be done in the case of indigenous people without coming into direct conflict with the aim of preserving their cultures.

What, then, is to be done? The UN Sub-Commission on the Prevention of Discrimination and Protection of Minorities endorsed a Draft Declaration on the Rights of Indigenous People which was submitted to the Commission on Human Rights in 1994 and was accepted by the Human Rights Council in 2006. The draft declaration is a fairly radical document. It affirms the right of indigenous people to self-determination, although it interprets this as the right to self-government in accordance with their own culture and traditions within the sovereign territory of the state that incorporates them. It affirms also their right to the means necessary to finance their self-government. The recognition of the right to self-government in accordance with their traditional cultures includes their right to the full recognition of their laws, traditions and customs; their right to manage their lands, territories, waters and coastal seas traditionally owned or occupied and used by them; their right to the restitution of lands taken from them or to fair compensation; and their right to determine their own membership.[35]

In effect, these rights entitle indigenous people to maintain, or be helped to return to, the way of life they followed prior to their subjection to more powerful and elaborate civilizations and their states. Should indigenous people be given such a special status in international society? One can understand the motivation for so doing: namely as compensation for the injustices they have suffered and as a remedy for the semi-degraded state they live in on the margins of modern societies. But the absurdity of so doing consists in the Declaration's invalidating all the other human rights for these people and according them a legally privileged status in their host states. The Declaration would set an extremely undesirable precedent for all other minorities inclined to illiberal practices and indeed for illiberal peoples everywhere. At the very least, the document ought to spell out the fact of the exceptional exemption from respect for human rights requirements given to indigenous people and the reasons for allowing it.

But are the reasons valid? The difficulty lies in devising alternative ways of treating indigenous people that respect their minority culture and help them to integrate with the larger society as free and equal citizens. However, it may be that the authors of the Declaration are living in the clouds. For, many indigenous peoples' way of life has been already irredeemably penetrated and transformed by the surrounding economy and culture and the attempt to restore traditional ways of life would seem neither practicable nor desirable. Of course, where it is viable it could be better protected and assisted. Yet, if it is not viable without substantial subsidy, such support cannot be seen as a duty of states but only as compensation for past wrongs.

In any case, is this a sensible long-term policy? Is it being seriously suggested that these people should live indefinitely in their stone-age cultures? Of course, they are given the right to choose to integrate with the larger society, but the problem arises from the great difficulty of their doing so. Furthermore, doesn't the right to development of all peoples, to be discussed at length in the next chapter, recognize that it is in every people's interest to acquire the capacities of the modern state and economy, and their entitlement to the help of others to do so, in order to take their place as equals in national and international society? This must surely be the aim, but how to achieve it without destroying the people is another matter.

The relation of the right to self-determination to other rights

It is in principle absolutely clear what this relation should be and is stated to be in some of the relevant declarations and conventions. The right should be subject to the requirement that the people exercising it acknowledge a duty to respect the human rights of their members and that they are subject to the normal range of sanctions for failing to do so. Of course, in practice there has been no attempt to restrict the exercise of the right on these grounds, even when the colonial regime offered more protection for these rights than successor regimes were ever likely to provide. This has led commentators to assert the peremptory character of the right as admitting of no derogation under any circumstances. This view may be supported also by the primary position given to the right in the two major UN covenants on human rights. Yet, even if one accepts the right's *jus cogens* status in international law, it will still be the case that the new people enjoying the right thereby make themselves subject to the duty imposed on all states to respect and promote human rights.

International society and its law understands the right in a statist manner, as we have shown, and with a sovereign state as the standard outcome. However, it is recognized in the 1970 Declaration and also in the draft declaration on indigenous people that there are forms of self-determination that fall short of political independence, such as a high degree of local self-government. We have discussed and commended such limited forms of self-government as appropriate ways of dealing with the problem of peoples who are not entitled under the statist conception to exercise any choice in this matter and yet who have developed a strong national will. We have also recognized the need in extreme cases of injustice to such national minorities to accept the moral case for, if not the legal entitlement to, secession.

Yet, all these arrangements still demand of those enjoying them the duty to recognize and advance human rights.

6 | *The right to development and development assistance*

The objective of development is to create an enabling environment for people to enjoy long, healthy and creative lives.

Mahbub ul Haq[1]

The denial of human rights is inherent in poverty, something which is powerfully recorded in recent studies, such as Voices of the Poor.

Deepa Narayan[2]

Right to development (RTD)

Declaration on RTD

The 1986 Declaration on RTD was adopted by a vote of 146 to 1 (the US), with 8 abstentions (including Germany, Japan and the UK).[3]

The preamble of the Declaration calls in support the UN Charter provisions. These are contained in:

- Article 55, which states that the UN shall promote (a) high standards of living, full employment and conditions of economic and social progress and development; (b) solutions of international economic, social, health and related problems; and international cultural and economic co-operation; and
- Article 56, which says that all members pledge themselves to take joint and separate action in co-operation with the organization for the achievement of the purposes set forth in Article 55.

The preamble also recognizes that development is a 'comprehensive economic, social, cultural and political process', and it calls for efforts at the international level to promote and protect human rights to be accompanied by efforts to establish a new international economic order (we discuss in detail below what this means).

136

Article 1 of the Declaration defines the right to development as:

an inalienable human right by virtue of which every human person and all peoples are entitled to participate in, contribute to and enjoy economic, social, cultural and political development in which all human rights and fundamental freedoms can be fully enjoyed.

It also states that the human right to development implies the full realization of the right of peoples to self-determination, including their full sovereignty over their natural wealth.

Article 2 asserts that 'the human person is the central subject of development and should be the active participant and beneficiary of the right to development'. It also states that all human beings 'have a responsibility for development, individually and collectively, taking into account the need for full respect for their human rights and fundamental freedoms' and 'they should therefore promote and protect an appropriate political, social and economic order for development'. It adds that 'states have the right and duty to formulate appropriate national development policies ... on the basis of the population's active, free and meaningful participation in development and in the fair distribution of the benefits'.

Article 3 says that states 'have the primary responsibility for the creation of national and international conditions favourable to the realization of the right to development'. It also calls, as the preamble, for 'a new international economic order based on sovereign equality, interdependence, mutual interest and cooperation among all States'.

Article 4 requires states to take steps, individually and collectively, to formulate international development policies and to promote the more rapid development of developing countries through effective international co-operation.

Article 6 reaffirms all states' duties to respect CP and ESC rights, and the indivisibility and interdependency of all human rights. States must eliminate obstacles to development resulting from failure to observe CP as well as ESC rights.

Articles 8 requires states in undertaking development to ensure 'equality of opportunity for all in their access to basic resources, education, health services, food, housing, employment and the fair distribution of income', and that 'effective measures be taken to ensure that women have an active role in the development process'.

To summarize the most important points as we see it:

- The primary responsibility for the creation of the conditions favourable to development is that of the developing state, although all states have a duty to co-operate to promote development. This could be understood as making international aid conditional on a developing state adopting policies that are favourable to development.[4]

- The human person is identified as the central beneficiary of the right to development, even if 'peoples' or collectives of 'human persons' are entitled to some rights, such as full sovereignty over the natural wealth and resources in terms of territory.

- The document's idea of development is extremely broad: it consists in an economic, social, cultural and political development that realizes all human rights and fundamental freedoms. Development is, thus, not purely economic. This view of development is in line with the view adopted by the international community today.

- In view of this, the process of development must ensure respect for CP rights as well as equality of opportunity for all in regard to education, health services, food, housing, employment and the fair distribution of income. Development cannot therefore involve a trade-off with CP and ESC rights since, by definition, development includes respect for these. Whether we can still prioritize some rights over others is a question addressed later in the chapter.

- Finally, RTD implies a 'new international economic order' based on sovereign equality, interdependence, mutual interest and co-operation among all states.

What is the international legal status of the RTD?

Some international law scholars, such as M. Bedjaoui, an Algerian international lawyer who has been President of the International Court of Justice, claim that the right to development has attained the definitive status of the rule of law, its legality deriving from the UNGA Declaration of 1986.[5] This is not the general view, however.

To be sure, UNGA Declarations can acquire the force of law, as we saw with the Declaration on the Granting of Independence to Colonial Countries and Peoples. But this legal status was acquired not by itself but because its fundamental principles were reproduced in a succession of other UN instruments on the subject or related subjects and not opposed by other states. The cumulative effect of these references and reaffirmations indicated its acceptance as binding state practice having the force of law.

It is obvious that the Declaration on the Right to Development has not acquired this status.

The only time the RTD appears uncontested as a legally binding principle is in the 1981 African Charter on Human and Peoples' Rights (hence it is only applicable to its parties), which predated the 1986 UN General Assembly Declaration.

Western countries have not been sympathetic to the idea of the RTD and have opposed it from the beginning. The US voted against it in 1986, and many Western states abstained. It has also been the subject of much critical comment by international lawyers. Moreover, even today when human rights and development are linked together, it appears that the RTD is rarely, if ever, addressed explicitly in the common studies and strategies on the question of development, including the World Bank's and IMF's Poverty Reduction Strategy Papers, the World Bank's Comprehensive Development Framework, and the UN Development Assistance Framework for each country.[6] The RTD is also rarely mentioned in international conferences and summits on development, including those by specialized agencies (World Health Organization, International Labour Organization, United Nations Educational, Scientific and Cultural Organization, etc.) and UN funds and programmes (UN Development Programme, UN Children's Fund, etc.).[7] The Vienna, Millennium Development Goals and Durban Declarations are rare examples. The RTD does not even feature as an important right in human rights campaigns by non-governmental organizations, most of them preferring to campaign on specific rights (such as debt relief or women's rights).[8]

So why has the right been so ignored (at best) and opposed (at worst), except in a few declarations which paid it lip service?

There appear to be two reasons for this. First, the main gist of the Declaration on the Right to Development is to reaffirm the two already existing covenants, the ICCPR and ICESCR, and the indivisibility and interdependence of all human rights and freedoms. As a practical tool, it is hence not as useful as the two covenants which specify the content of the rights and their limitations. Second, the Declaration includes a number of claims that are not to be found in the other two documents. In particular, it states that:

- states should put in place national development policies aimed at a fair distribution of the benefits resulting from development (Article 2(3));

- states should ensure, at the national level, a fair distribution of income (Article 8); and
- states should promote 'a new international economic order [NIEO] based on sovereign equality, interdependence, mutual interest and cooperation among all States'(Article 3).

The first two points seem to require welfare policies within the states, independently of international co-operation (supposedly the way the welfare policies developed in the Western world). The third point, Article 3's call for a new international economic order, may explain Western states' opposition to the RTD as outlined in the Declaration. While what Article 3 actually says about the new order is anodyne enough, the appeal to the idea recalls the demands of the less developed countries in the early 1970s for such a new order, which were strongly resisted by the developed world.

At that time the economic order was seen by the developing countries as unjust and exploitative because the capitalist countries owned and controlled most of the world's resources (or certainly were seen to do so) and were, thereby, held to be restricting the full economic self-determination of the former colonial and other poor countries. The main elements of the call for a new international economic order were:

- the stabilization of commodity prices at an equitable level;
- preferential treatment for the less developed countries' industrial products;
- greater access of less developed countries to financial resources;
- greater participation in decision making in financial institutions;
- facilitation of technology transfers;
- expropriation without compensation.

A standard justification for these demands was that the less developed countries' poverty was caused by capitalist and colonialist exploitation. These claims were repeated, and the demands further inflated, in the interpretation of the RTD by international lawyers such as the aforementioned Bedjaoui.

Probably because of the call for the new international economic order, the Declaration was also understood to be affirming an unconditional right of the less developed countries to international financial support. In the circumstances, there is little wonder that the developing countries were reluctant to accept that the RTD imposed any legally binding obligations on them, although they did not deny that the Charter and the ICESCR did require them to engage in some kind of economic international co-operation on aid.

Today, however, things have changed considerably, and the idea of a new economic order does no longer appear central to the approach of the developing countries to international economic relations. This is due to a number of factors. First, as Harris points out, there has been:

a failure of high expectations for the state-driven model of economic development, the collapse of communism and the emergence of new commercially-oriented middle-classes challenging the NIEO-focused state classes in developing countries.[9]

Second, this demise of the state-driven model of economic development in many developing countries was accompanied by developments improving considerably the status and role of the developing countries in the global economy. In particular:

- domination of the world economy (including industry) is shifting from the older industrial economies (such as the US, Western Europe and Japan) towards industrializing economies in East Asia, China, the Pacific, Asia and Latin America. Thus, it is estimated that by 2050, the so-called E7 economies (the seven largest emerging market economies, China, India, Brazil, Russia, Indonesia, Mexico and Turkey) will be larger than today's G7 countries (US, Japan, Germany, UK, France, Italy and Canada);[10]
- the demand for commodities and energy from the fast-growing economies of Asia – China in particular – have led to commodity prices rising enormously. After being flat or even negative from 1980 to 2004, they have risen since then by 50 per cent;
- oil prices are at record levels;
- Asian countries invest increasingly in the West and elsewhere: indeed, around 80 per cent of the flow of net savings in the world today comes from Asia, the Middle East and Russia.[11]

Many of the demands of the new international economic order have thus been satisfied by the market forces themselves, without any need for organizing along the lines advocated in the 1970s: rises in commodity prices at well above an equitable level; specialization by the developing countries in industrial products (not just export of commodities); greater participation in world financial institutions and investment flows. It is difficult to claim today that the developed world controls most of the world's resources; or that poverty in less developed countries is caused by capitalist and colonialist exploitation (we look in more detail at the question of poverty below). Calls for expropriation without compensation have also stopped.[12]

Accordingly, there are no longer any significant calls by the less developed countries as a movement for a new economic order (even if individual states still refer to it occasionally). Does this mean that Western states could or should now stop objecting to a legally binding RTD? We answer this question by considering what the use of a separate RTD would be, on top of the ICCPR and the ICESCR.

Why a separate RTD?

The reason to have a separate RTD is, we would suggest, to bring together a number of different rights, already existing separately at the international level: CP and ESC rights, the right to self-determination and, most importantly, the right of developing nations to receive (conditional) development assistance from developed countries.

While the first two sets of rights (CP and ESC, and the right to self-determination) are explicitly provided for by, respectively, international covenants (ICESCR, ICCPR) and customary international law, the right of developing nations to receive development assistance from developed countries is nowhere set out explicitly as a norm of international law. As we said in the introduction, it can only be deduced from other international law sources, in particular Articles 55 and 56 of the UN Charter.[13]

The right to receive (and give) development assistance is furthermore controversial, and not likely to be accepted easily by the international community. Indeed, as we discuss below, aid is presently given on charitable and self-interested grounds.

However, we believe that the whole point of having a separate RTD would be precisely to bring out the fact that international assistance is necessary in order to make CP, ESC and self-determination rights a reality for all states and their people; and that the giving of aid is required (not voluntary) under international law. The goal of RTD, based on norms of self-determination and civil, political, economic, social and cultural rights, would ultimately be, in this case, to establish welfare rights, such as those recognized domestically by the liberal welfare state, at the international level.

Of course, the mutual obligation of citizens at the domestic level rests on the effective creation of secure and stable legal and political orders, and it might well be argued that any international welfare obligations must rest on similar conditions. Thus, states would surely be under no requirement to give aid to countries that threaten their security or that of their citizens. Similarly, they would not be obliged to pour money into the pockets of ruling cliques that merely embezzle it for themselves and do nothing for their populations or spend the money in inappropriate ways or do not have the capacity to engage in effective development (as has been unfortunately so often the case: see our discussion of international aid below). However, there would still be an obligation on states to provide aid under certain circumstances when the recipient countries were doing 'the right thing', as agreed in the international 'compacts' we will discuss in more detail below.

Let us add that we must distinguish, of course, the issue of development from the question of reparations for colonial exploitation. The latter has nothing whatever to do with the former. If there were valid claims for reparations, then they would be valid even if there were no RTD. We ought also to distinguish questions of capitalist exploitation from the RTD. It may be that the capitalist countries have wrongly deprived the less developed countries of ownership and control of their natural resources. If so, this injustice should be remedied quite independently of whether there is an RTD. We saw anyway that with the disappearance of most socialist states and the rise to capitalist prosperity of many Third World countries, we don't hear much of this type of claim any more.

We can see, therefore, that most objections that developed countries may have had to a binding RTD as set out in the Declaration on RTD are no longer valid. There are no more calls for expropriation; no more calls for a state-driven model of economic development; and the new international economic order advocated within the Declaration – when stripped of its radical interpretations, which only some Non-Aligned Movement (NAM) countries are still insisting on, as we will see in our discussion of recent research into RTD – is arguably just another name for an ideal international legal order of the kind we outline. We conclude therefore that the Declaration ought to be made the basis for a binding international convention (the way the UN Declaration on Human Rights gave way to the ICCPR and ICESCR). The next section will discuss how there is little likelihood, nevertheless, of this happening in the near future; and how 'soft-law' (recommendations and principles lacking legal status but creating a strong expectation that their provisions will be respected and followed by the international community) commitments by states may be instead more suitable at the present time to advance the cause of human rights. It will do so in the context of outlining past and present development strategies, as well as strategies that ought to be pursued in order to realize the aspirations of the Declaration on the RTD.

One last word on the concept of the RTD: that is, whether the right is a group or an individual right. The Declaration states, as we saw, that the central subject of development is the individual person. However, it also attributes the right not only to every person but also to all peoples, and by connecting the right to the right of peoples to self-determination again makes a people rather than an individual out to be the subject of the right. Yet, as we saw in the last chapter, there is no need for liberals to worry about a supposed right of peoples, or states for that matter, where the right of the collectivity can be clearly understood as grounded in the general will of the associated individuals and conditional on its observance of its members' individual rights.

Development strategies

Recent research into the implementation of the RTD

Since the late 1990s (hence after the end of the Cold War), a lot of thought has gone into the question of RTD implementation or, more precisely, into the question of how 'to move the RTD from general principles and political commitments to specific operational tools for development practice'.[14]

We will look at the UN bodies and posts responsible for such research, all established by the Commission on Human Rights.

Open-ended Working Group on Development and the independent expert

The mandate of the independent expert, A. Sengupta, was to present to the Open-Ended Working Group On Development (a political body established in 1998) at each of its sessions a study on the current state of progress in the implementation of the right to development, with the focus on specific topics.[15] Sengupta saw the right to development as 'a right to a particular development **process**, which enables all fundamental freedom and rights to be realized, and expands the basic capacities and abilities of individuals to enjoy their rights'.[16]

To implement the RTD, Sengupta suggested a step-by-step approach aimed at achieving three basic rights: the right to food, the right to primary education, the right to health. This approach would be 'part of a development plan in which no human rights are violated but at least some come closer to realization'.[17] The rights closer to realization are hence ESC rights: for Sengupta (as for us) realization of these rights must clearly be a necessary condition for the realization of all other human rights.

To implement development plans – and recognizing the importance of international co-operation as set out in the declaration on the RTD – Sengupta suggested 'development compacts' between the developing countries concerned and donor countries plus international financial institutions. Such compacts would consist of developing countries committing themselves to fulfil their human rights obligations towards their citizens, and of the donor countries and financial institutions providing resources, sharing costs and generally committing themselves to international action in the following areas:

• trade and access to markets;
• debt adjustment for the poorest countries;
• transfer of resources and technology;
• protection of migrants and labour standards; and
• restructuring of the international financial system to give the developing countries a greater share in power and decision making and to increase the flow of private capital to their economies.[18]

This all seems very sensible and in line with the concepts of RTD as set out in the Declaration on RTD. However, as Piron points out, there is a danger that 'development compacts' would simply duplicate already existing mechanisms at the international level, such as Poverty Reduction Strategy Papers, UN Development Assistance Frameworks and UN Common Country Assessments.[19] We will look at some of these mechanisms (in particular the Poverty Reduction Strategy Papers) in the section on Global Governance: suffice to say here that, unlike the suggested development compacts, they are not explicitly based on concepts of rights. Hence they may not fulfil exactly the same function.

Open-ended Working Group and the high-level task force on the implementation of the RTD

The task force was established in 2004 in order 'to provide the necessary expertise to the Working Group to enable it to make appropriate recommendations to the various actors on the issues identified for the implementation of the right to development'[20] or, in the words of its Chairperson-Rapporteur, Stephen Marks, to contribute to: 'mainstreaming the right to development in the policies and operation activities of relevant actors at the national, regional and international levels, including multilateral financial, trade and development institutions'.[21]

Its first task was to consider criteria for a periodic evaluation of Millennium Development Goal 8, global partnerships for development, 'with the aim of improving the effectiveness of global partnerships with regard to the realization of the right to development' (we discuss the Millennium Development Goals later in this chapter).

At the fourth session of the Human Rights Council in January 2007, the task force recommended a number of criteria for such an evaluation, having selected three partnerships: the African Peer Review Mechanism, the United Nations Economic Commission for Africa and Organization for Economic Co-operation and Development Effectiveness in the context of the New Partnership for Africa's Development, and the Paris Declaration on Aid Effectiveness.[22]

The criteria ('a milestone in the right to development process')[23] include (a) the extent to which a partnership contributes to creating an environment and supports a process in which all human rights are realized; (c) the extent to which a partnership values and promotes good governance, democracy and the rule of law at the international and national levels; (d) the extent to which a partnership values and promotes gender equality and the rights of women; (j) the extent to which a partnership recognizes mutual and reciprocal responsibilities between the partners; and (m) the extent to which policies supported by a partnership ensure the constant improvement of the well-being of the entire population and of all individuals, on the basis of their active, free, and meaningful participation in development and in the fair distribution of the benefits resulting therefrom.[24]

Whither RTD?

We saw that the aim of the recent UN research into RTD has been how 'to move the RTD from general principles and political commitments to specific operational tools for development practice',[25] and not how to lay a basis for an international binding instrument.

Indeed, there is little hope for such an instrument in the near future. In our view, this is as much due to the attitude of developing countries as to that of developed countries. While the latter do not want to commit themselves to a legal obligation towards aid, the former will not accept the idea of tied aid, and continue to put more emphasis on international rather than national efforts to promote economic development. Certainly, as Piron points out, many have no intention at all of implementing the RTD at the national level: they are only desirous to use it to make economic claims on the international community. For example, at the Human Rights Commission's and General Assembly's meetings:

NAM [Non-Aligned Movement] countries and China argue that RTD is a *right of states and a collective right of peoples to development*, and that it has an international dimension.[26] The RTD cannot be reduced to international development assistance, nor to national poverty eradication programmes. The responsibility for the RTD cannot remain at the national level: globalisation, international trade, foreign domestic economic policies, foreign debt and intellectual property rights constrain national development efforts. The international agenda should include: greater and more effective participation by developing countries in international decision-making, a truly open multilateral trade system reflecting development needs of all nations, a new international financial architecture releasing resources for productive investment, an effective prevention and response capacity to deal with international financial crises, and sustainable and integrated world wide economic growth.[27]

Unfortunately, these claims ('the RTD cannot be reduced to international development assistance, nor to national poverty eradication programmes ... international agenda should include greater and more effective participation by developing countries in international decision-making') together with the continued emphasis on non-conditionality, seem to take us back to the claims for the 'old style' 1970s new international economic order; and do not augur well for the willingness of developed countries to subscribe to such an RTD. More recently, during the consideration of the report by the Working Group:

- The Group of African States reaffirmed that 'only a non-fragmented approach, including equitable international trade rules and responses to energy, raw material and debt burden issues, could reduce the growing gap between developing and developed countries'; and called for 'international cooperation exclusive of conditionality'.[28]
- In the context of the Declaration on the RTD, the Non-Aligned Movement called for international co-operation 'that is not subject to conditionality, nor be treated as a matter of charity'.[29] In other words, for the Movement the RTD obligations ought to be one-sided: developed countries would have an obligation to provide aid, but developing countries would have no obligation to engage in responsible domestic policies. It seems to us that this is very much the case of wanting to have one's cake and eat it.
- The Non-Aligned Movement declared 'for the record that a majority of States [presumably all developing states] was in favour of an international legally binding instrument on the right to development', and that 'it should be reflected explicitly in the conclusions and recommendations of the Working Group'.[30]
- Finally, several delegates and groups reiterated their position that the work of the task force should contribute to an eventual elaboration of a convention on the RTD. However, other delegations and groups opposed any reference to starting work on drafting such a convention.[31]

Indeed, if one examines the attitude of developed countries towards actual development assistance, one can see that there is little likelihood presently of them accepting it as a binding obligation. For example, in the Organisation for Economic Co-operation and Development (OECD)'s *Shaping the 21st Century: the Contribution of Development Co-operation* (a document representing 'the collective views of development ministers, heads of agencies and other senior officials responsible for development co-operation'[32]), the motives given for official assistance are:

1. humanitarian: a compassionate response to extreme poverty and human suffering;
2. enlightened self-interest: political stability, social cohesion, human security; and economic prosperity in developing countries benefit

developed countries in terms of access to markets and international stability;[33] and

3. international solidarity: people from all nations can come together to address common problems, and deal with issues that know no borders, such as environmental protection.[34]

There is no mention of legal obligation, human rights, etc.

A recent publication by the World Bank, *Global Issues for Global Citizens*, also gives the 'enlightened self-interest' justification as the one why aid should be provided. The authors say:

given that some 2.5 billion to 3 billion people in developing countries (about half the current world population) now live on less than two dollars a day, the ability of these countries to take care of all their people is at present extremely limited and will remain so for some time to come. Unless the richer nations help them through increased aid and trade, growing social discontent and outright conflict in developing countries will fester and eventually spill across their boundaries.[35]

Again, human rights are not mentioned at all by the authors, not even in their 'Introduction to Global Issues: Why Care About Global Issues?' section. According to them, it is only because of the potential consequences of our inaction – economic, social, security, health and environmental problems we will face if we do not help developing countries – that we ought to provide development assistance.

The present 'development partnerships' between developing and developed countries and international development organizations (some of which we will examine below), are based on the same reasoning.[36] The OECD talks about 'stronger compacts for effective partnership', which would include: (i) joint responsibilities of developing and external partners; (ii) developing countries' responsibilities; and (iii) external partners' responsibilities.[37] It does not mention a legally binding RTD; and neither does the Monterey Consensus.[38]

Does it matter though? Maybe, as with so many other international issues (environmental ones being the best example), soft-law commitments of states towards international co-operation in development matters may be sufficient for the time being to help us move towards the goal to which both developing and developed countries supposedly aspire: realization of all our human rights.

To help us answer this question, we will now look at what form the actual development assistance has taken in the past, where it is going today, and how effective it has been. We start by outlining the original debate on development and human rights trade-offs, when development was seen in purely economic growth terms. We then look at the context in which development assistance takes place nowadays: the growing integration of the global economy, and institutions of global governance, in particular, the World Bank, the International Monetary Fund, intergovernmental compacts, and transnational corporations (global governance meaning 'the processes through which policies aimed at regulating international society are agreed')[39]. Finally, we examine the statistics on development assistance and ask how effective all these billions of pounds have been, in view of the recent trends in poverty reduction and general progress on the Millennium Development Goals.

Development and human rights trade-offs

Development in the immediate post-WWII era was seen in purely economic growth terms. Further, the standard view was (throughout most of the Cold War) that rapid economic development and human rights were incompatible.

According to that wisdom, rapid economic growth depends on political repression and mass poverty. The former was held to be necessary for the execution of the drastic economic transformations indispensable for achieving sustained economic growth, while the latter was an unavoidable consequence of the need to secure the resources from the population for the sake of investment.

It is helpful here to use an analysis by Donnelly of this view.[40] Donnelly divides it into three types of development/human rights trade-offs:

1. The needs trade-off: this is concerned with maximizing the funds available for investment at the expense of social programmes satisfying basic human needs.
2. The equality trade-off: this holds that economic inequality has to increase during the process of development within a society both because it is needed as an incentive to improved economic performance and because transferring income and wealth to the better-off increases the level of saving and hence makes possible an increase in the rate of investment.

3. The liberty trade-off: here the claim is that civil and political freedoms would make it impossible for the inevitably unpopular sacrifices needed for development to be carried through. Hence, they must be suspended.

These suspensions or neglect of human rights were believed, of course, only to be temporarily necessary. They would be rectified as development raised the general level of prosperity, increased the wealth available for social programmes and brought stability to society.

This strategy of trading off basic human rights for high growth came, however, increasingly under attack, as it so often clearly served the interests of repressive regimes without leading to a general increase in welfare in society. Successful economic development of countries like South Korea and Taiwan – which achieved rapid growth without huge inequalities and with increasing levels of welfare provision – was also taken to show that there was certainly no unavoidable needs and equality trade-offs.

Development scholars started to argue that the liberty trade-off was also unnecessary; and that, on the contrary, CP rights are needed:

- to implement reasonable development policies through providing for the flow of information about and evaluation of proposals; and to ensure a reasonable distribution of resources by preventing elites grabbing all the benefits or making catastrophic resource misallocation mistakes (China's coercive system having contributed to massive famines, for example).[41] Nowadays, the argument is cast in terms of CP rights helping to monitor a state's compliance with ESC rights and ensure that it realizes rights progressively as expeditiously as possible;[42]
- to guarantee social and cultural rights without which a stable social order cannot be maintained and chaos and retrogression take place; and
- in and of themselves by everyone, however poor.

As a result of these views, in the 1980s a shift started in the development strategies of UN agencies and Western governments, first to a more welfare-oriented approach which aimed at (i) increasing employment through using labour-intensive technology rather than large-scale industrial enterprises; (ii) fairer distribution of resources; and (iii) satisfying basic needs at a minimum level of the entire population;

and second, to an even more expansive view of development as 'human development'.

Following scholars such as Sen, it became generally accepted that the development process had to respect all human rights, including CP rights. It could no longer be identified simply 'with the growth of gross national product, or with the rise in personal incomes, or with industrialization, or with technological advance, or with social modernization'.[43] True development was about the expansion of the real freedoms people can and should enjoy. As the Human Rights Development Report 2004 stated years later:

People are the real wealth of nations. Indeed, the basic purpose of development is to enlarge human freedoms. The process of development can expand human capabilities by expanding the choices that people have to live full and creative lives. And people are both the beneficiaries of such development and the agents of the progress and change that bring it about. This process must benefit all individuals equitably and build on the participation of each of them. This approach to development—human development—has been advocated by every Human Development Report since the first in 1990.[44]

In line with this view, the United Nations Development Programme started to include, beginning in 1990, a Human Development Index in its annual Human Development Report. By measuring life expectancy, literacy, education, and standard of living for countries worldwide, the Index was thought to enable a better judgement of the impact of economic policies on quality of life.

In 2003, the UN Development Group adopted a 'Common Understanding on a Human Rights-based Approach to Development Cooperation'. This Understanding has to ensure that UN agencies, funds and programmes 'apply consistently a Human Rights Based Approach to common programming processes at global and regional levels, and especially at the country level in relation to the Common Country Assessment and United Nations Development Assistance Framework [a common programme and resource framework for UN development agencies and programmes]'.[45] More precisely, the Common Understanding states:

1. All programmes of development co-operation, policies and technical assistance should further the realisation of human rights as laid down in the Universal Declaration of Human Rights and other international human rights instruments.

2. Human rights standards contained in, and principles derived from, the Universal Declaration of Human Rights and other international human rights instruments guide all development cooperation and programming in all sectors and in all phases of the programming process.
3. Development cooperation contributes to the development of the capacities of 'duty-bearers' to meet their obligations and/or of 'rights-holders' to claim their rights.[46]

This integration of human rights into all UN programmes is also what is called 'mainstreaming human rights',[47] a process advocated by the Secretary-General since 1997 in a number of reform initiatives highlighting the relevance of human rights to development (such as in the well-known 2005 Report *In Larger Freedom: Towards Development, Security and Human Rights*). In 2005, the UN General Assembly's World Summit applied the concept of mainstreaming to individual states' activities and recommended including human rights in national development policies.[48]

As we will see in a moment, even international financial institutions, such as the World Bank and the International Monetary Fund, have started to think in terms of 'mainstreaming' human rights into their activities. As Sergio Pereira Leite explained in 'Human Rights and the IMF':

what exactly is a human rights-based development strategy? At the risk of oversimplification, one could define a rights-based approach to growth and poverty reduction as comprising six elements: (1) active protection of civil and political liberties; (2) pro-poor budgets and growth strategies; (3) policies geared toward ensuring that people receive adequate food, education, and health care; (4) broad participation in policy design; (5) environmental and social awareness; and (6) efforts to combat discrimination.[49]

'Active protection of civil and political liberties', as of all other liberties, is thus a *sine qua non* of today's development strategies. Clearly, there is no question any more about human rights/development trade-offs.

Does this mean, however, that development strategies ought to pursue the achievement of all these liberties at the same time; that one cannot pursue, say, 'policies geared toward ensuring that people receive adequate food, education, and health care' or 'pro-poor budgets and growth strategies' – that is, policies aimed at economic development – separately from pursuing all the other elements of human development strategy?

It is a difficult question to answer. On the one hand, human rights can only flourish in proper economic conditions; hence one ought to concentrate on achieving those. On the other, without the appropriate CP rights we may not be able to achieve such economic conditions in the first place. So it looks like one ought to pursue both CP and ESC rights together. The problem is that this may require too much expertise and resources from individual development institutions. It may therefore be better for these institutions (domestic or international) to specialize in the implementation of one set of rights or the other. We will see, however, how this can create problems of its own when we discuss the World Bank and the International Monetary Fund and the accusations directed at them that they neglect the impact on human rights of their economic development policies.

So what can be done? How are we to decide what comes first, chicken or the egg?

The way we regard it is as follows. We saw that the RTD requires us to establish welfare rights – such as are recognized domestically by the liberal welfare state – at the international level. The framework in which those rights are to be established is a liberal one, with the full recognition of CP rights; but the welfare rights themselves are the ESC rights, only possible to achieve when states have reached a certain minimum level of economic development. This is recognized indeed by the 'progressive realization' norm of the ICESCR. The role of the international community is, we believe, to help all states and all individuals to achieve (and whenever possible exceed) that level. This can only be done via pursuit of suitable economic policies at both international and domestic level that, while respecting other human rights, concentrate on achievement of economic indicators of welfare: for instance, a reduction in the poverty or amelioration in health (as sought by the Millennium Development Goals we discuss below). Hence we need institutions that specialize in the pursuit of these indicators, just as we have ministries at the domestic levels specializing in economic matters.

To be sure, other institutions ought to be responsible for overseeing the economic institutions, to make sure that they are not overlooking human rights in their pursuit of economic development, and that respect for human rights is written into their mandates. What these institutions ought to be – whether one of the present UN human rights bodies or a totally new body – is, however, another question we will not pursue here.

What we want to do now is ask how, given that human rights can only flourish in proper economic conditions, we can achieve such conditions in today's global free-market environment. Is globalization not inimical to the achievement of human rights? Does it not create great inequality and suffering? Do we need to direct and regulate it in the same way we regulate competitive markets at the domestic level?

These are all huge questions, to which we can do no proper justice here. We can only outline the main debates and arguments.

Globalization and human rights

It is not, by and large, the case that as a result of globalization the poor are getting poorer and the rich are getting richer, which is the rhetoric that is often used, and which I believe is mistaken. It may have happened in a few countries, but by and large, this is not the case. (Amartya Sen)[50]

For a period after WWII, it was widely believed that economic development depended on the building of large-scale industrial enterprises and on the support of state interventionism.

Originally based on the apparent economic success of the socialist economy in Soviet Russia and the reconstruction of the state-managed economies of Western Europe in the immediate post-WWII period, this belief resulted, it is widely held, in a collapse of the Soviet Union and the whole Eastern communist bloc in the late 1980s. Less dramatically, and more controversially, it also resulted in lower economic growth and higher unemployment in Western countries such as France and Germany that have continued to rely on considerable state intervention in the economy in more recent times.

This view of economic development is today on the whole discredited. The predominant belief is instead the same as Adam Smith's in his 1776 *Inquiry into the Nature and Causes of the Wealth of Nations:*[51] that is, that economic development is the result of free operation of competitive markets, with the state (or states) intervening only to construct a proper framework for such markets (ensuring property rights, anti-trust laws, transport infrastructure, education and defence).

The result of that belief has been, in recent years, an unprecedented economic growth; but also a growing interdependence between states through trade, financial integration, migration, temporary movement of service providers and information flows. This growing interdependence is known as globalization; and while welcomed by many, it is viewed by others as a great threat to the ability of governments to conduct appropriate domestic economic policies, and a cause of increased world poverty and inequality. In the naysayers' view, human rights and globalization are incompatible.

As the above quote by Sen indicates, this negative view of globalization is wrong. Empirical research makes clear that private-led growth is the most important cause of poverty reduction; hence, by and large, both poor and rich can benefit from economic growth brought about by globalization. Similarly, globalization does not have to stop governments from pursuing their preferred policies. They are simply less able to pursue them on their own, and may be required to do so by 'pooling' sovereignty with other states (the way the European Union has operated, for example). Furthermore – and somehow paradoxically – globalization also goes together with localization; a good example is the demand for autonomy by regions and communities such as seen recently within Britain by Scotland and Wales. And localization may mean more, not less, control by people over their own lives.

However, there is no doubt that there are problems with unregulated globalization. First, trade liberalization may lead in the short run at least to increased unemployment and lower wages, especially among the poor, who are often unable to take advantage of new economic opportunities or to protect themselves against negative shock.[52] As K. Dervis, the United Nations Development Programme Administrator points out:

The fact is that globalization, the global market economy delivers to the upper half; it doesn't really deliver to the poor people [in the short run]. In some cities in the developing world, you have 50 percent of young people unemployed ... You have to have ... institutions to accompany market development, to accompany what's happening in the technological and financial sphere, so that we indeed have a much more equitable and balanced human society.[53]

Second, while one of the most important determinants of growth is financial development, brought about by increased financial integration,[54] financial integration also entails global capital flows; and these, in turn, lead to a greater vulnerability to currency crashes, surges in inflation, falls in output, increases in unemployment, and so on. As a result, financial crises – such as we saw in Asia in the late 1990s – can hinder development and increase poverty in countries that open up their financial markets to world competition.

This is not an argument, however, against globalization, without which we would simply have lower economic growth full stop (and hence less resources with which to build our liberal welfare state throughout the world); it is rather an argument for certain domestic and international reforms (as also advocated by the United Nations Development Programme mentioned above). Domestic reforms required by developing countries would be those, for example, suggested in a recent paper prepared by the International Monetary Fund staff entitled 'Reaping the Benefits of Financial Globalization'. After considering data on financial globalization for the past thirty years, the paper concludes that:

[w]hereas advanced economies largely benefit from the free movement of capital, emerging market and developing countries should make sure they meet certain thresholds—which include the quality of their institutions and policymaking and their level of domestic financial development—before they open up their capital account. If they do not meet such thresholds, financial liberalization can lead to macroeconomic volatility.[55]

International reforms would include what the World Bank calls a 'genuinely global public policy',[56] conducted by a global body with the legal authority to exercise direct control over international transactions. Unfortunately, there is no such body, nor likelihood of one in the foreseeable future. There is no global central bank – such as the US Federal Reserve or the European Central Bank – that could provide liquidity globally; nor any other international body that could provide insurance, require and enforce uniform accounting standards or legislate financial disclosure requirements for firms issuing equity or bonds (all ways of regulating business at the domestic level).

An alternative (and more pragmatic) way to deal with those global financial issues would in this case be:

- to get countries to agree on and enforce common standards for financial regulation and supervision (already over sixty have been promulgated, according to the World Bank);[57] and
- to improve monitoring and surveillance of countries and international financial markets by the International Monetary Fund and other international institutions.

There is another way – besides contributing to economic growth – in which globalization contributes to human rights: through the growth of global civil society, including a global human rights movement.

Indeed, we now have 'a global network of government officials, activists, thinkers and practitioners, who share a common commitment to democracy, the universality of human rights and respect for the rule of law'.[58]

Looking at specific issues, advocacy groups' campaigns on global issues such as debt relief and a fair global trading system have raised peoples' consciousness of these problems all around the world. The campaign to reduce the debt burden of the poorest countries has been particularly effective. The Heavily Indebted Poor Countries Initiative, which we discuss below, was the result of a sustained campaign by the international coalition, Jubilee 2000, to cancel poor countries' debt by 2000; and the Multilateral Debt Relief Initiative was the result of a campaign by the international coalition Make Poverty History.[59] Even corporations, banks and private investors increasingly serve as 'transmission belts' for human rights norms. Contrary to the fears of many critics of globalization, and as we discuss more fully below, corporate social responsibility has become increasingly accepted as a core trait of global corporate citizenship.

Globalization and human rights are hence, in our view, not only compatible but go hand-in-hand together. Globalization increases enormously the opportunities for worldwide growth; and it exposes more and more people to international human rights norms. At the same time, for globalization to 'deliver' on those norms, it needs to be managed, the way domestic economies are managed, through fiscal and monetary policies, and regulatory practices. Who can manage globalization and how is the topic of our next section.

Global governance and human rights

Global governance, as explained earlier, refers to 'the processes through which policies aimed at regulating international society are agreed'.[60] In the absence of a global government, these processes will include international institutions and agreements, civil society campaigns and associations, and global partnerships (which would include governments, private sector and civil society organizations and international organizations).

The two principal groups of global governance institutions are the UN system and the international financial institutions: in particular the World Bank, International Monetary Fund and World Trade

Organization (which replaced the General Agreement on Trade and Tariffs (GATT) in the 1990s). Another important source of decision making in the economic sphere is constituted by the private sector, such as the transnational corporations. Yet another is that of inter-governmental or 'global' compacts, in which countries agree to work together toward global development goals and to prevent and resolve violent conflicts. In view of the perceived ineffectiveness and lack of legitimacy of many of the global governance institutions, the compacts (of which the Millennium Development Goals that we are going to analyse soon are the most prominent) play an increasingly important role.

International financial institutions

We have already examined the UN systems of relevance to human rights in the previous chapters. In this section, we focus on the global compacts and the main economic institutions of global governance: the World Bank, the IMF, and the transnational corporations.

The World Bank

It is important to recognize when there has been a defining moment for the international promotion and protection of human rights. One such moment, I believe, was when the World Bank Group recognized that it had an express role to play in the promotion and protection of human rights. (Mary Robinson, United Nations High Commissioner for Human Rights)[61]

The World Bank is a public international financial institution created at the end of WWII to help rebuild a ravaged Europe.[62] Its aim is to provide loans and credits to developing countries for projects that alleviate poverty and promote social and economic development. It does so by providing:

- financial assistance to governments: concessionary financing through loans and grants from its affiliate International Development Association (IDA);[63] and non-concessionary financing through the International Bank for Reconstruction and Development (IBRD);[64]
- loans and guarantees in support of private sector projects (some through the International Development Association and the International Bank for Reconstruction and Development, but most

through the International Finance Corporation and the Multilateral International Guarantee Agency); and
• policy advisory and analytical services and technical assistance.

Besides aid, other significant issues for the World Bank have been good governance and clean government, an effective legal system, a well-organized financial system, a social safety net and social programmes. But, until the 1990s, human rights *per se* were entirely absent from the Bank's agenda. This absence was due to the fact that, according to its original mandate, the Bank had to take into account only economic considerations while making decisions.[65] This meant, many argued, that if the Bank pursued human rights objectives it would be violating this mandate; and that its role was not that of a political or ethical reformer of its members. The Bank should only react, it was said, where given political events had significant economic effects or led to a breach of international obligations relevant to the Bank (such as those created by binding decisions of the UN Security Council).

Under its President James Wolfensohn (1995–2005), however, this view of which political events have significant economic effects was extended: first, to corruption, now considered as the biggest single inhibitor of equitable and effective economic development (and hence legitimately an economic and social issue); and second, to lack of press freedom and generally of freedom of expression, as it became clear that the more freedom there is – that is, the more opportunities to criticize and dissent – the more corruption can be controlled.

In 1998, the Bank started to make pronouncements on human rights, 'issuing statements' about how it supported the realization of human rights and how it believed that 'creating the conditions for the attainment of human rights is a central and irreducible goal of development'.[66]

Reflecting the Bank's new approach to development, the Comprehensive Development Framework and the associated Poverty Reduction Strategy Papers were created in the late 1990s.

The Strategy Papers are plans for reducing poverty, written by low-income countries themselves before they can qualify for the Bank's assistance. They are based on the Comprehensive Development Framework's four principles for designing and implementing effective strategies for economic development and poverty reduction – long-term, holistic vision, country ownership, country-led partnership; and results focus – which emphasize the interdependence of all elements of development: 'social, structural, human, governance, environmental, economic, and financial'.[67] The Bank bases its Country Assistance

Strategies, i.e. its plans for assistance to low-income countries, on the Strategy Papers. According to the Bank, the five principles on which the Papers in turn are based are:

1. They are country-driven, involving broad-based participation by civil society and the private sector as they are produced.
2. They are focused on outcomes that would benefit the poor.
3. They recognize that tackling poverty requires a comprehensive approach because poverty is more than just a lack of income: poor people also suffer from a lack of opportunity, security, and voice in decisions that affect their lives.
4. They are partnership-oriented in that they encourage the co-ordinated involvement of bilateral, multilateral and non-government organizations in the country's poverty reduction programme.
5. They are based on a long-term perspective for poverty reduction.

The Bank also helps businesses to uphold human rights and to operate in a 'socially responsible' manner. The International Financial Corporation website points out how, even though human rights have traditionally been the sole responsibility of government, increasingly businesses are expected to 'play a key role in upholding human rights and to carry out their operations in a socially responsible manner'; and how the Bank helps them to make human rights impact assessments, including developing, together with the UN Global Compact, the Guide to Human Rights Impact Assessment and Management, to be published by mid-2009.[68] We further discuss the question of businesses and human rights below.

All this indicates to what extent the Bank truly tries hard to 'understand ... the connection between human rights and development on several levels'.[69] In its *Frequently Asked Questions and Human Rights*, the Bank refers to 'a growing body of research from development experts that shows the linkage between human rights and development' and to the fact that many of its development partners are increasingly integrating human rights into their programmes.[70] It also refers to the 2003 *UN Common Understanding on a Human Rights Based Approach to Development*, the 2005 *UN Millennium Project Report*, the Secretary-General's 2005 Report *In Larger Freedom*, the 2006 World Development Report, *Equity and Development*, which 'explores the ways in which structural and distributional inequalities can hinder development', and to the substantial research linking economic outcomes to respect for human rights.[71]

Some research, the Bank says, has shown already back in 1997 that substantial violations of political and civil rights are related to lower economic growth.[72] In the same year, other research has shown respect for civil liberties to be connected with better performance of government projects.[73] Yet more research investigates the link between governance and human rights.[74] In the 'Legal Opinion on Human Rights and the Work of the World Bank' (January 2006) – apparently the first legal opinion issued by a General Counsel on any topic since 1995 – the former Senior Vice-President and General Counsel, Roberto Dañino, also confirms that 'human rights may constitute legitimate considerations for the Bank where they have economic ramifications or impacts', and refers to 'the facilitative role the Bank may play in supporting its members to fulfill their human rights obligations'.[75] In an article written a few months later, and based on the Legal Opinion, Dañino (by then no longer a General Counsel) goes further and claims that 'human rights are at the very core of the World Bank's mandate'.[76]

Without a formal approval by the Board, the Legal Opinion has an uncertain legal status. Nonetheless, as the present General Counsel, Ana Palacio, points out, there is no doubt that the Opinion marks:

a clear evolution from the pre-existing restrictive legal interpretation of the Bank's explicit consideration of human rights. It is "permissive": allowing, but not mandating, action on the part of the Bank in relation to human rights.[77]

However, despite the Bank's undoubted adoption of the human rights discourse, it is not clear to what extent the Bank really follows human rights considerations in its actual work and research. For example, a recent publication on the Bank's role in poverty reduction and development, *Global Issues for Global Citizens*, a 2006 publication of the Bank,[78] does not even have 'human rights' in its index, let alone address the issue of human rights and development explicitly. What it does recognize is that:

economic growth cannot be sustained without human development. Thus, investing in education, health, and gender equality and achieving the Millennium Development Goals are [sic]vital in helping to empower people so that they can better participate in the development process.[79]

This does not sound like a language of rights that would insist on human rights as an entitlement rather than, as here, simply as a desirable development.

There have also been criticisms of the Bank for ignoring the impact of its policies on women and gender issues;[80] continuing to approve loans to countries with well-known poor human rights records; and ignoring the environmental impact of many of its policies.[81]

Generally, as 'Righting the Bank's Agenda' concludes, despite the Bank's human rights rhetoric, civil society is 'cautious' about the Bank's commitment to human rights implementation in its own policies.[82] The Bank cannot be trusted:

not to finance activities that contravene international human rights law, to take full responsibility where the activities of the institution negatively impact or undermine the enjoyment of human rights, or to address its complicity in past abuses ... [not to] ignore ... the negative effects of Bank-funded large infrastructure, or extractive projects on the access to productive resources – like land and water – as well as the massive displacement related to these projects which have undermined the rights to food, water, health and housing, amongst others.[83]

There have also been calls for the unconditional cancellation of and reparations from the Bank for illegitimate debt lent to rights-abusing regimes; calls for the creation of a special optional protocol on economic, social and cultural rights, which would allow complaints to be heard at the international level for violations of the ICESCR; and demands that the Bank provide reparations for its complicity in projects resulting in grave abuses such as at the Chixoy dam in Guatemala, the Bulyanhulu gold mine in Tanzania, and the Sardar Sarovar dam in India.[84]

We think that some of these criticisms are rather unfair.

First, it is not clear how helpful it would be for the unfortunate citizens of a state with a 'rights-abusing' regime to have their country ostracized altogether by the international community and the international financial institutions such as the World Bank. It is at least arguable that the Bank's lending to such a state may contribute to its prosperity: so why should we call such lending 'illegitimate debt' *a priori*, when we don't yet know the impact of such lending? And if it is not *a priori*, then we simply cannot know, without the benefit of hindsight, whether a debt is going to be 'illegitimate' or not.

Second, the fact remains that, unlike many other UN bodies, the Bank does **not** have an explicit mandate to implement human rights; and it is restricted by its Articles of Agreement in how far it can go in influencing human rights (and hence political) developments in the countries in which it operates. The 'civil society' institutions recognize as much (implicitly if not explicitly). The Bretton Woods project says, for example (somehow inconsistently in our view with their previous arguments about how the Bank ought to expand its role), that:

[t]here are also fears that given its economic and political power and influence, the Bank may end up assuming a role as the arbiter of human rights violations, and burdening countries with an additional set of conditionalities based on human rights. Recently Kenneth Roth, Executive Director of Human Rights Watch, was careful to emphasise that the Bank's role is not to promote human rights *per se*, but rather that it should integrate a human rights approach into its policies, such as country assistance strategies.[85]

Following Palacio, we would see the Bank's role in the propagation of the liberal project worldwide as having three aspects: (i) to contribute to the realization of human rights in the areas in which the Bank operates (for example by reducing poverty); (ii) to adopt human rights as a normative baseline against which to assess relevant development policies and programming (for example so as to be able to decide whether a particular project violates the human rights of the people affected by it); and (iii) to support Bank members' 'actionable' legal obligations with regard to human rights – whether arising from international treaties or from national laws – where they relate to Bank policies and projects.[86]

Even this 'restricted' view of the Bank's human rights obligations is not going to be easy to implement: we all know how domestic governments struggle trying to determine how their particular policies will affect different sectors in the population (and hence how difficult it is to define the elusive 'public interest'). Further, it seems to us that the Bank's problem of how to incorporate human rights into its operations is symptomatic of the problem encountered at the international law level: there are many conflicting and unclear rules, applicable to different bodies at different times, and it is difficult to have a consistent framework that would satisfy everyone.[87] Sovereignty versus human rights is one example; the validity of the application of human rights conventions to international organizations such as the Bank – rather than states which are clearly bound by them – is another.[88]

This problem has been increasingly recognized by international human rights scholars and practitioners who are now looking for ways in which to define legally the relations between different international law institutions. It has been suggested, for example, that member states of the ICESCR might use the ICESCR and the obligations imposed by the Covenant as an 'international shield' to protect their population against international projects and policies that might negatively affect their rights.[89] We also saw that there are calls for the creation of a special optional protocol on economic, social and cultural rights, which would allow complaints of violations of the International Covenant on Economic, Social and Cultural Rights, to be heard at the international level and presumably also against international organizations such as the World Bank.

While all this is very useful, we think that maybe too much is being asked from the World Bank. After all, the Bank is not a world government, having a duty to implement all human rights (as set out in different international conventions) throughout the world. It is an international financial institution established by states, with a (fairly narrow) explicit mandate to take only economic considerations into account while making decisions; and expressly forbidden from interfering in a country's political affairs, and from allowing its decisions to be influenced by the political character of the member country. It is up to the states that created it to decide how and whether this mandate is compatible with its newly found duty to promote human rights; and change it if necessary.[90]

Meanwhile, it may be more useful to concentrate on the 'micro' within the Bank and ask, the way Sarfaty has, **why** the World Bank has not internalized human rights norms in its operations, despite its human rights rhetoric.[91] Somewhat surprisingly, Sarfaty gives, as an explanation, lawyers' 'inferior intellectual status at the Bank as opposed to economists', and, accordingly, 'a lower status of legal discourse over economic discourse'.[92] To remedy the situation, the lawyers are apparently now trying to 'translat[e] human rights into the dominant discourse of economics' or, in other words, to 'economize human rights'.[93] They are doing so mainly through developing human rights indicators and impact assessments, instead of concentrating on rights solely as obligations deriving from legal instruments. Her research shows, therefore, that for the World Bank to internalize human rights norms in its operations, it may be necessary to bridge a gap between lawyers and economists over how to define and interpret human rights in relation to the Bank's mission.

It may not be easy. As James Wolfensohn, probably the person most responsible for introducing human rights into the Bank (and originally a lawyer), admitted in a recent book on human rights and development, he still hoped to 'elucidate just what some of the issues are and what is the way forward in a debate that I've never fully understood'.[94] This does not augur well for the hapless economists.

The International Monetary Fund

As most of the issues relevant to international financial institutions and human rights have been discussed above, we will only have a cursory look at the question of the International Monetary Fund (IMF) and human rights. For the areas of collaboration between the Fund and the World Bank, we would refer our readers to the report on collaboration between the two institutions commissioned by the managing director of the Fund and the president of the Bank in 2006.[95]

The IMF is the other Bretton Woods institution besides the World Bank and, in its own words, the 'world's central organization for international monetary cooperation'.

The charter (Articles of Agreement) of the IMF directs it to promote international monetary co-operation and orderly exchange rate arrangements, facilitate the balanced growth of international trade, and help members resolve their balance of payments difficulties. To fulfil this mandate, the IMF employs surveillance of each member country's economic situation, conducted usually once a year; technical assistance; and lending.[96] As of July 2006, there were $28 billion outstanding loans to seventy-four countries, of which $6 billion represented loans to fifty-six countries on concessional terms.[97]

Controversially, the IMF loans are generally conditional on the adoption of appropriate policies to resolve a country's balance of payments difficulties (this is the so-called IMF conditionality), and to enable the government to repay the Fund. Many countries do not like those conditions; however, if they are in grave financial difficulties, they have few options but to comply. The IMF says that conditionality is a necessary way for it to monitor that its loan is being used effectively in resolving the borrower's economic difficulties, so that the country will be able to repay promptly, and to make the funds available to other members in need.

Up to the early 1980s, the IMF conditionality largely focused on macroeconomic policies. In the 1990s, this changed, largely as the result of reflections on the collapse of communism and on the links between political and economic reform. The IMF started to pay more attention to microeconomic factors: in particular, efficiently functioning competitive markets. This led it to the adoption of the so-called 'Washington consensus': a term that refers to policies promoted by the Washington-based institutions (the IMF, World Bank and the US Treasury Department), broadly associated with expanding the role of market forces and constraining the role of the state.

Critics of the IMF condemn it for adopting the 'consensus'; and accuse it of forcing governments to adopt policies that result in increased poverty and neglect of their citizens' human rights. They also accuse it of lending to governments with poor human rights policies. Additionally, the IMF conditionality has been attacked as Western imperialism, most notably by an ex-prime minister of Malaysia, Mahathir Mohamed.

The IMF defends itself by pointing out that by working to promote global growth and economic stability, it prevents economic crisis and hence helps to reduce poverty. In recent years, it has also established concessional lending facilities aimed at reducing poverty directly: the Poverty Reduction and Growth Facility and the Exogenous Shocks Facility.[98] In most low-income countries, the lending under the facility is underpinned by Poverty Reduction Strategy Papers. As we saw in our discussion of the World Bank, these papers are prepared by country authorities – in consultation with civil society and external development partners – to describe 'a comprehensive economic, structural and social policy framework that is being implemented to promote growth and reduce poverty in the country'. As an example, Rwanda's November 2000 Strategy Paper includes a framework for good governance that incorporates a human rights programme, as well as capacity for the country's Human Rights Commission. Other countries where the poverty reduction strategy deals with human rights explicitly include Bolivia, Cambodia, Cameroon, Nicaragua, Tanzania, Uganda and Vietnam.[99]

The IMF has also contributed greatly to debt relief under the Heavily Indebted Poor Countries Initiative and the Multilateral Debt Relief Initiative, both of which we will briefly look at below.

In terms of the relationship between its policies and human rights, the IMF believes that its role is (i) to focus on sustainable growth and a stable macroeconomic environment, in themselves supportive of human rights; and (ii) to encourage member governments and specialized agencies to work together towards designing development strategies that take human rights into account. It is adamant, however, that:

while human rights advocates should be given every opportunity to participate in PRSP [Poverty Reduction Strategy Papers] consultations, they should not expect the IMF to impose human rights conditions on its member countries. The IMF does not have the expertise required to make judgments in this area.[100]

At the same time, the Fund admits that 'the pursuit of economic, social, and cultural rights is an integral part of sound economic policies'; and hence inappropriate economic policies – unsustainable public deficits, high inflation, unrealistic exchange rates, wasteful subsidies, and obstacles to trade – are contrary to human rights.[101] This is why, it says: 'the work of the IMF should not be seen as a threat to human rights, but as a key contribution'.[102]

We certainly agree with this statement; and indeed, the relevant statistics seem to support the view that countries that have undergone the dreaded IMF conditionality might have benefited, on average, in terms of income growth and social expenditure.[103] However, we question the assertion that, while addressing the inappropriate economic policies of its member states, the IMF cannot also address the lack of the pursuit of ESC rights. How else indeed, without the latter – which are 'an integral part of sound economic policies' – can economic policies be said to be 'sound'?

It is true that the IMF sees its main contribution toward raising living standards as focusing primarily on macroeconomic stability and sustainable growth. However, as we pointed out, the Fund also gets involved in countries' 'micro' policies: in particular, through its stress on competitive markets and financial liberalization. Why should the IMF therefore have the expertise in those areas but not in the areas involving realization of ESC rights?

The answer may be that, as with the World Bank, human rights are seen as the (less-prestigious) domain of lawyers, not economists (who run the Fund to possibly an even greater extent than the World Bank). The economists (to many of whom very likely the discourse of human rights sounds like mumbo-jumbo) may indeed not have 'the expertise required to make judgments in this area'; but in that case, we would suggest that they should acquire it. To be sure, 'translating human rights into the dominant discourse of economics' may be more difficult for the IMF than the Bank, where, as we have seen, lawyers have started doing it already through developing tools such as human rights indicators and impact assessments.[104] But this is because development and human rights are nowadays accepted to go hand-in-hand. On the other hand, too many see economics and human rights:

at polar opposites in our post-Cold War society, with economics emphasising efficiency and the optimal use of resources, while human rights focuses [sic] on the dignity of the individual and the demands of justice and fairness.[105]

However, if ESC rights can be see as welfare rights, there is no problem surely with incorporating the question of their realization into economics (with its sub-disciplines of public and welfare economics). The problem economists would have to solve when incorporating ESC rights into their analysis would be the usual economic one, but specifically adapted to rights: that is, how to allocate resources in order to maximize ESC rights, subject to the usual budgetary, etc. constraints. There is no reason not to have such 'human rights economics': as a matter of fact, such a sub-discipline of economics could ideally include analysis of how to achieve CP rights, not just ESC rights. After all, we saw how the realization of most CP rights requires resources to the same extent sometimes as the realization of ESC rights.

Similarly, it could be argued that state parties to the ICESCR – or any other international human rights agreement – that do not pursue ESC rights as part of their economic policies are in violation of their international obligations; and that the IMF has an obligation not to aid countries that violate international law.

To be sure, as with the World Bank, there needs to be more consistency between international law norms and the international obligations of the IMF. In particular, there is a great need for clarification on the extent to which the IMF (and all other international financial institutions) is bound by human rights norms. To simply say, however, that 'the IMF does not have the expertise required to make judgments in this area' (i.e. the area of the realization of ESC (if not CP) rights), is, in our view, unacceptable. The World Bank lends money to countries for particular projects only; hence our belief, expressed above, that it should not be asked to approve the economic and social policies of these countries, unless they are relevant to the project in question. Its remit is too narrow. The IMF, however, asks countries to adopt particular macro- and microeconomic and policies before lending to them. It has therefore clearly a responsibility, we believe, to evaluate the impact on human rights of the policies it imposes.

Let us now move on to the discussion of an important new way in which states and international institutions have been trying recently to co-ordinate their actions with respect to human rights: the so-called global compacts. The best known of these are the Millennium Development Goals.

Intergovernmental global compacts

In order to take action on global issues, the international community agreed at the beginning of this century on a number of global compacts.[106] The distinguishing feature of these compacts is the fact that:

- they have clear and monitorable goals;
- they are UN sponsored, although not legally binding;
- they combine mutual roles and responsibilities of developing as well as developed countries; and
- they represent new partnerships among governments, civil society organizations and the private business sector to work together to achieve the agreed goals.

There are four compacts in particular: the Millennium Declaration adopted at the UN Millennium Summit in 2000; the Doha Declaration on Trade, adopted at the Fourth Ministerial conference of the World Trade Organization, in Doha, Qatar, in 2001; the Monterrey Declaration on Financing for Development, adopted at the International Conference on Financing for Development, Monterrey, Mexico, in 2002; and the Johannesburg Declaration on Sustainable Development, adopted at the World Summit on Sustainable Development in 2002.

As the Doha, Monterrey and Johannesburg declarations basically elaborate on some of the targets of the Millennium Development Goals – improved trading environment for developing countries; expanded official development assistance and debt relief; and progress toward environmental sustainability respectively – we concentrate our discussion on the Millennium Declaration Goals only. We will return to the discussion of the Monterrey Declaration in our section on development aid.

Let us just mention here that the Doha negotiations have still not concluded, after being suspended in July 2006 amid disagreements over access to agricultural markets and reductions in domestic support. However, early 2007 saw an informal agreement by the World Trade Organization members to restart the talks.

Millennium Development Goals

The Millennium Development Goals (MDGs) are a set of eight goals, adopted following the Millennium Declaration signed by 189 countries in September 2000 at the UN's Millennium Summit. The MDGs were reaffirmed at the UN's 2005 World Summit where countries committed to ensure that their development strategies were MDG-based.[107] In more detail, the MDGs are:

1. To eradicate extreme poverty and hunger, by reducing by half between 1990 and 2015:

   – the proportion of people living on less than $1 a day (from 27.9 per cent to 14.0 per cent);
   – the proportion of people who suffer from hunger.

2. To achieve universal primary education by 2015.
3. To promote gender equality and empower women, by eliminating gender disparity in primary and secondary education, preferably by 2005, and in all levels of education by 2015.
4. To reduce child mortality by two thirds among children under five between 1990 and 2015.
5. To improve maternal health, by reducing the maternal mortality ratio by three quarters between 1990 and 2015. Presently, women in high fertility countries in Sub-Saharan Africa have a 1 in 16 lifetime risk of dying from maternal causes, compared with women in low-fertility countries in Europe, who have a 1 in 2,000 risk, and in North America, who have a 1 in 3,500 risk of dying. High maternal mortality rates in many countries are the result of inadequate reproductive health care for women and inadequately spaced births.

6. To combat HIV/AIDS, malaria, and other diseases.
7. To ensure environmental sustainability, by:

   – integrating the principles of sustainable development into coun-
     try policies and programmes and reversing the losses of envir-
     onmental resources; and
   – halving, by 2015, the proportion of people without sustainable
     access to safe drinking water and basic sanitation.

8. To promote a global partnership for development, with aims such as:

   – an open, rule-based trading and financial system;
   – more generous aid to countries committed to poverty reduction;
   – relief for the debt problems of developing countries;
   – attention to the special needs of landlocked countries and small
     island developing states;
   – co-operation with the developing countries to develop decent and
     productive work for youths; and
   – co-operation with the private sector to ensure access to afford-
     able, essential drugs, and to make available the benefits of new
     technologies.

While each goal is important in its own right, they should be viewed
together as mutually reinforcing, with the fight against poverty clearly
depending on the achievement of all other goals.[108]

Since 2000, the MDGs have been referred to continuously in international fora dealing with development. This reflects their significance,
in particular the fact that:

- they have been agreed on by all member states of the UN, by the
  IMF, the World Bank and other multilateral development banks;
- they establish a consensus that poverty is the biggest challenge facing
  humanity; and
- they concentrate on co-operation by developed and developing
  countries and on increased participation of non-governmental organizations in the preparatory work.

More controversially, the MDGs can also be viewed as a means to
realize some of the main ESC rights and to meet the RTD.[109] As the
Committee on Economic, Social and Cultural Rights states, poverty in
particular – while not found as a term in any of the major international

human rights instruments – is a human rights issue, directly affected by the 'rights to work, an adequate standard of living, housing, food, health and education'.[110] The Committee defines poverty as:

a human condition characterized by sustained or chronic deprivation of the resources, capabilities, choices, security and power necessary for the enjoyment of an adequate standard of living and other civil, cultural, economic, political and social rights'.[111]

Hence, international human rights provide, in the view of the Committee, 'a framework of norms or rules upon which detailed global, national and community-level poverty eradication policies can be constructed'.[112] While the ESC rights are subject to resource availability and may be realized progressively, state parties have a 'core obligation to ensure the satisfaction of, at the very least, minimum essential levels of each of the rights'.[113] Without such a core obligation, the Covenant 'would be largely deprived of its *raison d'être*'.[114] The Committee adds:

the core obligations of economic, social and cultural rights have a crucial role to play in national and international developmental policies, including anti-poverty strategies. When grouped together, the core obligations establish an international minimum threshold that all developmental policies should be designed to respect. In accordance with General Comment No. 14, it is particularly incumbent on all those who can assist, to help developing countries respect this international minimum threshold. *If a national or international anti-poverty strategy does not reflect this minimum threshold, it is inconsistent with the legally binding obligations of the State party.*[115]

A number of the same points were made subsequently by other human rights bodies, most notably in the Office of the High Commissioner on Human Rights' Draft Guidelines on human rights approach to Poverty Reduction Strategies.[116]

All this would indicate that the achievement of Millennium Development Goal 1, at the very least, represents a human rights obligation on state parties to the ICESCR. It is unlikely that states will accept this view, however. As we saw, both developed and developing nations fear being held accountable for the realization of human rights, and having to put into place effective implementation measures (which they could do via, for example, 'national human rights institutions as part of the national participatory evaluation of the implementation of national poverty reduction strategies'),[117] as well as mechanisms to deal with non-compliance.

The use of 'soft law' through non-legally binding Millennium Development Goals may therefore be at present a more effective means of realizing those goals. We will be able to judge this better when we look at what happened to those goals in our section on Progress on the Goals. We will also be able to evaluate in that section the question whether it is sensible to have the Goals in the first place. Many argue indeed that it is not; that the Goals are simply pious utopian aspirations making the developed world feel better about itself, and that they promise more to the world's poor than they can deliver.

William Easterly, a former World Bank economist, worries, for example, that, were the Goals to fail (as he thinks they are likely to do), the resulting disappointment will discourage countries from continuing to implement development projects. He therefore suggests specific, smaller goals to concentrate on; for example providing enough vaccines to reduce malaria in Africa. He also calls for development agencies (both international ones such as the World Bank and individual domestic ones) to be made more accountable while providing aid to developing countries.[118]

Transnational corporations

For all the sour feelings that the acts of certain transnational corporations have aroused in developing countries where they have operated, there is one thing which, for a developing country, is even worse than to attract foreign direct investment (FDI): it is to attract none.[119]

We have seen how, since the 1990s in particular, global markets have expanded significantly as a result of trade and domestic liberalization and privatization. Needless to say, the transnational corporations (TNCs) have played a major role in this expansion, contributing to it through trade, financial integration, movement of service providers, information flows and labour migration.[120] It is estimated that there are currently more than 77,000 transnational corporations, with about 770,000 subsidiaries and millions of suppliers.[121]

The question we want to pursue here is what, if any, human rights obligations have these corporations towards their workers and the communities in which they set up their operations?

To answer this question, it is useful to examine a recent report on the question by Prof. John G. Ruggie, Special Representative of the UN Secretary-General on Business & Human Rights.[122] While it applies to business generally, it is obviously most relevant to the transnational corporations.

Before we do that, we want to note that Ruggie's appointment in 2005 by-then UN Secretary-General Kofi Annan, suggests a change in attitude towards globalization that occurred among human rights activists in the early 2000s. As a think-tank on global issues, Stratfor, points out, they have finally 'stopped seeing corporations as villains that needed restraint and began to see them as potential tools for positive change in globalization'.[123]

States' duty to protect against corporate abuse

Ruggie starts by saying that, under international law, it is nowadays accepted that states have a duty to protect against non-state human rights abuses within their jurisdiction, and that this duty extends to protection against abuses by business entities.[124] While the ICCPR and ICESCR did not specifically address the question of states' duties regarding business, the later treaties, such as the Convention on the Elimination of All Forms of Discrimination Against Women, the Convention on the Right of the Child and the recently adopted Convention on the Rights of Persons with Disabilities, did so. Article 2(e) of the Convention on the Elimination of All Forms of Discrimination Against Women, for example, requires states to take all appropriate measures (including legislation and judicial remedies) to eliminate discrimination against women by any 'enterprise'.[125]

UN human rights bodies such as the Human Rights Committee read similar obligations into other conventions, with respect to both business and other non-state actors. In its General Comment 31, the Human Rights Committee states that, under the ICCPR, 'the positive obligations on state parties to ensure Covenant rights will only be fully discharged if individuals are protected by the state, not just against violations of Covenant rights by its agents, but also against acts committed by private persons or entities'.[126] It adds that states could be breaching Covenant obligations if they fail 'to take appropriate measures or to exercise due diligence to prevent, punish, investigate or redress the harm caused by such acts by private persons or entities'.[127]

The states involved are either the states on whose territory the acts are being committed or states whose nationals are the victim or the actor.[128] The regional human rights systems also affirm the state's duty to protect against non-state abuse, including corporate abuse.[129]

Ruggie concludes that states, however, still 'either do not fully understand or are not always able or willing to fulfill this duty'. In support of his view, he quotes a recent Special Representative of the Secretary-General survey which shows that very few states have policies, programmes or tools designed specifically to deal with corporate human rights abuses (for example incorporating human rights criteria in their export credit and investment promotion policies or in bilateral trade and investment treaties).[130] Most rely instead on soft-law instruments such as the OECD Guidelines, or the International Finance Corporation's performance standards; and on voluntary (or self-regulatory) initiatives like the Global Compact, often inspired by NGO pressure, consumer activism or social labelling that informs consumers whether a product has been made with child labour.[131] We examine both soft-law instruments and voluntary initiatives below.

While international law imposes a duty on states to protect against corporate abuse, it does not impose direct legal responsibilities on corporations themselves (except possibly with respect to international criminal law).[132] To be sure, there have been efforts to create such legal responsibilities, such as the adoption on 13 August 2003 of the 'United Nations Norms on the Responsibilities of Transnational Corporations and Other Business Enterprises with Regard to Human Rights' by the Sub-Commission on the Promotion and Protection of Human Rights (Resolution 2003/16).[133] Under General Obligations, Art. 1, the norms state that:

Within their respective spheres of activity and influence, transnational corporations and other business enterprises have the obligation to promote, secure the fulfilment of, respect, ensure respect of and protect human rights recognized in international as well as national law, including the rights and interests of indigenous peoples and other vulnerable groups.

The norms are still awaiting adoption by the UN Human Rights Council.[134]

One of the problems is that while the norms reaffirm that states have the 'primary responsibility' to 'promote, secure the fulfilment of, respect, ensure respect of and protect human rights', a number of provisions appear to put corporate responsibility on a par with that of governments. For example, the commentary to paragraph 10 of the norms mentions that the transnational corporations are under a duty to 'encourage social progress and development by expanding economic opportunities – particularly in developing countries and, most importantly, in the least developed countries'.[135] This could be interpreted as encouraging the transnational corporations to act so as to influence the policies of the countries in which they operate.

As we will see in our section on 'radical proposals', some think this is the way to go in propagating human rights (including the RTD). Others, however, including Ruggie (and the authors), are unhappy about this view of corporate responsibility, as they believe it is governments that ought to have the primary responsibility for protecting and promoting human rights. States are also not likely to accept such an encroachment on their sovereignty and on the principle of non-interference.

Finally, we would like to mention a recent initiative on the business/human rights issue, announced in August 2007 by Ruggie and the International Finance Corporation.[136] The initiative consists of a study of the impact of investment agreements on citizens in the developing world. The study will examine, in particular, clauses in contracts between lenders and states that 'either freeze the human rights laws that affect investors, or that compensate investors for the costs incurred by complying with new human rights laws'. Indeed, many contracts have clauses that specify that a country cannot change labour, environmental or other laws after a project contract has been signed, or that do not allow a country to vary some of the terms of the contract even in cases of emergency (for example if a contract guarantees a specific water supply for an industrial project, states cannot divert that supply to humanitarian purposes in the event of drought). One of the recommendations of the report may be that governments should be able to override such clauses – through domestic or international legal instruments? – in order to avoid corporate human rights abuse. Without knowing much about the contracts in question, this seems to us a most sensible idea.

Soft-law standards

There is an increasing number of soft-law standards, reflecting the present view of transnational corporations as potential contributors to global human rights implementation.

The 2000 (Revised) OECD guidelines recommend that firms 'respect the human rights of those affected by their activities consistent with the host government's obligations and commitments',[137] including the host state's international commitments.[138] As a result of pressure by civil society, individuals are now allowed to make a complaint against a multinational firm operating under the OECD Guidelines to a national contact point, in a 'non-judicial review procedure'.[139]

The International Finance Corporation has eight performance standards that companies must meet if they want to qualify for the Corporation's investment funds. The performance standards include several human rights components.[140] If the project requires so, the Corporation may ask for impact assessments that include such human rights components, as well as community consultation. Here too, there is a grievance mechanism: anybody who believes that they have been negatively affected by a Corporation's project can raise their concern with a Compliance Ombudsman.[141]

However, most companies lack technical skills in the area of human rights impact assessment. In response to that problem, the International Finance Corporation and the International Business Leaders Forum, together with the United Nations Global Compact, developed the Guide to Human Rights Impact Assessment and Management.[142] The guide is a work in progress; and, as the Corporation states:

> this current draft version has been published to allow companies from different business sectors to test it in practice and for various stakeholders to comment. The experience gained from the road-testing will be used to further refine the guide. A revised version of the guide will be published by mid-2009.[143]

For companies in the extractive sector, there are also Voluntary Principles on Security and Human Rights. The Principles were initially launched in late 2000 and the 'multi-stakeholder process' was convened by the Governments of the United States and the United Kingdom, more recently joined by the Governments of Norway and the Netherlands. Participating non-governmental organizations include Amnesty International, Human Rights Watch and Pax Christi and most of the leading mining and oil and gas companies. The purpose of the Principles is 'to provide a framework within which companies can ensure the legitimate security of their employees and assets without adversely affecting the human rights of people living in communities close to company operations'.[144]

Self regulation

Again, there has been an increasing number of self-regulating measures in recent years, reflecting a growing corporate commitment to responsible corporate citizenship. Three such measures are: the 1999 UN Global Compact, the Global Reporting Initiative inaugurated in 2002, and the SA8000 social accountability system, instituted in 1997 by Social Accountability International (an international non-profit human rights organization 'dedicated to the ethical treatment of workers around the world').[145]

Starting with the SA8000 system: it is a voluntary standard for work places, based on International Labour Organization and UN conventions. To certify conformance with SA8000, every company must be audited and implement any necessary improvements. Once it does that, it can earn a certificate attesting to its compliance with SA8000. This certification provides a public report of good practice to consumers, buyers, and other companies. The Social Accountability International website states that it is highly complementary with the principles set out by the UN Global Compact as well as with the framework of the Global Reporting Initiative.

The Global Reporting Initiative is the *de facto* international standard (used by over 1,000 companies) for corporate reporting on environmental, social and economic performance.[146] The goal of the Global Reporting Initiative is to have all companies reporting on their economic, environmental, and social performance (the so-called 'sustainability reporting'), as routinely and comparably as they do on their financial performance.[147] In order to achieve this goal, the Reporting Initiative operates within a Sustainability Reporting Framework, developed by 'a large multi-stakeholder network of experts, in dozens of countries worldwide'.[148] The cornerstone of the Framework is the Sustainability Reporting Guidelines. The third version of the Guidelines – known as the G3 Guidelines – was published in 2006. To date, more than 1,000 organizations, including many of the world's leading brands, have declared their voluntary adoption of the Guidelines. Consequently, the G3 Guidelines have become, as already mentioned, 'the *de facto* global standard for reporting'.[149]

As for the UN Global Compact, it was first proposed by Kofi Annan in an address to the World Economic Forum in 1999. The Compact 'brings companies together with UN agencies, labour and civil society to support universal environmental and social principles'.[150] The idea behind it is to promote 'responsible corporate citizenship so that business can be part of the solution to the challenge of globalisation'.[151] Companies are asked to embrace and act, within their sphere of influence, upon ten principles in the areas of human rights, labour standards, the environment, and anti-corruption (derived, respectively, from UN Declaration on Human Rights, International Labour Declaration on Fundamental Principles and Rights at Work, the Rio Declaration on Environment and Development, and the UN Convention Against Corruption).

The first two principles of the Global Compact are that: (1) businesses should support and respect the protection of internationally proclaimed human rights within their sphere of influence; and (2) make sure that they are not complicit in human rights abuses. The remaining eight principles require businesses to: (3) uphold freedom of association and the right to collective bargaining; (4) eliminate forced and compulsory labour; (5) abolish child labour; (6) eliminate discrimination in respect of employment; (7) support a precautionary approach to environmental challenges; (8) undertake initiatives to promote greater environmental responsibility; (9) encourage the development and diffusion of environmentally friendly technologies; and (10) work against corruption.

The UN Global Compact participants are expected to produce an annual Communication on Progress report for shareholders and other stakeholders. This communicates their progress in implementing the ten Global Compact principles.

By the time of the Global Compact Leaders' Summit in July 2007, more than 4,000 organizations from 116 countries (among them trade unions, non-governmental organizations and some 3,100 businesses) had committed to the ten principles.[152] Increasing numbers of companies are also now disclosing annually how the implementation is taking place (otherwise risking being de-listed). More than 2,000 Communications from around 100 countries have been deposited with the Global Compact so far.[153] This is apparently two thirds of relevant businesses, assuming each company produces only one Communication (we could not get any figures confirming this). By comparison, in 2002, when only 2,200 companies had committed to the compact, no more than 38 of them developed Communications on Progress.[154] Companies are certainly taking the compact seriously.

This is good news for the liberal project. Businesses, as well as states and individuals, must be involved in propagating human rights around the world if we are committed to their effective implementation. Of course, many would argue that corporate codes of conduct are no substitute for national legislation or for international labour standards enforced around the world, especially in cases when they do set lower standards than the International Labour Organization and national law. They also should not be a substitute for the right of workers to organize and bargain collectively.

This is undoubtedly true: however, one must not underestimate companies' self-interest in self-regulation. A research report presented at the 2007 Global Compact Leadership Summit showed, for example, that companies that are considered leaders in implementing social, governance and environmental policies have outperformed the general stock market by 25 per cent since August 2005.[155] This is in line with considerable earlier research showing that companies that invest in such policies acquire an advantage over their competitors, given that today's 'sophisticated buyers will usually appreciate safer, cleaner, quieter [and produced under humane conditions] products before governments do'.[156] Having said that, companies may need to be made more aware of these advantages of being 'human-rights friendly'. As The Ethical Corporation reported in 2006:

A report issued earlier this year by WWF and the private finance focused NGO coalition BankTrack found only 20% of banks surveyed had introduced a human rights policy. Only Rabobank has committed explicitly to follow the draft UN Norms for Business, and not even they disclose how they will do so.[157]

However, 20 per cent is better than nothing: it may actually represent quite a significant figure given that the scrutiny of human rights impacts of businesses (in this case financial institutions) is only very recent.

Research also shows that multinational companies are often the leaders in improved working and environmental conditions (either in the country where they operate or in the country they come from). *The Economist* pointed out, for example, that:

companies harmonise up not down. In developing countries (never mind what the non-governmental organisations say) multinationals tend to spread better working practices and environmental conditions; and when emerging-country nationals operate in rich countries they tend to adopt local mores.[158]

Indeed, it is the local companies in developing countries that often pay no attention to human rights standards. For example, in a report issued in August 2007 China Labor Watch said that it was the eight Chinese toy manufacturers that were responsible for the recently discovered brutal working conditions of their workers: low wages, non-existent benefits, dangerous work environments and humiliating living conditions. To be sure, the response of a small number of transnational companies served by those manufacturers – including Disney, Bandai and Hasbro – could have been better. Hasbro 'could not be reached for an immediate comment'; and Bandai (a Japanese transnational company) refused to comment.[159] Only Disney said, promisingly, that 'it and its affiliates take claims of unfair labor practices very seriously, investigate any such allegations thoroughly and take remedial action'. Nonetheless, it is without question the transnational companies rather than the local Chinese companies (or Chinese government) that are likely to be the cause of their workers' improving working conditions.[160]

What is also a hopeful development is that the transnational companies are no longer exclusively Western. Increasingly, such corporations emerge from the developing world: mostly India, China, Brazil and Russia.[161] While this may cause short-term problems for the implementation of human rights (those companies being supposedly less aware of their human rights obligations than their Western counterparts or less willing/able to enforce them, at least within developing countries), these problems should be only temporary. Corporate social responsibility having evolved in line with economic and social globalization, non-Western companies (and consumers) everywhere are bound to become similarly aware of human rights issues (especially under consumer and non-governmental organizations pressure), and to model the 'good citizen' behaviour of their predecessors.[162]

Incidentally, this emergence of non-Western transnational corporations confirms another of our claims: that overall globalization benefits all countries, companies and consumers, not only the Western 'imperialists'. How precisely it does so, and who the main winners and, of course, the main losers are will be the topic of our last section in this chapter. First, however, we want to look at some recent 'radical' proposals of how to render businesses even more 'human-rights friendly'.

Radical proposals?

We have just seen how businesses are expected nowadays to respect human rights in their activities, via a global framework of legal norms (that impose duties on governments to control companies' behaviour), soft-law and voluntary standards. We have also seen how those businesses (and transnational corporations) are no longer exclusively Western, the idea of corporate social responsibility spreading to businesses all over the world.

However, even if businesses were to adhere to all these rules and standards in their sphere of influence, would it be sufficient? This is the question posed, among others, by Olivier de Schutter in his Chapter 'Transnational Corporations' in *Human Rights and Development*.[163]

De Schutter responds in the negative. Indeed, he thinks that, besides having to respect human rights in their activities, transnational corporations should also pay attention:

to the economic context in which they operate and the impact their investment may have on the general economic situation of the country concerned, for instance the level of unemployment or the debt-repaying capacity of the state.[164]

Thus de Schutter believes that businesses' economic responsibility ought to encompass the eradication of poverty and contribution to development (which, following Sen, he understands as a process ensuring the full enjoyment of all the human rights). As de Schutter says, transnational corporations:

have the potential to be important actors in development, not only in that they may contribute to the expansion of exchanges and therefore to economic growth, but also in that they may help fulfil a form of development oriented towards the expansion of human capabilities, of which human rights are both a main ingredient and a precondition'.[165]

So we are back to the question of RTD: what is it and, if it exists or should exist, who should have what obligations to fulfil it? Should the transnational corporations really have as their goal eradication of poverty and contribution to development in the countries where they operate? Shouldn't they rather concentrate on creating wealth (while guaranteeing human rights to their workers and those affected by their operations), rather than reorganizing the world according to the human rights model as interpreted by them? And wouldn't their telling countries what policies they should pursue interfere with state sovereignty and those countries' (hopefully) democratically elected governments; and hence give the corporations too much (unaccountable) power? Wouldn't it be better to use multilateral lending institutions to insist on a good governance commitment of borrower countries (assuming this were within their mandates), as we discussed in our section on the World Bank and the IMF?

Our inclination would be to say that businesses ought to concentrate on creating wealth, while guaranteeing human rights to their workers and those affected by their operations. We do think that telling countries what to do would interfere with their governments to far too great an extent and that transnational corporations do not possess (nor should possess) the legitimacy to do so; and that such governance questions are best left to relevant international organizations.

Let us now look at what has actually been happening 'in the real world' in terms of development assistance, development, and impact of aid. We hope that by doing so we will be able to see more clearly what may help us realize the right to development; and whether pouring untied aid into developing countries (as advocated by so many developing countries and non-governmental organizations) could be one such help.

Development assistance and effectiveness of aid

Despite the general perception that the level of development aid to the poor countries of the world from the rich has been woefully inadequate, there has been a huge flow of aid money over the years. In fact, if all this money had been wisely and productively invested, the world would indeed have made poverty history. For instance, it has been calculated that the sum of $568 billion has been given to African states in the last forty years and over $1 trillion (i.e. nearly twice as much) worldwide.[166]

To put this into perspective, the United States' 2006 GDP is estimated to be $11 trillion, the UK's just over $2 trillion, Russia's slightly less than $1 trillion and Turkey's $407 billion. The sub-Sahara's 2006 GDP as a whole was $709 billion.[167] For a sample of African countries in another recent study, aid was equal to an average of 14 per cent of GNP and 43 per cent of government spending.[168]

By comparison also, going back to the hugely successful 1947 Marshall Plan, $13 billion in economic and technical assistance (equivalent to $75 billion today) were given over the period 1947–53 by the US to help the recovery of the sixteen European countries that had joined in the Organisation for European Economic Co-operation.[169] America's contribution never exceeded 5 per cent of the GDP of recipient nations.[170]

On top of all that money in financial assistance, billions have also been given to developing countries in the recent years in debt relief: nearly $60 billion to Heavily Indebted Poor Countries alone by mid-2006.

Where have all these billions gone? What do we have to show for them today in terms of improved economies and other performance measures of developing countries? Have they really reduced poverty and inequality or have many – too many – of them ended up in the pockets of corrupt dictators or on running the dozens of aid agencies around the world?

These questions require a huge study, and we cannot hope to answer them here. By giving our readers some statistics on debt relief, financial assistance and recent development trends, as well as by referring them to a few studies conducted on the question of aid effectiveness, we simply hope to alert them to the complexity of the problem of poverty reduction and to the fact that aid may not always be the best solution to that problem.

Magnitude of aid

In the mid 1990s, the debts of the developing countries came to be seen as unsustainable: the debt-to-exports ratios of the poorest countries rose from below 250 per cent in the early 1980s, to 800 per cent of exports by the mid 1990s (equivalent to 160 per cent of gross national income).[171]

Due, in a great measure, to pressure from civil society, a joint IMF-World Bank Enhanced Initiative for Heavily Indebted Poor Countries (HIPC) was launched in 1996. Under this initiative, forty countries are potentially eligible to receive assistance: of these, twenty-nine are already receiving debt service relief totalling more than $59 billion (of which the Bank's contribution to date is about $14 billion).[172] Besides the debt relief by the IMF and World Bank, the Initiative proposes parallel debt relief on the part of official bilateral, private creditors, or other multilateral institutions.

More recently, at the 2005 Gleneagles summit in Scotland, the leaders of the Group of Eight major industrial nations proposed the Multilateral Debt Relief Initiative, to help the poorest countries advance toward the United Nations' Millennium Development Goals. The Initiative commits three multilateral institutions – the IMF, the International Development Association of the World Bank, and the African Development Fund – to cancel 100 per cent of their debt claims on countries that have reached, or will eventually reach, the completion point under the Initiative. In early 2007, the Inter-American Development Bank also decided to provide similar debt relief to the five Heavily Indebted Poor Countries in the Western Hemisphere. So far, £37 billion has been committed by the World Bank and $50 billion from all donors, effectively doubling the Initiative's relief.[173] We mentioned already that by mid-2006, nearly $60 billion in debt relief had been committed to countries that had reached the Initiative's decision point. Relief under the two initiatives is expected to reduce the debt stocks of these countries by almost 90 per cent.[174]

While this is all very worthy of praise on the one hand, on the other it raises fears that the programme does little to encourage poor countries to spend the borrowed money responsibly. On the contrary, it may lead them to borrow again and again hoping for new future debt relief, while engaging in disastrous public policies. As the World Bank points out: 'empirical analyses have ... indicated a strong positive relationship between debt distress (and hence the need for debt forgiveness) and poor policy and institutions'.[175]

Another risk associated with debt relief is that no one may actually want to lend funds to poor countries again in future, fearing that they would not be able to repay their debts. Between 1999 and 2003, for example, Heavily Indebted Poor Countries paid the equivalent of only a fraction of their total Official Development Assistance ($68 billion) in the form of debt service ($14 billion).[176] And if lenders stop lending to poor countries, debt relief simply would replace or even eliminate new loans, instead of representing – as one would hope – funds additional to other financial flows such as new debt.

There are therefore grave concerns in practice with writing-off poor countries' debts. Debt relief may not benefit them in the longer run: especially because, as with development assistance generally, it is increasingly argued that it is weak governance and inappropriate policies in developing countries that constrain growth, not lack of resources.

Let us look now at the other facet of development assistance or amount of debt (besides debt relief): financial assistance to developing states. We can divide development assistance into: (i) official assistance from the World Bank Group and the IMF (strictly speaking, the Fund does not provide 'development assistance' but 'financial assistance' in the form of loans to countries experiencing balance of payments problems; we find it useful, however, to include those loans, to get a picture of total assistance to developing countries); (ii) official assistance from the OECD Development Assistance Committee (DAC), the largest organized group of state donors; (iii) official assistance from non-DAC members; and (iv) private development assistance.

Official assistance from the World Bank Group and the IMF:

1. IMF, July 2006: provided $28 billion in outstanding loans to seventy-four countries, of which $6 billion to fifty-six countries on concessional terms in July 2006.[177]
2. International Development Association, 2005: provided $8.7 billion, of which Africa received $3.9 billion, South Asia, $2.9 and East Asia and Pacific, $1.1 billion. The corresponding figures for the fiscal year 2006 and 2007 are $9.5 billion and $12.8 billion, respectively.[178]
3. International Bank for Reconstruction and Development, 2006: lending commitments were $14.1 billion. Latin America and the Caribbean received the highest level of this lending, with $5.7 billion, or 40 per cent of total IBRD commitments, followed by Europe and Central Asia with $3.5 billion and East Asia and Pacific with $2.3 billion. Five countries – Brazil, China, India, Mexico, and Turkey – received a combined commitment volume equalling 52 per cent of such lending in fiscal year 2006.[179] The total figure for commitments in the fiscal year 2007 was $12.8 billion.

Official assistance from the OECD Development Assistance Committee (DAC):

1. Provided more than $106 billion in 2005.[180] That figure fell by 5.1 per cent in 2006, to $103.9 billion (which included $19.2 billion of exceptional relief to Iraq and Nigeria).[181] The fall suggests, as the

2007 Report on Millennium Development Goals points out, that aid delivery might be falling short of donor commitments at Gleneagles; and that doubling of aid to Africa by 2010 looks increasingly unlikely.[182]

2. DAC countries' official assistance as a share of their combined gross national income climbed from 0.22 per cent to 0.33 per cent in 2001–5. However, this is still well short of the target ratio of 0.7 per cent that rich countries pledged back in 1970 to move toward, and that all developed countries were urged to move toward under the Monterrey Consensus. Indeed, only five donors (Denmark, Luxembourg, the Netherlands, Norway, and Sweden) have met that target.[183]

Official assistance from non-DAC members:

1. In 2001–4, it increased to $3.7 billion.[184] Indeed, their aid (as opposed to DAC donors) is expected to double to over $2 billion per year by 2010, with emerging donors such as China.[185] Interestingly, much of this aid goes to infrastructure and productive sectors, no longer targeted by DAC donors.[186]

2. Saudi Arabia accounts for the largest share, with Korea, Kuwait, Taiwan and Turkey following behind.[187]

Private development assistance:

1. Grants from non-governmental organizations grew by more than 50 per cent in 2001–04, to more than $11 billion.

2. Private giving for tsunami-related humanitarian relief, for example, was $5.1 billion or 38 per cent of the total pledged.[188]

Adding all the figures together gives us a back-of-an-envelope figure of $161.8 billion in total development assistance to developing countries in one year (most probably 2005, for which we have most statistics). The *2007 Millennium Development Goals Report* gives a more accurate figure of net aid disbursements of $103.9 billion, equivalent to 0.3 per cent of developed countries' combined national income. These figures can be compared to the figures given at the beginning of the section; for example, Turkey's GDP in 2006 of $406 billion. Clearly, $161.8 billion (or $103 billion) in aid per year is a lot of money (even if it is not close to the promised 0.7 per cent of developed countries' GNP in aid).[189]

Today, indeed, low-income countries (unlike middle-income countries) rely mostly on development aid to finance their development. In many of them, shockingly from our point of view, aid finances a large share of government expenditure, possibly over 50 per cent;[190] and is a greater source of financial flows than non-debt. In Sub-Saharan Africa, for instance, aid was about $25 billion (in total) in 2004, as compared to $11.4 billion of non-debt private financial flows such as foreign investment and $7.7 billion of inward remittances.[191] It is difficult to see what incentives governments might have to raise revenue – and hence to aim for higher growth – or even to attract private investment in such cases.

We discuss further the question of efficacy of aid in the last section of this chapter. But first let's examine where developing countries lie in terms of recent development trends, in particular in terms of growth, inequality and progress with the Millennium Development Goals.

Progress toward the Millennium Development Goals[192]

Surprisingly, in view of the wide-ranging opinion (certainly of the anti-globalization activists) that globalization has impoverished the most needy and that aid is sorely inadequate, the figures show that the proportion of people living in extreme poverty has actually halved since 1980 (and, more recently, that the first of the Millennium Development Goals is on track);[193] and that the developing countries as a whole have experienced a solid 3.9 per cent annual growth in GDP per capita a year since 2000.[194]

As reported, however, in two recent publications, *Global Issues for Global Citizens*[195] and a joint Bank and International Monetary Fund report, 'The 2007 Global Monitoring Report: Confronting the Challenges of Gender Equality and Fragile States on the Millennium Development Goals', these figures both mask vast differences between regions; and also are not followed by similar successes with other Millennium Development Goals.

The main findings of the publications are that:

- Halving of extreme poverty is on track for 2015 globally, global poverty being projected to fall to 12 per cent from 29 per cent in 1990 and 18 per cent in 2004: a 'striking success' according to the

2007 report (in absolute figures, it is a decrease from $1.25 billion in 1990 to $985 million in 2004).[196]

- Some progress is being made in virtually all the Goals across all regions. Significantly, the post-2000 period in particular has seen major gains, 'indicating that the Millennium Development Goals compact has sparked a seriousness of effort that is bearing fruit'.[197]
- However, regional differences are sharp:
  - China, Cambodia, India, Pakistan, and Vietnam have experienced the greatest reduction in poverty. In China, for example, poverty fell from 64 per cent in 1981 to 14 per cent in 2002.[198] This huge reduction in poverty has been without doubt caused by those countries' fast GDP growth: confirming that growth is 'essential to reducing poverty, [even if] it isn't the only factor'.[199]
  - In Sub-Saharan Africa poverty declined from 46 per cent to only 41 per cent since 1999 (after having risen between 1981 and 2001 from 41 per cent to 46 per cent, at the same time as their GDP per capita fell by 14 per cent).[200]
  - The so-called fragile states – countries with weak governance and capacity – had actually made *negative progress* toward the first Millennium Development Goal by 2005.[201] Fragile states account for 9 per cent of the population of developing countries but 27 per cent of the extreme poor, nearly one-third of all child deaths and 29 per cent of twelve-year olds who did not complete primary school in 2005.[202] While extreme poverty levels in non-fragile states are estimated to decline to 17 per cent by 2015 – thus more than achieving the first Millennium Development Goals target – levels of extreme poverty in fragile states will remain at *over 50 per cent*, 'higher than the level in 1990'.[203]
- Generally, measured in absolute terms, the income gap between the rich and the poor countries has widened over the past several decades.[204] Income per capita in the world's high-income countries is, on average, 65 times that in the low-income countries.[205] The figures are better when the income gap is measured in relative terms. The poorest 40 per cent of the world population have nearly doubled their share of world income, while the richest 10 per cent have seen only a small increase in their share.[206] However, this result is mainly due to the strong economic growth in China and India; and the richest 5 per cent of the world's population still

receive about 33 per cent of world income, while the poorest 5 per cent receive only 0.2 per cent.[207]

- Some areas of gender equality and empowerment of women (the third Millennium Goal) have seen rapid progress, such as achieving educational parity for girls in school. But in other dimensions, including political representation and non-agricultural employment, performance falls short.[208] And yet, as the World Bank accepts, gender equality is most important because it 'makes good economic sense and because it helps advance the other development goals – including education, nutrition and reducing child mortality'.[209]

- There is much less progress in the human development Millennium Goals, such as education, health, and access to sanitation. While life expectancy in these countries has risen from sixty to sixty-five between 1980 and 2002:

  - Malnutrition remains the world's most serious health problem, with nearly one-third of all children in the developing world being either underweight or stunted;[210]

  - 1 child in 12 in developing countries dies before its fifth birthday, compared with 1 in 152 in high-income countries; and

  - 1 woman in 16 dies from complications of pregnancy and childbirth in Sub-Saharan Africa, compared to 1 in 3,800 in developed countries.

- In terms of the Human Development Index (a composite measure of well-being based on life expectancy at birth, knowledge, and income per capita, developed by the UN Development Programme in 1993), African countries in particular rank amongst the lowest and the trend for these countries is far from favourable.[211]

- Goal 8, the Global Partnership for Development, has seen mixed results:[212]

  - Debt relief has been very successful. As we saw already, by mid-2006, nearly $60 billion in debt relief had been committed to countries that had reached the Highly Indebted Poor Countries decision point, with the result that the debt stocks of these countries should be reduced by almost 90 per cent.[213]

  - With the continued collapse in trade talks, there has been little or no progress on liberalization of agriculture. However, manufacturing trade is less restrictive, owing to the steady reduction of tariffs. The result is, as the Report points out, that most economies are now less trade-restrictive than they were in 2000. The exception is a number of African countries.

• Expansion in global aid has come to a stop, and aid to Sub-Saharan Africa increased by only 2 per cent between 2005 and 2006. The Gleneagles summit's promises of higher aid to Sub-Saharan Africa (doubling of aid by 2010 or the UN target of 0.7 per cent of gross national income) are hence unlikely to materialize.[214]

The Report concludes that:

Nearly seven years after the Millennium Summit and five years after the Monterrey summit, there has yet to be a country case where aid is being significantly scaled up to support a medium-term program to reach the Millennium Development Goals.[215]

This is a problem particularly for fragile states, where aid constitutes the main source of development finance.[216] The weak performance of the 'fragile' states is, however, 'clearly linked to chronically weak institutional capacity and governance and to internal conflict'.[217] It is hence not clear in our view how pouring more aid into these states is going to help them improve their performance. 'Weak institutional capacity and governance' and internal conflict, combined with aid money pouring into a country seem to us a recipe for corruption and inefficiency.

To be fair, the Report advocates also, besides more aid:

1. Increasingly selective aid allocation 'on the basis of need (poverty) and the quality of policies (governance)';[218] and
2. Scaling up of 'quality' aid.

The latter requires greater coherence among donors, developing countries, and international agencies. In particular, it requires a more coherent 'aid architecture' – aid architecture being 'proliferation of donor channels, fragmentation of aid, ear-marking of funds' – to reduce the costs of fragmentation in areas such as aid quality and effectiveness. The average number of official donors has indeed *tripled* since the 1960s; and, since 1990, the number of countries with over forty active bilateral and multilateral donors increased from zero to over thirty. Emerging donors, such as China, are also expanding their presence rapidly.[219]

Indeed, there is a growing questioning of the effectiveness of aid, and of where all these billions go. We address some of the issues connected with this topic explicitly below.

Studies and proposals on the impact of aid

Evidence about the impact of aid generally is inconclusive.[220] As the World Bank says:

The evidence supporting the positive impact of aid is shaky at best. Some find aid to have a large positive impact on growth, while others find no or even a negative impact. A number of authors have claimed that aid only works in good policy environments [hence that mainstream (not emergency) aid should be directed only to countries with good economic management] while others refute that recipient country policies are a factor.[221]

Critics often suppose that it is donors who are responsible for aid being ineffective, using aid to promote their own exports or to pursue their own political and strategic objectives: Iraq and Afghanistan, for example, have accounted for over half of the increase in net official development aid from all donors during 2001–3.[222]

However, the available evidence shows most clearly that, in many of the recipient countries, aid has been used to support corrupt governments, the military, oppressive state apparatuses and bureaucracies; and that much of it ended in individual leaders' pockets. It is estimated that Zaire's President Mobutu Sese Seko alone embezzled $5 billion; Nigeria's President Sani Abacha, $2 billion to $5 billion.[223] A recent report in *The Times* reported that £15 *billion of aid a year*, according to the 2002 Tax Justice Network, is embezzled by the rulers of sub-Saharan Africa.[224] This could be, according to our back-of-an-envelope calculations, between 15 to 20 per cent, if not more, of total aid to those countries.

Studies also suggest that the $568 billion provided to Africa in aid in the past four decades have not had much impact on poverty there.[225] The huge inequality within those countries (as within Latin America and the Caribbean) seems to add to the problem: countries with high initial income inequality see a smaller positive impact of growth on poverty reduction than the countries with low initial income inequality.[226] In these countries, public spending on education and health often benefits the richest rather than the poorest.[227]

Our own inclination is to agree with those who believe that aid only works in good policy environments; and that these require free-market policies combined with a redistributive state. We have no doubt, for example, that the success of the Marshall Plan mentioned earlier was in the first place due to the free-market policies imposed on Western Europe in return for aid (these policies being also one of the reasons for which the Soviet Union rejected the Marshall Plan). The recipients had to agree to balance their budgets, stop inflation, stabilize their exchange rates at realistic levels, decontrol prices, eliminate trade restrictions and resist nationalization of industry.[228] As a result:

Economists today place far more weight on the economic reforms initiated by the Marshall Plan, and much less on the actual aid itself ... For example, ... [a] 1991 study by the Institute for International Economics concluded: "The Marshall Plan experience does not suggest that capital inflows – in the absence of economic reform – will lead to sustainable economic growth".[229]

Similarly, a colonial past and low initial levels of economic development have often been blamed for developing countries' low economic growth and poverty. This, to our mind, does not explain why countries such as South Korea and Malaysia – once as poor as Ghana and Kenya – are doing so much better today. Real income per head in the forty-eight countries of sub-Saharan Africa between 1960 and 2005 has risen on average by 25 per cent, but growth is thirty-four times faster in East Asia.[230]

As we also have said several times before, we do not believe that poverty can be abolished (and aid be effective) without economic growth. We saw when discussing the progress on the Millennium Goals that those who have done the best are those who have experienced highest economic growth. Preliminary estimates are that, for a sample of nineteen low-income countries, 1 per cent of GDP growth was associated with a 1.3 per cent fall in the rate of extreme poverty and a 0.9 per cent fall in the $2-per-day poverty rate.[231]

Fortunately, all countries seem to have benefited from the growth in the world economy in recent years (not experienced since the 1970s), even Sub-Saharan Africa, 'where the sustained and rising growth performance since the late 1990s is in sharp contrast to the weak performance evident over the last three decades'.[232] Of course, as we stated before, growth is not enough: it has to be accompanied by appropriate human rights policies. Nothing indicates this more than the fact that the highest rates of malnutrition, for example, are found in South Asia, where there has been nevertheless such a strong growth (much higher than in Sub-Saharan Africa).[233] However, growth is without doubt a necessary condition for reducing poverty. Additional untied aid in particular, in our view, is most unlikely to result in such a necessary growth.

This view seems to be accepted wisdom within the international aid community today. We have already mentioned the 2007 *Millennium Development Goals Report* and its conclusions on selective aid allocation and scaling up of 'quality' aid. Previously, widespread concerns about the effectiveness of aid had led to the 2005 Paris Declaration on Aid Effectiveness (following the 2003 High Level Forum on Harmonization in Rome and the 2004 Roundtable on Managing for Development Results in Marrakech).

In the Declaration sixty partner countries, thirty donor countries, and thirty development agencies committed, in 'an unprecedented level of consensus',[234] to an agenda specifying monitorable, time-bound actions to improve the quality of aid.[235] The commitments are organized around five key principles (ownership, alignment, harmonization, managing for results and mutual accountability) and focus on how to improve 'the efficiency of financial and administrative arrangements necessary to reduce transaction costs and improve aid delivery particularly in the light of donor commitments to scaling up aid'.[236]

According to the OECD, there are three reasons why the Paris Declaration will make a significant difference to the effectiveness of aid:

1. The Declaration goes beyond previous agreements, by laying down practical goals to improve the quality of aid and its impact on development, with fifty-six partnership commitments;
2. Twelve indicators of aid effectiveness were developed as a way of tracking and encouraging progress; and
3. The Declaration creates stronger mechanisms for accountability, by promoting a model of partnership through which donors and recipients of aid are held mutually accountable, and compliance in meeting the commitments will be publicly monitored.[237] This mutual accountability is indeed, 'the cornerstone of the new international aid architecture'.[238]

Without referring explicitly to human rights, the Declaration links the goal of improving the quality of aid with the achievement of Millennium Development Goals: which, we have seen, involve realization of human rights. Implementation of the Declaration will hence also help advance human rights.[239]

So far, however, not much has happened. As the World Bank concludes (and as appears to be still applicable at the time of writing this chapter):

[progress] in implementing the Paris framework at the country level has been mixed – only a few countries have seen substantive progress in the customization of several Paris indicators and targets to the country context. Vigorous implementation of the Paris agenda is needed to deliver more effective development assistance ... [240]

Ideally, more progress will be made in implementing the Paris framework by the time of the progress review of the Declaration, at the Third High Level Forum on Aid Effectiveness in Ghana in 2008.

Meantime, efforts are being made to fight what many might consider another (if not the) obstacle to effective aid: corruption. A draft Implementation Plan for Strengthening World Bank Group Engagement on Governance and Anticorruption was prepared at the time of writing this chapter, with the World Bank seeking feedback from any interested parties.[241]

Finally, we want to mention another study, commissioned by the OECD, entitled *Integrating Human Rights into Development: Donor Approaches, Experiences and Challenges.*[242] To quote the study at length:

Human rights also contribute to enhancing the effectiveness of aid. ... Human rights are fundamentally about challenging power relations. As a result, the approach can lead to explicitly [sic] recognition of the political dimensions of aid, not in a party political sense but, as with political economy studies, in terms of bringing the political dimensions of poverty reduction to the fore. New partnerships have been built by donors as a result, finding supportive ways of facilitating domestic change processes. A number of these contributions are not new to the development world; what human rights offer is a coherent, normative framework which reinforces 'good programming practices' by making them non-negotiable, consistent and legitimate.[243]

Conclusion

There is today a broad agreement within the international community on how to reduce poverty and achieve other Millennium Development Goals. In the words of the World Bank, this agreement 'rests on a framework of mutual accountability between developed and developing countries'.[244] This means that both developed and developing countries need to fulfil their part of the 'mutual accountability' bargain. In the case of developed countries, as the World Bank says, they need to ensure that:

- developing country producers have a better access to developed country markets;
- developing countries have a better access to international financial resources ('to boost investment in health, education, and infrastructure and to reduce vulnerability to external shocks and natural disasters');
- there is effective debt relief that would actually free up resources for investing in health, education, water and sanitation; and
- technological and scientific advances and medical research directly benefit the poor.[245]

For their part, developing countries need to follow sound policies 'and make a commitment to good governance, which is central to development'. For that to happen, among other things, they need to be accountable to their citizens 'for the delivery of services such as health, education, and infrastructure and for their use of resources'.[246]

We have three comments to make with respect to that 'mutual accountability agreement' on development strategies today.

First is that, while we would, of course, not dissociate ourselves from it (in view of our own arguments in favour of 'mutual accountability'), we believe that it does not emphasize sufficiently the most important source of poverty-reducing development: namely, the take-off into sustained economic growth accompanying the rise of a market economy that can benefit from globalization in the manner that has been recently so remarkable in the cases of China and India.

Second, we find it interesting that some of the elements of the agreement take us back to the old claim for a 'new international economic order' in the 1970s. We may recall that the main elements of the call for a new order were:

- the stabilization of commodity prices at an equitable level;
- preferential treatment for the less developed countries' industrial products;
- greater access of less developed countries to financial resources;
- greater participation in decision making in financial institutions;
- facilitation of technology transfers; and
- expropriation without compensation.[247]

While some of the elements of the call have been already realized (as we saw, for example, the stabilization of commodity prices at a more 'equitable' level) and others are obsolete (expropriation without compensation), yet other elements are precisely those of the agreement: greater participation in decision making in financial institutions, facilitation of technology transfers and preferential treatment for the less developed countries' industrial products (the latter in the modern guise today of a call for developing country producers to have better access to developed country markets). Another call relevant to the twenty-first century – to make the Intellectual Property Rights regime more equitable towards developing countries, especially when essential drugs are concerned – is also gaining traction, as 'developing countries are becoming critical players in shaping how the pharmaceutical companies will conduct business in the future'.[248] The developing countries might be getting their new economic order after all.

Third, while the 'mutual accountability' agreement concentrates on the economic aspects of development – poverty reduction and other Millennium Development Goals – it also commits, in our view, the developing and developed countries to the implementation of CP rights and the right to self-determination, respectively. Indeed, the right to self-determination can be deduced from the resolve that Poverty Reduction Strategies are to be 'country-owned';[249] and the CP rights from the general acceptance of Sen's view of development as an expansion of all human freedoms, and hence of CP rights as a *sine qua non* of development.

Further, it is clear that without CP rights it would not be possible to effectively monitor a state's progress on the Millennium Development Goals or its compliance with any other ESC rights. As the Office of the High Commissioner for Human Rights' Guidelines points out with respect to poverty reduction strategies:

if the poor are to enjoy the right to participate in poverty reduction strategies, they must be free to organise without restriction (right to association), to meet without impediment (right of assembly), and to say what they want without intimidation (freedom of expression); they must know the relevant facts (right to information), and enjoy an elementary level of economic security and well being (right to a reasonable standard of living).[250]

All this indicates, we believe, that the RTD is no longer just an idea but already to a great extent a reality. Like the UN Declaration on

Human Rights before the ICESCR and ICCPR, the (non-binding) Declaration on the Right to Development reflects in many ways generally accepted norms of state behaviour. And, also like the UN Declaration on Human Rights, the Declaration on the RTD might one day be succeeded by legally binding international documents.

We hope it will. To us, the right to development expresses in international terms the obligations, on the one hand, of members of a liberal society to ensure that everyone has adequate access to the resources that will enable them to exercise their freedom; and on the other, of members of aspiring liberal societies to promote circumstances most productive of successful development and realization of their peoples' human rights. It is hence, as we have so often said, an indispensable part of the liberal world project.

7 | *Women's international human rights*

Women are guaranteed equal rights with men in all respects under the Charter of the UN, which says that the peoples of the UN reaffirm faith in the equal rights of men and women, and Article 1(3) commits the UN to promote respect for human rights for all without distinction as to race, sex, language or religion. The Universal Declaration of Human Rights contains a similar affirmation (Art. 2), as do the ICCPR (Art. 2.1) and the ICESCR (Art. 2.2).

However, Article 16(3) of the Universal Declaration of Human Rights (UDHR) states that the family is the natural and fundamental group unit of society and is entitled to protection by society and the state. Some feminists believe that as nothing is said about the effect of family structure on the enjoyment by women of equal rights, this provision gives states *carte blanche* to give priority to the patriarchal family preservation over women's rights. At any rate, it shows the lack of seriousness about women's rights in the early documents.

Indeed, it is now widely held that the protection these instruments offered women against discrimination on grounds of sex was of little effect and that women's rights and women's issues were almost entirely neglected by the UN for many years.

Such criticisms could no longer be made after the coming into force of the Convention on the Elimination of All Forms of Discrimination Against Women: a convention that requires states not only to prohibit discrimination but also to take affirmative steps in order to achieve gender equality. As we will see, there is still much feminist criticism of the Convention directed at its adoption of liberal and supposedly male norms.

Convention on the Elimination of all Forms of Discrimination Against Women, 1979

In 1979, the UN General Assembly adopted the Convention on the Elimination of all Forms of Discrimination Against Women (CEDAW) with a total vote of 130 to none, with 10 abstentions.[1] The Convention was the culmination of more than thirty years of work by the United Nations Commission on the Status of Women (as well as 'decades of work by ... governments, and women's rights activists'),[2] originally established in 1946 as a sub-commission to the Commission on Human Rights. As a result of the pressure exerted by women activists in particular, the sub-commission was, however, quickly granted the status of full commission.

Because of its importance, CEDAW is often described as an international bill of rights for women.[3] It is also seen as 'the most authoritative UN Human Rights instrument to protect women from discrimination ... the first international treaty to comprehensively address fundamental rights for women in politics and public life, health care, education, equal pay, economics, employment, law, financial benefits and property rights, and equality in marriage and family life';[4] as well as a very effective tool that women around the world are using to bring about change in their conditions.[5] Thus, 'in nations that have ratified the treaty, CEDAW has proven invaluable in opposing the effects of discrimination, which include violence, poverty, lack of legal protections, along with the denial of inheritance, property rights, and access to credit'.[6]

The Convention defines discrimination against women as:

any distinction, exclusion or restriction made on the basis of sex which has the *effect* or purpose of impairing or nullifying the recognition, enjoyment or exercise by women, irrespective of their marital status, on a basis of equality of men and women, of human rights and fundamental freedoms in the political, economic, social, cultural, civil or any other field (Article 1)

By accepting the Convention, states commit themselves to undertake a series of measures to end discrimination against women in all forms, including:

1. To incorporate the principle of equality of men and women in their legal system, abolish all discriminatory laws and adopt appropriate ones prohibiting discrimination against women.
2. To establish tribunals and other public institutions to ensure the effective protection of women against discrimination; and, most importantly
3. To ensure elimination of all acts of discrimination against women by *persons*, organizations or enterprises.[7]

Looking at each article in more detail (and noting that Articles 2 and 16 are the most important articles in the Convention):

- In its preamble, CEDAW exposes its concern that, despite the above-mentioned commitments to the equal rights of women in the UN regime, discrimination against women continues to exist. It specifically states that a change in the traditional role of men as well as the role of women in society and in the family is needed to achieve full equality between men and women. CEDAW *aims thus at a radical change*: and we think elaborates the goal reasonably effectively in its substantive provisions.
- As we just saw, Article 1 defines discrimination as 'any distinctive exclusion or restriction made on the basis of sex that has the *effect* or purpose of impairing or nullifying the recognition, enjoyment or exercise by women ... on a basis of equality of men and women, of human rights and fundamental freedoms in political, economic, social, cultural, civil or any other field'. In other words, distinctions, etc. that have this effect – even if not on purpose – are outlawed. This includes distinctions that arise not solely from state action but action of groups in society.
- Article 2 says that this goal is to be pursued without delay and amplifies Article 1 in (e) and (f), stating that all appropriate measures must be taken to eliminate discrimination by *any person, organization or enterprise* and to modify or abolish existing laws, regulations, customs and practices which constitute discrimination.
- Article 4 contains an affirmative action or reverse discrimination clause as temporary measure.
- Article 5 requires state parties to the Convention to take appropriate measures.
- Article 10 concerns the particular field of education and lists specific goals such as (i) same conditions for career and vocational guidance and access to studies from pre-school age to higher education; (ii) access to the same curricula; (iii) elimination of stereotyped concepts of the roles of men and women at all levels by revision of textbooks and school programmes and teaching materials, and so on.
- Article 12 requires special provision for women in respect of preparing, confinement and the post-natal period, granting free services where necessary, as well as adequate nutrition.

- Article 14 requires state parties to take special account of problems faced by rural women and through women's non-monetized work in enjoying these equal rights.
- Article 16 requires state parties to do away with many fundamental traditional discriminations against and subordination of women regarding marriage and family relations.
- Articles 2(f) and 5(a) require state parties to modify customs and practices that discriminate against women, a most important step in the fight against discrimination.

Having regard to all this, it seems to us undeniable that CEDAW is a splendid and radical liberal feminist document, in spite of attacks on it by a number of feminist writers (mainly representing different 'feminisms' than the liberal one).[8] We will address the criticisms of CEDAW below. First, however, we want to discuss the vexed question of reservations.

Any state can ratify a treaty specifying certain reservations to it, thus showing that it does not wish to be bound by certain provisions of the treaty.[9] It cannot, however, make reservations that defeat the object and purpose of the treaty. Furthermore, the other state parties can enter objections to other states' reservations, so that the provisions to which the reservation relates do not apply as between the objecting and the reserving states to the extent of the reservation. The states objecting to a reservation can also of course oppose the entry into force of the whole treaty as between themselves and the reserving state in the first place.

While most states have ratified CEDAW,[10] there have been an exceptionally high number of reservations made to it by states ratifying.[11] Several countries have entered reservations to Articles 2 and 16 in particular; for example, Bangladesh and Egypt on grounds that they conflict with sharia law (Bangladesh subsequently withdrew its objection to Article 16). Saudi Arabia entered a general reservation stating that: '[i]n case of contradiction between any term of the Convention and the norms of Islamic law, the Kingdom is not under obligation to observe the contradictory terms of the Convention'.[12] And yet, one could reasonably claim that these reservations undermine crucial aspects of the Convention and should not have been allowed. As the

Committee on the Elimination of Discrimination Against Women (discussed more fully in our section on implementation) stated:

> Articles 2 and 16 are considered by the Committee to be *core provisions* of the Convention. Although some States parties have withdrawn reservations to those articles, the Committee is particularly concerned at the number and extent of reservations entered to those articles. The Committee holds the view that article 2 is central to the objects and purpose of the Convention. States parties which ratify the Convention do so because they agree that discrimination against women in all its forms should be condemned and that the strategies set out in article 2, subparagraphs (a) to (g), should be implemented by States parties to eliminate it. *Neither traditional, religious or cultural practice nor incompatible domestic laws and policies can justify violations of the Convention.* The Committee also remains convinced that reservations to article 16, whether lodged for national, traditional, religious or cultural reasons, are incompatible with the Convention and therefore impermissible and should be reviewed and modified or withdrawn.[13]

Somehow surprisingly, only a few countries objected to particular reservations; for example Germany, Mexico, the Netherlands and Sweden were the only states objecting to Bangladesh's reservation to Article 2, and Germany, the Netherlands and Sweden the only states objecting to Egypt's reservation to Article 2.[14] The reason these (seemingly unacceptable) reservations were agreed to must clearly have been a belief that it was better to allow the reservations and get the general commitment of as many states as possible to the convention, than to force these states outside the Convention altogether. Personally, we have our doubts on that policy, as it seems to us that it allows the state to claim that it endorses the principles and then do nothing about them.

The status of women under Islamic law

It is relevant here to discuss comments on the chapter on *Restrictions on Rights and Freedoms of Women under Islam* by Mayer.[15] Mayer makes a general contrast between the attitude of the Koran to women and the status of women in traditional Islamic law or the sharia as this has been developed through the centuries by Islamic jurists on the basis of the Koran and the Sunna (the sayings and doings of the Prophet Mohammed). She claims, and this we think is a widely held view, that the Koran actually increased women's status and rights relative to their traditional position in Arab society. Thus the Koran forbade female infanticide, restricted polygamy, limited abuses of the divorce laws by husbands, gave women ownership of the bridal dower, allowed women to inherit and control property, gave them the right to divorce their husbands. In effect, she says, women had full, if not completely equal, legal personality.

This status disappeared in the subsequent jurist-made law of the sharia. Those laws treated women as needing male tutelage, gave them subordinate roles in the family and secluded them in the domestic house. Child marriages were permitted, women had to be monogamous, and to obey their husbands, who had the right to beat them and withhold maintenance for disobedience. Divorce was made more difficult for women, men got custody of children, had unequal rights of inheritance, and so on.

Thus sharia law regarding women's rights and duties developed in tension with the Koran and the Sunna and in the direction of a strong patriarchal society with women having a substantially inferior status in the family and in Muslim society generally.

Mayer says that since the late nineteenth century Muslim elites, with the exception of Saudi Arabia, have sought to improve the status of women but that there have been some notable reactionary Islamic movements. In this context, she looks at what Islamic human rights schemes say about women's rights.

First, the Universal Islamic Declaration of Human Rights of 1981 affirms the human right to marry and found a family in conformity with one's religion.[16] This departs from the Universal Declaration of Human Rights and the ICCPR articles on the subject, which do not include any reference to religion. The effect of including the reference to religion is to limit the rights of women to marry. For, according to Islamic law, a Muslim woman cannot marry a non-Muslim man or a Muslim man a woman whose religion is not of the book. Also, apostasy leads to death and the annulment of marriage.

Second, the Universal Islamic Declaration of Human Rights states more generally that relations between spouses are governed by the law. If the law here is that of the classical sharia, this in effect reaffirms the subordination of women in patriarchal structures.

Mayer considers also the new Iranian Constitution adopted by the revolutionary Islamic regime. This affirms the dignity of women and women's rights. But again, those rights are those they have according to the law and the law is sharia law. Thus one of the first acts of the Khomeini regime was to nullify the progressive family law of the previous regime, to remove job opportunities for women in public and legal life, impose segregation on women, force them to wear the chador and to go out in public only if accompanied by a male relative. While some of these Iranian restrictions on women have been subsequently relaxed, Mayer concludes that Islamic human rights schemes and constitutions of the above type violate the Universal Declaration of Human Rights Article 1 guaranteeing equality between the sexes, Article 2 guaranteeing against discriminatory treatment, Article 7 on equal protection of laws, Article 16 on freedom to marry, and so on. She also believes that, in respect of being confined to home, they are denied many other freedoms guaranteed in the Universal Declaration and the subsequent conventions.

One general move that Islamists make in defence of these facts is that men and women are being treated equally by their laws in accordance with their different natures. But equality here means justly or fairly and requires different treatment precisely because men and women are perceived as unequal. So equality does not mean having the same rights but not having the same rights and indeed having unequal rights (on any view of the matter men have more rights than women) and a subordinate place in family and society.

We strongly believe that those Islamic schemes and constitutions are bad news for the UN human rights regime and show the sort of obstacles facing its implementation. However, it should be said that it is possible to give the sharia a very different, and indeed liberal, interpretation from the classical form being assumed here. We will discuss these matters further in Part III. Let us now turn to the question of the implementation of the CEDAW provisions.

CEDAW Committee

Under the Convention, a CEDAW Committee was established to oversee its implementation by state parties.[17] The Committee has twenty-three members elected by state parties on the basis of geographical distribution and having regard to the representation of different forms of civilization as well as principal legal systems. The members serve a four-year term, and they can be re-elected. They are experts in the field and not political representatives of governments.

Lawyers – who usually dominate these committees – constitute 50 per cent; the rest come from many fields, but usually with a feminist background of involvement with women's groups.

The Committee works as follows:

- State parties have to submit a report on measures they have adopted to give effect to the Convention and on progress made, within one year of ratification and then at least every four years or whenever the Committee requests.
- The Committee meets for two weeks to consider these reports and then submits an annual report through the Economic and Social Council to the General Assembly on its activities and may make suggestions and general recommendations based on examination of reports.[18]

From this we can see that the Committee's powers are very limited. It can't pronounce a state party to be in violation of the Convention and order an appropriate remedy. The only pressure it has to bring to bear on states lies in the public nature of its annual review of individual state reports. But the Committee can function effectively only with the general support of the state parties who provide the resources for it and who need to endorse the critical attitude it may take to particular state parties. It obviously can't afford to antagonize the majority of the state parties.

In fact, the Committee has pursued a policy of so-called constructive dialogue with state parties as the basis for its consideration of reports. This is the idea of the Committee and the state parties being together engaged in the joint enterprise of advancing the goals of the Convention, as opposed to the idea of a confrontational accusatory procedure. Still the Committee has adopted an adversary stance to state parties in some cases.

Nonetheless, the Committee does not appear to have engaged in making detailed suggestions to individual states about specific measures but has rather provided broad guidelines on measures the Committee wants state parties to take. Its policy has been to press states for accurate information about the condition of women and to take steps to discourage stereotyped attitudes to the role of men and women, especially in the media and educational systems. More recently, it has given special attention to the effects of the World Bank's and IMF's structural adjustment programmes on the position of women; and has taken the view that women's concerns must be integrally involved in any economic restructuring or development plan.

As usual with international law, the most effective implementation is, however, through domestic courts.[19] It is to be hoped that courts – and government agencies more generally – in all member countries will become much more aware of the issue of women's rights now that Security Council Resolution 1325 has come into existence (we discuss the resolution below). We now want to turn our attention to the discussion of one important area, explicit attention to which was lacking in CEDAW: that of violence against women.

1993 Declaration on the Elimination of Violence Against Women and the 1995 Beijing Declaration and Platform for Action

While insisting on equality for women and lack of discrimination against them in all areas of life, CEDAW did not explicitly acknowledge human rights abuses occurring in the private sphere, such as domestic violence, rape and sexual abuse. This was in line with the general attitude of the international community towards violence against women, considered by most governments largely 'as a private matter between individuals, and not as a pervasive human rights problem requiring State intervention'.[20]

To be sure, the CEDAW Committee made two general recommendations under Article 21 that directly linked gender-based violence and discrimination. General Recommendation 12 emphasized that the international community should implement anti-discriminatory provisions that already existed within the Convention to combat gender-based violence (so that Articles 2, 5, 11, 12 and 16 could be read as requiring the state parties 'to act to protect women against violence of any kind occurring within the family, at the work place or in any other area of social life').[21] Additionally, it required state parties to include in their periodic reports information as to what they were doing to combat violence against women at the national level. General Recommendation 19 stated that 'the definition of discrimination includes gender-based violence'; that 'discrimination under the Convention is not restricted to action by or on behalf of Governments' (Articles 2(e), 2(f) and 5), and that '[u]nder general international law and specific human rights covenants, States may also be responsible for private acts [of violence] if they fail to act with due diligence to prevent violations of rights or to investigate and punish acts of violence and for providing compensation'.[22]

However, many felt that this was insufficient and that an international document *explicitly* addressing the issue of violence against women by private individuals was also required. Many went further, and argued that the Convention as it stood reinforced existing patriarchal structures and perpetuated a public/private dichotomy that further oppressed women. As one of these writers, Hilary Charlesworth, said: 'issues traditionally of concern to men [political and economic] are seen as general human concerns; "women's concerns" [what happens within the family] by contrast, are regarded as a distinct and limited category'.[23]

As a result of similar feminist concerns, and in order to strengthen and complement CEDAW, the UN General Assembly passed a Declaration on the Elimination of Violence Against Women in 1993. Though not legally binding, the Declaration is viewed as a 'normative force' that influences international standards concerning violence against women (the way the Universal Declaration of Human Rights influenced international standards on CP and ESC rights); and it is widely accepted within the international community.[24]

The Declaration defines violence against women as:

Any act of gender-based violence that results in, or is likely to result in, physical, sexual or psychological harm or suffering to women, including threats of such acts, coercion or arbitrary deprivations of liberty, whether occurring in public or private life (Article 1).

Violence will include therefore rape, sexual abuse and marital rape, among other things.

The Preamble to the Declaration recognizes that effective implementation of CEDAW would contribute to the elimination of violence against women; and that the Declaration on the Elimination of Violence against Women 'will strengthen and complement that process'. It also asserts that violence against women is a manifestation of historically unequal power relations between men and women and that its eradication therefore requires an analysis not only of violent acts but also of the social conditions, institutions and norms which perpetuate them. Accordingly, a state party to the Declaration has a responsibility not only to refrain from engaging in or encouraging acts of violence against women but to actively intervene in and exercise due diligence in the prevention of such acts 'whether those acts are perpetrated by the State or by private persons' (Art. 3(c)).

Victims of domestic violence can now argue that human rights abuses are being condoned by the state that has not exercised due diligence in preventing such violence (Article 3c). Further, a state's failure to remedy the situation could be viewed as a failure to intervene actively in preventing, or as condoning, discriminatory practices amounting to human rights violations under various treaties. Failing to train police in matters of domestic violence or to provide accessible services, for example, can also be seen as a failure to exercise due diligence, and a breach of international obligations.

As a follow-up to the Declaration, a number of other events took place in the last years of the twentieth century, reinforcing the international women's rights regime.

In 1994, a Special Rapporteur was appointed by the Commission on Human Rights to seek and receive information on violence against women, its causes and consequences, to carry out field missions to various geographical regions in both an investigative and consultative capacity and to make recommendations for national, regional and international reform in relation to the elimination of violence against women.[25]

In the same year, the Inter-American Convention to Prevent, Punish and Eradicate Violence against Women (also called Convention of Belem do Para) was adopted by the Organization of American States.[26] The Convention recognizes all gender-based violence as an abuse of human rights, and provides for an individual right of petition and a right for non-governmental organizations to lodge complaints with the Inter-American Commission of Human Rights.[27] As Amnesty International points out, the Inter-American system can be seen therefore as 'pioneering in its reaffirmation ... of the State's international responsibility when it fails to investigate or punish with due diligence human rights violations committed by individuals, thus establishing a doctrine of particular relevance to women facing systematic violence within the family and the community'.[28] This is in line with other innovations of the Inter-American system, which we examine in Chapter 8.

Finally, in 1995, the Fourth World Conference on Women took place in Beijing.[29] In the Beijing Declaration and Platform for Action, the core document of the Beijing Conference, governments declared, among other things, that 'violence against women constitutes a violation of basic human rights and is an obstacle to the achievement of the objectives of equality, development and peace'. The Platform, adopted unanimously by representatives from 189 countries, is now considered one of the most progressive 'blueprints' for achieving women's equality, outlining 12 critical areas of concern, including violence against women. It also suggests corresponding principles and strategic actions to help governments in addressing the issue. In particular, governments agreed:

- to adopt and implement national legislation to end violence against women;
- to work actively to ratify all international agreements that relate to violence against women, including CEDAW;
- to establish shelters, legal aid and other services for girls and women at risk, and counselling and rehabilitation for perpetrators; and
- to adopt appropriate measures in the field of education to modify the social and cultural patterns of conduct of men and women.[30]

The Platform also called on media professionals 'to develop self-regulatory guidelines to address violent, degrading and pornographic materials while encouraging non-stereotyped, balanced and diverse images of women'.[31]

However, as the US was careful to point out, the Declaration and Platform do not create legal obligations. Instead, the US stated:

the Beijing Declaration and Platform for Action express important political goals that the United States [and other signatories] endorses. We reaffirm the goals, objectives, and commitments of the Beijing Declaration and Platform for Action based on several understandings. We understand [however] these documents constitute an important policy framework that does not create international legal rights or legally binding obligations on States under international law.[32]

It is all very well: but have all these fine declarations had any practical effect on women's rights worldwide? Without looking at individual countries and women's conditions in them (something which is beyond the scope of this study), it is really impossible to say. Certainly, the fact that there is an increasing awareness of, and agreement on, the importance of issues such as violence to the realization of women's human rights, is encouraging. What is even more encouraging, in our view, is the fact that women's issues are being taken seriously in international criminal law. As discussed in the next section, this means that perpetrators of gender crimes can no longer be assured of impunity.

Gender crimes

Less than a decade ago, it was openly questioned whether rape was a war crime ... Courageous and concerted actions of women around the world forced a sea change in international law, culminating in the recognition of gender violence as a human rights concern and in its codification as among the gravest international crimes in the Rome Statute of the International Criminal Court (ICC). (Rhonda Copelon, 2003)[33]

Rape and enforced prostitution are already listed in the Geneva Conventions as acts which women must be protected against. Article 27 of the Fourth Geneva Convention, relating to the protection of civilian persons in time of war, states thus: 'Women shall be especially protected against any attack on their honour, in particular against rape, enforced prostitution, or any form of indecent assault'. There is, however, no specific recognition of these acts as grave breaches.

As for the Statute of the Nuremberg Tribunal, it makes no mention at all of rape or any sexual or gender-based crimes. Rape is enumerated neither as a crime against humanity, nor as a war crime. Sexual crimes that took place during WWII were hence never prosecuted by the Nuremberg tribunal.[34]

It was only after the 1993 Vienna Conference on human rights and the Declaration on the Elimination of Violence Against Women, which made violence against women a priority in the human rights system, that rape started to be taken seriously in international law. To quote Radhika Coomaraswamy, the then United Nations Special Rapporteur on violence against women, stating in 2003: '[w]hile much remains to be done, the progress made since 1994 is extraordinary'.[35] This progress includes the recognition of rape (when widespread and systematic) as a war crime and a crime against humanity, as well as an instrument of genocide, in the statutes or jurisprudence of the international criminal tribunals and the international criminal court.

In particular, the Statutes of the Yugoslav and the Rwandan Tribunals (which we examine in Chapter 8) list rape as among the crimes against humanity; and recognize, through their jurisprudence, other forms of sexual and gender violence as war crimes and crimes against humanity.[36] The Rwandan Tribunal was also the first international tribunal to recognize rape as an instrument of genocide.

Following in the steps of the Tribunals, the Rome Statute recognizes rape, sexual slavery, trafficking (in particular in women and children), enforced prostitution, forced pregnancy, enforced sterilization and any other form of sexual violence of comparable gravity as war crimes in international and internal armed conflict as well as crimes against humanity when committed as part of a widespread or systematic attack on a civilian population (and by non-state actors as well as officials).[37] Persecution is also included as a crime against humanity; and gender recognized specifically as a basis for persecution.[38] Finally, rape and sexual violence are included in genocide (Article 6(b) Elements of Crime).

This brief overview of gender crimes today makes clear that violence against women is nowadays considered a serious international crime; and that since the days of Nuremberg 'where rape was too atrocious to mention' a lot indeed has changed.[39]

This is not to say, of course, that feminists can rest on their laurels. While on the books, law in this area seems to have been sparingly enforced; for example, twelve years after the Rwandan genocide, only ten persons have been convicted of rape, either in Rwanda or at the International Criminal Tribunal for Rwanda (ICTR).[40]

There is also the problem of not compensating sufficiently victims of sexual violence. Nonetheless, international criminal law in the last fifteen years or so has made important milestones. As Balthazar says:

> At the time of the Nuremberg trials, rape was grossly overlooked as a normal consequence of genocide, of war and was viewed as too atrocious to prosecute. Sixty years later, we know that rape can be a tool of genocide, the gravest crime against humanity. We also know that all those who incite violence against women, be they government leaders, business people, newspaper editors or women themselves, will be held accountable.[41]

Security Council Resolution 1325

The unanimous adoption of United Nations Security Council Resolution 1325 on 31 October 2000 was, according to many, a watershed in the evolution of international women's rights and peace and security issues.[42] This is because it was the first resolution ever passed by the Security Council that asked parties in a conflict to respect women's rights; to support their participation in peace negotiations and in post-conflict reconstruction, elections and government; and to end impunity for perpetrators of gender-based violence.

However, as the Global Justice Centre pointed out six years after the adoption of Security Council Resolution 1325, the Resolution has not achieved much so far.[43] For example, the 2006 Report of the Secretary-General on women, peace and security (27 September 2006) states that 'since the adoption of Resolution 1325, only 55 of 211, or 26.07 per cent, of country-specific Council resolutions include language on women or gender'.[44] The corresponding figure as of 15 October 2007 is 88 out of 287 or 30.66 per cent.[45]

Nonetheless, the widespread use of Resolution 1325 by women's groups indicates its great potential.[46] True, as the Resolution was not passed under Chapter VII, it is a non-binding resolution, that is it creates no enforceable obligations on the part of the UN member states. However, the reception with which it has met since its creation in 2000 shows that it is an example of soft law. It is to be hoped that the Resolution may therefore serve as the basis of future legally binding international agreements (the way the ICESCR and ICCPR grew out of the Universal Declaration of Human Rights); and as the basis for encouraging states to implement the already existing international agreements (such as CEDAW or the statute of the ICC) in their domestic legislation.

More specific recommendations made by a number of women's organizations and some member states are:

- The Security Council ought to develop monitoring mechanisms to ensure the systematic integration of Resolution 1325 in its work (best of all in its daily work): that is, the Security Council should include a systematic and express focus on the gender dimensions of conflict in every case that comes before it, and a Security Council member should be responsible for tracking implementation of the resolution.
- It should also have an independent international inquiry to identify those responsible for sexual violence against women.
- There should be specific funding from the general UN fund and from voluntary contributions for the implementation of Resolution 1325.

• Generally, gender should be used as an analytical tool for rethinking key policy initiatives, ideals, goals and actions.[47]

Feminist criticisms of international human rights

This section is concerned with criticisms of the women's international human rights regime, which are largely directed at its liberal character. It might be thought more appropriate to discuss these critiques in Part III's account of attacks on liberalism from within the Western cultural tradition. However, as they are focused on the women's international human rights regime, we have decided to include them here. We will discuss the criticisms under the following heads:

1. The public/private distinction;
2. The critique of equal rights and the focus on CP rights;
3. Difference feminism and liberalism as a male system of values.

There is an overlap between these criticisms, but it is still useful to formulate them separately.

The public/private distinction

This criticism is common to many forms of feminism. It holds that central to the liberal conception of law and rights is the distinction between a public and a private realm. This distinction is, then, identified with that between the domestic sphere of the home on the one hand and economic, political and legal activities that are carried on outside the home, on the other hand. The distinction, it is held, inherently discriminates against women because law and rights regulate the public realm, which is men's sphere, while the private realm is by definition one within which the state and its law may not intervene. As the private sphere is that of women, it is untouched by liberal rights regimes. CEDAW, as a thoroughly liberal document, does nothing to change this situation but merely seeks to ensure that women have the same rights as men in the public sphere, which is not theirs.[48]

What is true in this claim is that liberalism necessarily contains a distinction between what is a public and what is a private matter and that, allied with unreformed patriarchal family structures, formally equal rights for women will do little to alter their subordination to men. But just about everything else in the claim is false. The primary distinction within liberalism between public and private is one between what is a matter of individual choice, or the collective choice of voluntary co-operators, and what is required by public law or policy. This distinction is not identical with that between the domestic sphere of the home and what falls outside the home in society, economy or polity. Examples of standard matters of private (individual) choice in liberal society are the choice of a job, a religion, a political party, a club, friends and sexual partners. This is to say that a liberal society is one in which such choices are left to individuals to make and are not coercively imposed on them by political, religious or any other authority. Other choices are similarly private, although they are the collective choices of voluntary co-operators, for example the choice by members of a club of its internal rules and its premises, or the choice by a business enterprise of the goods and services it will offer. Of course, all such choices are subject to the constraints of public law. An individual may not secure the job or sexual partner he desires by the exercise of force or fraud. A club may not adopt rules involving physical punishments for their breach. A business may not offer some services without a public licence, such as gambling or drinking, or may not offer some services at all, such as sado-masochism or money-laundering.

The domestic sphere of the home is one in which there are many protected individual or voluntary collective choices: the choice of two people to set up home together, the choice of where to live, how to co-operate domestically, whether to have children, how to educate them, and so on. But just like any other protected choice, they are subject to public law constraints. Spouses may not use violence against each other or against their children. They may not refuse to educate their children. They may not use their domestic property so as to cause a public nuisance.

In the first place, then, the liberal public/private distinction is not restricted to the domestic/non-domestic division. In the second place, it is not the case that what is private is *ipso facto* not subject to public law constraints, as pointed out above. In the third place, the constraints are matters of public/political decision and may vary over time. Thus, not so long ago, in the UK, husbands were permitted to beat or rape their wives (but not to kill them), and parents to beat their children but not to kill them or sell them into slavery, although both the latter were permitted by ancient Roman law. Hence, the image presented by the feminist critique of a private realm which by virtue of the public/private distinction is necessarily beyond the public's purview is quite false. The public political voice may decide that behaviour previously permitted in the 'private realm' is no longer acceptable and thus change the law. It could not do this, if it were never allowed to take a view on what is going on in that realm in the first place. The public/private distinction contributes nothing by itself to the determination of what should or should not be permissible. This must be done by reference to other principles. Hence, it is pointless for feminists to attack the public/private distinction unless their aim is to abolish all private choice and make all choices public political ones, which does not seem to be their intention.

It may be said that these arguments fail to deal with the notion of a right to privacy. This is not just a right to make private choices but a right to a life in private that is beyond the prying eyes and inquisitive questions of outsiders. But while the right to privacy is no doubt a very important right, it can no more exclude all public political concern with what goes on in the privacy of the home, as though the right entitled one to commit murder, abuse one's children and take dangerous drugs, than the notion of a private choice can. In other words, together with the notion of a realm of privacy, one needs the idea of legitimate public political judgements as to what one may or may not be permitted to do in it.

Nevertheless, some feminists might still want to say that insofar as the public/private distinction includes the domestic sphere and this is the sphere of women, and even though the domestic sphere is subject to public political constraints on what is permitted in it, the whole scheme is still discriminatory because it prioritizes men's public concerns over women's private ones. However, what is at fault here is not liberalism but primordial patriarchal family structures. Furthermore, while it is true that liberalism, when first developing, simply applied its principles to men (actually, not even to all men) leaving the patriarchal structure of the family untouched, this attitude has been completely abandoned in the course of the nineteenth and twentieth centuries, as is clearly evidenced by CEDAW itself. The ideal of contemporary liberalism is for men and women to enjoy equal opportunities and share equal duties in both public and domestic spheres. Thus, when Susan Okin argues that the public/private distinction leads to the assumption that the rights-bearer is the head of a household, who is male, and that one of his rights is the right of privacy in his personal and family life, and that this assumption places serious difficulties in the way of protecting the rights of women and children, she is blaming liberal ideas for what are in reality patriarchal traditions.[49] It is not liberalism that is responsible for the assumption that there must be a single head of household who is necessarily male. The public/private distinction is perfectly compatible with each member of the family having an individual right to privacy and for the parents to be jointly and equally responsible for the private affairs of the household. Let us now shift the focus of the discussion to the idea of the equal rights of men and women.

The critique of equal rights and the focus on CP rights

Some criticisms of the principle of equal rights for men and women, as elaborated in CEDAW, hold that the idea of rights in itself and the ideal of equality of rights are essentially male legal and ethical constructs that are inappropriate for women. We will discuss these in the next section on difference feminism. Here we will concentrate on claims about the inadequacy of the formal conception of equal CP rights. The standard criticism is that the notion of equal rights fails to take account of the imbalances of power between men and women. This makes equality of rights not a real equality but a purely formal one. Underneath the umbrella of formal equality, men rule.[50]

This type of criticism can be, and was in fact first, applied to relations between men or between classes of men (as by Karl Marx and many others). The liberal answer has been, firstly, to acknowledge that the reality of equal rights does require that everyone attain a minimum level of welfare in terms of education, health and income to enable them to exercise their formal rights and make responsible choices for their lives. Secondly, for liberals equality does not standardly mean an absolute equality in power and wealth: a self-defeating political goal. It means rather that everyone has the capacity and should have the right to make their own decisions regarding their basic interests in job, sexual partner, religion and associates and to participate in collective decision making on public matters. Inequality of political power may still be a threat to individual rights but such threats are to be dealt with by institutional and legal checks on abuses of power and the vigilance of people in defence of their rights.

This liberal response reveals the hollowness of another criticism (to be found in Charlesworth and Chinkin[51]), namely that equality of rights prioritizes CP rights over ESC rights. Since the major forms of women's oppression take place in the economic, social and cultural spheres, such prioritization effectively subordinates women's interests and opportunities to men's. It is also claimed that in practice the international community has focused on the promotion of CP rights rather than ESC rights.[52] However, as we have argued above, such prioritization is not justified in liberal theory, nor is it justified by the UN's understanding of the relations between types of rights. It may not even be true that in practice the international community has given more attention to CP rights than to ESC ones, if we take into account the huge quantities of development aid and assistance that has been transferred to developing countries.[53] All that can be said truly is that it is easier to give some precision to universal rules regarding CP rights than it is in the case of ESC rights but this on its own hardly justifies the feminist criticism on this issue.

The principle of equal rights as applied to women has, of course, to deal with the question of the differential roles of men and women in the family and household. If women are in practice the primary child-carers and household managers, then these roles may substantially affect their equal opportunities even if the ESC rights are as good as they could be. There are two ways out of this problem (or some admixture of the two): one is to bring it about that men share family and household responsibilities equally with their partners; the other is to ensure that through nursery provision women have the real option of staying at home to care for their children or pursuing their careers in the non-domestic realm. If they genuinely choose the former when they have the real opportunity for the latter, then their being at home is not imposed on them but is a result of their responsible choice as to how they wish to live their lives. Whatever the difficulties on this issue, once again they are not the fault of the notion of equal rights for men and women but the result of problems in approaching its full realization.

Difference feminism and liberalism as a male system of values

Difference feminism was originally based on the view that men and women have different (if not necessarily fixed) natures and that these

different natures are the basis for men and women having fundamentally different interests and ethical conceptions. A standard view
of this difference is that women's identity is more closely tied to
emotions, feelings and bodily senses and expresses itself typically in
an ethics of care and love, while men's is focused on rationality,
abstraction and impersonality and is typically expressed in concepts of
law and rights. Modern state law and the notion of the sovereign state
articulate a male point of view. This law 'constructs the legal subject
as a rational individual in control of its cognitive capacities, inhabiting
a public sphere and abstracted from affective ties.[54] The notion of
individual rights in modern law as protecting individual choices over
goods and activities is a typical male one, while women's ethical
concerns are realized in relationships and through collective goods.

Difference feminism contains a conception of men and women that
was used for millennia as the basis for women's subordination to men
and their exclusion from the public political realm. Women are too
emotional, insufficiently rational and incapable of achieving the
standpoint of impersonal law. Of course, the feminists are using these
traditional differentiations in a context in which it is assumed by both
parties that justice requires equal respect. Given their different natures,
equal respect for women cannot involve subjecting them to forms of
life that are alien to them.[55]

It might seem that a social and political order that combines rights
with welfare and fosters personal relationships and emotional fulfilment within the structures of the modern state and its law would
constitute a viable combination of the two points of view and types of
values. Difference feminism would, then, only become the basis for a
criticism of rights if such a combination was still held to establish an
unjust subordination of women's interests to those of men and that the
ideal of rights had to be sacrificed in part or in whole to accommodate
the equal worth, or indeed superior standing, of feminine values.

Let us assume that there is a significant divergence between men and
women's natures along the lines suggested. This must be a difference
in the degree to which the 'masculine' and 'feminine' elements are
combined in human beings. It is surely absurd to suppose that women
are wholly without the capacity for rationality and abstraction and
have no interest in law, rights or entitlements. Equally absurd would
be to suppose that men have no emotions or feelings, do not care for
or love others and have no concern for collective goods. Of course, as

many have emphasized, these notions of the masculine and the feminine are to some degree social constructs that can be modified. Some writers even take the view that they are wholly social constructs and that there exist no essential natures of men and women or indeed of human being. However, it is difficult to see how any meaningful feminism can be based on such a view. If men's and women's 'natures' are socially constructed all the way down, then what is the 'woman' to whom injustice is being done by modern state liberalism?

Assuming, then, that there is a difference between the sexes and that it consists in a different balance between the emotional and rational capacities of individuals, the issue becomes whether women in respect of their rational and autonomous nature have an interest in rights and law. Similarly, the issue is whether men as in part emotional beings have an interest in personal relationships and collective goods. It seems to us that it would be wholly ridiculous to deny the existence of such interests. The problem, then, becomes whether within the system of rights characteristic of liberal society, the emotional needs and caring ethical dispositions of both women and men can be fulfilled.

In the first place, rights in no way exclude personal relationships of love and friendship. That there exists a basic framework of rights within which such relationships are carried on sets legal limits to the degree of oppression or exploitation that is possible within them but does not otherwise interfere with the relationship. If love and friendship are in trouble in contemporary liberal society, it is not because of the existence of a system of rights but more probably because of the hyperactivity of the modern world and the shallowness of many of its values.

In the second place, there are many professions in which care for others is still (or should be) a central concern, such as the medical, social work and teaching professions, not to speak of the huge range of charitable organizations. If they are increasingly subject to minute and bureaucratic regulation in some Western countries that drives out all the pleasure from the primary activity, this is not the fault of the notion of rights but of an excessive pursuit of accountability.

In the third place, the ethics of concern has already captured the public political sphere in the form of welfare liberalism. The attempt to expand this ethic in the public sphere to all activities by eliminating individual liberty rights is collectivist socialism, which is surely now generally accepted as an unmitigated disaster. Welfare liberalism expresses a collectivized concern for others and is far removed from the personal level of ethics that, it is suggested, women are most at home in. Yet, there is no reason why personal as well as general ethical concerns cannot be satisfied in liberal society.

Finally, some account has to be given by difference feminists as to the terms on which men and women are to live together if the terms are not to be liberal ones. Here, they tend to assimilate women's interests to those of cultural minorities and propose a type of polity in which all such groups are directly represented and required to negotiate *ad hoc* settlements with each other. Since such agreements will not be based on any common principles, they will be forms of *modus vivendi* based on relative power for which there seems to be little to be said from an ethical point of view.[56]

Conclusion

We believe, then, that the feminist critique of the liberal character of CEDAW, of international law and international human rights instruments generally, is seriously misconceived. The problem does not lie with the public/private distinction, the gender bias of liberalism, its abstract character or liberalism's being out of touch with the realities of power. The problem is one of the effective implementation across the world of the rights of women affirmed in these documents. But this is not a problem that is peculiar to women's international human rights. It affects the whole UN programme. The next chapter discusses what is actually being done to give effect to these rights and what might be done to improve the situation.

8 | The implementation of international human rights

In the preceding chapters of Part II we have described and analysed the main human rights that the international community, by and large, and through the auspices of the UN, has agreed that human beings and peoples have. On the face of it, this agreement constitutes an international consensus on liberal human rights. However, despite this apparent agreement on basic human rights, there are serious problems with their implementation. There are, of course, the difficulties in realizing socio-economic rights in poorer countries, which we have discussed in detail in Chapter 6 and will not return to in this one. Here our main concern is with the failure of many states, other organizations and individuals to abide by their commitments to respect and promote civil and political rights.

The UN organs responsible for implementation of human rights

There exists a large number of UN bodies with human rights responsibilities. Many of these are *ad hoc* and overlapping entities and procedures and most commentators agree that this development has not been sensible or helpful to the cause of human rights and that it needs substantial rationalization. We do not discuss what form this rationalization should take here; what we do is outline the most important of these institutions, regulations and agreements and their effectiveness.

As noted in Chapter 4, Article 1 of the UN Charter sets out the purposes for which the UN is established. These include the promotion and encouragement of 'respect for human rights and fundamental freedoms for all without distinction as to race, sex, language or religion'. Of the principal UN bodies, the two that are of main interest to us are the General Assembly (GA) and Economic and Social Council (ECOSOC), both of which possess independent powers to pursue 'the promotion and encouragement' of human rights issues. The General

Assembly has the power (i) to promote universal respect for, and observance of, human rights;[1] and (ii) to initiate studies and make recommendations regarding human rights.[2] The Economic and Social Council has the power to make recommendations on human rights; and to draft conventions.[3] Furthermore, the Council is called upon by Article 68 of the Charter to 'set up commissions in economic and social fields and for the promotion of human rights, and such other commissions as may be required for the performance of its functions'. Let us look at both of these bodies in more detail.

The UN General Assembly

The General Assembly is subdivided into six committees. Issues are typically discussed briefly by the entire General Assembly (during its annual regular sessions from September to December), and they are then referred to one of the committees for discussion, as appropriate. The most relevant committee for our purposes is the third committee (social, humanitarian and cultural). An important part of this committee's work focuses on the examination of human rights questions, including reports of the special procedures of the newly established Human Rights Council (see below).

The General Assembly has also established a set of subsidiary committees and organs concerned with special issues. Its most important creation in the human rights field is undoubtedly the post of *High Commissioner for Human Rights* (HCHR) in 1993. The High Commissioner heads the Office of the High Commissioner for Human Rights (OHCHR) and is the principal United Nations official responsible for United Nations human rights activities. The Office has the broad mandate to prevent human rights violations, secure respect for all human rights, promote international co-operation to protect human rights, co-ordinate related activities throughout the United Nations, and strengthen and streamline the United Nations' system in the field of human rights. In addition to its mandated responsibilities, the Office leads efforts to integrate a human rights approach within all work carried out by United Nations agencies.

The Economic and Social Council

The Economic and Social Council (ECOSOC) is a UN body established by Chapter 10 of the UN Charter. It has fifty-four member states elected annually for three-year terms by the General Assembly. The Council undertakes investigations of international economic and social questions and reports its conclusions and suggestions to the General Assembly and other organs of the United Nations for action.

The most important body responsible for human rights within the Economic and Social Council was until recently the Commission for Human Rights, now replaced by the Human Rights Council. In fact, the Commission became the main UN human rights organ (apart from the General Assembly) and ECOSOC served as a rubber stamp to its decisions. The Commission spawned a Sub-Commission which then created a system of special rapporteurs and working groups with mandates to find out the facts and make recommendations on a variety of issues or countries. At the same time, the Commission itself also produced working groups directly responsible to it. This array of entities dealing with human rights can be totally confusing and cries out, as already stated, for rationalization. The section below looks in detail at the Commission and its successor, the Human Rights Council.

Commission on Human Rights

The Commission has become a forum in which governments defend their record [sic] rather than examine them. After rejecting the system for a long time, repressive regimes have understood that the best way to protect themselves against any examination is to take part in it. So they participate more and more actively in the commission's work and combine efforts to better undermine it from the inside. Rwanda's Hutu regime, for example, was preparing the Tutsi genocide in 1994 at the same time as it got itself elected to the commission and to the UN SC. When the Mugabe regime in Zimbabwe was riding roughshod over the most fundamental rights in 2002, it not only managed to avoid a vote on a resolution about this, but it also succeeded in getting elected to the commission for 2003 thanks to the connivance of other dictatorial countries.[4]

Before its replacement in 2006 by the Human Rights Council, the Commission on Human Rights (CHR) had fifty-three members, who served for three-year terms and who were elected by the Economic and Social Council. The fifty-three seats were distributed as follows: African States: fifteen; Asian States: twelve; Eastern European States: five; Latin American and Caribbean States: eleven; Western Europe and other States: ten. Members served as representatives of governments and for the most part were not experts in the field.

The Commission met once a year for a six-week session when it issued resolutions and decisions. Its reports were usually hundreds of pages long, and besides the fifty-three members, several other states participated in their annual sessions as observers, as well as several international agencies, national liberation movements and non-governmental organizations with consultative status (overall thousands of delegates).

As already mentioned, the Commission was assisted by the Sub-Commission on the Promotion and Protection of Human Rights, individual experts, representatives, and special rapporteurs. After 1993, it was also assisted by the Office of the High Commissioner for Human Rights, which provided most of the administrative and substantive support needed for Commission meetings (including producing reports to support the Special Procedures and processing the Resolution 1503 complaints, both of which we discuss below). The UN High Commissioner for Human Rights (HCHR) played an active role, seeking to guide the work of the Commission from a perspective divorced from national political interests. This was because, while the Commission was fundamentally a meeting of government officials lasting six weeks, the Office of the High Commissioner on Human Rights is a permanent UN agency, and the High Commissioner on Human Rights is an individual appointed by the Secretary-General to determine how to ensure that human rights are adequately integrated into all of the UN's many functions.

The chief purpose of the annual meeting of the Commission was to determine the human rights agenda of the UN, mainly through writing, debating and passing resolutions. After 1967 these resolutions generally either condemned or praised activity in a certain field of human rights, cited specific countries as violators of human rights, and established mandates or working groups for the further study of other human rights concerns. Activities that extended beyond the Commission's annual six-week meeting were called Special Procedures.

Because of its high profile (in spite of its incompetence except in the immediate post-WWII period), it is worthwhile to have a closer look at the evolution of the Commission from 1946 till 2006, when it was replaced by the Human Rights Council.

1946–1967

The Commission was given a very broad mandate. It had the power to:

- formulate an international bill of rights;
- formulate recommendations for international conventions on human rights;
- protect minorities;
- prevent discrimination on grounds of race, sex, language or religion; and
- consider any other matter regarding human rights not covered by the above list of responsibilities.

Despite this broad mandate, till the late 1960s the Commission concentrated uniquely on its standard-setting role, claiming that it had no authority to act on the complaints of human rights violations that were directed towards it;[5] in other words, denying that there was any right of petition to it in respect of violations of human rights. The result of this claim was that while its standard-setting role was impressive and contributed to the cause of human rights everywhere, the Commission did nothing for the individual victims of human rights violations who had been sending petitions to it for its consideration since the inception of the UN. While complaints to the UN of human rights violations would be sent to the Secretary-General and forwarded by him to the Commission, information about the identity of the petitioners was removed and no action of any kind was taken by the Commission.[6] For those victims, indeed, the Commission represented 'the world's most elaborate waste-paper basket'.[7]

The Commission's decision to interpret its mandate as simply a drafting body for the General Assembly was, partly, based on a desire to avoid political controversy: in particular, to avoid getting involved in the Cold War and the apartheid and decolonization issues, so as to concentrate on producing an effective statement of human rights. The political issues were left to the General Assembly, which, as we have seen, set up its own committees concerned with apartheid, decolonization, and so on.

The main reason for the Commission's inaction was, however, the fact that for a long time the political will on the part of most of the member states to address the question of actual violations of human rights was lacking. The Western states, which enjoyed a comfortable majority in the UN at that time prior to the substantial decolonization of the European empires, felt themselves vulnerable to human rights investigations: the US in respect of racial discrimination; and Britain, France, Portugal, Belgium and other colonial powers, in respect of their treatment of their colonial subjects. At the same time, the communist bloc did not want an investigation into communist terror. So in effect an unholy alliance between the US racists, the European colonialists and the Stalinist terrorists defeated all attempts to get an effective precedent established.

1967–2006

After 1967, the Commission changed its approach to individual petitions on violations of human rights, accepting that it had a mandate to examine them. The main reasons for the change in its approach were:

- the enlargement of the Committee and the rise to a majority position in the UN of the Third World, both in the Committee and the General Assembly, together with the decision of the Third World countries that a more active human rights policy would be useful in the struggle against the racist regimes in Southern Africa and against the remnants of colonialism elsewhere;
- the US government's commitment around this time to an effective civil rights programme for its fifteen million black citizens; and
- a precedent being set by the adoption of a complaints procedure for two recent Treaty Conventions on human rights: the CERD (Racial Discrimination) in 1965 and the ICCPR in 1966. Both these conventions specifically allowed for individual and organizational complaints against state members of these conventions to be heard by committees set up for this purpose.

As a result of these moves, the General Assembly asked the Commission to give urgent consideration to ways and means of improving the capacity of the UN to put a stop to violations of human rights wherever they might occur, in other words, to the introduction of a general complaints procedure in respect of human rights. In fact, the Third World states only intended that the procedure should be directed at racist and colonialist states; but it was recognized that the arbitrary restriction of the procedures to only these abuses would be untenable.

In 1967 and 1970, ECOSOC adopted two new (permanent) procedures for the Commission. The so-called 1235 procedure of 1967 allowed the Commission to engage in public debate of gross human rights violations and to recommend to ECOSOC the condemnation of the responsible state. Such a resolution would seriously affect the prestige of that state. Under Resolution 1503, introduced in 1970, the Commission could investigate a consistent pattern of gross human rights violations such as genocide, apartheid, racial or ethnic discrimination, torture, imprisonment without trial on a mass scale, forced mass migrations. However, the sessions were held in private and the procedure was extremely slow and easily frustrated by repressive governments.

Predictably, the first countries to be subject to the new procedures were racist South Africa, Israel in respect of the occupied territories and the US-backed anti-communist Chilean government under Pinochet. Attempts to nominate Third World non-colonial, non-racist or non-right-wing states for investigation led to uproar and inaction. This was in effect the reason why as late as 1976–7 the Commission on Human Rights succeeded in completely ignoring publicly the massive horrors of the Pol Pot regime in Cambodia, the Idi Amin regime in Uganda, the Bokassa regime in the Central African Empire and the military regimes in Argentina and Uruguay. However, after 1979, under pressure from informed public opinion – and thanks to the high profile given to human rights issues by the US government under President Carter – the Commission began to be more even-handed and it discussed and condemned Nicaragua, Guatemala, and Equatorial Guinea.

The Commission also established a Special Procedures system of special rapporteurs or experts. These experts have been employed in two different contexts:

1. on fact-finding missions concerned with the state of human rights in a given state by an independent expert or group of experts for the purpose of gathering information vital to the 1503 or 1235 procedures;
2. on a thematic mandate allowing for the investigation of problems caused by human rights violations on a global scale, e.g. the rights of women. Working Groups (a group of experts) and/or special rapporteurs (individual experts) were chosen for these purposes. People appointed to the Special Procedures served in their personal capacity and not as representatives of their country.[8]

Finally, the Commission set up an Advisory Services organization to assist states in educating and training their personnel in the observance of human rights.

Unfortunately, none of these measures was able to make the Commission as effective as desired, mainly because of the presence of major human rights violators on the Commission and the politicization of the body. As the quote above made clear, during the years following the establishment of its Special Procedures until its extinction, the Commission became increasingly discredited, among activists and governments alike, for the membership on the Commission of countries such as Algeria, Syria, Libya and Vietnam, and more recently, China, Cuba, Zimbabwe, Russia, Saudi Arabia and Pakistan. These countries had extensive records of human rights violations, and were able to vote down resolutions condemning the violators. An example of such cynical abuse of the Commission was the election to the Commission in 2004 of Sudan while it was engaged in the massive ethnic cleansing and massacre of the inhabitants of its Darfur region.

In concluding his assessment of the Commission's procedures Alston says that it is difficult to accept that after half a century of concerted efforts, the principal UN procedures for responding to violations of human rights were quite as embryonic, marginally effective and unevenly applied as they were.[9]

The Human Rights Council

As we just saw, the Commission on Human Rights came under intense criticism because it had allowed some of the world's worst human rights abusers to sit as members. Accordingly, and after much discussion, the Commission was replaced on 19 June 2006 by the Human Rights Council (HRC), which assumed all its mandates, mechanisms, functions and responsibilities, including the Sub-Commission on the Promotion and Protection of Human Rights.[10] As many as 170 states voted for the Resolution replacing the Commission; four states voted against (the US, Israel, the Marshall Islands and Palau); Belarus, Iran and Venezuela abstained.

According to the Office of the United Nations High Commissioner for Human Rights, the main differences between the Commission and the Council are as follows:[11]

- In the UN 'organizational chart', the Commission fell under the Economic and Social Council, while the Council is a subsidiary organ of the General Assembly – an 'upscaling' of the status of human rights. Advocates of the Council hope that within five years it will rise further to become a principal organ of the UN alongside, among other bodies, the General Assembly, the Economic and Social Council and the Security Council.
- The Council meets in Geneva at least three times a year (including an annual main session) for a total of at least ten weeks. It also has the capacity to convene extra sessions as needed to address 'gross and systematic violations' of human rights more quickly than the Commission could, since it only met annually for one six-week session.
- The Council has forty-seven members only: thirteen from Africa, thirteen from Asia, six from eastern Europe, eight from Latin America and the Caribbean, and seven from a block of western Europe and other countries that includes Canada and the United States. Despite being smaller, the Council gives two more member seats to Asia and Eastern Europe, while cutting the representation from Western Europe and other countries (like Canada and the US) from ten to seven.
- Under the new system, a simple majority of all of the assembly's 191 member countries is required for admission, not just a majority of the countries that actually vote. The admission vote is carried out by secret ballot.
- The Council will carry out reviews 'on a periodic basis' of the human rights records of all countries in the General Assembly. Serious violators could be suspended from the council by a two-thirds vote in the General Assembly. Supporters say this will prevent countries from using their membership to shield themselves from censure. (There was no review process at all in the old UN Human Rights Commission.)

Nonetheless, the Council has been criticized mainly on the ground that the membership rules for the new UN Human Rights Council are not tough enough to ensure that rights violators will not get a seat. The US, for example (which voted against the Resolution establishing the Council), wanted members to be elected by a two-thirds majority (as the previous Secretary-General, Kofi Annan, had also wanted), rather than a simple majority. It also wanted any country under UN sanction to be explicitly prevented from joining the Council. But the initial proposals were watered down in subsequent politicking. The Council's procedures only call for members to 'take into account' the candidate member's human rights record.

While a number of countries – including Canada and the EU – and some human rights groups – such as Amnesty International – shared some of Washington's misgivings with the new Council, they ended up voting in favour, believing that the whole effort to reform the UN's human rights body might be scuttled if members agreed to reopen negotiations or postpone the vote. The UN High Commissioner for Human Rights – the former Canadian Supreme Court Justice Louise Arbour – also strongly supported the new Human Rights Council. Arbour wrote in February 2005 that 'failure to adopt the proposal threatens to set back the human rights cause immeasurably'.[12] She acknowledged that the new body is not an ideal blueprint, but stated that 'there is no reason to believe that more negotiating time will yield a better result'.[13] In her view, the new council will 'deal more objectively, and credibly, with human rights violations worldwide'.[14]

We leave it to our readers to decide for themselves, with the benefit of hindsight in a few years' time, whether this view was unduly optimistic. As for us, we are not inclined to be sanguine in the matter. We can only hope, together with the Peggy Hicks from the Human Rights Watch, that:

the council's second year [and the years after that] should be much more than a continuation of its first disappointing 12 months ... Continuing to ignore grave human rights abuses in places like Burma and Somalia is unacceptable.[15]

Treaty-based committees

In addition to the human rights bodies examined above, there is a whole range of committees set up under the international conventions, covenants or treaties on human rights. These bodies are not strictly organs of the UN since their authority derives from treaties made directly by the state parties to them. However, the committees are serviced by the UN Secretariat, and report directly to the General Assembly. These are the Committee on Economic, Social and Cultural

Rights, the Human Rights Committee, the Committee Against Torture, the Committee on the Elimination of Racial Discrimination, the Committee on the Elimination of Discrimination against Women, the Committee on the Rights of the Child, and the Committee on Migrant Workers.

All these treaty-based committees are, unlike the Human Rights Council and its predecessor, the Commission on Human Rights, committees of independent experts and not politicians, although they are still appointed by the state parties to the Convention. Most commentators agree that, unlike the Commission (and, we fear, the Human Rights Council), the committees – in particular the Human Rights Committee – have proved a success and are performing a valuable and important role in the field of human rights procedures.

The main functions of the committees are as follows:

1. To meet their reporting obligations, states must submit an initial report usually one year after joining and then periodically in accordance with the provisions of the treaty (usually every four or five years). In addition to the government report, the treaty bodies may receive information on a country's human rights situation from other sources, including non-governmental organizations, UN agencies, other intergovernmental organizations, academic institutions and the press. In the light of all the information available, the committee examines the report together with the government's representative. Based on this 'dialogue', the committee publishes its concerns and recommendations, referred to as 'concluding observations'.
2. Some of the treaty bodies may perform additional monitoring functions through three other mechanisms: the inquiry procedure, the examination of inter-state complaints and the examination of individual complaints.

Looking at the latter: the Human Rights Committee, the Committee on the Elimination of Racial Discrimination, the Committee Against Torture and the Committee on the Elimination of Discrimination Against Women can, under certain conditions, receive petitions from individuals who claim that their rights under the treaties have been violated. The drafting of an optional protocol to the ICESCR to consider individual complaints concerning non-compliance with the Covenant is also presently in progress.[16]

Any individual may bring a complaint before the relevant committee, provided that the state has recognized the competence of the committee to receive such complaints; and provided that the individual has exhausted all available domestic remedies before petitioning. Complaints may also be brought by third parties on behalf of individuals provided they have given their written consent or where they are incapable of giving such consent.

Once a petition has been accepted by the committee, information on the issue is sought by the UN Secretary-General and this is laid before the Working Group on Communications which reports to the full committee whose final decision is communicated to the parties. In this way, the committees, in particular the Human Rights Committee, have developed a solid body of jurisprudence relating to specific rights found in the Covenant.

However, none of the committees is a court with the power of binding decisions. The committees have no sanctions in case of non-compliance with their judgement against a state for violation of the relevant treaty provisions.

The committees also publish their interpretation of the content of human rights provisions, known as general comments or 'general recommendations' on thematic issues, methods of work, or reporting duties of state parties with respect to certain provisions; and they suggest approaches to implementing treaty provisions.[17]

Regional regimes on human rights

From the beginning of the UN's concern with human rights, it was intended that the general UN regime should be supplemented by regional organizations.[18] There are three main regional conventions on human rights: the European, American and African. There is a barely functioning fourth one: that of the Commonwealth of Independent States. We will briefly outline the main characteristics of each of these conventions.

European Convention on Human Rights 1950

This convention, which is concerned solely with CP rights (although it can be interpreted in such a way as to protect indirectly some ESC rights that overlap with CP rights),[19] was drawn up within the Council of Europe[20] and entered into force in September 1953. One of the essential features of the system is the right of individual complaint (as well as of state complaint: this option has rarely been exercised).[21] Originally only recognized by three state parties, recognition of this right became compulsory for all state members since Protocol 11 came into force in 1988.[22] As a result, today natural and legal persons (e.g. companies), groups or non-governmental organizations have a real right of action at international level to insist on the rights and freedoms to which they are entitled under the Convention. Without doubt, this right of action represents the highest degree of protection of all international agreements.

The European Court of Human Rights, which receives the complaints, makes judgements that are binding on the respondent states concerned. In Article 46(1), the contracting parties have undertaken to 'abide by the final judgments of the Court in any case to which they are parties'. Under Article 41, the Court has the power to afford just satisfaction (compensation and/or costs and expenses) to the injured party, in cases of a violation of the Convention. However, the Court has no power to order the respondent state to take specific measures in order to remedy the violation found. This is unlike the Inter-American Court of Human Rights (analysed further below), which, 'may rule if appropriate that the consequences of the measure or situation which constituted the breach [of a provision of the Convention] be remedied'.[23]

The responsibility for supervising the execution (or implementation)[24] of judgements lies with the Committee of Ministers of the Council of Europe (Article 46(2)).[25] Once the Court's final judgement has been transmitted to the Committee, the latter invites the respondent state to inform it of the steps taken to pay any just satisfaction awarded as well as of any individual or general measures which may be necessary in order to comply with the state's legal obligation to abide by the judgement.

The Commission has found it 'extremely difficult' to assess the degree of successful compliance with the Court's judgements.[26] We have also been unable to get any general statistics on that compliance.[27] Part of the problem may be the insufficient resources devoted to such an assessment: the Department for the Execution of the Court's judgements had, in 2002, nine lawyers in all, responsible for monitoring hundreds of cases in forty-four countries.[28]

However, the general perception of the operation of the Convention is that there has been a high degree of compliance with the Court's judgements. This is probably due to the fact that, as the Venice Commission reports, execution of judgements requiring just satisfaction (under Article 41) has rarely raised concern. Interestingly, this includes Russia which nevertheless was singled out by the Parliamentary Assembly of the Council of Europe in a February 2007 report as one of the two member states least co-operative with the Court (the other one is Turkey).[29]

More serious concerns have been raised by the (non) execution of broader measures (under Art. 46 (1)), falling within the margin of appreciation of the states.[30] Broader measures include individual or general measures, that 'may be categorized, generally, as follows: need to amend a legal situation; need to take appropriate action in respect of agents of the States; need to encourage an appropriate interpretation of domestic legislation; need to reopen domestic proceedings'.[31] Individual measures are those adopted to put an end to any continuing violations, and to redress their adverse effects not offset by the just satisfaction awarded to the applicant. General measures are those adopted in order to avoid new similar violations of the Convention.[32]

To enforce these measures, there are a number of tools available to the Committee of Ministers. These are:

- peer pressure: the most important, according to the Commission;[33]
- publicity: in particular, the adoption of 'interim resolutions' to exercise pressure on the government concerned by making public the fact that the state has not yet executed the judgement;[34] and
- suspension: as a last resort remedy, the suspension or termination of a state's membership by the Committee of Ministers.[35]

In 2000, the Parliamentary Assembly (another component part of the Council of Europe besides the Committee of Ministers, composed of 630 members from the 47 national parliaments) recommended the introduction into the Convention of a system of 'astreintes' (fines for delays in the performance of a legal obligation).[36] The European Community Treaty had introduced such a mechanism of financial penalties in 1993, to help ensure execution by Member States of the judgements of the Court of Justice of the European Communities. The

Venice Commission did not support this recommendation, however, as it considered it insufficiently feasible.[37]

American Convention on Human Rights 1969

The American Convention on Human Rights was adopted in 1969 and entered into force in 1978, thirty years after the adoption in April 1948 of the American Declaration of Human Rights and Duties. The Declaration was the first international expression of human rights principles, preceding the Universal Declaration of Human Rights by eight months. It also was the outcome of a long history of regional co-operation, dating back to the nineteenth century. As the Organization of American States (OAS) describes:

In 1826, Simón Bolívar convened the Congress of Panama with the idea of creating an association of states in the hemisphere. In 1890, the First International Conference of American States, held in Washington, D.C., established the International Union of American Republics and its secretariat, the Commercial Bureau of the American Republics – the forerunner of the OAS. In 1910, this organization became the Pan American Union. In 1948, at the Ninth International American Conference, participants signed the OAS Charter and the American Declaration of the Rights and Duties of Man.[38]

The 1969 Convention has been ratified by twenty-five of the OAS's thirty-five states, but not by the USA and Canada.

The rights included in the Convention are mainly civil and political. However, the Protocol of San Salvador, ratified by thirteen states, covers ESC rights.

The bodies responsible for overseeing compliance with the Convention are the Inter-American Commission on Human Rights and the Inter-American Court of Human Rights.

The Inter-American Commission is a permanent body, which meets in ordinary and special sessions several times a year. Its members are elected by the General Assembly of the OAS. It has the principal function of promoting the observance and the defence of human rights. It does so through the investigation of individual petitions, the observation of general, and the study of specific, human rights situations in member states and the publication of reports on them, and the submission of unresolved cases to the Inter-American Court of Human

Rights. Furthermore, the Commission has authority to investigate cases involving parties still not parties to the American Convention on Human Rights. To those countries, the Commission applies the American Declaration of Human Rights and Duties.

The Court of Human Rights issues opinions on matters of legal interpretation of the Convention, to give more in-depth guidance about the provisions of the articles and how states might implement them. This is its consultative (or advisory) work. In its contentious work, the Court adjudicates cases brought before it, in which a state that has accepted its jurisdiction is accused of a human rights violation. Where the state concerned has not accepted the Court's jurisdiction, the case can only be brought before the Inter-American Commission.

In contrast to the European Court on Human Rights, only a state party or the Commission has the capacity to bring a case before the Court's jurisdiction. There is no individual right of petition; and no direct victim representation before the court. Individuals who believe that their rights have been violated must first lodge their cases with the Commission and have that body rule on their admissibility. If the case is ruled admissible and the state deemed at fault, the Commission may serve the state with a list of recommendations to make amends for the violation. Only if the state fails to abide by these recommendations, or if the Commission decides that the case is of particular importance or legal interest, will the case be referred to the Court.

In spite of this lack of individual standing, the record of the system is impressive in view of the Latin American history of political violence, dictatorships and the past lack of support for the Convention by the political organs of the OAS.[39] The few studies available in English on the Inter-American system indicate to what extent the Commission has challenged the gross and systematic human rights abuses in the region.[40] The main tools it has used are country reports and on-site visits, and both the Court and the Commission have had recourse to precautionary and provisional measures that allow them to intervene in urgent cases to protect the life or physical integrity of victims under threat. Most of these tools, as well as the above-mentioned (in the section on the European Convention on Human Rights) right to rule that the consequences of the measure which constituted the breach of a provision of the Convention be remedied, are quite unique to the Inter-American Human Rights system and its great strength.

If a state fails to comply with a decision, the Court may notify the OAS General Assembly.

Significantly, the Commission has recognized that the main cause of the abuse of human rights in the region is extreme poverty and acute inequality of income. In its Annual Report 1979–80, for example, it states:

> When examining the situation of human rights in the various countries, the Commission has had to establish the organic relationship between the violation of rights to physical safety on the one hand and neglect of social and economic rights and suppression of political participation on the other. That relationship, as has been shown, is in large measure one of cause and effect. In other words, neglect of economic and social rights, especially when political participation has been suppressed, produces the kind of social polarization that then leads to acts of terrorism by and against the government.

African Charter 1981

The African Charter on Human and Peoples' Rights came into force in 1986 and has now been ratified by over forty states. It covers ESC as well as CP rights and also so-called third generation rights (development, satisfactory environment) and duties to an individual's family and society, the state and other legally recognized communities and the international community. As the African Union Message on Africa Human Rights Day (21 October, the date the Charter came into force) says, the Charter 'draws inspiration from international human rights norms and African values'.[41]

Oversight and interpretation of the African Charter is the task of the African Commission on Human and Peoples' Rights, established in 1987. The Commission's functions are limited to examining state reports, considering communications alleging violations, and interpreting the Charter at the request of a state party, the African Union (which replaced the Organization of African Unity, OAU), or any organization recognized by the Union.

The limited role of the African Charter is of course due to the fact that at the time the OAU adopted the African Charter very few African States (such as Gambia, Senegal, and Botswana) possessed a democratic regime respectful of fundamental human rights. However, some advance of democracy in several African states in the late 1990s initiated calls for stronger domestic and regional guarantees for the protection of human rights.

Accordingly, a Protocol to the Charter was adopted in 1998, providing for the creation of an African Court on Human and Peoples' Rights (ACtHPR).[42] The Protocol came into effect in January 2004, after ratification by fifteen member states. While the statute of the African Court has not yet been promulgated and a seat for the Court has yet to be determined, the first judges to the Court were elected in January 2006.[43] The Court had its first meeting on July 2–5 2006.[44]

Under the Protocol, individuals (and, unusually, non-governmental organizations) may bring cases, if at the time of ratifying it the state in question has made a declaration accepting the jurisdiction of the Court.[45] Also uncommonly, the Protocol provides that actions may be brought on the basis of any instrument, including international human rights treaties, which have been ratified by the state party in question.[46] Furthermore, the Court can apply as sources of law any relevant human rights instrument ratified by the state in question, in addition to the African Charter.[47] In other words, the African Court could in theory become the judicial arm of a panoply of human rights conventions concluded under the aegis of the United Nations or of any other relevant legal instrument codifying human rights (e.g. the various conventions of humanitarian law, those adopted by the International Labour Organization, and even several environmental treaties). Very few of those agreements contain judicial mechanisms for ensuring their implementation; therefore, at least potentially, several African states could end up with a dispute settlement and implementation control system stronger than the one ordinarily provided for by those treaties for the rest of the world.[48] In reality, of course, the likelihood of an effective human rights regime developing in the member states in the near future is very small.

Commonwealth of Independent States Convention on Human Rights 1995

The Commonwealth of Independent States (CIS) is an association of sovereign states, comprising Russia and other former Soviet republics. It was established in 1991 to help facilitate the dissolution of the Soviet Union. Its functions are to co-ordinate its members' policies regarding their economies, foreign relations, defence, immigration, environment and law enforcement. It has not been a success and is viewed by most observers as largely irrelevant and powerless.

The CIS Convention on Human Rights, which opened for signature in 1995 and entered into force in 1998, has not fared much better.[49] There is a Commission with the responsibility to monitor the execution of the Convention by issuing recommendations.[50] But the Commission's members are appointed representatives of the state parties; hence, the Commission cannot offer the required guarantees of impartiality and independence. The CIS Convention may also clash with the European Convention on Human Rights; in particular, there are fears that even though the Commission's recommendations are not enforceable, the use of the CIS Convention may jeopardize the effective use of the right to submit individual applications to the European Court of Human Rights. For this reason, the Assembly recommended those Council of Europe member or applicant states which are also members of the CIS not to sign or ratify the CIS Convention on Human Rights; and those who have already ratified the Convention to issue a legally binding declaration confirming that the procedure set out in the European Convention on Human Rights shall not be in any way replaced or weakened through recourse to the procedure set out in the CIS Convention on Human Rights. It also asked member states of the CIS and of the Council of Europe to keep their citizens informed about the difference in the legal nature of the mechanism of the European Court of Human Rights and the mechanism of the CIS convention.[51]

International criminal justice: the enforcement revolution

At the beginning of the twenty-first century, we might say of our times, it was the age of human rights, it was the age of genocide and torture, it was the era of abundance, it was the era of hunger, it was the dawn of global justice, it was the enduring night of deprivation and abuse. (James J. Silk paraphrasing Charles Dickens in *A Tale of Two Cities*)[52]

We have just discussed conventions on human rights established around the world in the post-WWII era and the enforcement mechanisms attached to them. We now want to look at another, this time a post-Cold War, phenomenon: establishment of international criminal institutions aiming to prosecute those responsible for war crimes and crimes against humanity (in the hope that such institutions will contribute to general deterrence and hence enhance human rights protection). These institutions include special international criminal tribunals such as in Rwanda and Yugoslavia, special courts such as those in East Timor, Sierra Leone and Cambodia, and of course the International Criminal Court (ICC). While all these institutions are recent, the model for them was the special tribunals set up after WWII in Nuremberg and Tokyo to try the Nazi and Japanese leaders for war crimes and crimes against humanity.

In this section, due to the lack of space, we examine only the two special international tribunals and the ICC itself, not the special courts. We also investigate universal jurisdiction, another tool available to states to pursue human rights abusers.

International Criminal Tribunal for Yugoslavia

The International Criminal Tribunal for the former Yugoslavia (ICTY) is a body of the UN established in 1993 by Resolution 827 (1993) of the UN Security Council to prosecute war crimes in the former Yugoslavia. The context to the establishment of the Tribunal is important: it can be seen as 'a judicial experiment, set up . . . as an alternative to active military intervention in Bosnia'.[53] Hence, unlike its predecessors at Nuremberg and Tokyo, the Tribunal was set up to sit in judgement on crimes that were still taking place.

The Tribunal, that functions as an *ad-hoc* court and is located in The Hague,[54] has jurisdiction over certain types of crime committed on the territory of the former Yugoslavia since 1991: grave breaches of the 1949 Geneva Conventions, violations of the laws or customs of war, genocide, and crimes against humanity. It can try only individuals, not organizations or governments. The maximum sentence it can impose is life imprisonment.

The Tribunal has attracted special attention for prosecuting former Yugoslav president Slobodan Milošević. Other individuals holding high political and military office have also been indicted, with the last indictment issued March 15, 2004 (the Tribunal aims to complete all trials by the end of 2008 and all appeals by 2010). The fact that individuals have been held accountable for war crimes and other serious violations of international law, regardless of their position, together with the fleshing out of several other international criminal law concepts not ruled on at all or not since the Nuremberg Trials – such as torture, enslavement, the laws of war applicable in internal conflicts – is undoubtedly one of the successes of the Tribunal.[55]

However, a number of criticisms have also been levied against the Tribunal. Besides a number of procedural matters (length of the trials,[56] cost,[57] etc.), the main complaints have been that:

- The Tribunal was established by the UN Security Council instead of the UN General Assembly. This allowed Milošević, for example, to claim that the court had no legal authority as it had not been created on a broad enough international basis.
- Furthermore, the Tribunal was established under Chapter VII of the UN Charter. The relevant portion of the Charter reads 'the Security Council can take measures to maintain or restore international peace and security'. It can be disputed whether a tribunal could be legitimately considered a 'measure to maintain or restore international peace and security'.[58] If it could not, then the SC acted *ultra vires* and the establishment of the Tribunal would have been unlawful.
- Contrary to its claim of having advanced reconciliation in Yugoslavia, the ICTY is perceived by many as dispensing 'victor's justice'[59] and engaging in a 'politically motivated show trial'. An apparently disproportionately large number of indictees are Serbs, whereas there have been very few indictments resulting from crimes committed against Serbs.
- The Tribunal has not prosecuted the citizens of any North Atlantic Treaty Organization (NATO) countries as a result of NATO's involvement in the Kosovo conflict. The Federal Republic of Yugoslavia (FRY), which has since become Serbia and Montenegro, filed a 1999 complaint with the International Court of Justice (ICJ) alleging that NATO had illegally targeted civilian institutions and infringed upon Yugoslav sovereignty. The ICJ did not decide the matter until December 2004, when it denied its own jurisdiction over the case because the FRY was not a party to the ICJ statutes when it filed the complaint.

The appearance of bias is supported by the fact that most of the Tribunal's funding comes from discretionary spending by the large NATO countries through the United Nations; and that it is NATO and European Union forces in the former Yugoslavia that are responsible for apprehending war crimes suspects. As the NATO spokesman Jamie Shea said himself in a since then oft-quoted statement:

NATO countries are those that have provided the finance to set up the Tribunal, we are amongst the majority financiers ... we want to see war criminals brought to justice and I am certain that when Justice Arbour goes to Kosovo and looks at the facts she will be indicting people of Yugoslav nationality and I don't anticipate any others at this stage'.[60]

Since so many consider the ICTY to be a political court and the puppet of Anglo-American geo-political interests, it is unlikely that the ICTY's verdicts will ever be regarded as impartial.[61] However, the question we need to ask is to what extent will today's perception of the Tribunal as dispensing 'victor's justice' matter in the long run. The Nuremberg and Tokyo Tribunals were seen equally – or perhaps much more – as show trials or weapons of revenge wielded by occupying forces. Yet, with time, the principle they established gave rise to a rudimentary international criminal justice system. It is to be hoped that the same will happen with the Yugoslav Tribunal. It may come to be seen, through the principles it elaborated in particular through its landmark prosecution of Milošević – the first time a head of state has had to answer to an international court for crimes he may have committed while in office – as a stepping stone to a more just world based on the rule of law rather than the rule of force. Certainly, the tribunal has already served as 'the prototype for a wave of institutions that have established international justice as a fixture in world politics',[62] one such institution being the International Criminal Tribunal for Rwanda which we now examine.

International Criminal Tribunal For Rwanda

In November 1994, eighteen months after the international tribunal for the former Yugoslavia had been established, the Security Council adopted Resolution 955 (1994) creating the International Criminal Tribunal for Rwanda (ICTR).[63] According to some, this was 'an act of expiation for not having done anything to halt the genocide in ... [Rwanda] while it was happening'.[64] The Resolution established 'an international tribunal for the sole purpose of prosecuting persons responsible for genocide and other serious violations of international humanitarian law committed in the territory of Rwanda and Rwandan citizens responsible for genocide and other such violations committed in the territory of neighboring States'. The Statute of the Tribunal (located in Arusha, Tanzania) is based on the Statute of the International Criminal Tribunal for the former Yugoslavia; and it applies to the period between 1 January 1994 and 31 December 1994.

The first trial at the ICTR started in January 1997. As of April 2007, the tribunal has handed down twenty-seven judgements involving thirty-three accused (among whom one prime minister, six ministers and several others holding leadership positions during the events in 1994).[65]

When it comes to evaluation of the Tribunal, it is generally credited with having made important contributions to international criminal jurisprudence, in particular in the area of genocide and sexual violence.[66] Thus:

• The tribunal was the first ever international court to interpret the definition of genocide (Akayesu case, 1998);[67]
• The Tribunal also underscored the fact that rape and sexual violence may constitute genocide in the same way as any other act of serious bodily or mental harm, as long as such acts were committed with the intent to destroy a particular group targeted as such;
• The guilty plea and subsequent conviction of Jean Kambanda, former Prime Minister of Rwanda, set a number of precedents. This was the first time that an accused person acknowledged his guilt for the crime of genocide before an international criminal tribunal. It was also the first time that a head of government was convicted for the crime of genocide; and
• The 2003 ICTR 'Media Case' was the first judgement since the conviction of Julius Streicher at Nuremberg after WWII in which the role of the media was examined in the context of international criminal justice.

Another notable achievement of the Tribunal has been its success in obtaining international co-operation for the arrest of suspects and the appearance of witnesses. To date, over 200 prosecution and defence witnesses from Africa, Europe and America have testified.

The main criticisms of the Tribunal have centred around:

1. Its inability to process all the cases falling within its jurisdiction. While as mentioned above only 27 judgements involving 33 accused

were handed down by April 2007 (and only 72 suspects arrested so far), over 120,000 people are in custody awaiting trial; and it is estimated that it could take well over 100 years to process them all.[68]

2. (As in the case of the Yugoslav Tribunal) its perceived ethnic bias, in that it has failed to charge Tutsis suspected of killing Hutus in the 1994 genocide.

3. Expense. At an estimated cost of $1.03 billion by the end of 2007, many feel that the Tribunal has not delivered and that the money would have been more productively spent elsewhere (e.g. on social programmes inside Rwanda).

Unlike the Yugoslav Tribunal, there has, however, been relatively little questioning of the legitimacy of the Tribunal compared to the Yugoslav Tribunal. This is probably due to the absence of any great power involvement in the Rwandan conflict: the Security Council resolution establishing the Tribunal may appear hence more as international justice in operation and less Great Powers' justice.[69]

International Criminal Court

The International Criminal Court (ICC) is a product of a multilateral treaty, and is *not* part of the United Nations (unlike the ICTY and ICTR, created in response to specific situations and in existence for a limited time period). It is the first ever **permanent** international institution with jurisdiction to prosecute individuals responsible for the most serious crimes of international concern: genocide, crimes against humanity and war crimes.

The ICC is based in The Hague, the Netherlands, although it may also sit elsewhere. It was established by the Rome Statute of the International Criminal Court. In accordance with its terms, the Statute entered into force on 1 July 2002, once sixty states had become parties. As of November 2007, 105 countries have become parties to the Statute.[70] The US is one of the countries that have refused to become a party and we will discuss its position further below, after explaining the workings of the Court.

The Court has jurisdiction over individuals accused of the crimes of genocide, crimes against humanity and war crimes, including those directly responsible for committing the crimes as well as others who may be liable for the crimes (for example by aiding, abetting or otherwise assisting in the commission of a crime).[71] The latter group also includes military commanders or other superiors whose responsibility is defined in the Statute. The Statute explicitly denies immunity to heads of state, declaring that 'official capacity as a Head of State or Government ... shall in no case exempt a person from criminal responsibility'.[72] The Court will determine its jurisdiction over the crimes of aggression at a review conference in 2009.

The Court does not have universal jurisdiction. It may only exercise jurisdiction in the following cases:

- the accused is a **national of a state party** or a state otherwise accepting the jurisdiction of the Court; or
- the crime took place on the **territory of a state party** or a state otherwise accepting the jurisdiction of the Court; or
- the United Nations Security Council has referred the situation to the Prosecutor, irrespective of the nationality of the accused or the location of the crime.

The Court's jurisdiction is further limited to events taking place since 1 July 2002. In addition, if a state joins the Court after 1 July 2002, the Court only has jurisdiction after the Statute entered into force for that state. Such a state may nonetheless accept the jurisdiction of the Court for the period before the Statute's entry into force. However, in no case can the Court exercise jurisdiction over events before 1 July 2002.

Even where the Court has jurisdiction, it will not necessarily act. The important principle of **complementarity** provides that certain cases will be inadmissible even though the Court has jurisdiction. In general, a case will be inadmissible if it has been or is being investigated or prosecuted by a state with jurisdiction. However, a case may be admissible if the investigating or prosecuting state is unwilling or unable genuinely to carry out the investigation or prosecution.

A country may be 'unwilling' if it is clearly shielding someone from responsibility for ICC crimes. A country may be 'unable' when its legal system has collapsed. In addition, a case will be inadmissible if it is not of sufficient gravity to justify further action by the Court.

State parties or the United Nations Security Council may refer situations of crimes within the jurisdiction of the Court to the Prosecutor.[73] The Prosecutor evaluates the available information and commences an investigation unless they determine there is no reasonable basis to proceed.

The Prosecutor may also begin an investigation on their own initiative: but the investigation must be authorized by a Pre-Trial Chamber. On the application of the Prosecutor, the Chamber may issue a warrant of arrest or a summons to appear if there are reasonable grounds to believe a person has committed a crime within the jurisdiction of the Court. Once a wanted person has been surrendered to or voluntarily appears before the Court, the Pre-Trial Chamber holds a hearing to confirm the charges that will be the basis of the trial. Following the confirmation of charges, a case is assigned to a Trial Chamber of three judges.

The accused is presumed innocent until proven guilty beyond reasonable doubt by the Prosecutor. The accused has the right to conduct the defence in person or through a counsel of their choosing. Victims may also participate in proceedings directly or through their legal representatives.

Upon conclusion of the proceedings, the Trial Chamber issues its decision, acquitting or convicting the accused. If the accused is convicted, the Trial Chamber issues a sentence for a specified term of up to thirty years or, when justified by the extreme gravity of the crime and the individual circumstances of the convicted person, life imprisonment. The Trial Chamber may also order reparations to victims.

Throughout the pre-trial and trial phases, the accused, the Prosecutor or a concerned state may appeal decisions of the Chambers as specified by the Statute, as they may also do following the decision of the Trial Chamber. Legal representatives of victims, the convicted person or *bona fide* owners of adversely affected property may appeal reparations orders. All appeals are decided by the Appeals Chamber of five judges.

As the Court's web site points out,[74] in the few years since it was established, the Court has developed 'into a fully functioning institution'.[75] Four situations have now been referred to the Prosecutor, all dealing with grave crimes in Africa. Three state parties (Uganda, the Democratic Republic of the Congo and the Central African Republic) have referred situations occurring on their territories to the Court, and the Security Council, acting under Chapter VII of the United Nations Charter, has referred a situation on the territory of a non-state party (Darfur, Sudan). After analysing the referrals for jurisdiction and admissibility, the Prosecutor began investigations in all these four situations. Let us quickly look at each one of those.

Uganda

In July 2005, the Court issued the first arrest warrants for top-level members of the Lord's Resistance Army (LRA), including its leader Joseph Kony, who has been recruiting child soldiers for years and using them in a merciless war in northern Uganda. The warrant of arrest for Kony lists thirty-three counts of crimes against humanity and war crimes.[76] The ICC does not have the power of arrest; such arrests are the responsibility of state parties. It is unclear how the Ugandan government will proceed with respect to the arrest. Kony refuses to negotiate with it to end what has been termed one of Africa's most brutal wars (more than two million people displaced) unless the ICC drops its indictments. As a result, a number of Ugandans, including victims of the LRA, are increasingly dissatisfied with the ICC, which they say fails to respect their desire for traditional reconciliation and is undermining efforts for genuine peace in their country.

Democratic Republic Of The Congo (DRC)

In March 2006, Thomas Lubanga Dyilo was surrendered to the Court by the Congolese government after a February warrant for his arrest. Lubanga, a militia leader in the country's northeast, has been charged with committing war crimes under Article 8 of the Rome Statute of the International Criminal Court. The crimes, committed in the DRC since July 2002, included 'enlisting and conscripting children under the age of fifteen and using them to participate actively in hostilities'. Human rights organizations have expressed concern that Lubanga will not be tried for other war crimes, such as rape. The hostilities refer to a decade-old conflict that has claimed more than four million lives in the DRC and has been described as one of the most deadly conflicts since the end of WWII. According to the latest news at the time of writing this chapter (October 2007), the ICC judges favoured a mid-February 2008 start date for the Court's first-ever trial.

Central African Republic (CAR)

In May 2007, the ICC Prosecutor announced the opening of a fourth investigation into grave crimes allegedly committed in the CAR, with the peak of violence occurring in 2002 and 2003. The Prosecutor's announcement points to a focus on sexual violence, referring to hundreds of victims telling of rapes and other abuses committed 'with particular cruelty'. Significantly, in an earlier decision of April 2006, the highest criminal court (Cour de Cassation) of the Central African Republic partly rejected an appeal against a decision of the Bangui Court of Appeal of December 2004, which held that only the International Criminal Court was able to try the serious crimes committed in the CAR since 1 July 2002. The Cour de Cassation held that the CAR justice system was unable to carry out effective investigations and prosecutions. The Office of the Prosecutor of the ICC had previously stated that it was waiting for the decision of the Cour de Cassation to decide whether to open an investigation in CAR, on the basis of the complementarity principle contained in the Statute of Rome.[77]

Darfur, Sudan

The UN Security Council referred the issue of Darfur to the ICC in March 2005 in response to ongoing reports from UN experts and others about atrocities (such as torture, murder and rape) committed against civilians on a mass scale, in a conflict estimated to have caused 200,000 deaths and 2.5 million displacements.[78]

In April 2007, the Court issued arrest warrants against Ahmed Harun, Sudan's humanitarian affairs minister (and recently appointed head of a committee to investigate human rights violations in Sudan, to the horror of many human rights advocates, including those within governments) and a Janjaweed militia leader, Ali Kushayb (also known as Abdal-Rahman). The judges decided to request arrest warrants instead of summons to appear, since they considered that Harun and Kushayb would not appear voluntarily before the Court. The two men have been charged with fifty-one counts of war crimes and crimes against humanity. The Sudanese government refuses to hand them over (it had detained Kushayb but released him following 'lack of evidence against him' in October 2007), claiming that the charges are 'false'.[79] The government has been accusing the ICC of 'increasing politicization', and claiming that it would never surrender any of its citizens for prosecution abroad. 'If there are any crimes, the place (to handle them) is Sudan (by) the Sudanese judicial system', Sudan's Ambassador to the UN is reported as saying.[80] This is the same judicial system that saw one of the accused being appointed head of a committee to investigate human rights violations. No need to say any more about the likelihood of the two accused being brought to justice in Sudan ...

As we can see, all of these investigations are of African countries. The main reason for this is that the prosecutor of the ICC has encouraged self-referrals; and only African countries have made them. Some international law experts also claim that it is the weakness of Africa's national legal systems that has led individual countries to refer situations to the ICC. Indeed, most African states have yet to implement the Rome Statutes in their domestic legislation, the first step toward retaining domestic jurisdiction for state parties to the Statute. As Olympia Bekou and Sangeeta Shah point out, 'strengthening domestic prosecutions so that the ICC does not have to intervene should be the ultimate goal of every state'.[81] Others say that despite the need for Africa to strengthen its domestic judiciaries, the continent is showing its commitment to international criminal justice; and that the African referrals to the ICC show 'the resolve the African governments have to say that impunity must end'.[82]

The position of the US
What is the US position on the ICC? Even though originally a supporter of the ICC, the US never ratified the ICC Statute because of the fear of the Republican administration under Bush that the ICC would be used for politically motivated prosecutions of US personnel abroad. This fear supposes that the officials of the Court would be unable to achieve the degree of impartiality that is absolutely necessary if the institution is to survive and flourish. It also ignores the principle of complementarity, which ensures that the United States itself would have the prior right to investigate and prosecute any US personnel accused of international crimes. Many question indeed whether the US is not more worried by the possibility of prosecutions arising from its record on the recent use of torture in Iraq, Afghanistan, Guantanamo and the processes of extraordinary rendition.

More recently, however, the US seems to be softening its stance on the Court. When the Security Council voted to refer the issue of Darfur to the ICC in March 2005, for example, the United States abstained rather than vetoing the referral. This meant that the United States, which, prior to 2005, had been engaged in a long-running effort to create a 'hybrid' UN–African Union Court to try Sudanese war criminals, moved 'from a posture of active opposition to the

very existence of the court to a position much closer to ...
acquiescence in the court's existence even though it had problems with
its conception'.[83] The United States even set up a formal channel of
communication between the State Department and the ICC to work
on Darfur (headed by the State Department's legal adviser, John
Bellinger II).[84]

The US also appears to have relaxed sanctions imposed on ICC
member countries that have refused to sign agreements with the United
States to forbid ICC prosecutions of Americans on their territory.[85]
For example, it was widely reported in the papers in late December
2006 that US military training programmes in many countries that
had been suspended because of their refusal to sign the agreements
were restored because the Pentagon concluded that the restrictions
were undermining efforts to combat terrorist threats.[86]

International criminal institutions assessed

What can we conclude on balance about international criminal
institutions?

It is clear that the establishment of these institutions – independently
of how presently inefficient and partial they may be – indicates a very
important recent development in the international community: an
increasing intolerance for the impunity of those individuals who commit crimes such as genocide and crimes against humanity. And it is as
clear that, without that intolerance and without the ability to pursue
individual accountability, an international human rights regime could
never be truly implemented. The international criminal institutions are
hence a necessary part of the human rights (or liberal) project.

However, it is also clear that, like any national institutions, the international legal institutions must be based on the rule of law and legitimacy. Most importantly, they must be seen as unbiased and just. This
is not the case: certainly not yet. It is to be hoped that this will happen,
and that the ICC in particular will be able to overcome these problems
of perception, as it expands (as of November 2007, it had 105 member
states), and as hostility towards it of states such as the US diminishes.

But of course international criminal institutions, no matter how
effective and fair, can never be the full panacea. They have to be supplemented by strong national courts (and possibly some kind of hybrids,
such as the Sierra Leone or Cambodian courts which unfortunately we
have no space to cover in our book). As acknowledged by the ICC

Statute with its complementarity principle, national courts ought to be the primary forum for dispensation of criminal justice. This is because, besides the problems mentioned above of legitimacy, etc., international courts cannot deal with the numbers of possible offenders alone; neither do they have universal jurisdiction. They are only applicable to state parties and for the period specified in their Statute.

National courts on the other hand, besides domestic jurisdiction over crimes committed within their territory or by their nationals, have another tool at their disposal to end impunity for gross violations of human rights: the exercise of so-called universal jurisdiction.

Universal jurisdiction

The principle of universal jurisdiction is the principle that national courts have the power (and duty) to try certain international crimes, irrespective of where they occurred and who they were committed by: crimes so grave and on such a scale that they can be seen as an attack on the international legal order, and their perpetrators as enemies of all mankind (*hostes humani generis*).[87]

In practice, the principle has allowed the prosecution of one country's officials by a second country for offences occurring on the territory or against the citizens of a third country. It is hence 'an exception to the general rule that a country must have some connection to conduct in order to regulate that conduct'.[88] Universal jurisdiction allows indeed a state to prosecute an individual in its courts where none of the traditional bases for jurisdiction (i.e. territorial, nationality, passive personality, or protective) exists.[89]

The principle of universal jurisdiction emerged as a customary international law norm with respect to the crime of piracy, possibly already from the seventeenth century.[90] The rationale behind it was that piracy was an egregious crime – violating a *jus cogens* norm of prohibition of piracy – that no jurisdiction could effectively prosecute because acts of piracy are committed on the high seas belonging to no state.[91] With the advent of international humanitarian and human rights law, the universal jurisdiction principle extended, first to other *jus cogens* crimes, then through treaties to lesser crimes than *jus cogens* (for example hostage-taking and hijacking).[92]

This extension created two main problems, however.

One is that there is no general agreement on what international crimes are covered by the universal jurisdiction principle derived from customary international law (rather than treaty law such as the Geneva Conventions 1949,[93] or Torture Convention 1987).[94] Many (probably the majority of) international lawyers would include among international crimes of universal jurisdiction, 'genocide, torture, war crimes, piracy, crimes against humanity and, less certainly, hostage-taking and hijacking'.[95] Others disagree. Higgins, for example, holds that beside piracy and slavery, the only other such offences are 'war crimes, crimes against peace and crimes against humanity committed immediately before or during war'.[96] Hence, the case of piracy and slavery apart, Higgins is limiting the application of the principle to the innovations established by the Nuremberg War Crimes Tribunals and subsequently endorsed by UN General Assembly resolutions.[97] If there is such disagreement amongst international law scholars, how can national judges – mostly untrained in international law – interpret what conduct is subject to universal jurisdiction, and ensure that prosecutions are not politically motivated?

The second problem posed by the extension of the principle of jurisdiction to crimes other than piracy is that there might be now several jurisdictions capable of, and willing to engage in, effective prosecution. In this case, the question arises which jurisdiction should receive priority when more than one seek to prosecute an individual for the same crime; and whether universal jurisdiction ought to be exercised only when there is no other jurisdiction capable of effective prosecution.

Certainly, the extension of universal jurisdiction to several international crimes and the uncertainty as to which these are presents substantial dangers. These are, in part, exemplified by the recent proliferation before the Belgian courts of international criminal suits arising from the courts' initial willingness to entertain cases occurring in the Rwandan genocide. The cases included lawsuits against former president George H. W. Bush and then-Chairman of the Joint Chiefs of Staff Colin Powell for acts in the first Gulf War; as well as against General Tommy Franks for alleged war crimes in the current Iraq war, and a lawsuit against former Israeli Prime Minister Ariel Sharon.

To be sure, the Belgians found it necessary to stop these applications soon enough, in some cases motivated to some extent at least by political realities; for example, in the American cases, following Secretary Rumsfeld pointing out 'how it would be difficult for US officials to continue to participate in NATO activities at NATO headquarters in Belgium if such harassment continued'.[98] However, independently of one's possible dislike of the Americans flexing their muscles, the fact that cases can be brought nowadays in any jurisdiction against anyone suspected of having participated in an international crime that may – according to the domestic court in question, but maybe not according to other courts – be subject to universal jurisdiction is cause for alarm (even if, we agree, it provides additional avenues to bring to justice those committing egregious international crimes).[99] As Morris points out:

If we have not seen grave abuses, the explanation may lie in the fact that the modern use of universal jurisdiction is in its nascent stages. The 'enormous potential of universal jurisdiction' is likely in the process of being recognised, not only by the well-intentioned states and organizations of the world, but also, by the malefactors ... [100]

An additional worry is that such malefactors may not only misapply international law (i.e. claim universal jurisdiction in a case when there is no agreement on one), but also carry out the prosecutions without due process, in countries with less respect for human rights and the rule of law than in the country of the alleged perpetrator of the crime in question.

All this leads us to think that universal jurisdiction should only apply when it is the only way to prosecute individuals in the absence of a relevant international criminal court (indeed, this is how it arose historically in the first place, with the absence of international criminal institutions till post-WWII). This means that, ideally, the ICC ought to become a universal criminal court. Only then would disagreements about what constitutes an international crime subject to universal jurisdiction stop, as international crimes for which individuals would be prosecuted would be those crimes set out in the ICC's statute.

However, until – if – such time comes, there is room for universal jurisdiction, imperfect as it may be. For those states that are not parties to the ICC and who are unwilling or unable to prosecute either their own nationals or other states' nationals who have committed crimes on their territory, the tool of universal jurisdiction in the hands of third states may be the only way to stop criminals escaping international justice.[101]

Non-governmental organizations

Views of non-governmental organizations (NGOs) range from their being saviours of the human rights cause to being no more than imperialist puppets (as many are heavily supported by private phil-anthropic institutions, such as the Ford or Rockefeller Foundations).[102] The truth lies somewhere in between, of course, as our discussion will show.

Let us start by asking what is an NGO?

In its broadest sense, the term 'non-governmental organization' is an organization that is not part of a governmental structure but a result of a voluntary association of interested persons.[103] Such organi-zations bearing on human rights encompass a wide variety of groups, ranging from corporate-funded think tanks, to community groups, grass-root activist groups, development and research organizations, advocacy groups, operational groups, emergency/humanitarian relief groups, and so on.

The major international non-governmental organizations (INGOs) concerned with human rights today include Amnesty International, Human Rights Watch, the International Committee of the Red Cross, the Anti-Slavery Society and the Commission of Churches. They gen-erally take the form of an international secretariat plus national sections which depend very largely on voluntary work. They work through the publication of special reports on general or individual cases, public statements, efforts to influence the deliberations of international gov-ernmental organizations (IGOs) like the UN, organize campaigns to mobilize public opinion and attempt to affect the foreign policy of states. Absolutely fundamental to their work is the gathering of information about abuses. They study the laws of a suspected violator state, the documents it submits, interview visitors and apparent victims, lawyers, government officials, and so on. Much of this is done on a private or confidential basis at first and the report produced on abuses may be sent to the offending government in the first instance on a private basis but there is always the threat of going public with the information gathered if the government is unco-operative. Crucial to successfully bringing pressure on a government is the mobilization of local groups in the violator state.

Since the mid-1970s, the non-governmental sector in both developed and developing countries has experienced a truly exponential growth.

Over 15 per cent of total overseas development aid is now channelled through non-governmental organizations;[104] and the number of international non-governmental organizations has increased from 6,000 in 1990 to 26,000 in 1999.[105] The main reasons for such a growth are:

- the end of the Cold War and triumph of the liberal model of a state based on the rule of law: in this model, individuals are free to associate to promote their own interests but also their 'principled concerns'; and the non-profit sector, including non-governmental organizations, is now expected to participate in the effort of development, alongside the state and the business world;[106]
- the public's increased awareness of global problems due to the global reach of today's media; and
- the advances in communications, especially the Internet, that allow immediate bonds between like-minded people across state boundaries.

The spectacular growth of non-governmental organizations has been accompanied by growing criticisms of their activities in recent years. Many of these criticisms are directed at international non-governmental organizations: their lack of accountability and transparency (thus causing some to call them 'the world's largest unregulated industry'[107]); their funding from Western governments and large multinationals undermining their independence and serving, even if not intentionally, the hegemonic interests of Western governments; their view of themselves sometimes as an alternative to the governments of the (developing) state they claim to be helping; their ideological biases (for example against Israel);[108] their undermining of local non-governmental organizations; their competition with each other, leading some of them to conceal information from the others in times of humanitarian crises;[109] their actually worsening the disasters they intervene in.[110]

In response to some of these criticisms, some non-governmental organizations have recently issued guidelines to humanitarian agencies during relief operations in a disaster, for example the International Federation of Red Cross and Red Crescent Societies' (IFRC) 'Code of Conduct',[111] the 'Humanitarian Charter and Minimum Standards of the Sphere Project'[112] and the 'Seven Principles of Accountability' of the Humanitarian Partnership Accountability International (HAP-I).[113] The main principles contained in these (voluntary) instruments are: humanitarian imperatives come first; aid is given regardless of race, creed or nationality; aid will not be used to further a particular political or religious standpoint; and there will be accountability to both those being assisted and those providing resources. As far as we know, there are no guidelines for international non-governmental organizations engaged in other activities than relief operations.

Notwithstanding the validity of some or all of those criticisms, there is no doubt that the international non-governmental organizations have played on the whole a very important role in the human rights area, in helping draft UN declarations and conventions, in bringing pressure to bear on particular repressive governments, and in developing international public opinion on human rights.

Indeed, the UN had already recognized the potential importance of international non-governmental organizations back in 1945. Article 71 of the UN Charter provides that '[t]he ECOSOC may make suitable arrangements for consultation with NGOs which are concerned with matters within its competence. Such arrangements may be made with international organisations and, where appropriate, with national organisations after consultation with the Member of the UN concerned.' ECOSOC is the only UN body thus mandated to consult with NGOs.

Resolution 1296 (XLIV), 1968, updated by Resolution 1996/31, now forms the legal basis for decisions concerning the consultative status of NGOs.[114] Resolution 1996/31 adds a provision for granting consultative status to regional and sub-regional NGOs; and specifically encourages the engagement of NGOs from developing countries and from countries with economies in transition. Currently, there are 2,719 NGOs(!) with consultative status with ECOSOC,[115] as compared to 2,012 in 2000.[116]

ECOSOC has also a Committee on NGOs to review applications for consultative status and an NGO section to administer the consultative relationship. The nineteen-member Committee on NGOs uses various criteria to recommend general, special or roster status with the Economic and Social Council, including the applicant's mandate, governance and financial regime. Organizations that have general and special consultative status can attend meetings of the Council and circulate statements of a certain length. Those with general status can, in addition, speak at meetings and propose items for the Council's agenda, while NGOs with roster status can only attend meetings. In return, the organizations with general and special consultative status must submit a report to the Council every four years.[117]

In practice, the relationship of NGOs with ECOSOC and in particular the Commission on Human Rights has reflected 'a general acceptance by governments of the value added by NGO participation despite the frictions that inevitably occur'.[118] For example, NGOs have attended, and participated in, not only formal Commission sessions, but also negotiations on Commission resolutions. These practices are 'almost unheard of in UN processes in New York' and may be thought of as 'a unique *acquis* of the Commission'.[119] This view was confirmed by the ex-Secretary-General of the UN Kofi Annan when he stated, in his report to the General Assembly in 2005, that the Commission's 'close engagement with hundreds of civil society organizations provides an opportunity for networking with civil society that does not exist elsewhere'.[120] He further stated that '[t]he special procedures and NGO engagement are two aspects of the Commission that should continue with the Human Rights Council'.[121] Indeed, the Council incorporated those two successful aspects of the Commission into its work.

The Economic and Social Council in its resolution 1297 called on another body of the UN, the Department of Public Information (DPI), to 'associate NGOs with effective information programmes in place and thus disseminate information about issues on the UN's agenda and the work of the Organization'.[122] Since then, the Department has sought 'to reach people around the world' through the organizations, to help them thus better understand the work and aims of the UN. The Department's activities include 'weekly NGO briefings, communication workshops, an annual NGO conference and an annual orientation programme for newly associated NGOs'.[123] While to get consultative status with ECOSOC it is enough that a NGO's work covers issues on the agenda of ECOSOC, association with DPI also requires 'having effective information programmes in place and the ability and means to disseminate information about the work of the United Nations'.[124]

According to the Department of Public Information website, on 17 January 2007 there were 1,533 NGOs associated with it, out of which 634 were also associated with ECOSOC. Yet, 'only 251 of the 1,550 NGOs associated with the DPI come from the global south and

with the ECOSOC this ratio is even lower'.[125] These figures support
the charge against the NGOs that they are:

biased towards northern agendas, with southern-based civil society groups
often lacking the resources to represent themselves adequately in global civil
society networks and other forums. Indeed, global civil society still shows
many of the same patterns of inequality that exist around the world ... [and
i]t still tends to be the 'usual suspects' – well-established, northern-based
organisations – that the [the UN] ... consults.[126]

We can conclude that the NGOs are a mixed blessing for the human
rights cause. Indispensable on the one hand, they can also harm the
cause they espouse because of their 'northern' agendas, unaccount-
ability and prejudices. Like the businesses we discussed in our right to
development, they therefore clearly need regulation, to start with at least
of the voluntary kind. The procedures we outlined above are a step in
the right direction, even if limited only at the present to relief operations.
Whether there may be also a need for some soft-law standards provided
by governments (to the international non-governmental organizations
in particular) is another question, not addressed in this chapter.

We want to turn our attention now to the consideration of another
way through which the cause of human rights can be advanced worldwide: ethical foreign policy, that is policy used by individual countries to
try to improve other states' human rights record.

We start with a brief historical overview of the human rights policies of Western states after WWII, before looking at different rationales
for ethical foreign policy and the legality of its different instruments,
including humanitarian intervention.

Ethical foreign policy

Human rights policies of the liberal powers

The aim of a human rights foreign policy must clearly be to change
those laws and policies of other states that bear on the human rights of
their citizens. The standard basis for such a foreign policy is the belief
that a human-rights-based political association is in the best interests
of one's own citizens and in the best interests of the citizens of other
states. A world of such states will, thus, be more stable, secure and
just. This has been, on the face of it, the fundamental motivating factor

of the human rights foreign policy of the most powerful and influential of the liberal states, the USA.

As we know from our previous discussion, the USA was primarily responsible for the presence of human rights in the UN Charter and for the initial impetus for the UN human rights programme, on the grounds expressed by George Marshall that:

[g]overnments which systematically disregard the rights of their own people are not likely to respect the rights of other nations and are likely to seek their objectives by coercion and force.[127]

It has since had, since WWII, a human rights foreign policy that links respect for human rights to its own security and that has sought to build an international community of liberal states mutually committed to trade and the rule of law.

However, the US has not pursued this policy consistently. With the onset of the Cold War, short-term security considerations often qualified and undermined its longer-term beliefs about its interests. Thus, it distinguished between left-wing and right-wing authoritarian governments and was willing to support the latter, such as the Shah's government in Iran, Somoza's in Nicaragua, Pinochet's in Chile and various other Middle Eastern and East Asian anti-communist repressive regimes, despite their appalling human rights records.

Nevertheless, its policy towards the Soviet Union was, for the most part, based not solely on achieving military parity or even, under Reagan, military superiority, but also on the need to fight Soviet aggression by opposing the attractions of 'Western' liberty to the brutal and unaccountable rule of Soviet communism. For a period after Kennedy's government, and especially under Nixon and Kissinger, US policy towards the Soviet and Chinese governments veered towards a traditional unideological balance of power approach. But under Carter a veritable crusade for human rights was launched, which, although it antagonized the Soviet government, nevertheless achieved the remarkable result of a Soviet endorsement of CP human rights in the Helsinki Accords of 1975 in exchange for the West's acceptance (but not its legitimization) of the post-war territorial settlement.[128]

This Soviet commitment, much to their surprise, gave great encouragement, and 'official' sanction, to human rights movements throughout Soviet-controlled territory and thereby contributed substantially to the de-legitimization of the communist regimes. The Reagan government continued the human rights pressure on the Soviet Union to which it added an enormously expensive arms race that left the Soviet economy unable to compete and the Russians under Gorbachev and his successor ready to throw in the towel and abandon communism. This victory for 'Western' liberty was enshrined in the Charter of Paris of 1990, signed by thirty-four states, endorsing as the fundamental principles governing the post-Cold War world 'democracy based on human rights and fundamental freedoms, prosperity through economic liberty, social justice and equal security for all countries'.[129] The first two elements of this proclamation have been important components of subsequent US foreign policy, even contributing to the disastrous decision to invade Iraq in order to overthrow Saddam Hussein and provide a beacon of liberty in the Middle East.

So far, we have only mentioned the US: but of course almost all liberal-democratic states have a human rights strand in their foreign policies and their human rights policies have become more active in the post-Cold War world. For the most part, these policies have consisted in verbal rather than material sanctions, although making development and other aid conditional on a state's human rights record is widely used. General trade and investment embargoes have been rarely employed. They are not thought to be very successful and have the perverse effect of harming the people the policies are intended to help. The one significant exception to this claim is widely held to be that of apartheid South Africa, where the isolation of the regime and its European peoples, not only economically but also culturally and in sport, and from their former Western allies, is believed to have undermined their will to maintain their racial ascendancy. The failure of general economic sanctions against Saddam Hussein's Iraq led to the attempt to design so-called smart sanctions that are aimed at the repressive ruling elite rather than the population in general. These are now in place against Mugabe's Zimbabwe, but do not appear to have been successful.

Human rights foreign policies by the Western liberal-democratic states are resented by the states at which they are aimed. Indeed, in the view of some Asians in particular, such policies violate the non-intervention principle (which we discuss further below) and are destabilizing in their effects on international peace and security.[130] But this is obviously a self-serving argument. Certainly, there is little evidence that non-coercive human rights policies harm the interests of the 'intervening' state. For instance, the Australian government raised over 400 human rights issues with 68 governments in the single year 1998–9 without apparently suffering any deleterious consequences for such a high degree of 'intervention' in the affairs of other states.[131]

Nevertheless, Donnelly, for example, believes that few states are prepared to make more than modest sacrifices of their other foreign policy concerns for the sake of human rights.[132] Certainly, even such countries as Britain and France that still like to think of themselves as significant powers in international society run into the same temptations as the Americans to subordinate their long-term human rights interests to their shorter-term security and economic interests. The most egregious example of this in the British case has been its policy towards the Saudi Arabian autocracy, which it is excessively anxious not to offend for the sake of the enormously profitable and long-standing 'Yamama' arms deal with the sole remaining British major aerospace company. (We provide some further examples later when discussing ethical foreign policy and enlightened self-interest.) The Americans, also, are willing to ignore the Saudis' human rights record because of strategic and oil supply concerns. The French are notorious for their support for former French colonies in Africa that have become deeply corrupt and repressive regimes, for the sake of preserving French influence in the world. Such attitudes generate substantial inconsistencies in the human rights policies of the liberal states and, as we will see, cause widespread anger and cynicism about 'ethical foreign policies'.

On the whole, however, scholars such as Forsythe are, in our view, right in concluding that the foreign policies of states play a very important role in the promotion and protection of human rights.[133] Indeed, if states did not engage in such actions both individually and in UN fora, it is difficult to see that the activities of UN administrators or those of human rights NGOs would be of any effect. International society is still one in which it is states that count. Nevertheless, it must be emphasized that for the most part human rights policies are long-term ones. It is essential for the liberal states to go on insisting on the legal obligation and moral desirability of states to promote and protect human rights even if this does not have any immediate effect on a state's human rights record. Such a long-term commitment clearly had its reward in contributing to the eventual collapse of the Soviet Union and is necessary to maintain the values for which the UN and the liberal states are supposed to stand.

Let us now turn our attention to a more detailed analysis of (i) a number of different reasons a state may have for adopting an ethical foreign policy; and (ii) the legality of various ethical policy instruments, both non-coercive and coercive.

Grounds for ethical foreign policy

A country's foreign policy can be defined as a set of goals it pursues in its interactions with other countries. Traditionally viewed as mainly aimed at protection of national security and economic prosperity, there is a consensus today – as evidenced by the overview above – that these goals ought to include protection of human rights.[134] As Gelb and Rosenthal put it:

A new vocabulary has emerged in the rhetoric of senior government officials, Republicans and Democrats alike. It is laced with concepts dismissed
for almost 100 years as 'Wilsonian.' The rhetoric comes in many forms,
used to advocate regime change or humanitarian intervention or promote
democracy and human rights, but almost always the ethical agenda has at
its core the rights of the individual.[135]

The aim is, as stated earlier, to change those laws and policies of other states that bear on the human rights of their citizens.

There are two main reasons for the present consensus: enlightened self-interest and legality. Let us look at each one in turn.

It may indeed be in the longer-term interest of states to follow human rights objectives in their foreign policy (the same way it may be in their interest to contribute development assistance to developing coun-tries).[136] Thus, as countries become more interdependent, poverty and human rights abuses in one country can impact on another country. Quoting Wright, who refers to America and the way in which even 'progressive realists' today accept that *realpolitik* (i.e. politics based on practical considerations rather than ideological notions) might include human rights concerns:

Progressive realists see that America can best flourish if others flourish – if
African states cohere, if the world's Muslims feel they benefit from the
world order, if personal and environmental health are nurtured, if economic
inequities abroad are muted so that young democracies can be stable and
strong. More and more, doing well means doing good ... We can at least be

thankful that history, by intertwining the fates of peoples, is bringing national interest closer to moral ideals.[137]

There is no doubt that this view of international relations is correct: that we are all increasingly dependent on others' well-being for our own welfare. The problem with the pursuit of such a 'realist' ethical foreign policy is, however, precisely that it is based not on moral grounds but practical ones. This means that it can give way to a 'non-ethical' policy any time realist interests would so require; for example, when human rights abuses are committed by powerful states (since attempting to bring pressure on them may increase international tension or put an end to useful alliances); or when they are committed by small, 'insignificant' states (since what happens within them may have no impact on our own welfare). Under the 'enlightened self-interest' rationale for an ethical foreign policy, one may thus want to bring pressure on human rights abusers only (i) when this pressure benefits us directly; and (ii) it does not damage our other, 'more vital' interests. This is exemplified by the Clinton administration's 1994 Presidential Decision Directive (PDD) 25, which stated that 'the US would only participate in UN peacekeeping operations if they were in the national interest'.[138]

This is not a comfortable ethical position to occupy (even if it may be occupied by many other foreign ministries, including the British one).[139] Surely, a liberal state ought to pursue ethical foreign policy not because it serves one's enlightened self-interest but out of a sense of a moral and legal obligation (the same way it ought to provide development assistance to less developed countries, as we argued in our chapter on RTD).

We can, of course, expand the notion of the enlightened self-interest to include moral considerations. In this case, states would see their long-term interest in terms of being members of an international society bound together at least in part by a common acknowledgement of human rights. On this view, they have therefore an interest in promoting respect for human rights throughout this association, even if occasionally this may damage their short-term interests, turn powerful states against them, or waste their diplomatic efforts on 'unimportant' countries. The problem with this wide notion of the enlightened self-interest is, however, that it is unlikely to 'trump' short-term considerations: again, the example of British 'ethical foreign policy' comes to mind. Lip service has been paid to it at least since 1997, when the then Foreign Minister, Robin Cook, made a speech 'that started it all', in which he said:

[s]ecurity, prosperity and quality of life [environmental concerns] are all clear national interests. Britain also has a **national interest** in the promotion of our values and confidence in our identity. That is why the fourth goal of our foreign policy is to secure the respect of other nations for Britain's contribution to keeping the peace of the world and promoting democracy around the world. The Labour Government does not accept that political values can be left behind when we check in our passports to travel on diplomatic business. Our foreign policy must have an ethical dimension and must support the demands of other peoples for the democratic rights on which we insist for ourselves. The Labour Government will put human rights at the heart of our foreign policy.[140]

Many (such as Murray, who we refer to in endnote 139) would claim that the goals of 'security and prosperity' have, however, far too often 'trumped' in reality the goal of promoting human rights around the world. Self-interest, enlightened or not, is not a good basis for moral considerations.

The other reason there is a wide consensus today that states ought to follow an ethical foreign policy is their legal commitment to a variety of human rights instruments.

As we know, all states have ratified the UN Charter with its human rights provisions; most states are parties to various human rights covenants (the ICCPR and ICESCR in particular, but also covenants on Torture, Genocide, etc.); and many legal experts argue that human rights norms such as prohibition of torture or genocide have become part of customary international law to the same extent as the norms against slavery or piracy.

It is clear therefore that states act unlawfully when they commit human rights abuses. We also know that their individual officials can be pursued today, under international tribunals or universal jurisdiction, to account for those abuses. Does this mean, however, that states have a right, under international law, to use their foreign policy to put pressure on the offending states to stop their unlawful behaviour? Wouldn't such a policy go against the principle of non-intervention in the affairs of other states, **the** principle of the Westphalian system of states that has never been displaced by the human rights regime?

The principle of non-intervention can be found in Article 2(7) which states: 'Nothing contained in the present Charter shall authorize the United Nations to intervene in matters which are essentially within the domestic jurisdiction of any state'. According to the International Court of Justice, this principle means 'the right of every sovereign State to conduct its affairs without outside interference ... the principle forbids all States or groups of States to intervene directly or indirectly in the internal or external affairs of other States'.[141]

Whether ethical foreign policy violates the principle of non-intervention must hence depend on the meaning of 'matters which are essentially within the domestic jurisdiction of any state', and 'intervene ... in internal ... affairs'. In other words, are the human rights of a state's citizens an 'internal' affair of a state? Or is it rather that, having been made binding in international law by the consenting states themselves, the human rights obligations of a state are now by definition of concern at the international level to both the relevant international institutions and to other states?

We believe that it is the latter; and that states engaging in gross human rights violations cannot claim that these are matters of purely domestic jurisdiction. They are clearly breaching international law, in many cases committing international crimes; and the only question is how far other states can go in responding to those breaches (as opposed to international institutions, whose powers are clearly delineated under particular human rights treaties).

Certainly, there is no doubt that there is a general duty on all states to ensure observance of human rights. As the International Court of Justice stated in a famous case, *Barcelona Traction*, the obligation of states to ensure observance of human rights is *erga omnes* (i.e. is binding on all states and also has the status of peremptory norm (*jus cogens*)):[142] it is incumbent on every state in relation to the international community as a whole and every state has a legal interest in the protection of human rights.[143] We also saw that all states are required to promote human rights globally, having bound themselves to the protection and advancement of human rights in the UN Charter; and, having enumerated them subsequently in detail in the Universal Declaration on Human Rights (taken today to reflect customary international law). Furthermore, state parties to the ICCPR, ICESCR, and all the other human rights conventions are bound, of course, to observe human rights contained in these treaties. The conclusion is clearly that, as the 1993 UN World Congress on Human Rights in Vienna affirmed: 'the promotion and protection of all human rights is a legitimate concern of the international community'.

What is more difficult to determine, however, is what form this obligation to ensure observance of human rights can take under international law. We turn towards this task in the section below, where we consider the legality of various foreign policy instruments.

Before we do that, we want to deal with one serious objection one may have to using foreign policy to enforce moral values: that is, the danger that powerful states may hide behind human rights rhetoric to act in their own self-interest or impose their own values on other states. This danger is clearly described below in two quotes, the first one (80 years old) by Carr:

Theories of social morality are always the product of a dominant group which identifies itself with the community as a whole, and which possesses facilities denied to subordinate groups or individuals for imposing its view of life on the community. Theories of international morality are, for the same reason and in virtue of the same process, the product of dominant nations or groups of nations. For the past hundred years, and more especially since 1918, the English-speaking peoples have formed the dominant group in the world; and current theories of international morality have been designed to perpetuate their supremacy and expressed in the idiom peculiar to them.[144]

and the second one (recent) by Putin:

From the point of view of stability in this or that region or in the world in general, the balance of power is the main achievement of these past decades and indeed of the whole history of humanity. It is one of the most important conditions for maintaining global stability and security ... I do not understand really why some of our partners ... see themselves as cleverer and more civilised and think that they have the right to impose their standards on others ... The thing to remember is that standards that are imposed from outside, including in the Middle East, rather than being a product of a society's natural internal development lead to tragic consequences, and the best example is Iraq.[145]

To be sure, from the point of view of the contemporary international human rights regime, both Carr and Putin have got it wrong. The standards are the ones the states themselves have agreed to and are only failing to comply with. They are not imposed from outside.[146] Nonetheless, it is clear that one has to be very careful how one acts, and that any unilateral action, or an action by a group of states seen as powerful by others (such as Putin's Russia) is fraught with danger. Mutawi, a Middle-East specialist quoted in Pilger expressed this danger well when he said, back in 2000:

While it is acceptable to call for the trial of Iraqi officials ... it is apparently not acceptable that officials of the UN, the US, the UK and culpable others should even be called to account ... The very notion of human rights in the west is corrupted ... selected rights can be championed while others are ignored.[147]

He also calls this 'a "bastardisation" of human discourse'.[148] Following the invasion of Iraq in 2003 and the subsequent accusations of torture, extraordinary rendition and Guantanamo Bay, many more, we fear, would feel that way about human rights.

In addition, as MacDonald, Patman and Mason-Parker point out, foreign policy 'exists, in the first place, as the instrument of a distinctive political process and environment'.[149] Nearly by definition, even ethical foreign policy based on human rights conventions cannot express uniform human rights values, but must reflect the culture and morality of the country using it. We have seen, indeed, that even within the ambit of the European Convention on Human Rights – which yet applies to states coming from similar traditions – state parties are allowed a 'margin of appreciation' when applying the Convention within their own borders. How likely is it that a state's foreign policy is not going to, in some way or another, reflect its own interpretation of human rights norms?

Having said that, does this mean that we want to abandon ethical foreign policy altogether? Surely not. This would be throwing the baby out with the bath water. Surely, we do want states to be able to intervene in situations when other states commit gross and persistent abuses of their citizens' human rights (an example springing to mind at the time of writing this chapter is Burma; prior to that, Rwanda) and when the Security Council, for whatever reason (most of the time political), is not acting; but we do of course want them to intervene lawfully and effectively.

While we look at the question of lawfulness below, it is beyond the scope of this book to discuss an effective ethical foreign policy. All we want to say is that, hopefully, the precedent of international criminal tribunals (in particular the ICC) will clarify some of the criteria for the conduct of an impartial ethical foreign policy in the area of international criminal law at least; for example, the ICC's Statute setting out what are the elements of each crime should put an end to an arbitrary interpretation of international crimes by each state.

The question we want to ask now is in what ways can states intervene lawfully in the affairs of other states? We answer this question by looking first at which non-coercive foreign policies are allowed under international law (by non-coercive we mean short of actual aggression); and second at whether there are any circumstances under which coercive foreign policies are allowed in order to remedy a situation of gross and persistent abuse of human rights (this is the case of the so-called humanitarian intervention).

Legality of ethical foreign policy instruments

Non-coercive policies

Not surprisingly, the various moves possible in terms of increasing pressure on states not respecting their citizens' human rights, short of actual coercion, are the same as for other foreign policy objectives. They are, in order of ascending gravity (in our view):

- confidential representations;
- joint representations with other governments;
- restrictions on sporting and cultural contacts;
- reduction in military and economic aid;
- trade sanctions;
- withdrawal of ambassadors; and
- breaking diplomatic relations.

Except for trade sanctions that could breach World Trade Organization rules (when not imposed by a Security Council resolution), none of these actions violates the principle of non-intervention discussed above. The International Court of Justice stated, for example, in the *Nicaragua* case:

Nicaragua has also asserted that the US is responsible for an 'indirect' form of intervention in its internal affairs inasmuch as it has taken, to Nicaragua's disadvantage, certain action of an economic nature. The Court's attention has been drawn in particular to the cessation of economic aid ... the 90% reduction in the sugar quota for US imports ... and the trade embargo ... While admitting in principle that some of these actions were not unlawful of themselves, counsel for Nicaragua argued that these measures of economic constraint add up to a systematic violation of the principle of non-intervention ... The Court ... is unable to regard such action on the economic plane ... as a breach of the customary law principle of non-intervention.[150]

Various other policies are also undertaken sometimes:

• aiding the legal internal opposition to the government;
• aiding non-violent illegal opposition; and
• aiding armed opposition movements.

Because they can be viewed as direct intervention in the internal affairs of a country, these last are of dubious validity under international law and are certainly unlawful when breaching the norm of no use of force in international affairs. Quoting the International Court of Justice, again in the *Nicaragua* case:

The support given by the US ... to the military and paramilitary activities of the contras in Nicaragua, by financial support, training, supply of weapons, intelligence and logistic support, constitutes a clear breach of the principle of non-intervention ... an armed attack must be understood as including not merely action by regular armed forces across an international border, but also the sending by or on behalf of a State of armed bands, groups, irregulars or mercenaries, which carry out acts of armed force against another State of such gravity as to amount to ... an actual armed attack conducted by regular forces or its substantial involvement therein ... the mere supply of funds to the contras, while undoubtedly an act of intervention in the internal affairs of Nicaragua ... does not in itself amount to a use of force [but it amounted to illegal intervention].[151]

Provision of strictly humanitarian aid to persons or forces in another country, whatever their political affiliations or objectives, is, however, not unlawful if provided equally to rebels and others in need.

Let us now look at coercive measures, such as the controversial case of humanitarian intervention.

Humanitarian intervention

Humanitarian intervention is an armed intervention in the territory of another state in order to protect the citizens of that state from being massacred or from extreme suffering and anarchy.[152] Is such intervention lawful under international law?[153]

At first view, the answer would seem to be no. As we know, any armed attack breaches the norm of non-intervention; and the only time states are allowed to use force against other states is either in self-defence or on the authority of the Security Council acting to protect international peace and security. But we also know that there is another norm of international law, which conflicts with that of non-intervention: this is the norm that says that the promotion and protection of all human rights is a legitimate concern of the international community.[154] In a liberal world order, shouldn't this norm 'trump' the norm of non-intervention? Shouldn't humanitarian intervention be hence used as yet another tool of an ethical foreign policy?

As we will see, there is no straightforward answer. While most international lawyers would agree that there is no right to unilateral humanitarian intervention, that is, by one or more states without the UN Security Council's authorization, most would argue that there is a right to collective humanitarian intervention, that is, to an intervention carried out or authorized by the Security Council. There is also a push within the international community to develop some kind of criteria to allow states to engage in humanitarian intervention, as proposed in a report on 'Responsibility to Protect', which we discuss below.

We will now outline the main arguments relating to both kinds of humanitarian intervention (collective and unilateral). To be sure, collective humanitarian intervention is not properly speaking a case of foreign policy (which, as you may remember, we defined as a set of goals an individual country pursues in its interactions with other countries). However, it can be seen as an example of the 'collective' foreign policy of liberal states towards those states unwilling or unable to protect their citizens from gross human rights violations. It is also a part of humanitarian intervention generally. It hence needs to be included in any discussion of coercive ethical foreign policy.

We start with a historical overview of what customary international law on humanitarian intervention was prior to the establishment of the UN.[155]

Some international legal authorities hold that humanitarian intervention was justified under customary international law prior to the establishment of the UN. If so, and if such a right has not been extinguished by the UN Charter, then humanitarian intervention must still be part of customary international law.

The supposed founder of modern international law – Grotius – affirmed the legality of unilateral humanitarian intervention. Of course, in the period in which Grotius was writing there could be no such thing as collective humanitarian intervention authorized by the competent global organization as there was none, unless we think of much later interventions authorized by the Great Powers, of which there was an instance in the 1860s that we shall come to.

Grotius' principle effectively affirmed that the exclusive sovereignty of the state stopped at the point at which an outrage upon humanity begins. However, what Grotius and other classical writers such as Vattel had in mind under the heading of an outrage upon humanity was attacks on religious minorities. Hence the right of intervention was at that time a right to act to protect persons of the same faith as oneself from actions that violated the conscience of mankind.

There are a number of cases cited in defence of the existence of a right of unilateral humanitarian intervention dating from nineteenth-century interventions in the Ottoman Empire by some combination of European Powers. There was a British and French intervention in the Greek uprising against the Turks in 1827; and a major intervention by all the Great Powers – Britain, France, Prussia, Austria and Russia – in the 1860s in Syria to protect Christians from massacre. There were also frequent bilateral interventions in this area justified by Treaty rights extracted from the Turks by the European states to protect Christians in the Ottoman domains.

It is certainly clear that an appeal to humanitarian reasons as justification for dictatorial interference in another state's affairs was widely used in the nineteenth century, particularly by the British. And it seems that many international jurists accepted humanitarian intervention defined as intervention to prevent actions that shocked the conscience of mankind as lawful under international law although others rejected it as incompatible with state sovereignty.[156]

But it has to be pointed out that in this period there was a right of states to wage war against each other as a matter of national policy. So it is doubtful that most of the cases cited could be understood as genuine cases in which intervention occurred for purely humanitarian reasons rather than out of a desire of the intervening powers to create spheres of influence in the unravelling Ottoman Empire. Commentators tend to consider the Syrian case of 1860–1 by the combined Great Powers as the only clear case of humanitarian intervention.

The contemporary Dutch international jurist Malanczak concludes a study of this issue by holding that the right of humanitarian intervention did not become an accepted part of customary international law prior to the UN. While states like Britain might have claimed such a right, it was never generally accepted by the international community and so could not be held to be part of customary international law.[157] Most (although not all) international jurists would agree with this view.

Let us now look at humanitarian intervention under the UN Charter.

The Charter recognizes as legitimate use of force only cases of self-defence and threats to international peace and security. Humanitarian reasons are not recognized and hence would seem to be illegal.

Some jurists argue that the UN Charter in principle only prohibits armed actions directed against the political independence and territorial integrity of another state and so does not preclude the use of force to protect human rights if the sovereignty of the state whose territory is invaded is preserved. For example, because Serbia retained its sovereignty over Kosovo at this time, the armed intervention of NATO did not violate the UN rules on the use of force as it was fulfilling a Charter duty to protect human rights.[158]

This seems to us fairly specious reasoning. As Greenwood says, the answer to the question of the legitimacy of humanitarian intervention would until recently have been a clear no, and a majority of jurists would have rejected the view that the UN rules on the use of force allowed it to protect human rights.[159] Thus, a much cited (in Britain) British Foreign Office Review of the position in 1984 held that the overwhelming majority of contemporary legal opinion comes down against the right of humanitarian intervention for three main reasons:[160]

1. The UN Charter and international law do not specifically incorporate such a right.
2. State practice at best provides only a handful of cases of humanitarian intervention and on most assessments none at all.
3. On prudential grounds the scope for abusing the right is high, that is the use of humanitarian arguments to justify interventions that are anything but. This was certainly a recurrent feature of state practice prior to 1945; and, although of course not mentioned in the Report, also of state practice during the Cold War by states such as the US, with its 'history of using military force for various

purposes and attempting to justify it (unconvincingly) in the name of [not humanitarian intervention but] advancing democracy, particularly in Central America during the 1980s'.[161] The US is of course using the same rationale now with respect to Iraq: having invaded in 2003 on the spurious grounds of pre-emptive self-defence (because of a presumed existence of weapons of mass destruction in Iraq), it now appears to justify the invasion on humanitarian grounds.[162]

However, the situation has changed since the end of the Cold War and the consequent increased co-operation of the five permanent members of the Security Council. The exercise of the Security Council's enforcement powers, which until then had been mostly prevented by the Soviet-American rivalry, became suddenly possible. This resulted in a reinvigorated Security Council adopting many more measures than before and, most importantly, adopting measures in the humanitarian area which, a few years earlier, would have been practically unthinkable.

In particular, the Security Council began to include, in the notion of threats to international peace and security, refugee flows, humanitarian disasters and even human rights abuses. For example Resolution 688 in 1991 required Iraq to desist from attacking the Iraqi Kurds and to allow humanitarian organizations into the area because of the threat to international peace and security. Resolution 794 in 1992 justifies a US-led armed intervention in Somalia on the grounds that attacks on famine relief measures threatened international peace and security. In a number of other cases, the Security Council endorsed or acquiesced in *ex post facto* armed interventions on humanitarian grounds such as those of the Economic Community of West African States (ECOWAS) in Liberia and NATO in Kosovo. In the latter case, the Security Council rejected by twelve votes to three the Russian motion supported by China and Namibia condemning the intervention as illegal.

Such cases (and others that followed, for example, Sierra Leone) have given rise to a general consensus today that humanitarian intervention is lawful when authorized by the Security Council under Chapter VII of the UN Charter on grounds of a threat to international peace and security. However, there is no consensus on what criteria should be used in order to justify the violation of the principle of non-intervention.

There is also no consensus at all on the legality of unilateral humanitarian intervention. While a few believe that there is a right to unilateral humanitarian intervention, many more claim that there is no such right: but that, while not legal, such a right may, when exercised in extreme circumstances, not be condemned by the international community. If this were to happen on a regular basis over time – and assuming a new rule on the use of force could emerge alongside the Charter – unilateral humanitarian intervention may actually become an accepted part of customary international law.[163] In our view, this is, however, unlikely.

Both questions of collective and unilateral humanitarian intervention were addressed in the highly influential International Commission on Intervention and State Sovereignty (ICISS) Report,[164] endorsed in the 2005 World Summit Document. The Report finds that growing state and regional organizational practice, as well as Security Council precedent suggest an emerging guiding principle that:

intervention for human protection purposes, including military intervention in extreme cases, is supportable when major harm to civilians [such as mass murder and ethnic cleansing] is occurring or immediately apprehended and the state in question is unable or unwilling to end the harm or is itself the perpetrator.

The ICISS Report argues further that such intervention would not violate the principles of non-intervention and state sovereignty. This is because, in its view, sovereignty entails responsibility: each sovereign state has a responsibility to protect its citizens. If it is unable or unwilling to do so, the responsibility – as well as the right to intervene – passes instead to the international community. In other words, there can be no sovereignty without responsibility.

The report suggests a number of criteria for determining whether to intervene militarily or not: a just-cause threshold criterion, four precautionary criteria and an authority criterion. As they have been widely analysed and commented on, we need to look at each of these criteria in turn.

Responsibility to protect (R2P)

Just-cause threshold

To warrant military intervention, there must be an extraordinary level of human suffering, as evidenced by either large-scale loss of life, which can be actual or anticipated, with genocidal intent or not, or by large-scale ethnic cleansing actual or anticipated, whether carried out by killing, forced expulsion, acts of terror, or rape. Possibility of anticipatory action is necessary as, without it, the international community would be placed in the ethically unacceptable position of having to wait until genocide begins, before being able to take action to stop it.

Four precautionary criteria

The four precautionary criteria put forward by the ICISS report are:

1. **Right intention**: the primary purpose of the intervention, whatever other motives intervening states may have, must be to halt or avert human suffering.
2. **Last resort**: military intervention can only be justified when every non-military option for the prevention or peaceful resolution of the crisis has been explored, with reasonable grounds for believing lesser measures would not succeed.
3. **Proportional means**: in compliance with humanitarian law, the scale, duration and intensity of the planned military intervention should be the minimum necessary to secure the defined human protection objective. This means that the action taken has to be commensurate in scale with its stated purpose, and in line with the magnitude of the original provocation.
4. **Reasonable prospects**: there must be a reasonable chance of success in halting or averting the suffering which has justified the intervention, with the consequences of action not likely to be worse than the consequences of inaction.

Right authority criterion

The United Nations Security Council is the most appropriate body to authorize military intervention for human protection purposes. The task is hence not to find alternatives to the Security Council as a source of authority, the ICISS Report says, but to make the Security Council work better than it has. One of the ways would be to ensure that when there would otherwise be majority support for intervention, a permanent member of the Council should abstain from using its veto to block the intervention unless the state has a vital national interest at stake which it would have to justify publicly.

The report points out that there are only two other institutional solutions available, were the Security Council for any reason unable or unwilling to act. One is consideration of the matter by the General Assembly in an Emergency Special Session; the other is action by regional or sub-regional organizations under Chapter VII of the Charter within their area of jurisdiction, subject to their seeking subsequent authorization from the Security Council (as happened with the West African interventions in Liberia in the early 1990s and Sierra Leone in 1997).

As for unilateral humanitarian intervention, the report does not actively endorse intervention in circumstances when all possible attempts to obtain Security Council authorization fail. Instead, it leaves open the question as to which of the two evils is the worse: the damage to the international order if the Security Council is bypassed, or the damage to that order if human beings are slaughtered while the Security Council stands by. It seems to suggest, however, that it may be the latter: and that if states act in the absence of a Security Council authorization and get it right (i.e. fully respect all the necessary criteria and intervene successfully, as happened, many would argue, with the NATO intervention in Kosovo), the international community may accept the intervention *post facto*.

The report suggested that one of the next steps for the international community ought to be a declaratory UN General Assembly resolution giving weight to the above principles and the whole idea of the 'responsibility to protect (R2P)' as an emerging international norm. Spurred on in a large measure by a huge support for the R2P from civil society,[165] (but also governments such as that of Canada and Britain) an Outcome Document was adopted at the World Summit by the UN General Assembly in September 2005, committing states to the basic principles of the R2P report. In particular, paragraph 139 stated:

we are prepared to take collective action, in a timely and decisive manner, through the Security Council, in accordance with the Charter, including Chapter VII, on a case-by-case basis and in cooperation with relevant regional organizations as appropriate, should peaceful means be inadequate and national authorities are manifestly failing to protect their populations from genocide, war crimes, ethnic cleansing and crimes against humanity.[166]

Importantly, the General Assembly was also willing to accept a 'redefinition of sovereignty',[167] by stating in paragraph 138 that '[e]ach individual state has the responsibility to protect its populations from genocide, war crimes, ethnic cleansing and crimes against humanity'. Sovereignty hence no longer means a state can do anything it wants within its jurisdiction. Sovereignty entails responsibility; without responsibility, there is no sovereignty.

Importantly, the position of the UN Special Advisor on the Prevention of Genocide was also created at the Summit, reinforcing this view of state's responsibility sovereignty.[168]

Merely a year later, the Security Council followed the General Assembly's example. In its (unanimous) Resolution 1674 on Protection of Civilians in Armed Conflict of April 2006, the Security Council reaffirmed 'the provisions of paragraphs 138 and 139 of the 2005 World Summit Outcome Document regarding the responsibility to protect populations from genocide, war crimes, ethnic cleansing and crimes against humanity'.[169] According to some, this development has 'codif[ied] R2P principles into the UN system'.[170]

Subsequent to the Resolution, the Security Council invoked R2P for the first time in country-specific resolutions relating to Darfur. This included the unanimously adopted Resolution 1769 authorizing the deployment of a 26,000-strong United Nations–African Union force to Sudan's western Darfur region. The resolution invokes Chapter VII to authorize the United Nations–African Union Mission in Darfur's (UNAMID) use of force to protect civilians.

The Security Council has, however, been unable so far (October 2007) to vote on a resolution that would, for example, address the human rights situation in Burma (Myanmar).[171] This has been due to vetoes by both China and Russia, who argue that Burma (Myanmar) does not pose a threat to regional peace and security and that what happens within it is an internal affair of the country. They also argue that 'while Burma (Myanmar) is facing a serious human rights and humanitarian situation, other bodies, such as the Human Rights Council, should hear these concerns'.[172]

The issue was indeed addressed by the Human Rights Council on 2 October 2007, when it adopted by consensus a Resolution criticizing the government of Burma (Myanmar) for recent violence and calling for an urgent investigation by the UN Special Rapporteur for human rights in the country. During the session, the UN High Commissioner for Human Rights, Louise Arbour, noted that in the 2005 World Summit Outcome Document, UN member states agreed that the international community has a responsibility to protect civilians against grave crises, no matter where they occur.[173]

We are not sure, however, whether the situation in Burma, terrible as it is, does fall under the criteria suggested by R2P. We would think that the just cause threshold of 'large-scale loss of life' may not be met in this case, in which 'only' maybe thousands at most, as opposed to hundreds of thousands in Darfur, have been killed.

The problem is, as the R2P website points out, that '[w]hile many of the Council's members speak favorably about R2P, others still resist applying it to the Council's work. As a result, the Council has not yet considered how R2P will be used to guide its actions'.[174] The Council clearly needs to develop guidelines as to what constitutes 'large-scale loss of life' as well as all the other R2P criteria.

Not surprisingly, there has been a mixed scholarly reaction to R2P proposals. Some commentators see the proposal as a watershed; some criticize it as being too radical; yet others as too conservative. Many fear that the R2P principles would legitimize politically motivated interventions, especially on the part of the major powers. Others point out that without multinational standing forces (yet unforeseeable for a long time in future), the lack of operational capacity will stop the principle from being practically implemented.

Whatever the case may be, it seems to us that the proposal undoubtedly reflects a growing (and welcome) trend in international relations to accept, in principle at least, that a state's sovereignty in the field of human rights is not unlimited and can be subject to certain conditions (even if some countries such as China and Russia make sure that the conditions are rarely met). As the R2P website states, '[i]n 2005, world leaders agreed, for the first time, that states have a primary responsibility to protect their own populations and that the international community has a responsibility to act when these governments fail to protect the most vulnerable among us'.[175]

This is a very important agreement.

However, it is clear that the question of how this responsibility is going to be discharged in practice is not going to be answered for a long time. One practical solution in the immediate future may be to encourage regional organizations – the European Union, the Organization of American States, the African Union – to accept the responsibility to protect civilians from humanitarian disasters by authorizing armed intervention in the territories of their members.[176] The question would remain, however, what to do if the organizations refuse to act; or abuse their responsibility by acting out of other motives than humanitarian ones.

Conclusion

There is a widely held view among commentators on the present international human rights regime that there exists an international consensus on human rights norms but that at the same time there remains a high level of non-compliance with these norms. The problem, then, is to make conduct conform to the accepted beliefs.[177]

It seems to us that this view is seriously misleading. It is true that there was, in the first instance, a *nem. con.* vote in support of the 1948 Universal Declaration on Human Rights and that there has subsequently been a high level of ratification of the UN-sponsored human rights covenants. Furthermore, there was a *nem. con.* endorsement of the Vienna Declaration at the end of the 1993 UN Vienna Conference on Human Rights, which reaffirmed the universality of human rights with only a modest acknowledgement of the need for sensitivity to cultural context in their interpretation. The Vienna Declaration also re-endorsed the UN interdependency thesis regarding the relation between the various types of rights, thus excluding the legitimacy of picking and choosing among rights to suit one's state.

This shows that when challenged to break ranks with the official UN view and justify their actual non-compliance, no state was willing to do so. But this may not indicate a serious commitment to the UN human rights values. Given that many of the states that voted for the official view were persistent, flagrant and unrepentant violators of the UN human rights, the vote surely suggests the belief on their part that they have nothing to lose by endorsing norms that they have no intention of following, since they are confident that they will suffer no serious consequences from their non-compliance. It is easier for them to accept the norms and not follow them than to dissent openly from them. In other words, it reveals a high degree of cynicism about human rights on the part of the violators.

However, this was exactly the attitude of the Soviet Union in signing up to the Helsinki Accords, which yet had the most unexpected and unpalatable consequences for them in contributing to the de-legitimization of their regime.[178] Could the same thing happen again? The circumstances, especially the economic circumstances, for the most part, are not the same. The pseudo- or post-communist regimes, as also the Islamic ones, allow a degree of capitalism and in many cases their economies are, at present, buoyed up by very high mineral prices. Their collapse or conversion to liberal values is hence most unlikely in the future. Nevertheless, liberals must hope, and must act in the hope, that in the long run the result will be similar. Furthermore, in order to discuss sensibly how liberals should face the challenge of non-compliance, we need to make some distinctions between the different types of violators and take a view on the causes of human rights abuses.

There are, in the first place, the ideologically based anti-liberals. These comprise:

- the remaining communist regimes (North Korea, Cuba), together with the pseudo-communist regimes that allow a degree of capitalism but limit to a greater or lesser extent other essential liberal freedoms, such as speech, association, religion, political participation, and have an inadequate record on the rule of law (China, Vietnam) and the 'fundamentalist' Islamic regimes (Iran, Saudi Arabia); and
- the 'cultural distinctiveness' states (Malaya, Singapore, some authoritarian Middle Eastern and African states. China is partly in this camp and even Russia under Putin shows signs of it).

In the second place, there are the authoritarian regimes that are not obviously based on a permanent anti-liberal ideology:

- the development dictatorship states where this used to be a widely accepted justification for temporary illiberalism, but is no longer because of a very mixed record. Nevertheless, the argument is still, sometimes, applied to states like China and Russia; and
- more or less temporary law-and-order dictatorships, often of a military character. These have been widespread in Latin America, Africa, the Middle East and parts of Asia.

In the third place, there are failed states, in which there is large-scale human rights abuse that cannot be attributed to the state since it has collapsed. As should be clear from the above remarks, states may appear in several categories at the same time.

As to the causes of these human rights abusing regimes or situations, the ideologically based ones are on the face of it to be understood in terms of their ideologies. Communism, in our view, is essentially illiberal. However, as regards Islam and the cultural specificity arguments, there is no such clear case to be made from Islamic, Confucian, etc. values for anti-liberalism. As we will argue in Part III, it is perfectly possible to develop liberal versions of these beliefs, so that the adoption of an illiberal understanding is, to some degree, a matter of choice governed by other considerations such as faithfulness to tradition, hostility to the 'West', or even class interests. Development dictatorships are clearly the product of belief in the need for authoritarian regimes to deliver economic benefits. This leaves us with the ragbag of law-and-order dictatorships and failed states, arising from ethnic, religious and class conflicts, often, but not always, in conditions of relative poverty or from ambition, corruption and greed.

What, then, should liberal states do to advance the liberal project in the light of these distinctions? We need, first, to remind the reader what we believe is the sensible goal of the liberal project at the international level for the foreseeable future. This goal is the creation of a world of liberal-democratic states. The aim is not to establish a world federal state with a liberal character. This may well come about at some point in the distant future. But it should not be the basis of present plans or aspirations. For one thing, such a world state would need ideological coherence, which, in our view, and contrary to the widespread assertion of an international consensus on human rights, we do not yet have.

So, the obvious preliminary step in a world of sovereign states is to transform all of them into liberal democracies. A world of liberal-democratic states would, of course, require international institutions, such as already exist, for the regulation of their interactions and the settlement of their disputes. No doubt these would need substantial reform. This is above all true of the Security Council, which at present institutionalizes the hierarchical differentiation of states through the establishment of the veto powers. In the first place, this officially sanctioned hierarchy no longer reflects the actual distribution of power in the world and, secondly, it is in conflict with the fundamental equality of states that should characterize a liberal international polity.

The legalized hierarchy exists because of the realities of the international security situation. There is no international sovereign that is capable of enforcing the rule of law and that is also accountable to its subjects. There are only more or less powerful states each of which is ultimately responsible for its own security in a potentially hostile world. The more powerful are not going to impose an equality on themselves in the absence of reasonable guarantees for their security.

Such guarantees cannot be forthcoming in a world of heavily armed states, some of which are authoritarian regimes that do not have to justify their foreign policies to their people, and have potentially hostile attitudes to each other and the liberal democracies. A world of liberal-democratic states, by contrast, would eliminate both these sources of international conflict and provide the context in which liberal reform of international institutions could be carried through. Liberal-democratic states are not in the habit of engaging in military adventures against each other. This may be because they have not been around long enough to make an adequate comparison with the behaviour of authoritarian states possible and because their security concerns have been overwhelmingly directed towards combating threats from illiberal powers. A world of liberal-democratic states could, in the absence of others to fight, turn upon each other. But this seems unlikely.[179]

If the long-term goal is a world of liberal-democratic states recognizing each other as equals and pursuing their prosperity and security together through common institutions, what should liberal states do in the present to promote this goal?

First, they should accept the character of the present international regime for the promotion of liberal human rights, that is, the fact that each state has a primary responsibility for the advancement of human rights in its territory. Only in regard to exceptional crimes against humanity may it be permissible for other states, or the international community collectively through the Security Council, to intervene coercively in a state's territory for the sake of protecting human rights or through the actions of the ICC. Standardly, both the UN and other states can pursue only non-coercive policies directed at influencing the policies of non-complying states. This combination seeks on the one hand, an effective prevention of the worst violations of human rights, and on the other, to preserve a world of sovereign states each responsible for the organization of its internal affairs, although answerable to the critical evaluation of the international community.

In the second place, the liberal states must make sure their own houses are in order before undertaking to criticize the human rights record of others. It cannot be emphasized too strongly how stupidly, as well as unlawfully, the Americans have acted in creating and maintaining the Guantanamo detention centre, denying the detainees their basic human rights. This symbol of the hypocrisy and double standards of the liberal powers, together with similar policies justifying and promoting the kidnapping and torture of suspected terrorists through the process of extraordinary rendition, has severely undermined liberal states' criticism of the human rights abuses of others. It enables a major human rights abuser such as President Putin of Russia to sneer at the liberal states for thinking themselves to be more civilized than the Russians while running or servicing such illegal camps.[180]

The American attitude displayed in such violations of international law is more generally to be condemned. It expresses a belief that as the liberal state *par excellence* and the only benign superpower, it must be free to take whatever steps it deems necessary to preserve world order. It is above the rule of law, while seeking to impose that rule on others. It is reluctant to submit itself to the international criminal courts and human rights covenants that it promotes internationally for others, on the grounds that its officers must be free from the harassment subordination to the court would be likely to produce, while its constitution already contains its own and superior scheme of rights. Such American exceptionalism is repugnant to American leadership in the pursuit of a liberal order of the world.[181]

Of course, in extreme emergencies, illiberal measures have to be taken for the sake of the security of individuals and the liberal state (and international human rights covenants allow that, as we have seen, in their derogation and limitation provisions). But the terrorist threat is not as yet an extreme emergency except in some parts of Iraq, which is largely the result of foolish and deceitful policies.

In the third place, the liberal states must recognize that the liberal project for world order is unavoidably a long-term one, which they need to pursue with patience and persistence and not be seduced by tempting short-cuts, such as the dream of a post-invasion liberal-democratic Iraq, or alternatively by retreating into the security of an exclusive liberal-democratic bloc opposed to the rest of the world. In other words, it should be a policy of promoting respect for human rights through the various forms that we have been discussing in this chapter: the UN fora, non-coercive foreign policy initiatives, full support for the ICC and encouragement for the work of the human rights non-governmental organizations, while being prepared to engage in collective, or even unilateral, humanitarian intervention if urgently necessary.

Such policies should be as consistent as possible. Obviously, the NATO powers cannot act towards Russia or China in the way in which they acted in the territories of the former Yugoslavia or are now acting in Afghanistan. But this is not a reason for turning a blind eye to what the Russians have been doing in Chechnya or with regard to the rule of law and civil freedoms more generally. Similarly cowardly policies should be avoided in respect of human rights abusive countries, such as Saudi Arabia, which for strategic or economic reasons are deemed 'friends'.

The greatest international asset possessed by the liberal-democratic states is the nominal commitment of all states to the liberal human rights norms. They should not allow these norms to be watered down by accepting arguments from cultural specificity that are supposed to justify giving priority to Islamic or Confucian, etc. values over human rights.

The non-discrimination principles of the human rights covenants and declarations forbid faith-, ideology- or gender-based limitations on individual freedom, and states should be held to account through the UN and the foreign policies of the liberal powers, as they will be by the human rights non-governmental organizations, for the systematic violation of these principles.

This anti-cultural specificity claim is quite different from the view, which we wholeheartedly support, that the liberal human rights norms can be justified from many diverse philosophical, religious and cultural standpoints. In Part III we explore some of the problems in doing this, but we believe it to be perfectly possible and much to be encouraged. In this sense, while in this book we have argued that liberalism is an invention developed in the West, we hold much more strongly the view that its norms and practices, being of universal value rather than an exclusive possession, can be appropriated by, and integrated with, other cultures without there being any implication of cultural imperialism by the West. The spread of liberalism throughout the world should no more be seen as a case of cultural imperialism than the spread of the principles of national self-determination or state sovereignty have been. The only cultural ground for objecting to such transfers is the Herderian belief in the superiority of pure cultures uncontaminated by foreign elements.[182] Such a view is both completely unrealistic and utterly myopic.

Some commentators on ethical foreign policy argue that because of the multiplicity of human rights abuses around the world, the liberal states should focus their efforts on some rather than others. Vincent, for example, proposes the following two criteria:

1. What are the worst cases of human rights abuse?
2. Which cases hold the best prospect of positive response to international attention?

He believes that, on this basis, the liberal states should concentrate on subsistence rights.[183] Donnelly, in the first edition of his work, similarly believes that states should focus on major and systematic violations of human rights.[184] He recommends that the right policy towards major abusers be one of positive non-involvement. Others think that cutting ties with abusive states is a mistake, since to do so runs the danger of losing all influence over that state. The problem is that the most effective policy will be, in some cases, to disengage, as was probably true of apartheid South Africa, and in others, to remain involved while maintaining diplomatic pressure. There may hence be no general rules to apply to individual situations, which makes implementation of an ethical foreign policy even more difficult.

As to the question of priorities, we have already made clear that development aid to lift the poorest countries into sustainable economic growth should be a major ongoing concern of the liberal states. There will also no doubt be major human rights emergencies that require immediate attention. But such ongoing and more temporary commitments should not be a reason to ignore other persistent abuses such as systematic violations of civil freedoms.

However, we do believe that, in general, it is more important to concentrate on promoting the rule of law and civil freedoms than in trying to get democracy established. There are those who think of democracy as necessarily accompanied by the civil freedoms. But this is quite incorrect. Democracy just means the rule of the people through a majority or by a government that is representative of the majority. Without liberal guarantees of individual freedom, such a democracy can be every bit as tyrannical for individuals and minorities as any individual despot.[185] So, rather than pressing for democracy and hoping that liberalism will accompany it, one should first seek the consolidation of civil freedoms and the rule of law as the conditions of a desirable democracy. Such priorities are also sensible in respect of the concern for sustainable development, since they are essential to the stable, long-run functioning of a market economy.

With regard to specific human rights international governmental organizations, we believe that the transformation of the Commission of Human Rights into the Human Rights Council has been of little help in bringing serious pressure to bear on major human rights offenders and that another attempt should be made to introduce the reforms initially proposed by the USA. These were first that members of the committee should be experts in the field and not government officials, and second that any country under investigation for serious human rights abuse should not be eligible for election or if already a member should have its membership suspended during the enquiry. The present operation of the Human Rights Council must surely spread cynicism about international human rights and encourage states to mouth the rhetoric while continuing to do as they please. Support must be built up among UN human rights staff and sympathetic countries for these absolutely minimum requirements of a respect-worthy UN implementation regime on human rights.

We believe also that regional organizations that have sponsored human rights regimes, such as the Council of Europe, the Organiza-tion of American States and the African Union should be encouraged to take a more active stance towards human rights abusers. Thus Russia has consistently ignored adverse judgements of the European Court of Human Rights regarding its conduct in Chechnya (except for paying, as we saw, the amounts of the required just satisfaction to the victims concerned) without any action being taken by the Council of Europe responsible for the oversight of the European Convention.[186] The African Union has recently instructed Senegal to bring to trial on its behalf the former President of Chad for crimes against humanity, but otherwise its record in bringing pressure on the massive human rights abusers in Africa has been lamentable. Furthermore, it is most disappointing that there is no Asian Convention on human rights and this should be remedied.

None of these measures look likely to be rapidly adopted but we reiterate that those committed to the international liberal project must be in it for the long term and must be willing to persevere in spreading the word and promoting the practice. This book, we hope, will be a contribution to that cause.

PART III

Critique and defence of liberalism

9 | Western critiques of liberal human rights

We have been presenting the liberal project as both a distinct theory and a practice of political association. This project has become the dominant ethic in the West and has taken fairly effective root in some non-Western countries and also, officially, in the UN. Yet there have been and still are many who reject liberalism's beliefs and values on principled grounds. In this final part of the book, we aim to identify the main theoretical opposition to rights-based liberalism in Western and non-Western intellectual traditions and to provide reasons to rebut such criticisms and for everyone to commit to the liberal project.

In this chapter, we will discuss the utilitarian, communitarian, Marxist and authoritarian arguments against liberal human rights. While differing substantially among themselves, of course, they do share a basic objection to the idea of human rights. This is the view that the attribution of human rights to individuals involves the untenable belief that individuals possess these rights absolutely and independently of considerations of the collective good. These critics differ over what they emphasize are the implications and consequences of this untenable belief, but their objections have to do with the way in which absolute and independent possession of rights misconstrues the proper relation of individuals to each other and to the common good.

The answer to these critics is to show that the view attributed to human rights theorists is not one that they have to hold or indeed that they should hold. The human rights theorist ought to say that individuals possess these rights only as part of a general system of equal rights through which each individual's right is related to the rights of others and regulated from the perspective of the coherence, harmony and security of the whole system.

The utilitarian critique

The original utilitarian onslaught was by Jeremy Bentham on the tradition of natural rights that we discussed in Part II of this work. Bentham was an indefatigable explorer and propagator of the utilitarian idea in the late eighteenth and early nineteenth centuries and secured for this doctrine a very influential position in British thought in the nineteenth and twentieth centuries.[1] His most explicit and vituperative attack on the idea of natural rights is contained in his *Anarchical Fallacies*, in which he discusses the Declaration of the Rights of Man and the Citizen, as proclaimed by the French revolutionaries of 1789.[2] This is the second major political document – the American Declaration of Independence being the first – that appeals to the idea of natural rights as the basis for a radical transformation of political tradition. According to Bentham, the appeal to natural rights is an anarchical doctrine destructive of good government because it incites citizens to reject the constraints on their natural passions that it is the function of government to provide through a system of law. He calls the logic of the natural rights doctrine 'a perpetual vein of nonsense flowing from a perpetual abuse of words' and in a well-known phrase he dismisses it as nonsense and the idea of imprescriptible natural rights as 'nonsense upon stilts'.[3]

Bentham begins his detailed criticism with a disparaging commentary on Article 2 of the French Declaration, which says: 'the end in view of every political association is the preservation of the natural and imprescriptible rights of man. These rights are liberty, property, security and resistance to oppression'.

Bentham interprets the first sentence to mean that (i) there are rights prior to government, (ii) such rights cannot be abrogated by government and (iii) governments are created by contract in order to preserve such rights and governments that exist in any other way are illegal and may be resisted. He rejects (i) outright and hence (ii) also. Men without government, he says, are like the savage nations of New South Wales. They have no habit of obedience and hence no government, no government and hence no laws, no laws and hence no such thing as rights. Without rights there will be no security and no property. There will be, however, a perfect liberty in the sense that the liberty of individuals will be unconstrained by law. At the same time, this will be a situation in which the liberty of each person will be constantly threatened by the power of others. So, no one will enjoy security and the level of happiness will be very low. In other words, a world without government will be an anarchical Hobbesian world in which every man is at war with every man.

Bentham has, of course, his own utilitarian criterion for evaluating government. What we should say, according to Bentham, is that, if it is advantageous to society that there should be such and such rights recognized in law, then governments should enact such laws, and vice versa. Furthermore, in order to determine the question of what is advantageous to society or not, we need to know the details of time and place and the specification of the proposed rights and not some vague general description of the right as expressed in the French revolutionaries' appeal to liberty, property, security, etc.

Even if there could not be any rights prior to government, legitimate government could still come into being through a contract. Yet, Bentham rejects this part of the doctrine also. The idea of the contractual origin of government is false because there never has been such a contract and it is in any case beside the point, since to evaluate and legitimate government we need to ask, not how it came into being, but whether it is contributing to the happiness of society. In addition, and in accordance with his views on the relation between rights, law and government, he holds that contracts come from government and not government from contracts.

Bentham understands the doctrine of natural rights, as affirmed by the French revolutionaries, to involve the idea that each person's right is absolute and unbounded. The natural right to liberty of individual A is an unbounded liberty, so also is individual B's natural right, and so on. This means, in effect that each person has a natural right to do anything he pleases; and hence a natural right to kill or injure others or to seize their possessions should he wish to do so. It is the idea of a natural right to liberty as a free-for-all, in which, of course, right has no meaning other than as the absence of any duty not to act as one pleases. Bentham raises the possibility that, in order to avoid the absurdity of the natural right doctrine, it should be understood as intending that rights should be limited by law, once government has been created. However, he rejects this interpretation on the grounds that it contradicts the express declaration that the rights are imprescriptible.

Furthermore, the obvious intention of asserting these rights is to limit the reach of government and law, so it would be senseless to suppose that government could determine these limits.

Bentham examines the unbounded nature of natural rights in more detail, taking each right separately. First, in regard to liberty, he holds that liberty and law are antithetical, since the latter imposes obligations and hence restricts liberty. If I have a right protected by law, then, this imposes an obligation on another not to violate my right and thus restricts his liberty. Since laws distributing rights *ipso facto* limit other people's liberty, they necessarily contravene their natural and imprescriptible rights.

With regard to the natural right to property, Bentham argues that to have a property right is to restrict other's liberty in respect of the thing owned. So, the right must be to some thing in particular: a house, a piece of land, and so on. If the natural right is a right to property in general but to nothing in particular, a person must either take what he wants without a specific right to that thing or starve. Since the affirmation of the natural right says nothing as to what anyone's legitimate claims are, the inference must be that every man has a natural right in everything. But what is everyman's right is no one's right.

Finally, in regard to the natural rights to security and resistance to oppression, Bentham sees these as incompatible with all laws that authorize the punishment of offenders and hence as incompatible with government itself and thus as the culmination of the absurdity of these anarchical fallacies.

It is obvious enough, given the understanding of natural and human rights that we have been promoting in this work, what our response to Bentham's critique will be. In the first instance, his claims as to the necessarily unbounded nature of the natural rights are clearly wrong. Each person's right is limited by the equal right of others. But this view has to be given some substance. In regard to liberty, if we understand the equal right to mean that everyone has the right to do whatever he pleases, we get Bentham's conclusion. So, we need to be able to specify some natural limits on each person's liberty to do as he pleases, arising from the existence of others with rights. These limits deny legitimacy to acts that involve the exercise of force or fraud (except when force is used in self-defence) or as Locke put it, acts that harm another in his life, liberty, health or possessions. These are, admittedly, still very general formulae, which need to be given much more detail in order to be justiciable in a court of law. The main problem lies in determining an initially just starting-point from which specific actions of others can be reasonably characterized as unjust invasions of a person's liberty, rather than as responses to the aggressions of another. But the idea of a natural right here is a right that any legitimate system of positive law must, first of all, ensure that there is a fair initial distribution of liberty between persons, treating everyone as an equal and, in the second place, such a system must provide an equal protection to everyone's liberty from acts of force and fraud and, finally, that the liberty of an individual may not otherwise be curtailed except insofar as restrictions may be necessary for the operation of a government and the safeguard of public order, health and morals as discussed in Chapter 4 above.

In respect of property, Bentham is, of course, correct that the natural right must be understood as a right to acquire rights to particular things and hence must specify a natural mode of legitimate acquisition. This is what Locke attempts to do, while Grotius and Pufendorf allow that beyond the natural right of first occupation more extensive rules governing legitimate possession can arise only through general consent. However, the trouble with a first-occupancy principle together with free transfers unaffected by force or fraud as the natural foundation legitimizing a system of positive legal ownership is that the actual history of property transfers in the past has been a sorry tale of force and fraud. Hence, it would be impossible to establish on the basis of such principles who are the current rightful possessors of anything. In addition, the principles do not in themselves have anything to say about ensuring fair access to possessions on the part of everyone. If everything is already (justly) appropriated at a certain point, and others are born into such a world who find that they have no means of acquiring any property through 'the work of their hands or the labour of their bodies', they will have had their natural right to preserve themselves through the acquisition of property violated. Thus, the historical principle of first occupancy and free transfer would at least have to be supplemented by social and economic rights guaranteeing fair access to everyone.

This brief discussion makes it clear that the question of just natural principles governing property acquisition and transfer requires fuller consideration, to which we will give further attention in the final chapter. However, that there should be much dispute over such principles does not support Bentham's contention that the idea of a natural right to property is empty because the right must necessarily be unbounded. The problem arises, as in the case of liberty, from the difficulty in specifying a naturally fair initial distribution of property. All that we need to say here is that a natural right should be understood as a right that any legitimate system of positive law should ensure fair access, treating everyone as an equal, with equal protection and no restrictions other than those necessary to protect the rights of others, the needs of government, and so on.

With regard to the natural right to security and the claim as to its incompatibility with government-legislated and enforced punishments, Bentham again totally fails to do justice to the natural rights theorists. Their view is that one has a natural right to defend oneself against violators of one's natural rights; and that in view of the general insecurity of a state of nature, it is rational for persons to together support the institution of a government with the authority to elaborate and enforce a system of laws based on natural principles. Such a scheme will increase everyone's security. Bentham's mistake is again to suppose that everyone's right is necessarily unbounded, so that any governmental law will violate that liberty.

Insofar as natural rights constitute natural principles for determining in broad terms the structure of a legitimate politico-legal order, it is not clear that Bentham is in such deep disagreement with the natural rights theorists, once we have rejected his view of natural rights as necessarily unbounded. For, as a liberal (of a classical turn), he espouses the same general principles regarding liberty, property and security as they do. Of course, he does not see these principles as expressing natural rights but rather as subordinate ones for organizing society derived from the fundamental principle of utility, which tells us to establish that order of society that will have the best consequences from the perspective of the general happiness. Nevertheless, the secondary principles can be seen as natural ones based on reason and experience. They are natural in the sense that they are the principles best adapted to human nature for the achievement of the general happiness.

In this way, rights-based liberalism and utility-based liberalism might be thought to approach each other. However, a standard rights-based criticism of utilitarianism is that by appealing to what serves the general happiness, the utilitarian accepts in principle the reasonableness of sacrificing some people's happiness to the greater happiness of others. If what maximizes the total happiness is a policy that imposes poverty and misery on a few, then this is acceptable from a utilitarian point of view because that point of view is not concerned with the claims of each person as setting a limit on what anyone else may do to him. Utilitarianism does count everyone's happiness and unhappiness in the calculation of the total – so everyone is to count for one and nobody for more than one – but it allows for the overriding of some people's interest in happiness if doing so will be counterbalanced by a greater amount accruing to others. This fails to treat each person as valuable in herself rather than as a contributor to the general good.

The utilitarian *per contra* accuses the rights' theorist of rule fetishism since he insists on inflexibly sticking to the rule of rights even when their observance in a particular case will have deleterious effects on the general utility. However, some utilitarians can be as fetishistic about rules as any rights' theorist could require by holding that only strict adherence to the rule of rights will, as a matter of fact, maximize the general utility. Furthermore, most rights' theorists, and the various declarations and covenants of human rights, allow that it may be necessary on occasion to suspend the protection of certain rights for the sake of the general good. So, despite their mutual hostility, there is a tendency, as we remarked in our introduction, for the two theories to approach each other in practice.

Where they still differ, of course, is in the ground they give for rights. The rights theorist holds that the maximizing principle of utilitarianism is unsatisfactory because what serves the general good may be very unjust to particular individuals and that no social scheme can be defensible if it cannot be justified to each person subject to it from his perspective as an individual with his own separate natural interests. The affirmation of natural or human rights as inherent attributes of individuals is one way of expressing this requirement. The rights protect the basic natural interests of individuals as separate beings with their own individual identities and destinies, whereas the idea of the general good lumps all individuals together as constituting an undifferentiated sum of utilities in which the inherent separateness of persons is lost.[4] Nevertheless, the rights' theorist must remember that while the individual is this ultimately separate being, he can have no claim to any rights except as an equal member of a moral community of rights holders in which his rights are necessarily limited by the equal rights of others and are realizable only through the creation of appropriate politico-legal institutions.

The communitarian critique

The term communitarianism is standardly applied, in the first instance, to a body of theoretical writing critical of liberal individualism that appeared in English-speaking philosophy in the 1980s. Of particular note are the works of this period of Alasdair MacIntyre, Michael Sandel, Charles Taylor and Michael Walzer.[5] Subsequently, the term has been used also to refer to more practically oriented writings concerned with the re-invigoration of local community feeling and action rather than with the national community. As one would expect from the name of this doctrine, the emphasis of these writers is on the importance of community in the lives of human beings, which they see liberalism as incapable of doing justice to. This stress on community has two aspects: a sociological and a moral thesis.

The sociological thesis is the primary one. It is the claim that human beings are essentially social beings. By this is meant that their nature as human beings as well as their particular identity as this or that human being is constituted by relation to the community of which they are members. Liberals are taken to deny this. For instance, it is said that the account by the natural rights theorists of the seventeenth century, as well as by contemporary writers such as Robert Nozick,[6] of a state of nature that obtains prior to the formation of political society, shows that they believe that individuals naturally exist as fully formed human beings independently of society. Similarly, the enormously influential contemporary liberal theorist John Rawls in his employment of the idea of an original position in which independent, rational and autonomous individuals reach agreement on reasonable principles of social co-operation, reveals the same assumption that human beings' identities are constituted independently of society and that society is the product of a contract by such persons. By contrast, the communitarians hold that human beings are born into and necessarily formed by a community and that how an individual comes to think of himself and his interests will be determined by the range of possibilities available to him in the beliefs and practices of his community. An individual self is not an inherently separate and independent rational entity but a being embedded in the thick fabric of a particular communal life.

Communitarians hold that the consequence of liberalism's false view of the nature of human beings is that social life is corrupted and undermined. Society is atomized by being dissolved into its separate individual atoms rather than held together by a rich nexus of constitutive relations through which the identity of each member is tied to that of others and the whole. The liberal atoms will be connected only externally through relations of self-interest, as typically realized in the market economy but now spreading throughout society. Individual rights held against society are the hallmark of this corruption because they protect the individual in the pursuit of his interest from intervention by society or other individuals and hence entitle him to act selfishly. Such a society cannot recognize a genuine common good that unites the members and subordinates their selfish passions. On the contrary, liberal society can be held together only through compromise between selfish and hence conflicting interests.

Some of these themes are barely distinguishable from Marxist ones, which we will discuss shortly. But the communitarians of the 1980s are not Marxists. Unfortunately, they tell us very little about the proper organization and moral constitution of genuine communities. They accept, of course, that there will be a plurality of properly constituted communities. But that would still be compatible with their having a common, if general, moral form. This is the point at which the second aspect of the communitarian doctrine arises. This is the moral thesis. It holds that human beings should act in accordance with the norms and values of their socially constituted identity. In fact, insofar as liberalism is avoided and community properly established, individuals are more or less bound to act in the morally required way. For, if they have been adequately socialized, they will conceive their identity and interests appropriately. The most explicit of the communitarians on this subject is MacIntyre. Communitarian morality, according to MacIntyre, is one of roles and functions. Individuals are members of families. They are fathers and mothers, husbands and wives, sons and daughters, brothers and sisters; and these identities specify their rights and duties towards other members of the family and as family members towards society at large. They will also exercise a trade, business or profession, such as farmer, craftsman, merchant or soldier. These roles will have standards of conduct and specific virtues attached to their performance, which the role bearers will be expected to meet or aspire to attain. Furthermore, being a member of an independent community, as distinct from fulfilling particular roles within it, is itself a role with appropriate virtues belonging to it, such as loyalty, patriotism and public-spiritedness.[7]

Since a functionalist view of morality suffers from obvious defects, it is not surprising that on the whole the communitarian critics of liberalism are so reticent about the nature and content of communitarian ethics and speak of it only in the most general terms by commending the strength of communal attachments and loyalties and the thickness of communal identities as compared with the thinness and weakness of the identities and relations of liberal individuals. Nor is it surprising to find that these writers, reared in great liberal academies, begin soon enough to backtrack from the implications of their strong communitarianism in order to allow that individuals have the capacity to reflect upon and critically engage with the practices and beliefs of their community.[8] For the obvious shortcoming of a strong communitarianism is that the structure of society as a whole and of particular groups within it may be unjust and oppressive. But if persons' identities and interests are constituted by their roles in society, then there is no scope for anyone to stand back from their embeddedness in their roles and subject them to criticism from an ideal point of view. Since it is not just liberals but peoples throughout history who have engaged in the activity of constructing ideal standards for evaluating the justice of, or perhaps simply justifying, the particular arrangements of their society, the strong communitarian thesis of embeddedness seems hopelessly wrong.

However, the ideal standards appealed to may themselves be communitarian in nature: that is to say, they may treat individual self-fulfilment and happiness as achievable only through fulfilling a function in a community that is structured in accordance with supposed natural differences between human beings. Thus, within the family it may be held that there is a natural division of labour between man and woman based on their different natures. In society, it may be claimed that one can identify different classes of person that reflect their different natural abilities and dispositions. If everyone occupies the place for which he or she is naturally fitted, then the ideal will be achieved in actuality. Plato's *Republic* gives classic expression to such a communitarian ideal.

The caste beliefs of Hinduism constitute another example. These ethical conceptions, nevertheless, presuppose the capacity of at least some individuals to stand back from their embeddedness in their actual social relations and beliefs to reflect upon the ideal.

A more modern communitarian ideal is that of organic nationalism. According to this doctrine, humanity is naturally divided into nations and each nation ought to govern itself in conformity with its cultural traditions. Individuals are born into and achieve their good only through service to the nation. Since nations differ, and are characterized by both a distinct ethnicity and a separate culture, there is no substantive universal socio-political order, as in Platonism or Hinduism, that all nations must conform to in order to realize the good. Each has its own national ideals. What is common, however, is the universal ethical truths, that humanity is divided into organic natural wholes, that nations should govern themselves and that individuals achieve their good as part of the self-governing nation.

Contemporary communitarianism in its initially strong form before its adherents start backing away from its unsavoury implications really only makes sense as a form of organic nationalism. It is organic nationalism without ethnicity and so a purely culturally based nationalism. Humanity is naturally divided into cultural communities and individual identities and interests are constituted as parts of such wholes. By implication such wholes should be self-governing. The dangers of such a view arise from its denial of the ethical claims of members of the society who are not culturally pure. Since to be a member of the community is to be constituted by relation to its culture, those who do not so identify themselves or who do not participate in it cannot be genuine members and so are not entitled to the rights of members. Just as traditional ethno-cultural nationalism leads to the creation of second-class citizens, ethnic cleansing or even genocide, because few, if any, states are ethno-culturally pure, organic cultural nationalism would tend towards a similar discrimination against culturally impure elements.

If one tries to avoid this conclusion by allowing that what are broadly called cultures may be internally diverse and conflicting, so that the identity of the culture is subject to indefinite contestation, the advantages of cultural communitarianism disappear. The community's identity in a substantive sense would become unclear. Individuals could not securely identify themselves and their interests and achieve their self-determination by relation to the fixed standard of the community's good, since what this was would be in dispute among them. One possibility, at this point, would be to hold that the individual's fundamental cultural identity should not be conceived in terms of his membership of the overall political association but in terms of his membership of cultural subgroups that have their own distinct and coherent identities. This suggestion forms the basis of recent attacks on liberalism from a so-called multi-cultural point of view. This multi-cultural critique of liberalism we will consider shortly.

So far we have not challenged the communitarian conception of the asocial nature of liberal man. But, in fact, this view is quite false. Liberals need not reject the communitarian's sociological thesis. They can perfectly well accept the claim that human beings develop their human capacities only through being born and brought up in communities that provide them with secure attachments, teach them a language and ways of thinking about themselves, their society and world. If the natural rights theorists of the seventeenth century and contemporary Rawlsians believe differently, then they were and are clearly wrong. However, it is not necessary for them to have held or to hold such an absurd position. What they cannot accept is the full embeddedness thesis. They must hold that in the development of their human capacities for reflective thought, individuals can distance themselves from their particular identifications and understandings and think of themselves and their interests from a much more general point of view. As we have already claimed, such a move from a more or less unreflective identification with one's community and its practice and beliefs towards a more detached standpoint from which one views one's own community from a universal perspective is possible even within an overall communitarian ethic such as Platonism.

So, there seems no reason why all theorists, including rights-based liberals cannot accept the sociological thesis as an account of the necessary conditions of the intellectual, emotional and moral development of human beings while holding at the same time that human beings possess the inherent capacity to transcend their initial embeddedness in the particular and to come to evaluate the particular from the standpoint of the universal. Such a claim, however, assumes that the standpoint outside the individual's community is one from which a genuinely universal truth can be reached. This is the point at which communitarians are inclined to take a relativist direction. MacIntyre, in particular, develops this line, but it is essential for all to take if their position is not to collapse immediately before the apparent facts of human transcendence towards the truth.[9]

If it is held that the self embedded in the fabric of a particular communal life must necessarily orient itself in the world through the beliefs and practices of that community, then one must deny that there is any standpoint outside a person's community and accessible to her from which she could evaluate its beliefs and practices in terms of truth and goodness. Among the beliefs of a community are likely to be general statements about what is good and bad, virtuous and vicious, which serve to legitimize the community's way of life. A member of that community will absorb these beliefs and make truth claims on their basis. These truth claims, however, will be valid only within the perspective of the beliefs of that community. A community in which patriarchy is deeply embedded will hold that women should not have the same education and opportunities as men, and statements made from within the patriarchal viewpoint will be true for those who hold those beliefs. But they will be false for members of a liberal community who hold that men and women are fundamentally equal and should have equal opportunities.

On this view, there is no genuinely impartial general standpoint from which particular beliefs of a community can be evaluated in terms of truth and goodness. General standpoints from which apparently objective claims are made are themselves aspects of a community's system of beliefs and anyone making such claims will not be distancing himself from his community but will remain embedded in it. General statements about values from within a perspective of this kind are ideologies that purport to justify a particular way of life but in fact only express its commitments at a general level.

We will discuss the inadequacies of this type of relativism in the next chapter when we consider the claims of cultural relativism as a response to the clash between a Western-based liberal human rights culture and non-Western values. But the communitarian view that the self is necessarily embedded within the particular community it is formed by seems, once again, obviously false. Quite apart from the fact that entities such as 'the British community' are far from being homogeneous units of belief but rather include divergent and conflicting views, some of which may involve the radical criticism of the community in question, it is clearly perfectly possible, and not even extremely rare, for someone formed in one tradition of thought to come to reject it and to convert to some alien body of beliefs: for instance, to move from being a Western-type liberal to becoming a Muslim fundamentalist.

In one sense, such a person can be said to have acquired a new Muslim self or identity that is constituted in relation to the beliefs and practices of Islam. He is not the same person that he was. But this self-evidently paradoxical statement reveals that, in another sense, the convert is the same person who before his conversion possessed a liberal identity. To make sense of this combination of sameness in change, we need to distinguish two levels of personal identity. At one level, a human being is an individual psycho-physical organism that is born at a certain time and has a unique spatio-temporal history until death. As a human being whose human capacities have been developed, it is a self-conscious, language-speaking and reason-giving individual organism. This is the basic level of identity in terms of which we can say that a person is one and the same being throughout his life. This level combines individual uniqueness with the general form of human identity. This description refers to the fact that, at this level, the unique individual has, apart from his unique spatio-temporal history, no differentiating features. It is one individual human being just like any other. We will call it the general individual.

The other level of personal identity involves the particular relations and experiences of these general individuals over time. One person will differ from another in terms of such particularities. As self-conscious language speakers, such persons will identify themselves by reference to the particular features that are important to them and that in this sense can be said to constitute their identity. Belonging to particular groups will standardly be present in such self-identifications. Clearly, these particular identities can change radically over time without destroying the sameness of the general individual. In a functioning human being these two levels do not just lie alongside each other but are synthesized: a human being is a unity of generality, individuality and particularity.

The point of raising these matters about personal identity in this context is to show how naturally a self-conscious, reason-giving being understood in the above way can distance itself from its particular identifications and think of itself from a general point of view. In doing this, persons are abstracting from their particular identity and thinking of themselves as human beings in general with the capacities and interests that are peculiar to such beings: in other words, as general individuals. From this perspective, they can raise the question as to what interests such persons have in associative living and how they can best organize their social lives. The answer that is arrived at from such a perspective may, of course, not be a liberal one. It may, indeed, involve claims as to the differential possession of the human capacities, as in Platonism. But the naturalness with which human beings can take up this perspective shows that the communitarian cannot blithely assert that human beings are wholly constituted by their particular communal identities. This is clearly false. At most the communitarian can maintain that there is nothing much of substantive interest that can be said at the general level and that there are many different particular answers that are compatible with such a meagre generality with no way of showing that one answer is better than another.

Such a position would be disputable. Furthermore, it would take us well away from the communitarian criticism of liberalism. For, it is difficult to see why liberalism couldn't be one of the possible ways of filling out the meagre generality. Liberalism, we have shown, is compatible with the acknowledgement of the importance of particular communities in the development of individuals' human capacities. In addition, its appeal to the capacity to abstract from particularity to general conceptions of human being has been vindicated even if its particular prescriptions from that perspective are not conclusive.

The communitarian might still claim that the liberal's conception of the basis of community, because of its general, abstract and thin nature, cannot do justice to the importance of communal attachments in human lives or to the necessity for the development of strong communal loyalties for the viability of human associations. However, from the general standpoint the liberal standardly argues for the rational necessity of political association and for the existence of a plurality of such associations. Thus, human beings, in becoming aware of who they are, will necessarily find themselves members of such particular communities and will naturally develop appropriate attachments and loyalties. From the liberal general standpoint, nothing is said about how to group people in particular associations but most thinkers have come to accept ethnicity and culture as relevant but not determining considerations. Yet, in a sense this does not matter. However human beings are collected together in particular associations, they will have to develop strong loyalties and commitments in their members if they are to sustain themselves as independent self-governing entities over time. From a liberal point of view these commitments must be subject to the overriding ethical requirements of liberal community. But there is no reason to suppose that acceptance of such overriding principles will sap or undermine the strength of their attachment to their particular communities any more than a commitment to any other ethical principles will.

Multi-cultural communitarianism

A liberal society is perfectly compatible with the flourishing of many different cultural sub-groups within it provided that the sub-groups respect liberal norms and treat their members as having the right to dissociate themselves from the group should they so wish. The recent development of an anti-liberal multi-culturalism springs from the application of the strong communitarian idea of individual identity to an individual's membership of the sub-group rather than to his membership of the political community. The primary cultural identities of individuals are said to be constituted in relation to such sub-groups and the political association is conceived as a forum within which the representatives of the sub-groups enter into negotiations with a view to achieving peaceful accommodation. The entities that are promoted as the bearers of these primary identities are ethno-cultural minorities either long established or of recent immigration and also other groupings that have come to have a degree of political importance arising from being seen as the victims of discrimination in liberal society, such as blacks, women, homosexuals, the disabled, and so on. Liberalism, because of its constitution of the political realm on the basis of human beings' supposed abstract general identity, is said to deny political relevance to these cultural identities and so excludes them from political participation. By doing this, liberalism secures the unchallenged interests of the dominant class, which is held to be that of white middle class males. Hence, liberalism cannot do justice to these groups and must be opposed. Groups must be the bearers of rights, especially in the political realm.[10]

This form of multi-culturalism is deeply antagonistic to the idea of an overarching national identity, let alone one that is subject to liberal norms. Given the primacy of the sub-group, any larger identity would have to arise from the achievement of a *modus vivendi* among the groups in a particular political forum, now known as the state, and would have to remain subject to rejection or re-negotiation by any sub-group. This, of course, reverses the appropriate relation between national and group identity as this has been standardly understood. National identity trumps other group identities on the traditional view. No doubt, this could have deeply illiberal consequences, which is why national identity should itself be subject to liberal principles. Equally obviously, such a communitarian multi-culturalism would protect internally illiberal groups from having to respect the rights to freedom and equality of their members.

What is fundamentally wrong with this is the communitarian idea of identity that it adopts. We have criticized this idea in the last section. But it also quite misrepresents the way in which liberalism treats sub-groups. Members of groups in a liberal state are perfectly free to organize themselves politically in order to promote their group interests in the political domain by seeking changes in public policy or legislation. The pursuit of group interest in politics is subject to two sets of constraints. Firstly, proposals must not violate the fundamental commitments of liberalism to the equal civil, political, social and economic rights of everyone. Secondly, within the area of legislative indeterminacy left by the first constraint on acceptable laws, groups must accept the resolution of conflicts of interest by majority decisions arrived at through a fair system of representation based on equal individual civil and political rights. The willingness to accept majority decision-making, albeit within liberal constraints, requires that the group attach greater weight to its membership of the national community than to its sub-group within it.

A more modest claim for the special recognition of cultural difference, over and above what is obviously required by liberal norms, would be one made on behalf of cultural minorities whose values are not incompatible with liberalism but whose members are disadvantaged relative to the majority in terms of their ability to compete on fair terms for positions of wealth and status. The demand would be for preferential treatment of the members of such groups so that they could enjoy fair equality of opportunity. However, this would not give special recognition to the culture as such but to its members as disadvantaged individuals. While such preferential treatment is acceptable in principle under liberalism, it is difficult to administer fairly – since the benefits of such schemes tend to accrue to the better-off members of the disadvantaged group – and without generating high levels of resentment among the majority population.

A certain kind of anti-liberal feminism can be understood as an example of the group identity argument. In its eighteenth and nine-teenth century origins, feminism consisted in the application of liberal principles to women. Women were conceived as having the same nature and interests as men and were therefore entitled to the same liberal rights.

Radical feminists from the 1970s opposed the liberal assimilation of women's claims on the grounds that the liberal conception of the person did not reflect women's nature. This nature had been obscured by millennia of patriarchal rule and needed liberation from patriarchal society before its true content could be revealed. But whatever it turned out to be, the radical feminists were certain that it would not be liberal in character. Whereas liberalism was based on impersonal rationality and abstraction, a woman's ethical life was rooted in her body and its emotions. Given that women are not individuals in the liberal sense, then the multi-cultural arguments against the possibility of political justice for non-liberal groups within a liberal polity would apply to women also. They also count as a discriminated against 'minority' and deserve special representation in the political sphere.

The appropriate answer to all these claims as to the differentiated particular identity of cultural groups (women, blacks, etc.), is that although there is no doubt that these differentiating particular features exist, all these human beings are general individuals as well as having such particular identities and on that basis are capable of thinking of themselves and their interests from a general point of view as human beings.[11]

The Marxist critique

Karl Marx's major work of his maturity, *Das Kapital*, is an elaborate theoretical and practical critique of economic liberalism. But we are not going to attempt a brief critique of this critique. Suffice it to say that Marx's theoretically based predictions regarding the inability of the capitalist economies to go on increasing the production of wealth and raising the standard of living of the workers have been shown by events to be hopelessly wrong-headed. The critique of liberalism that we will focus on is the one to be found in his early work before his turn to economic theory and most clearly expressed in an essay on the Jewish question.[12] In our view the assumptions of this essay remain an integral part of the later economic work.

In this essay Marx is responding to an article by a contemporary fellow radical thinker, Bruno Bauer. Bauer had claimed that there were no grounds for the political emancipation of the Jews (i.e. granting them the vote), because the emancipation of the Jews was a religious problem. The Jews, Bauer held, should first emancipate themselves from their religion, so that both Jews and Christians could live simply and truly as free human beings. This would constitute a truly human emancipation. Jews have a right to emancipation only as human beings and this requires emancipating themselves from Jewishness. By such religious emancipation Bauer does not mean necessarily that people should cease to have religious beliefs but rather that religion should not involve membership in groups determinative of their identities but become a purely private affair.

For Marx, the crucial point about the modern liberal state is precisely that, through a policy of toleration, it can liberate itself politically by abolishing all religious qualifications for political membership and participation, thus distinguishing people's political identity from their religious identity, without liberating people from their religion. It is pointless, then, for Bauer to demand, in the context of the liberal state, that people be liberated from religion before they can be liberated politically, since the whole point of that state is the separation of political emancipation from other sorts of emancipation.

Of course, Marx agrees with Bauer that what is needed is a complete human emancipation. However, to achieve this, the liberal state must be abolished. Furthermore, Marx is not primarily interested in the religious sphere but in the economic one. He uses religion as an example of liberal state practice that applies much more significantly in the economic sphere. Here, the modern liberal-democratic state – he was thinking primarily of the USA, and France in its more revolutionary moments – liberates the state politically from private property by giving everyone the vote and making them citizens whether they are rich or poor, property owners or proletarians.

This is not, of course, a genuine human emancipation from private property for Marx because people still relate to each other in the economic sphere as property owners and proletarians. Thus, while democracy promises human freedom, it is only an illusion of it, since it leaves men tied to the inequalities and dependencies of civil society. Translated to the economic sphere, Bauer's proposal amounts to saying to the capitalists and proletarians, first liberate yourselves from property and market relations and then you can be truly emancipated politically. For Marx, this makes no sense unless state and economy are transformed at the same time.

The political annulment of private property in fact presupposes the continued existence of private property because the liberal state is founded upon the distinction between a public, communal world of politics in which the common good of all is supposed to be pursued, and a private world of economy, religion, and so on, in which individuals seek their private good. Under this conception, man leads a double life. Marx calls it a heavenly and earthly one, a life as a citizen where he is valued as a communal being and one in civil society where he is a private individual, treats others as means to his ends and degrades himself into a means to the ends of others through their relations in the market. This dependence on market forces, Marx describes as a process in which one becomes the plaything of alien powers or, less dramatically, of money.

Marx identifies this division between private and public life with the distinction in the French revolutionary Declaration of Rights between the rights of man and those of the citizen. The rights of man to freedom are not based on the union of man with man but on their separation. They are rights to be a separate and hence limited individual. It is best expressed through the right to private property which is a right to exclude others from one's possessions and hence a right of selfishness. Others appear as a limitation on one's freedom, and equality means only an equal right to selfishness.

Political community on this liberal view of man is in effect only an abstract ideal framework external to individuals and the only real bond holding them together is need and private interest. The political community, while purporting to realize the common good, is in actuality degraded into serving the interests of egoistic man. This is because political man is not a real being but only an abstract fictional being.

Real emancipation for Marx, then, involves abolishing the distinction between public and private life:

The actual individual man must take the abstract citizen back into himself and, as an individual man in his empirical life, in his individual work and relationships become a species-being; man must recognize his own forces as social forces, organize them and thus no longer separate social forces from himself in the form of political forces. Only when this has been achieved will human emancipation be completed.[13]

Marx's idea of a complete human emancipation here looks as though it requires a collective organization of the economy of a society as a single enterprise. His later work suggests such a view more strongly and this is, of course, how his political disciples attempted to realize his idea. Once again, we will not attempt to comment on the economics of this scheme. We are in any case primarily interested in the ethical content of this idea of human freedom and how it stands in relation to liberalism. The supposed ethical superiority of the communist idea obviously has to do with the way in which it conceives the relation of individuals to community compared with the liberal idea of this relationship. The clue to Marx's conception lies in his use of the term 'species-being'. This is an idea he takes directly from his older German contemporary and philosopher, Ludwig Feuerbach. Feuerbach was an atheist who held that historically human beings had constructed a notion of God as the possessor of the ideal attributes of perfect knowledge, goodness, mercifulness and justice.[14] Human beings then aspired to imitate God's perfection as best they could. But according to Feuerbach, the divine attributes are in fact the defining or essential attributes of humanity transposed onto a transcendent being and thus alienated from themselves as an essential moment in their acquisition of self-knowledge. For human beings to come to full self-knowledge and freedom, they must overcome this alienation by bringing back their essential powers into themselves and recognizing them as their own powers.

Feuerbach did not, of course, mean that separate individuals could achieve the divine perfection in their individual lives. The divine powers were the attributes of humanity as a whole, understood as a series of human beings spread over time and into the future. Human beings are a species-being, according to Feuerbach. By this he means that they are conscious of themselves as members of a species. Hence, when an individual who has overcome his alienated existence understands the true relation of the value of his human powers to the species as a whole, he will see that his worth as a particular individual consists in his contribution to the development and perfection of the powers in the species over time. In other words, the individual's ethical significance consists in his connection with the other individuals in the series and thus as an addition to the goodness realized in the whole.

Feuerbach claimed to be a materialist but in applying the Feuerbachian idea to labour and the economic sphere Marx rejected Feuerbach's claim and asserted his own better title to the name. According to Marx, what is essentially human is not so much the activity of mind – the traditional view of idealists – but labour. Hence as a species-being an individual's labour has value only as part of social labour. An individual worker realizes his own nature and fulfils himself only through his connection in the labouring process with other workers. However, under capitalism the value of the individual worker as part of the social whole is alienated because the interdependence of workers in the process of social production is achieved through the alienating force of market relations governed by money. Money is the alien god to which the powers properly belonging to humanity are attributed.

The essential ethical idea here is an organicist one which is to be found in most pre-liberal thinking in Western and other traditions. The individual has no worth in himself but only through fulfilling a function as part of a larger whole. What is peculiar about the Feuerbachian-Marxist use of this idea is that there is no attempt to give it a determinate structure by specifying particular functions within the whole and giving relations between them a hierarchical form. The whole is just a temporally extended series of undifferentiated individuals.

What is wrong with this ethical idea? First of all, there are some obvious misrepresentations of liberalism centred on the claim of the inherent selfishness of liberal rights. Liberal rights, of course, allow the individual to pursue his own interest as he sees fit. But he must do so within a framework of rights that requires him to respect others as equally valuable beings and to recognize that he has rights only as a member of a community of equal rights-holders. Furthermore, there is no reason to suppose that human beings will exercise their rights within the framework of equal rights in purely self-centred ways. They will, naturally, in accordance with their natural sociability – a feature Marx clearly presupposes – enter into co-operative relations of all kinds, including economic ones.

Secondly, Marx makes much of the distinction between private and public spheres under liberalism. He sees correctly that this is an essential aspect of it. He believes, however, that the public power under liberalism expresses an empty, because purely abstract, idea of the common good. Since the public power actually exists, its actual content will be determined by the dominant interest, which is that of the capitalists. This view is substantially misleading. The liberal common good is at the most general and abstract level constituted by the system of equal freedoms and opportunities. But this system has to be given concrete reality in and through the public power of a par-ticular state. Furthermore, this power has to give specific determin-ation to the basic rights in a detailed system of legislation and there will naturally be disagreement among the citizens as to what is the fairest and best interpretation of the general principles. In this process different interests will seek to promote their case. A decision pro-cedure is required to resolve disputes which all have to accept as binding on them. The institutions and procedures through which the public power operates will then be essential parts of the common good. The actual laws, if they are to be accepted by all as binding, must be capable of being understood as not unreasonable interpret-ations of the system of equal freedom. Such interpretations are likely to favour some interests over others but a liberal-democratic system will give other parties the opportunity to combine to reverse this bias.

While Marx substantially misrepresents liberal ideas and practices, he is nevertheless working with a fundamentally different ethical idea from that of liberalism. As we have characterized it above, it is the idea of the ethical worth of individuals as consisting in their contri-bution to a social whole, which is in effect the total social production. We have, of course, argued that the liberal idea is also best understood in terms of an ethical whole: the community of equal rights-holders. But the liberal idea treats persons as having a right to choose for themselves how they shall live, within the limits of the community of rights-holders, without further regard to their contribution to the whole. The idea of the community of rights-holders does not involve an appeal to any substantive content (such as the total social production). It requires only that the members respect each other's worth as autonomous choosers of their own lives. In this sense liberalism can be said to treat individuals as having worth in themselves.

The authoritarian critique

The authoritarian critics of liberalism attack it for affirming the equality and freedom of human beings. They believe that human beings are profoundly unequal and need hierarchy and submission to an authority that cannot be represented as springing from themselves. While sharing a powerful contempt for the idea of human beings' equality and freedom, they provide different justifications for the subjection of the great majority.[15]

The first major thinker to develop this line of criticism was Joseph de Maistre, a Savoyard Catholic aristocrat writing at the end of the eighteenth century in response to the upheavals of the French Revolution.[16] He believes that human beings are naturally evil and that their refractory wills need to be broken by an overwhelming force that must come from an authority external to the people. This is best provided for by a religiously grounded monarchy. The liberal Enlightenment of the seventeenth and eighteenth centuries, believing in the natural goodness of human beings, had attempted to liberate the people from religious and monarchical authority and to make government depend on the consent of the governed. Because this ran contrary to human nature, the effort culminated in the horrors of the French Revolution.

Carl Schmitt, writing first under the liberal Weimar regime in Germany and then under the Nazis, expressed similar conclusions from different premises.[17] For Schmitt, life is essentially conflictual, involving a radical distinction between friend and enemy. Liberals believe that conflicts can be resolved through the compromise of interests, rational discussion and mutual toleration of different values. This is illusory because life itself acquires its meaning and value through decisions that designate some other group as the enemy. The decision, supported by appropriate mythical constructions, creates the unity of one's own group and steels its members to do battle. Leaders are essential to make these decisions and to express the unity of the popular will. In this sense, a dictatorship of the fascist type, as exemplified by Hitler, is more democratic than the elected governments of

parliamentary democracies, which are characterized by endless discussion and conflicts of interest. Like de Maistre's, Schmitt's vision is
one of the unavoidable brutality of life for which liberals have no
stomach and against which they have no defence. De Maistre and
Schmitt are inegalitarians primarily because they believe that life is
violent and that a degree of order and unity can be achieved only
through the strong imposing their will and vision on the rest. To do
this, they have to acquire or inherit some legitimating myth for their
rule and sufficient control of force to compel the subjection of the
majority.

The fascists, whom Schmitt at least partially endorsed, believed in
authoritarian government and the inevitability of conflict and war,
while also excoriating liberal democracy. But they were extreme
nationalists who took seriously the idea of the inherent unity of the
national community and claimed political authority and the right to
rule on the grounds that they constituted the elite of that community.
In that sense, they were primarily communitarians in their rejection of
liberal democracy and only secondarily authoritarians.[18]

A somewhat different type of inegalitarianism is represented by the
late nineteenth-century German thinker Nietzsche.[19] Nietzsche believes
in the natural superiority of some men to the rest of humanity. This
superiority consists in their achievement of the autonomy that liberalism might be thought to attribute to all persons. For Nietzsche, it is
only the rare few who can become true legislators for their lives and
hence self-dependent beings. The great mass of humanity is incapable
of taking such responsibility for itself and needs instead to identify
itself by relation to its community and the community's values. They
are essentially dependent beings and as such despised as a herd in need
of a master. The morality of the herd is egalitarian, since that belief
relieves it of the pain of recognizing its own inferiority and submission. Yet, the herd still needs to submit to a coercive authority and be
ruled from above.

An interesting and quite influential version of the Nietzschean
vision of human inequality is to be found in the thought of Leo
Strauss, a twentieth-century German-American academic philosopher.[20] For Strauss, the superior beings are genuine philosophers who
pursue truth unshackled by respect for communal values and public
opinion. Indeed, he sees the needs of philosophy and society to be in
conflict with each other. Philosophy needs complete freedom of

enquiry, while society requires coercive authority, fixed values and the subjection of its members to its order. Philosophy uncovers truths that if publicized to the masses would undermine the herd's belief in and submission to society's coercive institutions. Thus philosophy rejects religious belief and reveals that all societies are founded on a criminal seizure of territory that naturally belongs to all. But without the backing of religious and other legitimizing myths, the herd will refuse to submit and society will disintegrate. Since philosophers need an orderly society to pursue in peace their elite activities, they should communicate among themselves in esoteric languages regarding the truth, while publicly lending support to the communal values they reject. They must help tame the herd, not by ruling directly as Platonic philosopher kings, but by covertly advising sympathetic rulers on the needs of the masses.

The reader may think that the question of human inequality or human equality is not open to rational debate but is simply a matter of a person's fundamental value commitments. However, before adopting such a view, it should be recalled that the liberal does not make the absurd claim that human beings are equal in respect of their potentialities or achievements. With regard to any human attribute, liberals can accept that some human beings can and do achieve more than others. This even applies to the capacity for autonomy. Since autonomy should be understood, not as an all-or-nothing feature of human beings, but as admitting of degrees of realization, the liberal assertion of equality amounts only to the claim that all normal human beings have a sufficient capacity for autonomy, if given a fair start in life, for it to be better for them to take responsibility for the major choices in their lives regarding work, friendship, marriage, religious or other affiliations and support for political parties, than for them to be subject to some elite authority in these matters. This is compatible with the acceptance that there are some superior intellects that have a much deeper understanding of the values involved than the ordinary person and that such superior beings should even be selected as the leaders of society but only so long as they remain responsible to the people for their actions through some such institutions as those of liberal democracy.

Of course, it is always possible that equality will be understood as the enemy of excellence and distinction in all spheres because it is taken to mean that each person's understanding and valuation of anything is as good as anyone else's. But there is no reason to attribute such a ridiculous view of equality to liberalism and less reason to fear its domination of a society that is liberal as well as democratic than in a pure democracy. Liberalism protects individuals' freedoms, including the freedom to pursue excellence.

10 | *Liberalism and non-Western cultures*

This chapter has a broader scope than that of a consideration of critiques of liberal human rights from non-Western cultural perspectives. It will cover some of these but it will also examine attempts to show that liberal practices can be endorsed from non-Western cultural perspectives. The latter literature claims either that there already exists an overlapping consensus of the major world cultures on human rights or that there would be no great difficulty in constructing one. An overlapping consensus in this context would be a consensus on the desirability of the actual practices prescribed by the United Nations human rights regimes but one that was supported in diverse ways by the different religious or metaphysical theories of the world's cultures.

We believe that such a consensus is both possible and highly desirable. A consensus on human rights of this kind has come about in the West, although some parties to the consensus, such as the Catholic Church, have joined it only recently. However, we believe also that some of the literature on non-Western adherence to a human rights consensus is quite naïve about the content of the United Nations human rights requirements and tends to ignore its liberal core consisting in the civil freedoms. Once the human rights regimes are identified in terms of this liberal core, the conflict between liberalism and non-Western traditional ethical cultures becomes more apparent and an overlapping consensus on human rights will be seen not to be possible without the transformation of those traditions by liberal ideas. This is indeed what happened in the West, so there is nothing peculiar in the clash between liberalism and non-Western traditional culture.

Our claim, it should be remembered, is not that liberalism was inherent in traditional Western culture, but rather that it involved a fairly radical reformation of that culture.

Liberalism is, nevertheless, indigenous to the West and imported into non-Western societies through the West's hegemony in international society. It is, therefore, fairly easy for non-Western peoples to see liberalism as alien to their cultures. Furthermore, the UN human rights programme with its liberal core can appear as just a continuation of the liberal universalism that accompanied the expansion of the European society of states in the nineteenth and early twentieth centuries to include independent non-European states, such as the Ottoman Empire, China, Japan and Siam (Thailand) and led in the name of the standard of civilization to the imposition of the hated unequal treaties described above.

Yet, the Western origin of liberalism should not of itself be considered a reason for non–Western societies to reject it. Societies and cultures regularly and successfully borrow from each other. A recent and very relevant example is the willing adoption from the West by non-Western societies of the sovereign state form. The proper test for liberalism should not be whether it is alien but whether it is a better form of social and political life under modern conditions of sovereign states and market economies than available alternatives from the point of view of the nature and interests of the human beings who are the members of those societies.

Before entering on these discussions of the possible clash between liberalism and non-Western cultures, we will consider and reject a move that, if justified, would render the discussions pointless. This is the standpoint of cultural relativism, which, while accepting the incompatibility of the different world ethical cultures, denies that there is any neutral ethical ground from which they can be compared and evaluated. Each position is perfectly valid from within its own perspective and there is no culture-independent standpoint from which one can be shown to be superior.

Cultural relativism

Cultural relativism supposes that the world can be reasonably clearly divided into distinct cultures with different systems of belief and values. These different systems cannot be evaluated from the point of view of their truth and falsity, because truth and falsity, right and wrong are terms that are given their meaning from within one of these cultural perspectives. That women should not have the same educational opportunities as men is true for the Taleban but false for the liberal and there is no absolute standpoint from which such relative judgements of truth can be transcended and an authoritative judgement delivered. No doubt the relativist can allow that there exists a degree of overlap between some or all cultures that makes meaningful cross-cultural dialogue possible. But he must still hold that that the areas uncovered by any overlap constitute significant elements of unbridgeable beliefs.[1]

There are two ways in which the above claim of cultural relativism can be understood. According to the first way, when one judges from within the Taleban perspective that women should not have equal opportunities with men, the scope of this judgement extends only to the members of the Taleban society. On this view, the Taleban would allow that non-Taleban are perfectly entitled to follow quite different values. On the second version, the scope of the initial judgement is universal. The judgement that women should not be treated equally with men applies to all peoples everywhere. At the same time, the liberal's contrary judgement also applies universally. These universal judgements, however, are valid only from the relevant cultural standpoint. They are not true absolutely but only relative to the appropriate framework. Yet, from within the framework the judgements have universal scope.

The second version of cultural relativism is a two-level account. At the first level judgements are made with universal scope and thus appear to be anything but relativistic. At the second level, it is recognized, in reflecting on the variety and oppositions of first level judgements that, while having a universal form, they are true only relative to their cultural perspective. It is at the second level that relativism is endorsed. The first version of cultural relativism is a single-level account. Judgements at that level are recognized to be valid only for believers. The judgement always contains an implicit reference to the group of persons who believe it. So, to the judgement, 'drinking alcohol is wrong', should be added 'for us', with the implication that it is perfectly OK for everyone else.

The trouble with the single-level version is that, as applied to ethical judgements, it cannot do justice to the authoritative nature such judgements have for believers. When we say that torture is wrong or religious intolerance is bad, we do not mean that torture is wrong for us but OK for you, or that it is OK for you to persecute people of different religious faith but not for us. That would be to treat ethical beliefs as operating like social customs, such as shaking hands on being introduced as opposed to bowing. Not behaving in accordance with the relevant customs in one's society marks one out as ill-bred and ill-mannered or merely ignorant but not as a morally bad person, which would be the case if, contrary to our moral values, we believed someone to be guilty of torture. We recognize that the authority of the social custom for us derives simply from its being the customary practice of our society. Other people have different customs and it would not be appropriate for them to treat each other in the way that we do. But the authority of moral judgements is not like that. We believe that we should not engage in torture because it is wrong for human beings as such to engage in torture.

This feature of moral judgements is acknowledged by the second version. On that version, judgements at the first level have the appropriate universal authority and it is only second-level reflection that establishes the relative nature of the first-level universal judgements. However, once a person moves from the first to the second level can he go on asserting the universal scope of his first-level judgements? When he says that from our perspective it is wrong for the Taleban to discriminate against women but from their perspective it is required, and that there is no way of showing the superiority of our perspective over the Taleban's except from within our assumptions, he surely cannot maintain the initial unqualified confidence in the (universal) rightness of his first-level judgements. When he, unreflectively, condemns the Taleban from his liberal standpoint, the confidence he has in this judgement depends on his belief in the superiority of the liberal standpoint to that of the Taleban. But when, from the second level, he reflects on liberalism and Talebanism and concludes that neither can be said to be superior to the other because there is no culture-independent standpoint from which one could make such a judgement, he cannot return to the first level and continue to make first-level judgements with universal scope as though nothing had happened. He must now surely accept at the first level that the liberal assumptions are no better than those of the Taleban and hence that judgements made from them cannot be supposed to apply to non-liberals. What he is left with is just the difference between our beliefs and their beliefs, where the authority of our beliefs just consists in the fact that they are ours. In this respect, then, our ethical beliefs become just like social customs, which we happen to have and which it would be boorish or ill-mannered for us not to follow but which have no claim on others who do not share them. In other words, the two-level form of cultural relativism is not self-sustaining and must collapse back into the single-level version.

Perhaps we should accept single-level cultural relativism, including its costs in terms of the reduction of our moral beliefs to the level of local custom. However, the costs would be very substantial, consisting in the loss of the whole domain of our moral concepts. And there is an alternative. This is to hold that ethical belief systems claiming universal validity in respect of how human beings should best live their lives are much more open to discussion and contestation from other perspectives than the doctrine of cultural relativism allows. Thus with regard to the opposition between liberals and Taleban over women's place in society, much hangs on the understanding of women's nature and capacities relative to men's, together with the implications to be drawn from any differences for women's participation in society. On these matters there is considerable empirical evidence and hence room for discussion between open-minded liberals and Taleban. Of course, insofar as the ultimate ground for the Taleban position on women's difference is a non-moral drive to subordinate women to men's will, then they will not be open-minded and cannot consider themselves to be possibly wrong, unless they can come to recognize and question the justifiability of that motivation. It is one of the aims of this book, that, by attempting to make the assumptions, principles and practices of liberalism as clear as possible in themselves and in relation to the alternative positions of liberalism's critics, we will make discussion of these fundamental matters more open and more rational.

Islamic conceptions of human rights

Much Islamic literature on this subject, as distinct from Western commentators on Islam, holds that the Koran and other authoritative texts recognize human rights. For instance, the Universal Islamic Declaration of Human Rights issued by the Islamic Council of Europe in 1981 states that '1400 years ago Islam gave to humanity an ideal code of human rights'.[2] Similarly, Mawdudi, an influential early-twentieth-century scholar from the Indian sub-continent and defender of the Islamic faith against Western ideological hegemony, states that 'Islam has laid down some universal fundamental rights for humanity as a whole which are to be observed and respected under all circumstances'.[3]

In fact, what is appealed to in support of such claims is a set of divine injunctions to human beings issued through God's messenger,

Mohammed, such as not to kill without just cause, to keep one's covenants, to give full measure, to help the needy and render justice. It is usually accepted that the language of the divine texts does not include terms that we can directly translate as human rights. However, the assumption being made is that the types of duty listed above establish rights in the beneficiaries from their performance. Thus, if one has a duty not to kill without just cause, the beneficiaries of this duty are all innocent human beings and they can all be said to have a right as an innocent human being to life. Of course, one problem here is what is to count as an innocent human being. If one deserves to die because one rejects Islam and opposes its political imposition, this supposed right is nothing like what is meant in the Western-originating discourse on natural/human rights in which the right to life means the right not to have one's life taken by another except in self-defence or retribution for a life taken. But let us suppose, for the moment, that the Islamic injunction amounts to the same thing as the liberal human right. We would, then, clearly have a divine command that would endorse the same moral actions as the liberal human right.

Donnelly and others deny that rights can be understood as the correlative of duties in such a way that, if we have a list of duties, then we necessarily have a list of corresponding rights. Donnelly further objects that if the duties are seen as owed to God and not to other human beings, then it is not human beings who have the rights but God. For something to be the right of someone, it must be possessed or owned by that person.[4]

One problem with this denial of the status of human rights to divine commands is that the natural rights of John Locke and other seventeenth-century writers are grounded in God's commands to human beings to preserve themselves and others. Thus, all the natural rights are derived from a duty and that duty is owed to God. On Donnelly's line of argument, then, Locke should not be thought of as a theorist of natural rights: a fairly absurd conclusion. The solution to this conundrum, however, is simple. The right of a person to preserve himself can be affirmed as a right and yet derived from a duty, if the duty establishes an entitlement in that person held against other persons that they do not act so as to prevent him from preserving himself. Since Locke clearly intends this, there is no reason why we should not talk of the natural right of all human beings to self-preservation and to derive this right from a duty to preserve themselves and others. Furthermore, although the duty is owed to God, because it establishes a legitimate claim in each person against every other person, we can say at the same time that the duty is owed to other human beings also. It is owed immediately to them and ultimately to God.

The fact, then, that neither the Koran (nor for that matter the Old Testament) actually uses the language of rights but only that of duties, in no way excludes the addition of that language to one's understanding of the texts. What difference does it, in fact, make if one supplements the set of divine commands with the language of rights? The language of rights shifts attention to the subject who immediately benefits from the performance of the duty and by emphasizing his entitlement to make claims against a violator of the duty, raises his moral standing. But while this does give the individual subject more weight than in a simple duty system, it is still very far from transforming the moral scheme into a liberal-individualistic one. The trouble with Donnelly's and other Westerners' approach to this issue is that it identifies the language of human rights with liberal moral notions. We believe that there can be different accounts of human rights and that liberalism is only one. Later on in this chapter we will give an account of a system of human rights that involves the notion of a differentiated humanity possessing differentiated human rights. On the Donnelly view, this is completely confused. Human rights must be the attributes of undifferentiated and equal human beings. However, we see no necessity for this restriction provided the appropriate qualifications to the idea of human rights are made explicit and the commentator refers to the hierarchical or liberal version as it may be.

In the case of Islam, there appears to be a degree of differentiation in the ascription of human rights also. Thus, Khadduri says that 'Human rights in Islam as prescribed by the divine law are the privilege only of persons of full legal status. A person with full legal capacity is a living human being of mature age, free and of Muslim faith'.[5] This means that unbelievers and slaves do not have full human rights. Unbelievers (if they are people of the Book, i.e. the Bible: thus Christians and Jews) have rights to life, property and religion but not being members of the Muslim community have fundamentally inferior legal status. Slaves have only a right to life. Women have rights defined by their inferior position within the family and society. While the differentiated rights of women and slaves can be understood in terms of a traditional hierarchical conception of the natural social order, the male Muslim community itself is understood in egalitarian terms. Indeed, Islam treats all male human beings as fundamentally equal in the sense that all (except the justly enslaved!) can become equal members of the Muslim community by accepting Islam.[6] The unbelievers, then, put themselves outside the community of the equal faithful by rejecting God's message and so it is appropriate that they do not have the full rights of membership of those who do follow God's commands to human beings.

Human rights understood in this way, in terms of the prescriptions of the Koran and the Sunna,[7] are likely to have problems when faced with the requirements of the Universal Declaration of Human Rights and the UN's covenants on civil and political rights, which all Muslim states have endorsed except Saudi Arabia. Saudi Arabia has, however, ratified the subsequent major covenants on human rights. Furthermore, many have adopted constitutions or declarations of human rights which claim to be both Islamic and at the same time to incorporate the rights laid down in the UN bills of rights. Since we have taken the view that the latter express a liberal conception of human rights, their compatibility with an Islamic conception as understood above would seem to be most dubious.

Let us consider, then, more closely recent Islamic constitutions and declarations for their handling of liberal claims. We are referring to the following documents (some of which we have mentioned already in Part II): the 1979 Constitution of the Islamic Republic of Iran;[8] the Universal Islamic Declaration of Human Rights of 1981; the Cairo Declaration of Human Rights in Islam of 1990[9] and the Basic Law of Saudi Arabia of 1992.[10] The standard approach in these documents is to begin with the affirmation of many of the rights proclaimed in the international law of human rights and then to qualify them by the use of Islamic criteria. In other words, rather than just expressing the principles of traditional Islamic law in the form of a set of rights in the manner described above, they recognize the challenge presented to traditional Islam by the international law of human rights but seek to limit its impact by appeal to the requirements of Islamic law.

The international law of human rights does, of course, allow restrictions on many rights but these limits are reasonably clearly specified and never permit limitation by the requirements of a religion. Thus the freedoms of expression, association, peaceful assembly, and so on, can be subject to limitations imposed by law and necessary for respect for the rights of others, protection of the national security or public order, health and morals. However, in the Islamic documents the rights can be enjoyed only within the limits of the sharia, which is standardly understood as binding Islamic law derived directly from the Islamic sacred texts of the Koran and the Sunna. On this basis anything that is deemed to be incompatible with Islamic law is not permitted.

Here are some examples of apparent restriction of rights in the Iranian Constitution: Article 21 states that 'the government shall guarantee the rights of women in all areas according to Islamic standards'; Article 24 states that 'publications and the press may express ideas freely, except when they are contrary to Islamic principles'; Article 26 says that 'parties, groups, political and professional associations, as well as Islamic or recognized minority religious associations, are permitted provided they do not violate principles of independence, freedom and national unity or are contrary to the principles of Islam or the Islamic Republic'. In the Universal Islamic Declaration of Human Rights, the rights to liberty (Article 2a), to justice (Article 4a), to expression (Article 12a), to disseminate information (Article 12d) and many others are limited in their scope by the sharia. The Cairo Declaration states in Article 24 that 'all the rights and freedoms stipulated in the declaration are subject to the Islamic sharia'. Similarly, the Basic Law of Saudi Arabia states in Article 26 that the state will protect human rights according to the Islamic sharia.

The problem with these formulae is that they restrict fundamental freedoms by reference to the Islamic religion. This is directly contrary to the international law of human rights, which does not permit any discrimination between one person's freedom and another's on the basis of religion. However, whether discrimination does actually take place, or would take place, in an Islamic state depends on how the sharia is understood and interpreted. Thus, standardly the sharia refers to the classical codification of Islamic law based on the Koran and the Sunna by scholars and theologians that, according to tradition, was deemed to have been completed in the tenth century and was, therefore, not subject to further interpretation or modification.[11] This body of law clearly discriminates against women and religious minorities and justifies other actions contrary to the Universal Declaration of Human Rights such as the criminalization of apostasy from the Muslim faith.[12] But, in fact, there have been and are ways in which the classical sharia can be bypassed in the interests of modernity. One such method involves a pragmatic appeal to the general welfare of the Muslim community as the ground for introducing measures that appear to contradict the classical code. Nevertheless, the standing of the sharia is maintained by declaring it to be appropriate only for ideal circumstances such as reigned in the first Muslim community at Medina under the rule of Mohammed. Such an approach is used to avoid imposing the savage hadd punishments of amputation for theft, stoning for adultery and death for apostasy. Alternatively, the requirements for conviction in such cases are made so high that it is rare for them to be satisfied.[13]

The pragmatic method of reforming Islam, however, by preserving the ideal status of the classical sharia, leaves human rights in a vulnerable state. It is always open to Islamic movements to demand, as we now see them doing, the return to traditional Islam on the grounds that the present misfortunes of the Muslim peoples are due to the abandonment of its original historic path.

Another more radical and principled way has been adopted by committed Muslims who seek to liberalize Islam. This way involves treating the classical sharia as largely a human construction based on the sacred texts but not itself a direct expression of the word of God or of his prophet Mohammed. The Koran and the Sunna, on this view, articulate a spiritual and ethical message and declare general principles of conduct for the most part, rather than elaborate a detailed legal code of behaviour. The ethical spirit and the general principles have, therefore, to be interpreted by human beings who can only do so in the light of their changing historical circumstances.[14]

That traditional Islamic law is illiberal in certain respects is hardly surprising, since this was true of traditional Christianity and Western law prior to their transformation by liberal principles beginning in the seventeenth century but not adequately realized until the nineteenth and twentieth centuries. The fact is, however, that contemporary Islamic thinkers and publicists have been trying to gloss over the conflict by claiming that Islam has always recognized human rights and by issuing declarations and drawing up constitutions that appear to endorse the international law of human rights while subjecting it to an Islamic interpretation that may well eviscerate its liberal content. The liberal Muslim academic An Na'im describes the main areas of conflict between the international law of human rights and the sharia as traditionally interpreted as consisting in: (i) apostasy from the Muslim faith; this is to be punished by death according to the sharia and is thus incompatible with the fundamental freedoms of religion and expression; (ii) the status of non-Muslims; they are not full and equal citizens of an Islamic state. The people of the Book enjoy security of the person and property and religious communal autonomy under the protection and control of the Muslim community and subject to the payment of a special tax, but other unbelievers have no rights; and (iii) the rights of women; women, whether married or unmarried, are under the guardianship of men, have to cover themselves in public, cannot occupy public offices and are subject to inequalities of various kinds in matters such as divorce, inheritance, and serving as legal witnesses.[15]

Any Muslim who believes that a liberal Islam is achievable must claim that it is possible to re-interpret the Koran and reformulate the sharia so that it is compatible with liberal principles. An Na'im believes that it is, as do many other Muslims, although they cannot be said to be politically influential at the present time.[16] Fundamental to any such re-interpretation would be the adoption of the distinction between the sharia or true path, as expressed in the Koran and the Sunna and taking the form of ethical and religious spirit and general principle, on the one hand and the *fiqh* as the detailed code of law, on the other hand. The way is then open for the Muslim to interpret the general principles and spirit of Islam in a liberal direction by appealing to the circumstances of modernity. However, the case still has to be made that the Islamic spirit is susceptible to a liberal interpretation and, furthermore, certain passages of the Koran, which make what seem to be unequivocal statements regarding the inferiority of women,[17] the requirement of the cruel hadd punishments[18] and the subordination of non-Muslims,[19] have to be emasculated.

In respect of the former issue, the most plausible approach is to appeal to the Koran's stress on the special place given to man in God's creation and the consequent dignity that inheres in every person, together with its recognition of the equality of human beings independent of race, colour and ethnicity. Of course, what is problematic about the traditional understanding of this equality is its recognition of political inequalities based on the religious distinction between Muslims and non-Muslims. This raises serious questions about the political nature of the Islamic community, which we will address in a moment.

With regard to the Koran's explicitly illiberal passages, and especially in respect of the inequality of women, one way out has been to argue that the Koran in fact raises the status of women in relation to the existing customs of the Arabian tribal communities but could not proclaim a full equality in that historical context. Appealing again to the general Koranic spirit of emancipation, as applied to the very different circumstances of modernity, women's full equality should now be affirmed.[20] As to the hadd punishments, there seems no alternative to the adoption of some version of the pragmatic method, but in respect of the apparent intolerance of Mohammed to Muslim apostates, the Koran also famously affirms that 'there shall be no compulsion in religion'.[21]

However, the problem that the liberal interpreter faces on these matters is that the orthodox conception of the Koran holds that, as the word of God, the Koran was not created in time and so could not have a historical dimension, as the above interpretations require. This view only became the orthodox conception in the ninth century with the defeat and anathematization of the Mutazilists, before which time it was heavily disputed.[22] Obviously, it has to be rejected if the liberal interpretation is to succeed. It is, in any case, clear that some recent changes in the law of Muslim states that run counter to the Koran have been made in response to human rights claims. Thus slavery is accepted in the Koran as a perfectly normal part of Islamic society and is nowhere condemned, although those who free slaves are praised. But in accordance with the overwhelming international repudiation of slavery in the course of the nineteenth and twentieth centuries, it was made illegal even by such a bastion of Islamic conservatism as Saudi Arabia in 1962. This makes slavery appropriate for medieval Islamic society but not for the modern world. There seems no reason in principle, then, why Muslim societies should not proceed in the same way in regard to the three areas of major conflict described above between the international law of human rights and traditional Islam.

There is, however, said to be a prominent feature of traditional Islamic practice that is often regarded as a major obstacle to the liberalization of Islam. This consists in the fact that, when Mohammed moved the young Muslim community from Mecca to Medina because of persecution by the Meccan rulers, he became, by invitation of the existing Medinese inhabitants, their political and military leader as well as religious leader of the Muslims. As the Muslims soon became the overwhelming majority of the population of first Medina and subsequently of Mecca and all Arabia, through a combination of military success, political astuteness and religious ardour, there was a complete fusion of the political and religious community of Muslims under the leadership of Mohammed and his immediate successors, the so-called rightly guided caliphs. The suggestion is, then, that Islam is the law, not simply of a religious community, but of a self-governing community that is necessarily as much political as religious. Islam could, therefore, never accept the liberal exclusion of religion from politics and its limitation to the private sphere of individual choice and freedom, at least in the sense of treating non-Muslims as free and equal citizens of their state.

With regard to this claim, it should be noted in the first place that it is obviously not impossible to practise Islam as a non-political religion. This was, in fact, the practice of Mohammed and his followers in Mecca before their flight to Medina. It has also been its status in Turkey since the foundation of the secular Turkish Republic in 1925 and is also necessarily the case for all Muslims who find themselves freely practising their religion in liberal states. The claim must be, then, that this imposed non-political status is a violation of Islam's nature as an essentially political religion. In the second place, there are Muslims who do not accept this characterization of the political and religious elements in it. One of the most radical is 'Abd al-Raziq, an Egyptian writing in the early twentieth century, who argues that Islam is essentially a spiritual religion and that Mohammed's political rule in Medina cannot serve as a model for all subsequent Muslim communities, since it entirely depended on Mohammed's unique status as God's last prophet whose right to rule arose from his role as the medium of God's message. Since Mohammed's political successors could not inherit his prophetic status, the legitimacy of their rule could not depend on religious but only on social and political considerations of order and justice.[23] No doubt, this still leaves the general Koranic ethical principles of justice and benevolence as mandatory on Muslims. But these, being highly general, require substantive interpretation, one of which can obviously be liberal in character.

Clearly, a principled, as distinct from a pragmatic, liberal Islam has many obstacles to overcome in getting itself politically established. It was, no doubt, much less difficult for liberalism to become acceptable in the case of Protestant Christianity but it is surely no more impossible than it turned out to be for Catholicism to join the liberal consensus.

The East Asian values debate

This title has come to be used to refer to the controversy surrounding the claims of some recent East Asian ruling politicians and their apologists who object to the exercise by Western governments of diplomatic pressure to get them to respect the liberal core of the UN's human rights norms, namely the civil and political freedoms.[24] The Asian rulers and their supporters see the emphasis on civil and political rights as a reflection of the values and interests of Western society and as such inappropriate to Asian society whose values are quite different. They also claim that the rights to the enjoyment of one's culture, contained in the Universal Declaration of Human Rights and the ICESCR together with the rights of their sovereign states entitle them to interpret the international law of human rights in accordance with the traditional values of their societies rather than in accordance with the wishes of the West.

In addition, it has been argued that the civil and political rights at issue presupposed a high level of economic development and that the East Asian societies were warranted by their economic situation in giving priority to economic, social and cultural rights; that the authoritarian governments of these societies were not only more in tune with Asian traditions but were also needed to hold these states together and achieve national unity. Finally, and perhaps inconsistently, a major theme has been the social destructiveness of Western liberalism in itself.

This type of discourse was most prominently deployed by the long-term rulers of Malaysia and Singapore in particular: Mahathir Mohammed and Lee Kuan Yew. But similar ideas were propagated in Indonesia under Suharto and by successive governments in China. All these countries had or still have a dominant executive power that to different degrees controlled parliament and the judiciary and strictly regulated and limited the civil and political freedoms of their peoples beyond anything acceptable in a liberal society. In Malaysia under Mahathir, Western values were contrasted with those of Asian society and criticized for allowing an unfettered freedom to individuals that licensed a highly individualistic way of life in which morals became a private affair and selfish passions could be freely indulged. Asian society, on the other hand, valued authority and order above democracy, the interests of the community and the duties of subjects above individual rights and the satisfaction of individuals' passions. Furthermore, in Asian society the social order was grounded in shared and public moral values derived from a transcendent religion.

In Malaysia the cultural tradition is Islamic. In neighbouring Singapore, the inspiration for very similar claims is Confucian. Under the leadership of Lee Kuan Yew, a paternalistic government that promotes a well-ordered society and economic growth is considered more important than democratic rights and civil freedoms.[25] Yew thinks that liberal individualism, which protects the right of individuals to do as they please, has led to the erosion of the moral underpinnings of society and the diminution of personal responsibility, resulting in the breakdown of civil society with its huge increase in drug-taking, violence, vagrancy and unbecoming behaviour in public. Human beings, it is argued, possess both a shared sense of right and wrong but also a propensity for evil that needs to be controlled by an authority that is external to their will rather than an expression of it. Asian society provides for this nature by deeming community to be more important than the individual, by emphasizing the duties of subjects rather than their rights and by endorsing such values as filial piety, thrift, industry and loyalty in the extended family. Yew says that the fundamental difference between East and West consists in the fact that the individual in the former is conceived as existing in a network of family, extended family, friends and wider society, while in the West the individual is seen as a separate and independent being.

The general aim of this discourse was to defend the Malaysian and Singaporean governments against criticisms of their poor record on civil and political rights. The main thrust of the justification was threefold: first, Asian societies and polities were illiberal because liberalism was alien to their culture and values and in any case was destructive of social cohesion and order even in the West; second, economic growth and political stability were more important concerns of Asian societies than liberal freedoms in general but especially at the present time when these societies were trying to create strong modern states and dynamic modern economies; and third, as sovereign states they had the right to interpret international human rights law as they thought

fit. The latter points were also propagated by the Indonesian government under Suharto and by Communist China.

The latter claims would appear to contradict the official UN doctrine on the indivisibility and interdependence of civil and political,
economic, social and cultural rights. We discussed this doctrine in
Chapter 4 above and concluded that it could not be used to preclude a
substantive discussion of the merits of prioritizing certain rights under
certain conditions: a discussion we postponed to the chapter on the
right to development. But the good faith of the arguments of the Asian
rulers on prioritization may well be doubted in the light of their
general hostility to liberalism. Furthermore, their rejection of the
relevance of liberalism on cultural grounds does not look very con-
vincing given their willingness to appeal to their rights as sovereign
states, since the latter conception is as much a Western import as
liberalism itself. Indeed, some Asian commentators on the debate deny
that the Asian-values ideologues have any genuine concern for traditional Asian values, since they are quite prepared to ride roughshod
over them in the interests of creating a strong modern state and
economy.[26]

However, assuming that there is a cultural difference between
traditional Asian communitarianism and liberalism, we wish to point
out that communitarian values are not peculiarly Asian. They are also
the pre-liberal values of European society that have been resurrected
from time to time in Europe and on occasion in extremely vicious
forms. At the same time, the reader can recognize that the Asian
critique of liberalism is very similar to Western critiques and largely a
misrepresentation and misunderstanding of the liberal order. The
critique ignores the fact that (i) liberalism is a norm-governed form of
social life in which the scope of any individual freedom is subordinated to the collective system of equal freedoms; (ii) a liberal society of
equal individuals has to be realized through individuals' membership
of a state and that such states cannot survive without the members'
commitment to the common good and hence loyalty to the nation as
composed of their fellow-citizens; (iii) liberal individuals must learn to
control their passions so as to be able to respect the rights of others,
perform their duties to society and acquire the virtues that enable
them to co-operate successfully in all sorts of voluntary associations,
from marriages and families to commercial enterprises, that is, such

virtues as trustworthiness, honesty, justice and temperance; and (iv) liberalism is in no way incompatible with belief in a transcendent religion as the ultimate ground of the liberal order. This was how it was first conceived and can still be conceived. Furthermore, even if contemporary justifications of liberalism standardly eschew a religious basis, they cannot do without a firm moral foundation that explains why the members of liberal society should acknowledge their obligation to interact on the basis of liberal principles.

It is nevertheless true that traditional Asian values, as well as traditional pre-liberal European ones, seem to conceive the relation of individual to community in quite different ways from liberalism: the former are said to see the community as an ideal organic harmony and the individual solely in terms of fulfilling a function or role in the whole that determines his or her rights and duties. On this view, the individual is related to the community as part of a larger organism as the hand is to the whole body. Liberalism conceives of community as a unity of equal individual co-legislative wills. The unity arises from the recognition by individuals that their rights depend on the whole system of equal rights and that the system must be expressed and supported through their joint wills acting together. Furthermore, within liberal society individuals find their place through the exercise of their individual freedom in regulated competition or association with others, albeit through forms of social life such as families, religious groups, economic and social enterprises and ethnically based communities which may pre-exist liberalism but which liberalism transforms. This contrast between organic and individualist conceptions of community will be pursued further in the next two sections.

Confucianism and human rights

While the protagonists of East Asian values had in mind Islamic as well as Confucian beliefs, the attempt to appropriate Confucianism for the conservative authoritarian cause forms part of a long-established debate over the compatibility of Confucianism with modern forms of socio-economic and political life. The famous nineteenth-century German sociologist, Max Weber, claimed that Confucianism served as a substantial obstacle to the development of modernity in China and in the early twentieth century many Chinese reformers took a similarly negative view of Confucianism in relation to their aspiration to transform China under the influence of Western liberal models.[27] The negative view was at first enormously reinforced by the attitude of the communist regime established in the 1950s and manifested in extreme form in the infamous Cultural Revolution's attempt to extirpate every vestige of Confucian thinking from Chinese society.

However, since the death of Mao Ze Dong, the repudiation of the Cultural Revolution and the abandonment of much communist orthodoxy in the successful promotion of a dynamic Chinese capitalism, the ruling communist party, anxious about its legitimacy, has substantially revised its attitude to Confucianism and now justifies itself in part by reference to the supposedly authoritarian traditions of Chinese Confucian culture.[28] At the same time, many contemporary Chinese intellectuals, critical of the communist regime's suppression of civil and political freedoms, continue to see Confucianism as undesirable from a modern point of view because of its hierarchical, elitist and authoritarian nature. They are also inclined to see this so-called 'third wave' of conservative Confucianism as an 'overseas' phenomenon that is not characteristic of the mainland Chinese, apart from the government itself.[29]

While these opposed parties at least agree on the politically conservative nature of Confucianism, there have been increasing efforts to develop a middle position by exploring the resources within Confucianism for a Confucian endorsement of human rights. It is, of course, not being proposed that one can find the notion of human rights within the classic Confucian texts, but rather that basic Confucian values are not essentially antagonistic to a liberal rights regime, as both the rejectionist and the conservative camps agree in asserting. It should, thus, be possible to elaborate a Confucian justification of human rights and hence for Confucianism to join an international consensus on the UN human rights regime.

Most of the literature of this mediating type concentrates on the thought of Confucius himself and of his most influential disciple, Mencius. So, let us first try and characterize historical Confucian ethics in a way that might be acceptable to all parties. We believe that it expresses the ethical ideal of a well-educated and cultivated gentleman who lives in a well-ordered and harmonious society and respects others in accordance with their due in the five core human relations: those of ruler/minister, father/son, elder brother/younger brother, husband/ wife, friend/friend. The gentleman is motivated by a sense of duty to live in the right way irrespective of personal advantage and to serve his community by participating in public affairs as an official or adviser to his ruler. He is, indeed, a superior moral being who acts as a model for others and a society will be well-ordered if it is governed by such men of virtue who secure obedience to their rule by the force of moral example rather than through coercive law. A gentleman is not necessarily of superior birth. Confucius himself accepted suitable students from any class to instruct in the right way to live, while Mencius held that all men possessed the moral potential to become virtuous beings in the Confucian mould and hence to participate in public affairs. Of course, the poor are unlikely to have the opportunities or resources to become well-educated and cultivated beings and so will have little chance of approaching the Confucian ideal.[30]

We will now consider the reasons often given for thinking that Confucian ethics is unavoidably hostile to human rights understood in the standard liberal version. To begin with, it is widely claimed that Confucian ethics has a communitarian character and involves a role-based conception of a person and social values that is incompatible with liberal individualism. Although the liberal individual develops a consciousness of himself and of moral requirements in the first place through his embeddedness in family and other social relations, he has to learn to abstract himself from such a rootedness in particular relations and think of himself as one individual among others with the right within a general system of equal rights to choose for himself his order of values including, to some degree, the relative value he attaches to family relations. The communitarian conception of the person in his roles denies that the person is anything apart from the identity he has within the given roles. Similarly, communitarian values emphasize the harmony produced through the integration of individuals' interests in the common good by way of the integration of their role-defined interests in the structure of the whole.

A second charge is that the Confucian conception of social relations at all levels – family, government and society – is hierarchical with the implication that this is incompatible with the egalitarianism and democracy inherent in human rights. It is at the same time thoroughly elitist. It is primarily concerned with the achievement of moral excellence and the rule of beings of superior moral virtue. It is true that the production and dominance of such beings in society will result in a well-ordered and harmonious association through which all will benefit. Yet, this outcome is dependent on the formation and rule of the elite.

Third, the Confucian social ideal is that of a family writ large and the proper relations between family members is to be understood in terms of the exercise of the appropriate virtues in which the idea of rights has no place and is indeed incongruous. The spirit of family life is that of love and harmony rather than one of self-assertion and defensiveness characteristic of social relations conducted through rights. The appeal to rights turns society into a conflictual and litigious arena, while Confucianism emphasizes the values of mediation and consensus-building as a means of resolving conflicts.

Against these claims regarding the incompatibility of Confucianism and human rights, it is argued by some writers that the communitarian conception of personality is in itself not incompatible with liberalism. Thus Tu Wei-Ming, quoting J. Cohen, holds that human rights can be derived from the communitarian notion of a person as the centre of the five core relations.[31] For, on that conception a person has dignity and worth as a moral agent in and through his exercise of the core roles. He can, then, be said to be entitled to civil rights as the conditions necessary for his achievement of worth in the fulfilment of his roles. At the same time, constitutional restrictions on rulers, such as the political human rights, can be understood as conditions for the exercise by rulers of their Confucian duty to act for the good of society.

Other writers, such as Joseph Chan, accept that a role-based conception of personality and morality does constitute a bar to a possible justification of human rights from a Confucian perspective, but deny that the Confucian notion of moral agency is purely role-bound.[32] According to Chan and others, Confucius views human beings first and foremost as moral agents with the capacity to care for and sympathize with others. This capacity is standardly manifest in the five core personal relations, but it is not limited to them. It is to be exercised in impersonal relations such as helping a stranger in trouble. According to Mencius, 'the benevolent man loves others and the courteous man respects others', even when those to be loved or respected are not in a personal relation to the agent. Confucius says that to be benevolent is 'to love all men'. One can find also in

Confucius and Mencius expressions of the golden rule such as 'do not impose on others what you yourself do not desire'. This shows, according to Chan, not that human beings have rights as such in Confucian ethical thought, but that it is wrong to argue that Confucianism cannot accommodate the notion of human rights because it is a purely role-based conception of ethics.

In our view, the Chan argument is superior to that of Tu Wei-Ming. What is fundamental to a liberal human rights conception is that an individual human being can think of himself outside his roles as just one moral agent among others with moral duties and aspirations that transcend those arising from the core roles. This element of a general morality is clearly present in Confucian ethics in the injunction to adopt an attitude of benevolence towards others whether they are strangers and thus related to one as any man or whether they occupy one of the five core roles. In the latter case, the general moral attitude is manifest in the exercise of the virtues associated with one's roles; in the former case its realization will be determined by principles derived from the employment of the golden rule.

However, the existence of the element of general morality governed by the golden rule, while being necessary, is clearly not sufficient of itself to generate liberal human rights. Furthermore, the crucial obstacle to that move is the element of role-based morality. Because the latter lays down roles that the agent must fulfil, it deprives him of the fundamental freedom central to liberalism of determining for himself, within the limits of the rights of others and the needs of social union, how he shall live his life and how he hopes to achieve for himself an appropriate balance of human goods. In other words, the golden rule would have to be understood as generating, as the fundamental rule of conduct between moral agents, the principle of equal freedom, which, in the formulation of Thomas Hobbes, is the command to give up as much freedom towards others as you wish others to give up towards you. This would involve the restructuring of the social order – the institutions of family, economy, society and polity – in accordance with this principle. This does not mean that social and economic forms of life are so very different in liberal and non-liberal societies: they both have families, religious institutions, similar social and economic enterprises and governments. It is rather the way in which individuals relate to these forms of life that undergoes substantial change in the liberalization of a society.

The second argument against Confucianism's compatibility with human rights was that it is inherently hierarchical and elitist. With regard to the first part of this claim, it is undoubtedly the case that the traditional Confucian roles are conceived hierarchically, within both the family and polity and that, if they are an essential aspect rather than a historically contingent feature of Confucianism, then indeed Confucianism would be incompatible with the liberalization of these forms. But many commentators hold that Confucianism historically manifested itself in hierarchical form only because its ethic had to be realized in a feudal and patriarchal society. In a democratic society, the same values would support the equality inherent in the liberal family and political structures. As evidence of the non-hierarchical nature of Confucianism, it is pointed out that the Confucian gentleman of superior virtue was not necessarily of superior birth and that Mencius believed in the moral potentiality of everyone to achieve virtue. Furthermore, the golden rule is appealed to as an expression of the fundamentally equal nature of moral agents, since it denies that it is morally acceptable to exclude oneself from the application of rules that everyone else is subject to.

Finally, with regard to equal political rights, it is said that Confucius believed in the importance of limits on government authority, since he wanted the elite advisers to remonstrate with the ruler if he failed to set the right example to his subjects of how to live or if he failed to pursue policies that served the good of the people, while Mencius went so far as to justify the overthrow of unjust rulers. The requirement on rulers to serve the good of the people is said to be implicitly democratic, since it is easy to move from the principle of government for the people to government by the people, or their representatives, as the best way to achieve the former.[33]

In considering these claims, we should first like to remind the reader that on our view of liberalism, its fundamental equal civil and political rights are not at all incompatible with the existence of the kind of hierarchies that are essential for the maintenance of due authority in government, family and other social structures. Liberalism requires only that such authority is either accountable to its subjects in the case of politics or to legally enforceable limits in the case of family, educational and other social structures, or entered into and escapable from on a voluntary basis. Similarly, liberalism is not against the pursuit of moral or any other excellence, provided that it is pursued without violating anyone's equal rights. The superior being in moral or any other virtue has no right to rule unless she can secure the support of her fellow citizens or accepts rights-based limitations on her powers.

While respect for authority and the pursuit of excellence are perfectly compatible with liberalism, what a liberal Confucianism would be required to acknowledge is sufficient capacity and virtue in every person to give her an entitlement to make her own decisions regarding the basic relations and commitments of her life. Liberalism does not reject the view that there are universal human goods and that family is one of these and excellence in some field is another. But it recognizes that there exists a plurality of such goods and no natural hierarchy or harmony between them, and hence individuals must have the right to choose what range and order of them they wish to pursue in their lives. Can Confucianism accept such equality and pluralism? Here, the claim attributed to Mencius would seem to be the crucial one as regards equality – namely that everyone has the moral potential to be a virtuous person. Such a view is attributed to Confucius also as an interpretation of his saying: 'by birth close together, by practice far apart'. The implications of the golden rule would in addition seem to support such a claim.

A non-hierarchical plurality of human goods is a different issue, however, which goes to the heart of an illiberal conception of social harmony. If the educated and virtuous gentlemen have knowledge of an objectively valid order of human goods, in the manner of Plato's conception of the philosopher guardians of his ideal republic, then it is difficult for them to accept the right of all and sundry to make decisions for their own lives on such matters. On the contrary, the good of society clearly depends on moulding them to the given forms. Yet, the rejection of such an objective order of values does not mean that liberalism entails relativism of values and disharmony of society. A liberal society will undoubtedly be noisier and more confusing than one run by a Plato or a Lee Kuan Yew. But it is not equivalent to anarchy and social breakdown. Its order is produced through the observance of the liberal limits and the willingness of the members to accommodate each other's rights-based claims in the interests of social union. As to the question of an objective order of substantive values, it is surely acceptable to say that even if such an order exists, it is not certainly known by any human beings and hence cannot serve as the legitimate basis of a coercively enforced social system. The possibility of such objectivity should then be open to debate within the rules of liberal society. It does not seem to us particularly difficult for a contemporary Confucian to accept such a position.

The final reason for doubting the compatibility of Confucianism and human rights was the family character of the Confucian ideal which makes the rights-based model of human association inappropriate. In this regard, Chan argues that the attribution of basic rights to family members does not in itself destroy the family ideal of mutual care and social harmony but constitutes a safeguard against oppression should the family relationship break down. Basic human rights as a fall-back against social and political oppression are thus fully compatible with the Confucian ideal. The fact that Confucians seek to resolve family and social conflicts through mediation rather than litigation is also perfectly compatible with the acceptance of rights-based litigation as a safeguard should mediation fail or take an unfair or oppressive form. In this regard, we entirely endorse Chan's view of the way in which Confucian 'family values' can be supported rather than undermined by a rights regime.

In general, many of those who seek a Confucian basis for human rights also see elements of the Confucian tradition as capable of providing a corrective for some of the evils that are said to beset contemporary liberalism in the West: namely, its excessive individualism, competitiveness and moral and social disorder. A liberal Confucianism would support a much greater respect for family and communal authority than is current in the West without rejecting the equal individual rights that are fundamental to liberalism. This may well be so. There is no doubt that the social fabric in Western individualistic countries is in need of substantial repairs. But we have consistently argued that liberalism does not presuppose an asocial individualism or an absolutism of rights or a relativism of values and is not incompatible with a proper respect for family and communal values. Where the fault lies is no doubt a complicated matter, but understanding is not helped by the identification of liberalism with a complete relativism of values and an extreme relaxation of social discipline.

So, what would a Confucian justification of liberal human rights look like? We suggest that it would appeal to the benevolent moral motivation of the Confucian gentleman who seeks the right way to live, which is now to be found in respect for others' equal autonomy, while setting them examples of rightful choice and moral excellence regarding the traditional human goods of family, friendship, education and self-cultivation, wealth, public service, conflict mediation, and so on. Contrary to Weber's judgement, it seems to us that Confucianism can more easily be adjusted to a liberal but somewhat conservative world than the other non-Western ethical cultures we are considering in this chapter.

Hinduism and human rights

In a well-known essay called 'Is the Notion of Human Rights a Western Concept?' Panikkar contrasts the Western liberal view of human rights with what he calls an Indian view of social order.[34] He describes the latter as a conception of human rights because it constitutes an account of the necessary conditions of a life of human dignity and thus occupies the same ethical ground as the standard UN view of human rights. What he calls the Indian conception he takes to contain ideas that are present not only in Hinduism but also in Jainism and Buddhism. It is probably best to identify it as a simplified version of classical Hinduism.

As we have already indicated, Donnelly and other Western theorists are adamant that what is being referred to in such a discourse is a set of duties and not rights and that the latter term only applies in liberal-individualist discourse. This claim is, in our view, not compelling. There is a perfectly accepted and meaningful use of the term rights in which the rights of a person are tied to his fulfilment of a role or function, such as the rights of a judge to sentence convicted criminals to some form of punishment. Given this acceptable usage, if we find a discourse that gives to human beings roles not in this or that contingent social order but in a universally valid ideal order that bestows human dignity on those who fulfil its requirements, then the entitlements attached to the roles can surely be seen as rights pertaining to their non-contingent human nature rather than to a contingent social identity. At any rate, we shall follow Panikkar in being prepared to use the term human rights to refer to the entitlements arising from individuals' positions in an ideal social order. Since the order in the Indian conception is hierarchical in nature, we shall call this view of human rights the hierarchical conception.

Fundamental to this perspective is the idea of a cosmic order into which all beings fit in accordance with a hierarchy of being. Human social order is to be understood only in terms of its place in the cosmic order of things. Individual human beings have their place in the human order and through it in the larger order. What maintains or gives coherence to a thing in this order is the dharma of the thing or its dharmic character. Justice is what gives human relations an orderly form; hence justice is the dharmic character of the human order. To be concerned with the dharmic character of a being such as a human being is not a matter of asserting its rights against other individuals or against society, as Panikkar supposes is true of the Western conception. It is rather a matter of a being's rights within the appropriate order. Human beings have rights on this view but their rights are defined by their proper place in the whole. Rights in this sense are not absolutized and treated as the attributes of independent individuals – the supposed Western view again – but are relative to a being's position in an order. Indeed, Panikkar is prepared to say that rights are not just attributes of human beings; all beings have rights insofar as they have their proper place in a cosmic order of being. Given that the order of being in the Indian conception is hierarchical, then the rights will not be equal rights but differentiated according to a being's place in the order.

Panikkar says that rights in the Indian conception are duties as much as rights. A being has a right to occupy the position in the social and cosmic order to which it is entitled by its nature and a right to carry out the functions appropriate to that position. At the same time it has a duty to do the very acts it has a right to do. Rights and duties under this conception coincide. While Panikkar clearly misrepresents the absolute nature of human rights in the Western conception, he is correct to point out the difference in the understanding of the relation of rights and duties in the two views. For, although in the Western view, contrary to what Panikkar believes, it is true that a person has rights only insofar as he has duties also, the duties are owed to others to respect their rights, while one's own rights are entitlements to act in ways that are not themselves duties. This is because the liberal rights are in the first instance freedoms, which one is not under a duty to exercise in any specific way or to exercise at all if one does not so wish. Under the Indian conception of roles and functions, one has a duty to perform in accordance with one's role.

The objection might still be made to Panikkar's use of the term human rights to apply to the Indian conception that they can't be human rights because they are not the same rights for all human beings. This differentiation of rights, however, follows the differentiation of human beings according to the roles they are fitted to perform by their nature. Human beings have naturally different roles. Some should attend to human beings' spiritual needs, others should rule, a further class should farm the land and act as merchants and the remainder perform the menial jobs. The different roles attributed to men and women by nature is the most enduring element in this traditional conception. The rights human beings have by their human nature are their human rights. Since this nature is not the same in each person, their rights cannot be the same. Yet they hold these rights by virtue of their (differentiated) human nature, so it is not unreasonable to call them their human rights.

Panikkar makes much of the different understandings of the nature of the human individual under the Western and Indian conceptions. The Indian view recognizes the dignity of the human person. But the person is not the same as the individual. The personality of a human being in the Indian view is defined in terms of his relations to others through the roles he occupies. He exists as a person only through a network of relations. Adopting the metaphor of a net, Panikkar says that the individual should be conceived as an individual knot around which the entire fabric of the net is woven. Taken in abstraction from the net, that is, by separating the individual knot from the net, one would have destroyed the worth of the knot and seriously damaged the net. An individual human being on this conception, then, has worth and dignity only in fulfilling his function in the order of being.

On the Western conception, according to Panikkar, the individual has worth in himself as an independent being and hence his rights must be understood as absolute, since they are not relative to his participation in any social order. We have already challenged that interpretation of the Western view. We have argued that the only coherent way to understand individualistic human rights is as the equal rights of members of an ideal moral community of human beings, so that each person's right is relative to the equal rights of others. In himself, as an independent being, the individual has no rights. Nevertheless, there is a sense in which, on the Western view, the individual can be abstracted from his ideal relations to others and still thought of as having interests and capacities that are of supreme importance to the person himself. That is to say, each person has natural interests as a separate being with his own independent destiny in the world, in life, liberty and access to resources and the natural capacity to choose for himself an appropriate balance of human goods. These features underlie and are presupposed by his entitlement to equal rights in an ideal community of human beings. They ensure that the fundamental rights through which that membership is expressed will be freedom rights.

The Indian view apparently denies that any meaning can be given to the idea of the individual abstracted from the social order. Yet, it is not necessary, or sensible, for adherents of that view to say this. It is perfectly possible to make sense of someone, torn from his Indian network of relations and bereft of any moral support from others, having natural interests as a separate being in life, liberty and access to resources and exercising his capacity for self-control and self-direction to escape from his situation. All the Indian need say about this, is that these natural interests are best satisfied by human beings in the ideal social order and that this social order is a hierarchical one because human beings are naturally unequal in regard to the relevant capacities. The difference between the liberal and the hierarchist, then, turns on the notion of human equality. The liberal does not deny the existence of natural hierarchies of capacity but believes that they can and should be made subordinate to the idea of human beings' equal freedom, while the hierarchist doesn't believe that a social order structured by equal rights is possible. It would be against nature.

It should be noted that, while Panikkar initially holds that the liberal and Indian views of an appropriate social order for human beings fall completely outside each other, so that the problems to which liberalism provides solutions simply do not arise for traditional societies governed by the Indian-type metaphysics, he ends by accepting that the liberal conception of human rights is more appropriate for the modern technological world. He believes only that it is wrong to impose that conception of human rights on societies that have not undergone the modern socio-economic transformation. This is not much different from our own view of the matter, so that Panikkar can hardly be presented as a critic of liberalism. The value of his article lies rather in his clear articulation of a traditional non-liberal and non-Western cultural standpoint.

Panikkar's account of classical Hinduism treats it as a pure role-based conception of ethics. As we have already argued, this would ensure its total incompatibility with liberalism. But other writers deny that classical Hinduism is a purely role-based view. Thus Sharma maintains that it has a general element, which turns out to be not dissimilar to the general element of classical Confucianism that we discussed in the last section.[35] This general element is said to consist, in the first place, in the view of dharma as meaning the pursuit of rightness as an end in itself. In other words, it expresses a moral point of view on life distinct from the socially useful or advantageous. In the second place, rightness or dharma is not just manifest in the duties of a person's caste. It is also present in duties common to all and owed to all, irrespective of a person's station in life. In this respect, Sharma claims that the highest importance is attached to the following moral qualities: truthfulness, non-stealing, purity and the restraint of the senses. These duties are enjoined on all men without regard to caste and the degree of excellence achieved in their performance is the sign of human dignity and worth.[36]

This general element is, in itself, fully compatible with the hierarchical order of the caste system. One acts as a moral agent by fulfilling the particular duties of one's station, and the general duties to be truthful, honest, pure and sensually restrained in one's relations to all human beings, not for the sake of advantage but because it is the right way to live. However, if one's life is entirely filled by relations of caste, then one's performance of the general duties of being truthful, honest, and so on, will be carried out only in those relations. One will not have the ethical experience of acting morally towards another human being just as an undifferentiated person in need of help, for example.

The transformation of the general element in Hinduism to the point at which it can endorse a liberal point of view, then, requires in the first place an expansion of the area of social life which is not dominated by caste but in which persons have to relate to each other as moral equals, for instance as buyers and sellers in a market, which is no respecter of caste dignity, or as travelling strangers potentially in need of help. The good Samaritan in the Christian biblical story is the traveller who stops to help another just because he is a suffering other and irrespective of the other's particular identity. Yet, such moral equality is not in itself sufficient to generate the liberal point of view, if it runs parallel to something like a caste system. The latter denies this moral equality by marshalling people into a hierarchy of life functions on the basis of birth rather than on the basis of the free activity of equal moral beings who enjoy reasonably fair initial opportunities. Insofar as such role-based illiberal inequality is engrained far more deeply in the Hindu mind than a similar type of inequality is in Confucianism, the conflict between Hinduism and human rights will be that much greater. On the other hand, India has had a much longer and deeper experience of Western rule and political values than China ever had and its constitution enshrines the liberal human rights, while the recent impressive achievements of Indian capitalism cannot but make the social ground more and more suitable for the flourishing of liberal values.

Buddhism and human rights

Insofar as Buddhism is an offshoot of Hinduism, it would seem, in its rejection of the caste system, to involve the development of Hinduism's potential for moral equality and thus to be much more amenable for use as a justificatory theory of liberal human rights than Hinduism itself. This is the view of Charles Taylor. In his article on the possibility of an overlapping consensus on human rights from Western and non-Western perspectives, he suggests that the reformist Buddhist, Phuthatthat, has been developing Buddhism as just such a basis for a democratic society and a system of human rights.[37] Nevertheless, this Buddhism does not seek to transform the traditional Buddhist teaching but rather to return to its doctrines regarding the unavoidability of suffering, the illusion of the self and the goal of Nirvana. The crucial elements in the Buddhist doctrine that Taylor associates with a defence of democracy and human rights are its emphasis on the responsibility of each person for his or her own enlightenment and a new application of the Buddhist doctrine of non-violence as a ground for the requirement to respect the autonomy of each person. Simon Caney in another article similarly emphasizes the Buddhist stress on individual responsibility and non-violence as providing a Buddhist ground for human rights norms.[38]

The trouble with these accounts is that the Buddhist philosophy is traditionally an ascetic doctrine that promotes enlightenment through the overcoming of desire (rather than through disciplining by reason as in the Kantian philosophy) and while it no doubt stresses individual responsibility for the attainment of enlightenment and the wrongness of violence, the social and political order within which individuals are encouraged to seek their enlightenment seems irrelevant so long as it leaves them free to pursue the Buddhist path. Buddhism developed and flourished in traditional hierarchical societies and seems perfectly compatible with the maintenance of those relations. Caney describes its social ethics as enjoining people to observe five main precepts: not to kill, steal, commit adultery, lie or drink alcohol. Caney believes that these precepts are evidence of the convergence of Buddhist ethics with human rights norms. However, the five precepts are compatible with both hierarchical and liberal egalitarian socio-economic orders. At most they show that the Buddhist moral code is indifferent to the type of social order in existence. This is no doubt because of its concern for individual enlightenment through the overcoming of desire. The observation of the ethical precepts are a necessary preliminary step in that direction.

Of course, similar remarks may be made about traditional Christianity with the substitution of individual salvation for individual enlightenment. Perhaps, just as Christianity was the religious form within which the liberal natural rights doctrine first emerged, Buddhism could be the form within which a similar social doctrine of human rights could develop in Buddhist countries. According to Charles Taylor, this is already happening in the work of the Thai Buddhist, Sivak. From one point of view, Buddhism is more suitable as a metaphysical basis for human rights than Confucianism, Hinduism or even Islam, since in its primary spiritual concerns it is wholly indifferent to a hierarchical social order, which the others to different degrees are committed to. However, from another point of view its ascetic commitments would seem to make it an implausible basis for a radical transformation of the social order. Perhaps all that is required of Buddhism, and perhaps all that Christianity provided in the West, is a metaphysical endorsement of a social transformation that has been brought about in other ways. In this respect, there would seem to be no difficulty.

Conclusion

The liberal-individualist aspirations of the UN programme have generated two types of response from persons defending or merely expressing the point of view of traditional non-Western cultures. One is more or less outright opposition, as in some adherents of Asian values, orthodox Islam and classical Hinduism. The other is the claim that the specified non-Western culture already recognizes human rights, as in the case of many Islamists, or can be reasonably adapted to endorse the same norms, as in the accounts of Confucianism and Buddhism that we have considered. In the case of the Islamists, we have shown that the orthodox Islamist version of human rights is in flat contradiction with the UN programme on several points and in general spirit. In the case of classical Confucianism, Hinduism and Buddhism, and indeed of Islam, we have attempted to show how they might be transformed so as to join an international consensus on liberal human rights. We believe that, in their classical forms, these non-Western ethical cultures are in substantial discord with the liberal norms of the UN bills of human rights. We believe, nevertheless, that they can be liberalized. We believe, of course, that they should be liberalized and will give in our last chapter our reasons for thinking that (under modern socio-political conditions) liberal norms offer the best basis on which human beings can associate.

As we see it, the main challenge that both Western and non-Western anti-liberal doctrines present to liberalism is the view that the unity of the political community must be based on the possession of a substantial or thick truth about the human good, such as is offered by traditional Christianity or Islam or Confucianism or Marxism, or indeed Platonism and many other illiberal doctrines. Without such a unifying ethical substance, political association will not be possible. Furthermore, if one possesses the truth on this matter, then one is entitled to rule. Those who reject the truth have no right to their political freedom or even full civil freedom.

11 | *In defence of liberalism*

We have been presenting liberalism in this book as the best form of human association for the modern world: that is to say a world composed for the most part of medium-sized independent states whose economies are organized on the mass scale of the national or international unit rather than through small-scale and tightly knit bodies such as the guilds or manorial villages. Since individuals have ceased to be integrated into and protected by such modest and relatively static communities but have to find their feet in a larger and more fluid mass governed by a powerful bureaucratic state, both individuals and their societies will do better if the former enjoy the basic liberties and welfare rights endorsed by liberalism.

This is, however, only a utilitarian justification for liberal regimes. We see such pragmatic claims as necessary but not sufficient grounds for an adequate defence of liberalism. The form of social and political life that constitutes liberal practice has to be expressed also in terms of principles that establish its distinctive character and these principles have to be defended against their critics. We have already in our previous chapters covered much of this ground. We have, we hope, made clear what we take liberal practice to be, both nationally and internationally, what its principled commitments are and the weakness of most attacks on them. In this chapter, we aim to bring the main points of these discussions together in a clear and simple exposition of what we think is the best theoretical account of liberalism. We shall end with an attempt to meet the major challenge to liberalism presented by the claim that ethical or religious truth is more important than freedom as the basis of political association.

Liberalism and principled toleration

The fundamental attitude of liberalism can be seen as coming into being through the recognition by the adherents of rival truths of the superiority of mutual toleration over the struggle for domination. The generalization of mutual toleration produces the idea that people should be free to make their own choices as to how to live their lives, provided that their choices do not involve a violation of the equal freedom of others. To justify the commitment to such an idea, we need first of all to substantiate the claim that human beings have the appropriate capacities to found their principled association on the basis of mutual respect as free and equal. We have been interpreting the relevant notions of freedom and equality to require only that normal human beings, if given adequate conditions of nurture, are sufficiently able to take the major decisions of their lives for themselves for it to be wrong to subject them to the coercive authority of others in these regards.

This idea of a sufficient capacity for autonomy in each person doesn't suppose that some people are not better informed, more intelligent and wiser than others in particular matters or overall, nor that most people would not benefit from advice in making their decisions. The issue is whether some adults, whether parents, religious leaders, politicians or aristocrats, should be entitled to coerce other adults into conforming with choices that are not their own. Liberalism rejects this on the grounds, first, that everyone has a sufficient capacity to make reasonable decisions, even if the actual decisions are not always the right ones and may sometimes be disastrous. But second, liberalism requires each person to take full responsibility for his own life and participate in the determination of the collective life. The ultimate justification for this is that the related capacities for autonomy, rationality and responsibility are the distinctive human capacities, so that a fully human life for each person must involve their exercise. Illiberal societies deny this essential human activity to a greater or lesser degree. Under liberalism, human moral and political association is understood as realized through the recognition of the equal worth of each person as an autonomous being responsible for his own life and for sharing in the collective life.

In the third place, apart from the higher order values of freedom and equality, liberalism recognizes that there are many human goods and that these can be realized through different lives. There is no natural hierarchy of such lives, such as the Platonic-Aristotelian-Christian privileging of the contemplative life. This pluralism of human goods, then, provides another reason why individuals must choose for themselves how to pursue the good in their lives and why it is wrong for one person to be in a position to impose his choice of the good on others. Finally, liberalism takes the view that to grant coercive authority to some to make choices for others without being responsible to those subject to them is bound to lead to massive abuses.

The affirmation of the freedom and equality of human beings as the foundation of just association does not mean that liberalism believes that society is created by independent individuals entering into a contract to establish it. Liberals can perfectly well accept the obvious truth that human beings are born into, and their human capacities and identities are developed in, ongoing societies with their own cultures and traditions. Human beings attach, and identify, themselves, in the first instance, by relation to such particular communities. But they standardly develop a more universal identity by reference to The Gods or God or Reason or some such notion. In other words, human beings' capacity for reflective thought gives them the possibility of detaching themselves from a total embeddedness in membership of a particular community and of thinking of themselves in more general and abstract terms. Liberalism's principles, grounded in a general account of human interests and capacities, is one such universalizing viewpoint. Yet, it is absurd to think of the universal standpoint as somehow substituting for the particular community and hence abolishing it. The principles qualify a person's membership of it and require the community's reform only insofar as its organization does not already conform to the new values. From its general standpoint, liberalism justifies the existence of particular states and hence endorses the sentiments and commitments appropriate to a vigorous and flourishing self-governing community, which in its internal arrangements respects liberal principles.

Liberalism is perfectly compatible also with the recognition of moral and political authority, contrary to what some of its enemies assert. It is, in effect, a particular account of such authority. Moral authority lies in the moral community of equal rights' holders. Since individuals have rights only as equal members of this ideal community of human beings, a particular claim can be shown to be legitimate only if it is authorized from that standpoint. Standardly, the authorization will have to be traced through the laws of the claimant's political community. This is because liberalism conceives the actualization of the ideal community as necessarily taking place through such particular political communities, which interpret and enforce the general principles. A particular political association, then, derives its authority in part from its justification from the moral standpoint – it conforms to liberal principles. But it must also derive its authority from its character as the expression of the general will of the collection of people gathered in the territory controlled by the state whose authority is in question.

The idea of the liberal individual is frequently criticized by anti-liberals for its unrealistic notion of autonomy. Just as the liberal community is characterized and ridiculed for its supposed lack of concreteness, so the liberal individual is represented as a detached and abstract free will making essentially arbitrary choices about the life of the human being in which it is embodied. However, the generalizing capacity here is the ability of the reflective individual to stand back from his embeddedness in the decisions of the moment and to think of his life as a whole. From that standpoint, he can reflect on the sort of person he is already, the potentialities he has and the opportunities that are available to him and make long-term choices regarding the life he would most like to lead in the light of his circumstances. These choices, which are of course revisable, aim to be realizable and in that sense realistic. They are clearly not arbitrary, since they are based on the particularities of each individual. A person achieves autonomy insofar as he takes control of his life in the way described. Liberalism holds that all normal human beings have this reflective capacity, although its adequate and fair exercise in a complex modern economy and society requires a reasonable degree of education and opportunity and the enjoyment of the liberal human rights.

This conception of human autonomy is not essentially secular, although it is largely presented in such terms in the contemporary English-speaking philosophical literature. It can be endorsed from the point of view of a religion that believes in a creator God. All one has to say is that God created human beings with the nature and capacities that they now have or that he created a world in which in the course of evolution human beings would develop with such capacities. Since beings with that nature must be part of his plan in creating the world, he must want those beings to organize their life together through the exercise of their capacities. Autonomous human beings can recognize their dependence on God for their possession of the nature they have and surrender themselves to God's will even in exercising their God-given autonomous powers.

Similarly, one can revise a hierarchical conception of the cosmic order of being by treating the rank occupied by humanity as filled by fundamentally equally worthy autonomous beings. The appropriate roles that such beings would have to fill in order to achieve their nature and fulfilment would give pride of place to their membership of the moral community of equal rights' holders, while their more particular roles in human societies would be determined by the exercise of their autonomy rather than be assigned to them by birth.

The interpretation of freedom and equality

We have emphasized throughout this book that liberalism's general principle needs a public authority that will both enforce individuals' rights effectively but also arrive at an interpretation of the principle, as it applies to the variety of human interests, that is binding on all those subject to the particular interpretive authority.

What is at issue in this matter is a conflict between the claims of freedom and equality. It may be puzzling that there should be a conflict between freedom and equality when the fundamental principle is supposed to unite them. The trouble arises from the exercise of individual freedom and is particularly acute in economic affairs. Thus, suppose we interpret equal freedom as the equal individual freedom to use one's legitimately possessed resources as one pleases, so long as one does not engage in force or fraud, and that these initial resources are equal. The exercise of individual freedom to trade will quickly produce greater and greater inequalities as a result of differences in individuals' ambition, hard work, talent and luck. If one thinks that equality demands the continuous enjoyment of an equality of resources, as some egalitarian liberals do, then one will have to ban freedom to trade. Correspondingly, if one believes that freedom to trade is what is important, then one will have to accept the consequent inequalities. The two extreme positions here would be the collective organization of production and exchange and the equal distribution of income on the one hand, and on the other, an unrestricted individual freedom to trade with unlimited inequality. Most contemporary liberal societies go for an arrangement that is somewhere around the middle of this continuum and we do not disagree with that disposition. Our aim is not to argue for a particular interpretation of equal freedom in economic matters as the best one, but to emphasize how disputed this area is within a broadly liberal perspective of equal freedom and how a liberal society must expect not to be able to reach a general and lasting agreement on the appropriate balance between freedom and equality. It will need to accept that binding political resolutions of the dispute will have to be made and revised as circumstances and opinion change over time.

Even if it is possible to resolve these disagreements through political compromises, the theoretical problem remains as to why there is a conflict between freedom and equality if they are supposed to be united in the foundational principle. Could this conflict mean that in its foundations liberalism is not a coherent conception of a moral and political community? What this conflict reveals is that a community of free and equal autonomous beings must be realized through a political form in which the members together take responsibility for deciding what is an appropriate balance between the values of individuality-affirming freedom and a community-affirming equality. Neither value can be abandoned or wholly subordinated to the other without the abandonment of the very idea of a moral community of individual rights' holders. Individual freedom without community possesses no moral substance while community without individual freedom would be a pure tyranny.

In this context, we wish to consider a standard charge against liberalism made by both left- and right-wing communitarians, and Western and non-Western critics, that it is essentially an expression of a selfish materialism. It is, of course, true that the liberal capitalist market offers potentially huge rewards to enterprising, self-seeking conduct in competition with others. The market requires its participants to have regard to their own interests and places responsibility on each person to fend for himself and not depend on the goodwill of others. But it is absurd to object to such motivations and concerns in their entirety, since they are fundamental to human nature. A more sensible policy, and one fully in accord with contemporary liberalism, is to ensure that some of the gains from the successful operation of markets are used to guarantee that no one is made worse-off as a result of the competition. The market is not a zero sum game in which a gain to one person is necessarily a loss to some other. Hence, we all have a long-term interest in the efficiency, enterprise and innovation that market competition promotes, provided that welfare safeguards are in place.

The charge of selfish materialism, then, ignores, in the first instance, that individual freedom rights, whether in the economic or other spheres, are rooted in the idea of a moral community of equal rights' holders. This community requires individuals to value others as their equals and hence behave towards them by respecting their rights, which are now standardly understood to include welfare rights. Nevertheless, what can be truly said of the form liberal concern for others takes is that it has an impersonal or cold character as compared with the 'warm' mutual care of members of small, close-knit medieval communities. However, quite apart from the obvious tensions and oppressions that are likely to be present in such communities, they are not an option in the modern world and in any case the point is supposed to be the selfishness of liberal life, not the impersonal nature of its concern for others.

In the second place, liberal freedoms in no way discourage individuals from exercising their natural sympathies and pursuing their natural interests in forming close friendships and making other commitments of a non-commercial and non-impersonal nature to others. In fact, such voluntary associations proliferate in liberal society. One of these of especial importance is the family. However, a fairly widespread contemporary criticism of liberal society by non-Westerners in particular is that the family unit is being undermined by the licentious sexual mores that liberalism has either promoted or tolerated through its defence of individual freedom. Yet, while there is no ground in liberalism for re-criminalizing such forms of sexual conduct as adultery, there are other types of social control besides legal coercion and it seems to us that at some point the interests of liberal society in maintaining the health of the family must trump the interests of individuals in sexual freedom. This is because of the central importance of the family in the reproduction of liberal individuals who possess the moral character and self-discipline necessary for the successful reproduction of liberal society itself.

This issue raises, however, not only the question of the selfish character of individual freedom rights under liberalism but a second general problem in interpreting the liberal principle, namely the limits to individual freedom arising, not from the need to respect the equality of others, but from the need for the liberal ethical idea of a community of equal rights' holders to be realized through the life and institutions of particular independent political communities. The interests of such communities are referred to in the UN human rights documents in terms of public order, morality and the general welfare of a democratic society. Public order is essentially concerned with the maintenance of the conditions under which the members of the community can go safely about their legitimate private business on the one hand and peacefully carry out the public business on the other. Individual freedom may have to be restricted on both counts. An example of the former are drinking laws that limit the time or place of consuming alcohol. Examples of the latter involve restrictions on public demonstrations or meetings and constraints on the activities of particular organizations or individuals deemed to be threats to public order or the general welfare of a democratic society. Just as there is no exactly right point at which the claims of individual freedom and those of other-regarding equality must be balanced, so also the balance between individual freedom and the needs of public order and welfare cannot be exactly settled, but will depend on the particular conditions and dangers facing a community and require the exercise of practical political judgement more than philosophical rigour.

As regards the question of the interest of liberal society in the institution of the family and the relation of that interest to the legitimate claims of public morality in matters of sexual conduct and display, much depends on the interpretation of the empirical evidence that is available. This concerns the best family structure for the nurture of a new generation of liberal individuals, the effects on this family of different degrees of sexual freedom, the effects of the widespread availability of pornography and the general sexual character of much ordinary advertisements and public entertainment. We do not accept that individual freedom is the only value that counts here. We believe that there is a genuine public interest concern involving a balance between the interests of individuals in freedom and the interests of society in the maintenance of the conditions for its successful reproduction. Where that point lies depends, as we have said, on an understanding of the empirical evidence. But it also involves the exercise of practical political judgement as to what can best be done in the particular circumstances of one's own community.

Freedom of choice and human goods

Liberalism values individual choice. It seeks to promote social outcomes that are as far as possible the result of the free choices of individuals by themselves or in voluntary association with others. So one might think that liberalism is committed to the view that whatever is chosen by individuals that does not violate the rights of others or the needs of the liberal community for its security and flourishing is good. In other words, liberalism holds that only freedom and equality are objective human goods and otherwise what is good is relative to the chooser. This view is neither necessary nor sensible for liberalism to adopt. The only reasonable view is that there are objective human goods and human evils. There are natural human evils such as fear, pain, suffering, poverty, an early death, ugliness and ill-health and social evils such as disgrace, contempt, degradation, humiliation, hatred, loneliness, failure, ignorance and unhappiness. Human goods are similarly natural and social and include such things as life, pleasure, health, beauty, love, friendship, achievement, knowledge, wealth, family and happiness.

If individuals are left free to choose for themselves how to live their lives, so long as they do not harm others, some will choose lives that are likely to end badly. Illiberal societies seek to limit people's choices by a conception of the good for human beings. Even if liberalism is committed to the idea of a plurality of good human lives, the plurality is not unlimited. Should it not, then, restrict choice to the range of good things, or rather to the acts and activities that can be counted on to lead to the enjoyment of the good things and the avoidance of the evil? This conclusion does not follow. If liberalism is to work, it must tolerate beliefs and actions that do not harm others and are not a threat to the (liberal) society. So, it must tolerate those whose views are extremely hostile to liberalism provided that they do not engage in actions that imperil its life and security. Liberal society must, of course, promote the understanding and acceptance of its own values by its members, but not by coercion. So also, if individuals choose lives that bring evils upon them of natural or social kinds but which do not violate others' rights, then liberalism must prefer that such people are free to make their errors than that they are prevented from falling into evil by a paternalist authority. This does not mean that a liberal society should not promote the education of its people in the nature of human goods and evils. It should, indeed, do these things but not coerce people into conforming to recognized paths to the attainment of the goods.

The justification for this toleration must be that, for liberalism, the possession by all of the freedom to take responsibility for their own lives is a more important value than the values that would be realized if all were subject to coercion in following the good. It is more important because, as we have argued above, autonomy is, first, the distinctive human capacity, so that a fully human life is one that is realized through its exercise and second, it is possessed to a sufficient degree by all normal adults for each to count as equally worthy of respect in regard to it.

The choice of liberalism over its competitors

The above discussion is designed to defend liberalism as a perfectly coherent and viable conception of human community and to point to the values on which it is based. However, this leaves it open for someone to maintain that, although liberalism is possible, it is not the best form of human association even under modern conditions. Some other conception of society is better because it is based on the substantial ethical truth as to how human beings should live. As we have argued, liberalism is built in a sense on a compromise between rival versions of the truth and an agreement to live together on the footing of a mutual respect for each other's freedom. The agreement involves the construction of an idea of ethical community as grounded in a shared notion of the human good that differs from the rival ones in being a thin conception rather than a substantial one. It is thin because its fundamental values are those of autonomy and equality, the meaning of which is to leave each party as equally free as possible to determine how he shall pursue more substantial human goods and, in respect of decisions that have to be made collectively, to make them accountable to the community of equal rights' holders.

The liberal conception of ethical community might seem vulnerable, then, to the insistence of one or other of the claimants to substantial ethical truth that liberalism is nothing more than a compromise with the truth with which it will have nothing to do. Such a claimant believes that they possess the truth as to how human beings should live and have the duty to fight for its implementation. The main challengers to liberalism in the West at the practical level during the recent past have been the authoritarian nationalists, whose extreme form was fascism, and the communists. As both these movements had a strong 'communitarian' character – in the former case manifesting itself as a belief in the ethical unity of the ethnic nation and in the latter as a belief in the ethical unity of the workers – it is tempting for the liberal to seek to defend liberalism against them by attacking 'communitarianism' in general. The trouble with this approach is that the proper defence of liberalism against communitarianism in general consists in showing that liberalism is perfectly compatible with the value of community and this we have done. But this merely returns us to the standoff between a liberal conception of ethical community as grounded in a thin shared notion of the good and the nationalist-fascist and communist thicker notions.

So, how do we demonstrate the superiority of liberalism to these other views? One way would be to seek to refute each conception separately by showing that the beliefs in the ethical unity of the ethnic nation, the workers, and so on are unsustainable. This is no doubt an important part of a complete defence but it would take us into too much detailed polemic against an indefinite number of opponents and would in any case probably be inconclusive because of the difficulty in establishing decisive arguments in this field. A more attractive approach would still be to seek a general argument as to why the adherents of a thick ethical belief, which they claim to know to be true, should yet not try to impose the belief on others who reject it. The lack of decisive arguments in this area, as just mentioned, suggests that the way to do this is precisely to argue for the unavoidable uncertainty of judgements of truth regarding thick ethical notions. This may be called by some a moderate scepticism and by others a reasonable pluralism. However, the same objection applies to such reasoning, namely that it will have no effect on the adherents of the 'truth', who will simply claim that they have certain knowledge.

Another possibility for establishing a knockdown argument for liberalism against its opponents is through an appeal to the notion of autonomy. If we can show that human beings have the capacity for autonomy and that all normal human beings possess it to a sufficient degree to take responsibility for their lives, will we not have demon-strated the necessary superiority of liberalism? The problem here is that none of the anti-liberal doctrines, except what we have called authoritarianism, need deny that human beings have the capacity for autonomy. They will simply argue that autonomy in the ethical realm requires that human beings direct themselves in accordance with the truth or, in other words, in accordance with the principles of ethical community. Since even liberalism must hold this view of ethical autonomy, we are returned once again to the opposition between the conditions of liberal community and those of the variety of anti-liberal communities.

We propose, then, to challenge head on the claim that the possession of ethical truth entitles one to impose the truth on others, either in the form of coercing people to accept the truth or by subordinating those who reject the truth to the rule of the truth-sayers. We assume, in the first place, that it is possible to live in accordance with the 'true faith' in a liberal society that allows its members to pursue the good as they think fit so long as they do not violate the rights of others. Thus, whether the others conform to what you believe to be the truth does not directly affect your ability to live as you believe you are ethically required to do. So, by what right do you seek to impose your beliefs on others when they leave you perfectly free to follow your own? The adherent of the truth here might reply that liberalism itself reserves the right to enforce its (thin) conception of the good on the members of liberal society. Hence, liberalism has no grounds for objecting when other systems of belief do the same. Liberalism, however, claims that its system of coercive rule involves the minimum degree of coercion compatible with an orderly and viable ethical community. Anything less coercive would, in effect, be a state of anarchy and in such a state, while there would be no legal constraints on freedom, everyone's freedom would be *de facto* severely circumscribed. You seek to legally limit freedom beyond what is necessary for the existence of an ethical community, the liberal would say, and you have no justification for this excess degree of coercion.

What might the adherent of the truth reply to this challenge? He might say that he is coercing the non-believers into doing the right thing for their own good. But this is an implausible position to adopt. Doing the right thing out of fear or for the sake of conforming to the majority or the dominant will is not a motive that should get one any ethical credit. To count as making the unbelievers ethically better off, they would have to come to do the right thing for the right reason, which is that they believe it to be right. Coercion has little chance, then, of improving their ethical welfare. Suppose that the adherents of the truth say with St Augustine that there is no worse death for the soul than having the freedom to err. On this view, coercion is absolutely required to prevent the faithful from straying from the true path. Without this protective fence many people would be tempted to explore paths that would lead them to eternal damnation. It is not those who are compelled to enter the fenced area or those who keep within the fence through fear of terrestrial punishment who are benefited but all those who because of the existence of the fence do not begin to entertain any doubts about the 'truth' as it is transmitted to them.

The good achieved here can be conceived in individualist or communal terms. In the first case, it is individual believers who benefit. However, in order to do so, each must be led by the policy to narrow his vision of human possibilities to what is prescribed by the authoritarian shepherds. But the policy can still only be said to bring ethical benefit to the faithful if they sincerely yet unreflectively believe what is prescribed. It must be sincere, because it is quite possible that everyone publicly endorses and practises a prescribed faith, although in fact no one in their hearts believes it to be true, but at the same time no one is sufficiently confident that the others share his disbelief to dare to express it publicly. Cleary, there is no ethical benefit for persons in such a situation.

Assuming, then, that belief is sincere yet unreflective, there are two obvious criticisms of this defence of coercion for the sake of protecting the faithful from error. The first is that while the coercive authorities believe they have the truth, they may be wrong in whole or in part. How can they be so confident that they have the truth when, as is likely to be the case, most of humanity disagrees with them, and when the only serious test of whether one's beliefs are superior to others is through an open, free and critical dialogue between them? It is not that open dialogue is bound to produce the truth but that without it, the chances of finding oneself committed to error are very high. However, we have already admitted that someone who is absolutely certain that he possesses the truth will not be persuaded by such arguments, which, in effect, ask him to suppose that he might be wrong.

The second argument appeals to the consequences for a community of closing down debate over its beliefs. The beliefs will become lifeless dogmas without the capacity to invigorate the intellectual or practical life of those who profess them. This is indeed the whole point of the coercion. It is necessarily intended to stop people raising questions about the faith. It may be said that in the past the great mass of uneducated believers could not have been expected to acquire the learning that would have enabled them to explore the grounds and meaning of their faith. It sufficed for them to believe and to live in the way required of the faithful. However, in a coercive system designed to protect the faithful from error, the educated will have to be more closely policed than the herd. Furthermore, to treat the mass of believers as an unthinking and irrational herd in societies in which everyone could be educated to a reasonable level of knowledge and reflection on the practices and beliefs of his society is another matter altogether. It is only the authoritarians of the type described in Chapter 9 who hold that there will always be a herd whose members do not wish to reflect but want only some authoritative belief to which they can commit themselves and through which they will be bound in unity to each other. This greatly underestimates the capacities and interests of most people.

However, in our view, it is most probably the combination of the belief that one possesses the truth with the conviction that the unity a political community requires must be founded on an authoritative creed of a metaphysical or religious type that motivates the coercers. This is well expressed by Plato thus: 'it is better for everyone, we believe, to be subject to a power of God-like wisdom residing in himself or failing that imposed from without in order that all of us being under one guidance may be so far as possible equal and united'.[1] In this view, imposing the good on everyone produces two goods; first, everyone is brought into contact with the true path and second, all are united under a common rule. But the force of this combination rests on the unawareness or rejection of the liberal alternative to a faith-based community.

The above arguments have assumed that it is possible for the adherent of the truth to follow the prescriptions of his faith in a private capacity within a liberal state. Hence, why should he impose his beliefs unnecessarily on others? But this may not be possible. One's thick ethical 'truth' may require a politico-legal form for it to be the effective way of life of its adherents. In that case, liberalism and the other belief-systems would be in direct competition. This is true of ethno-nationalism and its fascist variations. The ethical truth here is that the nation must be governed in accordance with its ethno-cultural values and this is incompatible with its being governed by liberal norms. This is also true of hierarchical conceptions of order that are based on inherited position rather than on natural distinction, which liberalism can accommodate insofar as the hierarchies are open to all under fair conditions and are accountable for their conduct. Traditional Islamic law, as well, contains rules that cannot be lived privately by Muslims: these are those provisions of its criminal law that conflict with liberal norms, such as the hadd punishments, the killing of apostates and the legal rules discriminating against women, not to speak of those that subordinate non-Muslims to Muslim domination.

In such cases, there is no general argument that can be deployed against all. The liberal has to attempt to refute each in turn. Thus, as regards ethno-nationalism he has to show, as we have done in Chapter 9, that its strong communitarian claims about personal identity are false and that the limited truth in nationalism can be integrated into liberalism. The same can be done for hierarchical belief systems. The claims for a sufficient capacity for autonomy in everyone have to be affirmed and the limited truth of hierarchy integrated into liberalism. In respect of Islamic law, it is not possible for liberalism to maintain its commitment to the fundamental values of free and equal citizenship and allow parallel legal systems for some of its members. Muslims can, of course, within liberal society privately continue their family organization if this is done within liberal law and with the consent of their women who will have received an education in their liberal rights. The killing of apostates and other criminal provisions can only be claimed to be necessary for the practice of the Islamic faith because they are held to be commanded by God through his prophet Mohammed in the Islamic sacred texts. Outside that context, the persecution of apostates can clearly be seen as an attempt to preserve communal unity and as obviously unnecessary for the following of the faith on a voluntary basis. Given the supposedly divine nature of Islamic law, the liberal can only question the meaning or the contemporary relevance of such laws in the sacred texts or the goodness of a God who issues such commands.

The same has to be said of the belief in the right of Muslims to rule over non-Muslims. Insofar as this is based on the view that those who reject God's messenger and message have no rights or lesser rights than the faithful, then the liberal can argue that it is for God, not men, to punish those who deny him. But if God is taken to have commanded such subjection in his message to the faithful, then non-Muslims everywhere can only reject such unjust decrees and stand up and fight for their equal freedom.

Notes

Introduction

1 The application of liberal ideas to heterosexual and homosexual conduct is, however, only a recent phenomenon in the West. Whether one believes that the degree of sexual freedom, now widely accepted, is a good or bad thing must turn on what one thinks its consequences are for the stability of the family and the reproduction of responsible liberal individuals.

2 Universal Declaration of Human Rights in *Basic Human Rights Documents* (Geneva: Office of High Commissioner for Human Rights, 1998).

3 See especially Leif Wenar's distinction between orthodox and practical conceptions of human rights. The former looks for a philosophical ground in some principle such as the general utility or human autonomy. On the practical conception, 'human rights define the boundaries of legitimate political action' in some actual arrangements. L. Wenar, 'The Nature of Human Rights' in A. Follesdal and T. Pogge (eds.), *The Real World of Justice* (Dordrecht: Springer, 2005). Mervyn Frost also takes a practice-based conception of human rights. See M. Frost, *Constituting Human Rights* (London and New York: Routledge, 2002).

4 Quoted in H. Kamen, *The Rise of Toleration* (London: Weidenfeld and Nicholson, 1967), p. 14.

5 J. Locke, *Two Treatises of Government* (Cambridge University Press, 1964), Bk. II Ch. 5.

6 This is not to say that liberty and equality are independent and radically conflicting values within liberalism. As we have seen, the fundamental liberal value is that of an equal liberty. It is the different conceptions of equal liberty that give more or less weight to economic liberty relative to equality.

7 Plato, *The Republic* (Oxford: Clarendon Press, 1941), Part III. With regard to Islamic states, we are thinking in particular of the constitution of the Islamic Republic of Iran which gives ultimate oversight in all matters of policy to a supreme leader, who is a religious figure, together with a Council of Guardians composed of religious specialists. See J. Kelsay, 'Civil Society and Government in Islam' in S. Hashmi (ed.), *Islamic Political Ethics* (Princeton University Press, 2002), p. 16.

8 J. S. Mill, *On Liberty*, ed. G. Himmelfarb (Harmondsworth: Penguin, 1974).

9 We discuss the utilitarian theory further in Chapter 9.

1 The contextual origin of liberal thought and practice

1 The distinction between thick and thin conceptions of the self, although without using those terms, was influentially made by M. Sandel, *Liberalism and the Limits of Justice* (Cambridge University Press, 1982), pp. 59–65 and 179–83. For a similar distinction applied to moral principles, see M. Walzer, *Thick and Thin: Moral Argument at Home and Abroad* (University of Notre Dame Press, 1994).

2 We place truth in inverted commas to indicate that what we mean by truth here is only the view that is supported by the best reasons.

3 The individualism of Renaissance thought consists mainly in its attachment of much greater creative significance to the individual human being than is apparent in other cultural periods and societies, the supreme example of which is Pico della Mirandola's *Oration on the Dignity of Man*, quoted in J. Burckhardt, *The Civilization of the Renaissance in Italy* (New York: Harper Torchbooks, 1958), pp. 351–2. The individualism of the Reformation is present in Luther's principle of the priesthood of all believers. However, the main reformed churches avoided the libertarian implications of the principle by applying it only to believers in the 'true' faith as defined by the visible church under the guidance of its leaders supported by the state. See J. S. Whale, *The Protestant Tradition* (Cambridge University Press, 1959), pp. 110–15.

4 We discuss the problems of incorporating contemporary aboriginal societies in a liberal states system in Ch. 5.

5 See Q. Skinner, *Foundations of the Modern State* (Cambridge University Press, 1978), especially the Conclusion to Vol. II. Also R. von Friedeburg (ed.), *Murder and Monarchy* (Basingstoke: Palgrave Macmillan, 2004), pp. 16–28; A. Passerin d'Entreves, *The Notion of the State* (Oxford: Clarendon Press, 1967), pp. 96–113; G. Poggi, *The Development of the Modern State* (Stanford University Press, 1978), pp. 72–7.

6 C. Tilly, 'Reflections on the History of European State-making' in C. Tilly (ed.), *The Formation of National States in Western Europe* (Princeton University Press, 1975), pp. 34–5; A. Watson, *The Evolution of International Society* (London: Routledge, 1992), pp. 152–68.

7 Poggi, *Development of the Modern State*, Ch. 3.

8 *Ibid.*, Ch. 4; C. J. Friedrich, *The Age of the Baroque* (New York: Harper Torchbooks, 1952), pp. 17–21; N. Davies, *Heart of Europe: The Past in Poland's Present* (Oxford University Press, 1984), pp. 265–6.

9 W. H. McNeill, *The Pursuit of Power* (Oxford: Basil Blackwell, 1983), pp. 87–94; N. Davies, *Europe: A History* (London: Pimlico, 1997), pp. 518–20; Tilly, 'Reflections', pp. 73–6; S. E. Finer, 'State and Nation-building in Europe: The Role of the Military' in Tilly (ed.), *Formation of National States in Western Europe*.

10 Poggi, *Development of the Modern State*, pp. 60–1.

11 J. Bodin, *The Six Books of the Commonwealth*, abridged and translated by M. J. Tooley (Oxford: Basil Blackwell, no date), pp. 25–36; T. Hobbes, *Leviathan* (Oxford: Basil Blackwell, 1952), Ch. 18 and p. 219. The claim is being made in recent historical literature on the origins of the modern doctrine that it derived from the influence of some Renaissance humanists' interests in the absolutist Roman law concept of *dominium* in property and from the Romans' justification of pre-emptive war. See R. Tuck, *The Rights of War and Peace* (Cambridge University Press, 1999); F. Kratochwil, 'Sovereignty as *Dominium*' in G. M. Lyons and M. Mastanduno (eds.), *Beyond Westphalia?* (Baltimore: Johns Hopkins Press, 1995); C. Brown, *Sovereignty, Rights and Justice* (Cambridge: Polity Press, 2002), pp. 27–31.

12 The main exponents of the Divine Right theory were R. Filmer, *Patriarcha, and Other Writings*, edited by J. P. Sommerville (Cambridge University Press, 1990), and J. B. Bossuet, *Politics Drawn from the Very Words of Holy Scripture*, translated and edited by P. Riley (Cambridge University Press, 1990).

13 For Machiavelli's republicanism, see his *Discourses on Livy*, translated by H. C. Mansfield and N. Tarcow (Chicago University Press, 1996).

14 For medieval agricultural and manufacturing organization, see H. Pirenne, *Economic and Social History of Medieval Europe* (New York: Harcourt, Brace and World, Inc, first published 1933), Chs. 3 and 6; M. Weber, *General Economic History*, translated by F. Knight (George Allen & Unwin, no date), pp. 69–79 and Chs. 9–11: B. C. Tandon, *Economic Development of Developed Countries* (Allahabad: Chaitanya Publishing House, 1967), Chs. 2 and 3. However, both Anthony Black in his *Guilds and Civil Society in European Political Thought from the Twelfth Century to the Present* (London: Methuen, 1984), Chs. 1–6 and Alan Macfarlane in his *Origins of English Individualism* (Oxford: Basil Blackwell, 1978) and again in *The Culture of Capitalism* (Oxford: Basil Blackwell, 1987), Ch. 7, take a more qualified view of the dominance of guilds in medieval society. Macfarlane, indeed, argues that 'the majority of ordinary people in England from at least the 13th century were rampant individualists, highly mobile ... economically rational, market-oriented and acquisitive, ego-centered in kinship and social life'. *Origins of English Individualism*, p. 163.

15 For English development see S. T. Bindoff, *Tudor England* (Harmonds-worth: Penguin, 1950) pp. 122–7, and G. R. Elton, *England under the Tudors*, 3rd edn. (London: Routledge, 1991), pp. 238–51. On the importance of the Netherlands see W. W. Rostow, *How It All Began: Origins of the Modern Economy* (London: Methuen, 1975), pp. 39–41 and 109–11, and I. S. Michelman, *The Roots of Capitalism in Western Civilization* (New York: Frederick Fell, 1983), Ch. 6; C. H. Wilson, 'Trade, Society and State' in E. E. Rich and C. H. Wilson (eds.) *Cambridge Economic History of Europe*, Vol. 4: *The Economy of Expanding Europe in the 16th and 17th centuries* (Cambridge University Press, 1967), pp. 491–516.

16 On mercantilism see M. Weber, *General Economic History*, pp. 347–52; Rostow, *How It All Began*, pp. 37–66; Wilson, 'Trade, Society and State', pp. 498–530; Tandon, *Economic Development*, Ch. 4; W. Grampp, *Economic Liberalism* (Random House, 1965), pp. 48–89.

17 H. Kamen, *The Rise of Toleration* (London: Weidenfeld and Nicholson, 1967), p. 20.

18 J. B. Bury, *A History of Freedom of Thought* (London: Oxford University Press, 1952), pp. 61–2; Kamen, *The Rise of Toleration*, pp. 54–5 and 77–82.

19 Kamen, *The Rise of Toleration*, pp. 24–9 and 136–47.

20 *Ibid.*, pp. 175–190; Bury, *History of Freedom of Thought*, pp. 75–7.

21 S. Pufendorf, *Of the Relation between Church and State* (London: J. Wyat, 1719); J. Locke, *The Second Treatise of Civil Government and A Letter Concerning Toleration*, ed. J. W. Gough (Oxford: Basil Blackwell, 1948).

22 Locke, *Second Treatise and Toleration*, pp. 126–32.

23 Locke, *Second Treatise and Toleration*, pp. 155–7.

24 A. Passerin d'Entreves, *Natural Law* (London: Hutchinson's University Library, 1951), Ch. 1.

25 Aquinas, *Political Writings*, ed. A. Passerin d'Entreves (Oxford: Basil Blackwell, 1959), pp. 99–127. For a historical account of the Great Chain of Being, see A. Lovejoy, *The Great Chain of Being* (Cambridge, Mass.: Harvard University Press, 1936). Our account of Aquinas and the seventeenth-century natural rights theories is greatly influenced by J. B. Schneewind, *The Invention of Autonomy* (Cambridge University Press, 1998).

26 Montaigne's scepticism is to be found throughout his famous essays. See M. de Montaigne, *Essays: A Selection*, translated and edited by M. Screech (London: Penguin, 1993).

27 H. Grotius, *De Jure Belli ac Pacis; Libri Tres*, (War and Peace) translated by F. W. Kelsey (Oxford: Clarendon Press, 1925).

28 Grotius, *War and Peace*, Bk. II, Ch. XX.xliv-xlv, pp. 510–13. See also his *The Truth of the Christian Religion*, translated by J. Clarke (London, 1827).

29 Grotius, *War and Peace*, Bk. I, Ch. III.viii.2, p. 104. We follow Schneewind's account of the Grotian problematic closely, Schneewind, *Invention of Autonomy*, pp. 70–3.

30 Grotius, *War and Peace*, Prolegomena, vi.

31 *Ibid.*, Bk. I Ch. II.i.1, p. 51 and Ch. I.iv, p. 35.

32 *Ibid.*, Bk. II Ch. II.ii-vii, pp. 186–94.

33 *Ibid.*, Prolegomena, viii-ix.

34 *Ibid.*, Bk. I Ch. I.x, pp. 38–9.

35 *Ibid.*, Prolegomena, xii: see also Bk. I Ch. I.x, pp. 38–9.

36 J. Locke, *Two Treatises of Government* (Cambridge University Press, 1964), Bk. II, paragraph 6.

37 The distinction between negative and positive freedom or liberty is famously emphasized by Sir Isaiah Berlin in his much discussed lecture on 'Two Concepts of Liberty'. Our use of these terms should not be taken as endorsing the implications that Berlin finds in them. See Sir I. Berlin, *Four Essays on Liberty* (Oxford University Press, 1969).

38 Grotius, *War and Peace*, Prolegomena, xv-xvii.

39 *Ibid.*, Bk. I Chs. III.vii-ix and Ch. IV.ii.

40 T. Hobbes, *Leviathan*, pp. 82–3.

41 *Ibid.*, Ch. 43 and pp. 139 and 219.

42 S. Pufendorf, *De Iure Naturae et Gentium*, translated by C. H. Oldfather and W. A. Oldfather (Oxford: Clarendon Press, 1934), Vol. II, Bk. II, Ch. 2, *passim* but especially p. 176, paragraph 12. Locke, *Two Treatises*, Bk. II, paragraphs 19 and 123.

43 Locke, *Two Treatises*, Bk. II, Ch. 5.

44 *Ibid.*, Bk. II, paragraphs 240–3.

2 The Westphalian society of sovereign states

1 For views on the significance of the Peace of Westphalia, see A. Watson, *The Evolution of International Society* (London: Routledge, 1992), pp. 186–9; A. Osiander, *The States System of Europe 1640–1990* (Oxford: Clarendon Press, 1994), Ch. 2, *passim*; T. Nardin, *Law, Morality and the Relations of States* (Princeton University Press, 1983), pp. 57–8; C. Brown, *Sovereignty, Rights and Justice* (Cambridge: Polity Press, 2002), pp. 22–6.

2 Osiander, *States System*, pp. 72–7.

3 *Ibid.*, pp. 123–9; Watson, *Evolution*, pp. 198–201. By the balance of power here is meant the establishment and maintenance of an equilibrium between the most powerful states that is sufficient to prevent the emergence of a hegemon.

4 K. J. Holsti, *Peace and War: Armed Conflicts and the International Order 1648–1989* (Cambridge University Press, 1991), pp. 89–91.

5 Holsti, *Peace and War*, pp. 92–3 and 103–4; M. Dixon, *Textbook on International Law* (London: Blackstone Press, 2000), p. 295.

6 Osiander, *States System*, p. 102.

7 *Ibid.*, Ch. 9, *passim*; Watson, *Evolution*, Ch. 21, *passim*; F. H. Hinsley, *Power and the Pursuit of Peace: Theory and Practice in the History of Relations between States* (Cambridge University Press, 1963), p. 225 and Ch. 10, *passim*; G. Simpson, *Great Powers and Outlaw States* (Cambridge University Press, 2004), pp. 93–115. Simpson argues powerfully that the Concert marks the beginning of a legalized hierarchy of states in international society, continued in the special status granted the Great Powers both in the League of Nations and in the United Nations.

8 For detailed discussions of the national problem in Europe, see M. Teich and R. Porter (eds.), *The National Question in Europe* (Cambridge University Press, 1993), especially Chs. 3, 6 and 7 on the Italian and German questions. See also Holsti, *Peace and War*, pp. 169–74.

9 T. Naff, 'The Ottoman Empire and the European States System' in H. Bull and A. Watson (eds.), *The Expansion of International Society* (Oxford: Clarendon Press, 1984). See also Hinsley, *Power and the Pursuit of Peace*, p. 232.

10 On the expansion of European international society into the world, see Watson, *Evolution*, Ch. 22, *passim*; Bull and Watson (eds.), *Expansion of International Society*, Parts I and II.

11 Dixon, *Textbook on International Law*, pp. 21–2; I. Brownlie, *Principles of International Law* (Oxford University Press, 1998), p. 3.

12 Dixon, *Textbook on International Law*, pp. 106–12.

13 A. Cassese, *International Law* (Oxford University Press, 2001), pp. 88–91; Dixon, *Textbook on International Law*, p. 166; but for a radically different view of equality, see Simpson, *Great Powers*, pp. 67–76.

14 Dixon, *Textbook on International Law*, pp. 113–4; Cassese, *International Law*, pp. 350–1.

15 Dixon, *Textbook on International Law*, p. 135; Cassese, *International Law*, pp. 89–90; but on the complexity of non-intervention see R. J. Vincent, *Non-intervention and International Order* (Princeton University Press, 1974).

16 Dixon, *Textbook on International Law*, pp. 24–48; Brownlie, *Principles of International Law*, pp. 4–30.

17 The creation of *ad hoc* international criminal tribunals and the establishment of the permanent International Criminal Court requires an appropriate qualification to this statement. See our discussion of these tribunals in Chapter 8.

18 Cassese, *International Law*, pp. 151–3 and 138–48; Dixon, *Textbook on International Law*, pp. 37–41; Brownlie, *Principles of International Law*, pp. 514–7.

19 Emmerich de Vattel, *The Law of Nations*, J. Chitty ed. (Philadelphia: T. and J. W. Johnson, 1863); Dixon, *Textbook on International Law*.

20 Dixon, *Textbook on International Law*, pp. 294–6; Cassese, *International Law*, pp. 229–33.

21 H. Bull, *The Anarchical Society* (London: Macmillan, 1977), p. 13.

22 The distinction is discussed in Bull, *The Anarchical Society*, pp. 13–16.

23 Brown, *Sovereignty, Rights and Justice*, pp. 64 and 66–75.

24 On realism, see J. Donnelly, *Realism and International Relations* (Cambridge University Press, 2000). The major modern realist thinkers are usually taken to be H. J. Morgenthau, *Politics among Nations* (New York: Alfred A Knopf, 1954) and K. N. Waltz, *The Theory of International Politics* (New York: Random, 1979).

25 T. Hobbes, *Leviathan* (Oxford: Basil Blackwell, 1952), p. 83.

26 Bull, *The Anarchical Society*, p. 16.

27 Quoted in Nardin, *Law, Morality and the Relations of States*, p. 61. For Burke, see his 'First Letter on the Regicide Peace', in P. Langford (ed.), *Writings and Speeches of Edmund Burke* (Oxford University Press, 1984), Vol. IX, p. 248. On Burke see also, D. Fidler and J. Welsh (eds.), *Edmund Burke's Writings and Speeches on International Relations* (Boulder, Colorado: Westview Press, 1999). For Kant, see H. Reiss, *Kant's Political Writings* (Cambridge University Press, 1971), p. 171.

28 T. Blanning, *The Pursuit of Glory* (London: Allen Lane, 2007), Part IV.

29 This view is supported by P. Starr, *Freedom's Power: The True Force of Liberalism* (New York: Basic Books, 2007), p. 116.

3 The growth of liberal universalism

1 G. Simpson, *Great Powers and Outlaw States* (Cambridge University Press, 2004).

2 Simpson, *Great Powers*, pp. 78–83. Simpson strongly dislikes liberal universalism which he sees as illiberal. But this is a confusion. A liberal polity is not required to tolerate illiberals who seek to destroy it. See our Introduction and Conclusion.

3 J-J. Rousseau, *The Social Contract*, translated M. Cranston (London: Penguin Books, 1968). For the ideal version, see Bk. I, Ch. 7, p. 63; however, Rousseau also treats the law of majority voting as determining the constitutional sovereign, Bk. I, Ch. 5, p. 59.

4 P. Starr, *Freedom's Power: The True Force of Liberalism* (New York: Basic Books, 2007), pp. 58–61.

5 H. Grotius, *De Iure Belli ac Pacis; Libri Tres*, (*War and Peace*) translated
   by F. W. Kelsey (Oxford: Clarendon Press, 1925), Prolegomena, p. 15.
6 Grotius, *De Iure*, Bk. I, Ch. 14, p. 44, and for the reference to Christian
   practice, Bk. III, Ch.7, p. 696.
7 Grotius, *De Iure*, Prolegomena, p. 17.
8 Grotius, *De Iure*, Bk. II, Ch.1, p. 171.
9 *Ibid.*, p. 184.
10 *Ibid.*, Ch. 22, p. 550.
11 *Ibid.*, Ch. 20, pp. 504–5.
12 *Ibid.*, pp. 505–6, 508–10, 521.
13 *Ibid.*, Ch. 23, pp. 565–6.
14 Grotius, *De Iure*, Bk. III, Ch. 1, p. 599.
15 *Ibid.*, Ch. 7, *passim*.
16 Grotius, *De Iure*, Bk. I, Ch. 4, p. 149.
17 *Ibid.*, Ch. 3, pp. 103–4.
18 *Ibid.*, Ch. 4, pp. 139–40, 148–50 and Bk. II, Ch. 25, *passim*.
19 This is Rawls' idea of the contractual foundation of a just society, which
   he sees as raising to a more abstract level the early modern contract
   theory. J. Rawls, *A Theory of Justice* (Oxford University Press, 1971),
   p. 10.
20 T. Hobbes, *Leviathan* (Oxford: Basil Blackwell, 1952), Ch. 13, p. 83.
21 S. Pufendorf, *De Iure Naturae et Gentium*, translated by C. H. Oldfather
   and W. A. Oldfather (Oxford: Clarendon Press, 1934), Bk. VII, Chs. 2–3.
22 *Ibid.*, Bk. VIII, Ch. 2, paragraphs 2–4.
23 *Ibid.*, Bk. VIII, Ch. 6, p. 1307.
24 *Ibid.*, Bk. IV, Ch. 6, pp. 571–2.
25 C. Wolff, *Ius Gentium methodo scientifica pertractatum*, translated
   J. H. Drake, (Oxford: Clarendon Press, 1934), Prolegomena, § 9–15.
26 Wolff, *Ius Gentium*, Prolegomena, § 16–20.
27 Wolff, *Ius Gentium*, Ch. 2, pp. 156–8.
28 Emmerich de Vattel, *The Law of Nations*, J. Chitty ed. (Philadelphia: T.
   and J. W. Johnson, 1863), Preliminaries, p. lxi.
29 Emmerich de Vattel, *The Law of Nations*, Bk. III, Ch. 3, p. 311.
30 *Ibid.*, Prelims, pp. lxi–lxiii.
31 *Ibid.*, Bk. III, Ch. 3, pp. 307–314.
32 H. Bull, B. Kingsbury and A. Roberts (eds.), *Hugo Grotius and International Relations* (Oxford: Clarendon Press, 1992), pp. 8–9.
33 I. Kant, 'Perpetual Peace' in H. Reiss (ed.), *Kant's Political Writings*
   (Cambridge University Press, 1971), pp. 103–4.
34 Reiss, *Kant's Political Writings*, p. 104.
35 *Ibid.*, pp. 100–2.
36 *Ibid.*, p. 99.

37 *Ibid*, pp. 104–5.
38 On these events, see P. G. Lauren, *The Evolution of International Human Rights* (University of Pennsylvania Press, 2003), pp. 38–46; A. W. B. Simpson, *Human Rights and the End of Empire* (New York: Oxford University Press, 2001), Ch. 3; E. Luard, 'Origin of International Concern over Human Rights' in E. Luard (ed.), *The International Protection of Human Rights* (London: Thames and Hudson, 1967), pp. 10–11.
39 Lauren, *Evolution of International Human Rights*, pp. 58–62; Simpson, *Human Rights*, Ch. 3; Luard, *International Protection*, pp. 13–14.
40 G. Gong, *The Standard of Civilization* (Oxford: Clarendon Press, 1984), *passim*.
41 On the rule of law, see, B. Z. Tamanaha, *On the Rule of Law* (Cambridge University Press, 2004), Ch. 3, *passim*; D. Lyons, *Ethics and the Rule of Law* (Cambridge University Press, 1984), Ch. 7, *passim*; F. Hayek, *The Rule of Law* (University of Chicago Press, 1960).
42 Lauren, *Evolution of International Human Rights*, pp. 98–101.
43 Luard, *International Protection*, pp. 11–13; Lauren, *Evolution of International Human Rights*, pp. 63–9; Simpson, *Human Rights*, Ch. 3.
44 Lauren, *Evolution of International Human Rights*, pp. 112–14; Simpson, *Human Rights*, Ch. 3.
45 Lauren, *Evolution of International Human Rights*, pp. 103–111.
46 J. Morsink, *The Universal Declaration of Human Rights: Origins and Intent* (Philadelphia: University of Pennsylvania Press, 1999), Ch. 1, *passim*; Lauren, *Evolution of International Human Rights*, Ch. 5, *passim*.

4 The UN and regional declarations and covenants on human rights

1 For a detailed history, see www.un.org/Overview/milesto4.htm and www.un.org/aboutun/charter/history/atlantic.shtml.
2 www.un.org/aboutun/sanfrancisco/. The defeated powers joined later: Italy in 1955, Japan in 1956, and the Federal Republic of Germany and German Democratic Republic in 1973. Switzerland became member of the UN only in 2002. See www.un.org/Overview/growth.htm.
3 Article 2(4).
4 Article 51.
5 See D. J. Harris, *Cases and Materials on International Law*, 5th edn. (Sweet & Maxwell, 1998), p. 861.
6 The Commission was established under Article 68 of the Charter, which required the Economic and Social Charter to set up commissions in the human rights and economic and social fields. The Article itself was included in the Charter largely as a result of pressure brought to bear on

the political leaders by some forty-two United States non-government organizations. The Commission (now replaced by the Human Rights Council) was thus one of the very few bodies to draw its authority directly from the Charter of the United Nations. Peter Bailey, www.universalrights. net/main/creation.htm. We discuss the Commission and the Council further in Chapter 8 on implementation.

7 E. Roosevelt, 'The Promise of Human Rights', *Foreign Affairs*, 26 (April 1948), 470–7, www.udhr.org/history/113.htm.

8 www.unhchr.ch/udhr/miscinfo/carta.htm.

9 Art. 29(3) adds: 'These rights and freedoms may in no case be exercised contrary to the purposes and principles of the UN'.

10 Added emphasis.

11 J. Morsink, *The Universal Declaration of Human Rights: Origins and Intent* (Philadelphia: University of Pennsylvania Press, 1999), Ch. 1.

12 www.udhr.org/history/113.htm.

13 *Velasquez Rodriguez* v. *Honduras*, Inter-American Court of Human Rights, Judgment of July 29, 1988, Series C No. 1, www1.umn.edu/humanrts/iachr/b_11_12d.htm; UN Human Rights Committee (UNHRC), *General Comment No 31: Nature of the General Legal Obligations imposed on States Parties to the Covenant*, 26 May 2004, UN Doc CCPR/C/21/Rev.1/Add.13, para 8: 'The article 2, paragraph 1, obligations are binding on States [Parties] and do not, as such, have direct horizontal effect as a matter of international law. The Covenant cannot be viewed as a substitute for domestic criminal or civil law. However the positive obligations on States Parties to ensure Covenant rights will only be fully discharged if individuals are protected by the State, not just against violations of Covenant rights by its agents, but also against acts committed by private persons or entities that would impair the enjoyment of Covenant rights in so far as they are amenable to application between private persons or entities. There may be circumstances in which a failure to ensure Covenant rights as required by article 2 would give rise to violations by States Parties of those rights, **as a result of States Parties' permitting or failing to take appropriate measures or to exercise due diligence to prevent, punish, investigate or redress the harm caused by such acts by private persons or entities**', www.unhchr.ch/tbs/doc.nsf/(Symbol)/CCPR. C.21.Rev.1. Add.13.En?Opendocument, emphasis added.

14 There is no general derogation clause in the Declaration, unlike in the ICCPR which has both limitation and derogation clauses. If you remember, the general limitation clause in the Universal Declaration (Art. 29(2)) states that: 'In the exercise of his rights and freedoms, everyone shall be subject only to such limitations as are determined

by law solely for the purpose of securing due recognition and respect for the rights and freedoms of others and of meeting the just requirements of morality, public order and the general welfare in a democratic society'.

15 The Article states: '1. In time of public emergency which threatens the life of the nation and the existence of which is officially proclaimed, the States Parties to the present Covenant may take measures derogating from their obligations under the present Covenant to the extent strictly required by the exigencies of the situation, provided that such measures are not inconsistent with their other obligations under international law and do not involve discrimination solely on the ground of race, colour, sex, language, religion or social origin.'

16 UN Human Rights Committee, *General Comment No 31*, para 10. In line with that clarification and that of the ICJ (see below), the Working Group on Arbitrary Detention concluded in its report to the Economic and Social Council of 15 February 2006 on the situation of detainees at Guantanamo Bay that 'accordingly, the particular status of Guantanamo Bay under the international lease agreement between the US and Cuba and under US domestic law does not limit the obligations of US under international human rights law towards those detained there. Therefore the obligations of the US under international human rights law extend to the persons detained at Guantanamo Bay', http://news.bbc.co.uk/1/shared/bsp/hi/pdfs/16_02_06_un_guantanamo.pdf. We discuss the Human Rights Committee further in our Chapter 8 on implementation.

17 ICJ, 'Legal Consequences of the Construction of a Wall in the Occupied Palestinian Territories', Advisory Opinion, *I. C. J. Reports* 2004 (9 July 2004).

18 Article 2(1): 'Each State Party to the present Covenant undertakes to take steps, individually and through international assistance and co-operation, especially economic and technical, to the maximum of its available resources, with a view to achieving progressively the full realization of the rights recognized in the present Covenant by all appropriate means, including particularly the adoption of legislative measures.'

19 Article 2(2): 'The States Parties to the present Covenant undertake to guarantee that the rights enunciated in the present Covenant will be exercised without discrimination of any kind as to race, colour, sex, language, religion, political or other opinion, national or social origin, property, birth or other status.'

20 Committee on Economic, Social and Cultural Rights (CESCR), *General Comment 3: The Nature of States Parties Obligations (Art. 2, par.1)*, Fifth Session 1990, www.unhchr.ch/tbs/doc.nsf/.

21 CESCR, *General Comment 3*, para 10. The Committee also points out that: 'In order for a State party to be able to attribute its failure to meet at least its minimum core obligations to a lack of available resources it must demonstrate that every effort has been made to use all resources that are at its disposition in an effort to satisfy, as a matter of priority, those minimum obligations', *ibid.*

22 Article 2(3): 'Developing countries, with due regard to human rights and their national economy, may determine to what extent they would guarantee the economic rights recognized in the present Covenant to non-nationals.'

23 Article 22: 'The Economic and Social Council may bring to the attention of other organs of the United Nations, their subsidiary organs and specialized agencies concerned with furnishing technical assistance any matters arising out of the reports referred to in this part of the present Covenant [Part IV] which may assist such bodies in deciding, each within its field of competence, on the advisability of international measures likely to contribute to the effective progressive implementation of the present Covenant.'

24 The Article reads: 'The States Parties to the present Covenant recognise that, in the enjoyment of those rights provided by the State in con-formity with the present Covenant, the State may subject such rights only to such limitations as are determined by law only in so far as this may be compatible with the nature of these rights and solely for the purpose of promoting the general welfare in a democratic society.'

25 Article 11(2): 'The States Parties ... recognising the fundamental right of everyone to be free from hunger, shall take, individually and through international cooperation, the measures, including specific programmes, which are needed: (a) To improve methods of production, conservation and distribution of food by making full use of technical and scientific knowledge by disseminating knowledge of the principles of nutrition and by developing or reforming agrarian systems in such a way as to achieve the most efficient development and utilisation of natural resources; (b) Taking into account the problems of both food-importing and food-exporting countries, to ensure an equitable distribution of world food supplies in relation to need.'

26 Article 23: 'The States Parties to the present Covenant agree that international action for the achievement of the rights recognized in the present Covenant includes such methods as the conclusion of conven-tions, the adoption of recommendations, the furnishing of technical assistance and the holding of regional meetings and technical meetings for the purpose of consultation and study organized in conjunction with the Governments concerned.'

27 Open-ended Working Group to Consider Options Regarding the Elabo-ration of an Optional Protocol to the ICESCR, 3rd session (Geneva 6–17 Feb 2006), www.ishr.ch/hrm/WGOPICESCR/3rdSession.pdf.

28 'In the exercise of his rights and freedoms, everyone shall be subject only to such *limitations* as are determined by law solely for the purpose of securing due recognition and respect for the rights of others and of meeting the just requirements of morality, public order and the general welfare in a democratic society', emphasis added.

29 'The States Parties to the present Covenant recognise that, in the enjoy-ment of those rights provided by the State in conformity with the present Covenant, the State may subject such rights only to such *limitations* as are determined by law only in so far as this may be compatible with the nature of these rights and solely for the purpose of promoting the general welfare in a democratic society', emphasis added.

30 'In time of public emergency which threatens the life of the nation and the existence of which is officially proclaimed, the States Parties to the present Covenant may take measures *derogating* from their obligations under the present Covenant to the extent strictly required by the exi-gencies of the situation, provided that such measures are not incon-sistent with their other obligations under international law and do not involve discrimination solely on the ground of race, colour, sex, lan-guage, religion or social origin', emphasis added.

31 Article 2(1): 'Each State Party to the present Covenant undertakes to respect and to ensure to all individuals within its territory and subject to its jurisdiction the rights recognized in the present Covenant, without distinction of any kind, such as race, colour, sex, language, religion, political or other opinion, national or social origin, property, birth or other status'; Article 3: '1. Each State Party to the present Covenant undertakes to respect and to ensure to all individuals within its terri-tory and subject to its jurisdiction the rights recognized in the present Covenant, without distinction of any kind, such as race, colour, sex, language, religion, political or other opinion, national or social origin, property, birth or other status'; Article 26: 'All persons are equal before the law and are entitled without any discrimination to the equal pro-tection of the law. In this respect, the law shall prohibit any discrim-ination and guarantee to all persons equal and effective protection against discrimination on any ground such as race, colour, sex, lan-guage, religion, political or other opinion, national or social origin, property, birth or other status.'

32 Having said that, ESC rights apply to all equally without discrimination. Article 2(2) states thus: 'The States Parties to the present Covenant undertake to guarantee that the rights enunciated in the present

Covenant will be exercised without discrimination of any kind as to race, colour, sex, language, religion, political or other opinion, national or social origin, property, birth or other status; and Article 3 says: 'The States Parties to the present Covenant undertake to ensure the equal right of men and women to the enjoyment of all economic, social and cultural rights set forth in the present Covenant.'

33 World Conference on Human Rights, June 14–25,1993. Vienna Declaration and Programme of Action, UN Doc, A/CONE 157/23 (July 12, 1993).

34 http://193.194.138.190/html/menu5/wchr.htm.

35 Bruce Porter, 'Socio-economic Rights in a Domestic Charter of Rights – a Canadian Perspective' (Wellington Park Hotel, 10 May 2001). This was part of a lecture series organized by the Committee on the Administration of Justice to inform the debate on a Bill of Rights for Northern Ireland.

36 M. Cranston, 'Human Rights, Real and Supposed' in D. D. Raphael (ed.), *Political Theory and the Rights of Man* (London: Macmillan, 1967). For discussions of this issue, see P. Jones, *Rights* (London: Macmillan, 1994), Ch. 7, *passim*; J. Waldron, 'Rights' in R. Goodin and P. Pettit (eds.), *A Companion to Contemporary Political Philosophy* (Oxford: Blackwell, 1993); J. W. Nickel, *Making Sense of Human Rights*, 2nd edn. (Oxford: Blackwell Publishing, 2007), pp. 95–8 and Ch. 9.

37 On this issue, see C. Fabre, *Social Rights and the Constitution: Government and the Decent Life* (Oxford University Press, 2000), Ch. 5, *passim*.

38 Two major exponents of this point of view have been R. Nozick, *Anarchy, State and Utopia* (Oxford: Basil Blackwell, 1974) and F. Hayek, *The Road to Serfdom* (Chicago University Press, 1944).

39 On the Indian and South African situations, see H. Steiner and P. Alston, *International Human Rights in Context*, 2nd edn. (Oxford University Press, 2000), pp. 283–99.

40 www.sfu.ca/~aheard/417/util.html.

41 K. Starmer, *Blackstone's Human Rights Digest* (London: Blackstone Press, 2001), p. 11; R. Clayton and H. Tomlinson, *The Law of Human Rights* (Oxford University Press, 2000), p. 278, 280.

42 K. Starmer, *European Human Rights Law* (London: Legal Action Group, 1999), p. 179.

43 Clayton and Tomlinson, *The Law*, p. 331.

44 See, e.g. J. McBride 'Proportionality and the European Convention on Human Rights' in E. Ellis (ed.), *The Principle of Proportionality in the Laws of Europe* (Oxford; Portland, Oreg.: Hart, 1999).

45 Starmer, *European Human Rights Law*, p. 171.

46 *Ibid.*, pp. 187–9; Clayton and Tomlinson, *The Law*, pp. 273–8; J. Wadham, H. Mountfield and A. Edmundson, *Blackstone's Guide to*

the Human Rights Act 1998, 3rd edn. (Oxford University Press, 2003), pp. 44–7.

47 Clayton and Tomlinson, *The Law*, p. 285; Wadham, Mountfield and Edmundson, *Guide to the Human Rights Act*, pp. 45–6.

5 The right of peoples to self-determination

1 R. Higgins, *Problems and Processes: International Law and How to Use It* (Oxford: Clarendon Press, 1994), pp. 111–13.

2 www.un.org/documents/ga/res/15/ares15.htm.

3 In an advisory opinion on the Western Sahara Case. *ICJ Reports 1975*, 68, p. 162.

4 I. Brownlie, *Principles of International Law* (Oxford University Press, 1998), pp. 514–17; A. Cassese, *Self-Determination of Peoples: A Legal Re-appraisal* (Cambridge University Press, 1995), pp. 133–40.

5 *Reference re: Secession of Quebec*, 2 S.C.R. 217 para 138 (1998), available on http://csc.lexum.umontreal.ca/en/1998/1998rcs2-217/1998rcs2-217.html.

6 The last-mentioned group declared independence from Serbia on 17 February 2008 and its secession has been recognized by the US and most European states. For a discussion of issues involved see e.g. C. J. Borgen, 'Kosovo's Declaration of Independence: Self-Determination, Secession and Recognition', *ASIL*, Vol. 12, Issue 2 (2008).

7 Reference re: Secession of Quebec, 2 S.C.R. 217 paras 134 and 135 (1998), available on http://csc.lexum.umontreal.ca/en/1998/1998rcs2-217/1998rcs2-217.html.

8 Higgins, *Problems and Processes*, p. 124.

9 UN Human Rights, Status of International Instruments, UN Doc. ST/HR/5, 1987, 9.

10 Cassese, *Self-Determination*, pp. 19–23; D. Orentlicher, 'Separation Anxiety: International Reponses to Ethno-Separatist Claims', *Yale Law Journal*, 23(1) (1998), Section III, *passim*.

11 Cassese, *Self-Determination*, pp. 122–4; R. Higgins, 'Post-Modern Tribalism and the Right to Secession' in C. Brolmann, R. Lefeber and M. Zieck (eds.), *Peoples and Minorities in International Law* (Dordrecht: Martinus Nijhoff, 1993), p. 33.

12 Quoted in P. G. Lauren, *The Evolution of International Human Rights* (University of Pennsylvania Press, 2003), p. 90.

13 Cassese, *Self-Determination*, pp. 27–31; H. Steiner and P. Alston, *International Human Rights in Context*, 2nd edn. (Oxford University Press, 2000), pp. 1257–63.

14 Cassese, *Self-Determination*, p. 31, footnote 58, emphasis added.

15 Borgen, 'Kosovo's Declaration of Independence'.
16 The secession of Kosovo and its recognition as of 10 March 2008 by thirty-three countries including the US and several major European countries is held by Serbia, Russia and China to set a highly undesirable precedent which they strongly oppose. The recognizing countries, however, deny that it does anything of the sort. See e.g. Borgen 'Kosovo's Declaration of Independence'.
17 Cassese, *Self-Determination*, pp. 79–86, 214–8, and 223–30. In the West Irian case there was some pretence of consent.
18 Cassese, *Self-Determination*, pp. 86–8, 206–11. Cassese is less unsympathetic to the UN's position than we are.
19 J. Donnelly, *Universal Human Rights in Theory and Practice*, 2nd edn. (Ithaca and London: Cornell University Press, 2003), pp. 25–6.
20 J-J. Rousseau, *The Social Contract*, translated M. Cranston (London: Penguin Books, 1968), Bk. II, Ch. 10, p. 95.
21 Rousseau, *Government of Poland*, translated W. Kendall (Indianopolis: Hackett Publishing, 1985). His 'Projet de Constitution pour la Corse' can be found in his *Oeuvres Completes*, Vol. III: Ecrits Politiques (Bibliotheque de la Pleiade: Editions Gallimard, 1964).
22 J. S. Mill, 'Representative Government' in *Utilitarianism, Liberty and Representative Government* (London: J. M. Dent, 1910), Ch. 16, p. 362.
23 Mill, *Utilitarianism*, pp. 360–1.
24 *Ibid.*, p. 361.
25 D. Miller, *On Nationality* (Oxford University Press, 1995), pp. 93–5.
26 Mill, *Utilitarianism*, p. 364.
27 J. G. Barnard, *Herder's Social and Political Thought* (Oxford: Clarendon Press, 1965), pp. 55–62.
28 J. G. Fichte, *Addresses to the German Nation*, translated by R. F. Jones and G. H. Turnbull (Chicago: Open Court Publishing, 1922).
29 There is a so-called civic conception of the nation. This is the nation understood as equivalent to the people where the people is defined in a statist manner. On such a view it would be impossible to raise the issues that we discuss in this section.
30 Y. Tamir, *Liberal Nationalism* (Princeton University Press, 1993), p. 66; A. Smith, *National Identity* (London: Penguin Books, 1991), Chs. 1–2, *passim*; Miller, *On Nationality*, Ch. 2, *passim*; J. Hutchinson and A. Smith (eds.), *Nationalism* (Oxford University Press, 1994), Part I: The Question of Definition. See especially W. Connor, 'A Nation is a Nation is a State is an Ethnic Group is a …'.
31 Quoted in T. Blanning, *The Pursuit of Glory* (London: Allen Lane, 2007), p. 293.

32 This approach owes much to A. Buchanan, *Secession: The Morality of Political Divorce from Fort Sumter to Lithuania and Quebec* (Boulder: Westview Press, 1991).
33 Steiner and Alston, *International Human Rights*, p. 1291 and pp. 1298–9.
34 W. Kymlicka, *Multicultural Citizenship* (Oxford: Clarendon Press, 1995), p. 18.
35 See www.un.org/esa/socdev/unpfii/documents/FAQsindigenousdeclaration.pdf

6 The right to development and development assistance

1 http://hdr.undp.org/hd/.
2 D. Narayan with R. Patel, K. Schafft, A. Rademacher and S. Koch-Schulte, *Voices of the Poor*, 3 Vols. (2001 and 2002), quoted in the 2002 *Office of the UN High Commissioner for Human Rights Draft Guidelines: A Human Rights Approach to Poverty Reduction Strategies*, www.unhchr.ch/development/povertyfinal.html.
3 D. J. Harris, *Cases and Materials on International Law*, 5th edn. (Sweet & Maxwell, 1998), p. 724, ft 27.
4 Note how Poverty Reduction Strategy Papers (PRSPs), which we discuss later, are close to that requirement.
5 See, e.g. M. Bedjaoui, 'The Right to Development' in M. Bedjaoui (ed.), *International Law: Achievements and Prospects* (Dordrecht: Nijhoff Publishers, 1991) p. 1182. Bedjaoui asserts further in his article that the RTD is not only a right in international law but that it actually is part of *jus cogens*.
6 L.-H. Piron, *The Right to Development: A Review of the Current State of the Debate for the Department for International Development*, April 2002, available at www.odi.org.uk/rights/Publications/right_to_dev.pdf
7 *Ibid.*
8 *Ibid.*
9 Harris, *Cases and Materials in International Law*, quoting Walde at p. 552.
10 J. Hawksworth, *The World in 2050: How Big Will the Major Emerging Market Economies Get and How Can the OECD Compete*, PriceWaterhouseCoopers (March 2006), p. 3. See also Committee on Economic Affairs and Development, 'Realising Both Economic Growth and Social Protection in Europe in an Era of Globalisation', Doc. 11366, (Parliamentary Assembly, 9 August 2007), para 24: 'The *Economist* predicts that China will be the world's largest economy in 2026 ... followed by the US, India, Japan and Germany, in that order, with

the UK just scraping in before Russia and Brazil', available at www. assembly.coe.int/Mainf.asp?link=/Documents/WorkingDocs/Doc07/ EDOC11366.htm.

11 Hamish McRae, 'Don't Blame MC for Steering Rates up, Global Liquidity is the Backseat Driver', _The Independent_, 24 May 2007, p. 48.

12 See, e.g. OECD, Directorate for Financial And Enterprise Affairs, Working Papers on International Investment, Number 2004/4, 'Indirect Expropriation' and 'Right To Regulate', _International Investment Law_, September 2004, www.oecd.org/dataoecd/22/54/33776546.pdf.

13 Remember that Art. 55 states that the UN shall promote (i) high standards of living, full employment and conditions of economic and social progress and development; and (ii) solutions of international economic, social, health and related problems; and international cultural and economic co-operation; and Art. 56 says that all members pledge themselves to take joint and separate action in co-operation with the organization for the achievement of the purposes set forth in Art. 55.

14 S. Marks, 'Report of the High-Level Task Force on the Implementation of the Right to Development On Its Third Session', (Geneva, 22–26 January 2007), A/HRC/4/WG.2/TF/2, para 54, http://ap.ohchr.org/documents/dpage_e.aspx?m=130.

15 www.unhchr.ch/development/right-03.html, para 54.

16 _Ibid._, emphasis added.

17 _Ibid._

18 _Ibid._

19 Piron, _The Right to Development_, www.odi.org.uk/rights/Publications/right_to_dev.pdf.

20 www.ohchr.org/english/issues/development/taskforce.htm.

21 Marks, 'Report of the High-Level Task Force on the Implementation of the Right to Development On Its Third Session', para 3.

22 _Ibid._, para 27.

23 Ms Kang Kyung-wha, Deputy High Commissioner for Human Rights, _Report of the Working Group on the Right to Development on its Eight Session_, 26 Feb–2 March 2007, Chairperson-Rapporteur: I. Salama, Human Rights Council Fourth Session, A/HRC/4/47, para 6, http://ap. ohchr.org/documents/dpage_e.aspx?m=130.

24 'Report of the High-Level Task Force on the Implementation of the Right to Development On Its Third Session', Annex II.

25 'Report of the High-Level Task Force on the Implementation of the Right to Development On Its Third Session'.

26 See our earlier comment on RTD as a group right or individual right.

27 Piron, _The Right to Development_.

28 'Report of the Working Group on the Right to Development On Its Eight Session', para 18, http://ap.ohchr.org/documents/dpage_e.aspx? m=130.

29 *Ibid.*, para 19.

30 *Ibid.*, para 33.

31 *Ibid.*, para 38.

32 Piron, *The Right to Development.*

33 Department For International Development, 'Eliminating World Poverty: Making Globalisation Work for the Poor', *White Paper on International Development*, December 2000, p. 14 [WPII] quoted in Piron, *The Right to Development.* The Department explains that enlightened self-interest means that states benefit from helping others lift themselves from poverty, as many of the world's challenges – war and conflict, refugee movements, the violation of human rights, international crime, terrorism, environmental degradation – are caused or exacerbated by poverty and inequality.

34 Piron, *The Right to Development.* See also www.oecd.org?dataoecd/23/ 35/2508761.pdf, p. 14.

35 V. Bhargava, 'Introduction to Global Issues' in V. Bhargava (ed.), *Global Issues for Global Citizens: An Introduction to Key Development Challenges* (World Bank, 2006), p. 18.

36 Piron, *The Right to Development.*

37 *Ibid.* See also www.oecd.org?dataoecd/23/35/2508761.pdf, p. 14.

38 See below.

39 Bhargava, 'Introduction to Global Issues', p. 2.

40 J. Donnelly, *Universal Human Rights in Theory and Practice*, 2nd edn. (Ithaca and London: Cornell University Press, 2003), pp. 196–9.

41 See A. Sen, *Poverty and Famines: An Essay on Entitlement and Deprivation* (Oxford: Clarendon Press, 1981).

42 *OHCHR Draft Guidelines, Human Rights Approach to Poverty Reduction Strategies*, www.unhchr.ch/development/povertyfinal.html.

43 Sen, quoted on the website of the Human Development and Capability Association, www.fas.harvard.edu/~freedoms/.

44 *Human Development Report 2004*, p. 127, http://hdr.undp.org/en/ reports/global/hdr2004/, emphasis added.

45 www.undg.org/?P=221.

46 www.unescobkk.org/fileadmin/user_upload/appeal/human_rights/UN_- Common_understanding_RBA.pdf.

47 'Mainstreaming human rights refers to the concept of enhancing the human rights programme and integrating it into the broad range of United Nations activities, also in the areas of development and humanitarian action', www. unhchr.ch/development/mainstreaming.html.

48 But see the criticism by some feminists of 'mainstreaming' women's rights in particular, e.g. H. Charlesworth, 'Not Waving but Drowning: Gender Mainstreaming and Human Rights in the United Nations', *Harvard Human Rights Journal*, Vol. 18 (2005), 1–18.

49 S. P. Leite, 'Human Rights and the IMF', *IMF Finance & Development*, 38(4) (December 2001), www.imf.org/external/pubs/ft/fandd/2001/12/ leite.htm.

50 www.asiasource.org/news/special_reports/sen.cfm.

51 A. Smith, *An Inquiry into the Nature and Causes of the Wealth of Nations*, 5th edn. (London: Methuen and Co., 1904).

52 Bhargava, *Global Issues for Global Citizens*.

53 www.undp.org/about/. The UN Development Project is the UN's global development network that links and co-ordinates global and national efforts to reach the Millennium Development Goals (which we discuss below), through a network of country offices in 166 countries. The Development Project also publishes annually a Human Development Report. The 2007 Human Development Report is entitled *Human Development and Climate Change* ('the greatest challenge facing humanity at the start of the 21st Century'), http://hdr.undp.org/en/.

54 As S. Claessens says: 'recent evidence has shown that a more developed financial system can help reduce poverty and income inequality', 'The Search for Stability in an Integrated Global Financial System' in Bhargava (ed.), *Global Issues for Global Citizens*, p. 61.

55 Quoted in P. Mauro and J. D. Ostry, *Putting Financial Globalization to Work*, IMF Research Department, August 16, 2007, www.imf.org/ external/pubs/ft/survey/so/2007/RES0816A.htm. It is interesting to see how the Fund's thinking has changed on the topic over the years. When one of the authors worked at the IMF desk at the Australian Treasury in the early 1980s, few ever questioned the benefits of unbridled financial deregulation. Undoubtedly, work by Stiglitz and other critics of 'unmanaged' globalization has contributed to the Fund's present cautiousness on the implementation of financial reforms in developing countries. See, e.g. J. E. Stiglitz, *Globalization and Its Discontents* (London: W. W. Norton, 2003).

56 Claessens, 'The Search for Stability' in Bhargava (ed.), p. 62.

57 Claessens, 'The Search for Stability' in Bhargava (ed.), p. 63. At least twelve of these standards have been widely adopted and are monitored for compliance today by the IMF and/or World Bank. The bodies responsible for standard setting include the Basel Committee on Banking Supervision (banking standards); the OECD (corporate governance); the International Association of Insurance Supervisors (insurance

regulation), the International Organization of Securities Commissions (securities market regulation) and Financial Action Task Force on Money Laundering. Standards for national bankruptcy procedures have also been issued.

58 *1999 Country Reports on Human Rights Practices*, Bureau of Democracy, Human Rights, and Labor, Department of State. (February 2000). See www.state.gov/g/drl/rls/hrrpt/1999/65.htm.

59 P. Chuhan, 'Poverty and Inequality' in Bhargava (ed.), *Global Issues for Global Citizens*, p. 43.

60 Bhargava, 'Introduction' in Bhargava (ed.), *Global Issues for Global Citizens*, p. 2.

61 'Foreword' in The World Bank, *Development and Human Rights: The Role of the World Bank* (The World Bank, 1998), p. 7.

62 The World Bank and the International Monetary Fund (IMF) were set up at a meeting of forty-three countries in Bretton Woods, New Hampshire, USA in July 1944.

63 IDA credits are grants and nearly interest-free loans (0.75 per cent annual interest) with repayments stretched over thirty-five to forty years, including a ten-year grace period.

64 IBRD – the original institution of the World Bank group, which consists today of IBRD, IDA, International Finance Corporation (IFC), and Multilateral International Guarantee Agency (MIGA) – raises most of its funds on the world's financial markets.

65 IBRD Art. 1, Purposes of the Bank, establishes the bank as a financial institution with a mandate for reconstruction and development. Art. IV, Section 10 prohibits the Bank from interfering in a country's political affairs and its decisions from being influenced by the political character of the member country; and Art. III, Section 5 and Art. IV, Section 10 say that only economic considerations shall be relevant to the decisions of the Bank and its officers, and these must be weighted impartially. http://web. worldbank.org/WBSITE/EXTERNAL/EXTABOUTUS/ORGANI ZATION/BODEXT/0,contentMDK:20049557~menuPK:64020046~ pagePK:64020054~piPK:64020408~ theSitePK:278036,00.html.

66 *Human Rights and Development: The Role of the World Bank* (1998), quoted on http://web.worldbank.org/WBSITE/EXTERNAL/EXTSI TETOOLS/0,,contentMDK:20749693~pagePK:98400~piPK:98424~ theSitePK:95474,00.html.

67 See http://web.worldbank.org/WBSITE/EXTERNAL/PROJECTS/STR ATEGIES/CDF/0,,pagePK:60447~theSitePK:140576,00.html. and http://web.worldbank.org/WBSITE/EXTERNAL/PROJECTS/STRAT EGIES/CDF/0,,contentMDK:20072662~menuPK:60746~pagePK:13 9301~piPK:139306~theSitePK:140576,00.html.

68 'IFC Leads Development of a Guide to Human Rights Impact Assessment and Management (HRIA)', www.ifc.org/ifcext/enviro.nsf/Content/OurStories_SocialResponsibility_HumanRights.

69 Frequently Asked Questions, Human Rights, on the World Bank website, web.worldbank.org/WBSITE/EXTERNAL/EXTSITETOOLS/0,,content MDK:20749693~pagePK:98400~piPK:98424~theSitePK: 95474,00. html.

70 *Ibid.* Last visited 17 August 2007.

71 See also Ana Palacio, the present General Counsel: 'It is now widely recognized that human rights have relevance for several other international goals, including development', 'The Way Forward: Human Rights and the World Bank', in *Development Outreach: Putting Knowledge to Work for Development*, June 2007, www1.worldbank.org/devoutreach/article.asp?id=388. But see 'Righting The Bank's Agenda', in *Bretton Woods Project: Critical Voices on the World Bank and IMF*: 'The Bank's claims that human rights are intrinsic in the World Development Report (WDR) 2006 on equity and development have been challenged by critics such as Desmond McNeill and Asun St Clair, who point out that the document makes modest, inconsistent and inexplicit concessions to the issue', www.brettonwoodsproject.org/art-538514.

72 R. Barro, *Determinants of Economic Growth: A Cross-Country Empirical Study* (Cambridge, Mass: MIT Press, 1997); R. Barro, 'Economic Growth in a Cross-Section of Countries', *The Quarterly Journal of Economics*, 106(2) (1991), 407.

73 J. Isham, D. Kaufmann and L. H. Pritchett, 'Civil Liberties, Democracy and the Performance of Government Projects', *World Bank Law Review*, 11(2) (1997), 219.

74 D. Kaufmann, 'Human Rights and Governance: The Empirical Challenge' in Alston and Robinson (eds.), *Human Rights and Development: Towards Mutual Reinforcement* (Oxford University Press, 2005).

75 http://web.worldbank.org/WBSITE/EXTERNAL/EXTSITETOOLS/0,,contentMDK:20749693~pagePK:98400~piPK:98424~theSitePK:954 74,00.html.

76 *The Legal Aspects of the World Bank's Work on Human Rights*, www1.worldbank.org/devoutreach/october06/article.asp?id=386.

77 Ana Palacio, 'The Way Forward: Human Rights and the World Bank', in *Development Outreach: Putting Knowledge to Work for Development*, June 2007, www1.worldbank.org/devoutreach/article.asp?id=388. Note that in another passage, however, Palacio agrees with Dañino that the articles not only permit but also in some cases require the Bank to recognize the human rights dimensions of its development policies and activities. She says: 'It is now clear that the Bank can and sometimes **should** take human rights into consideration as part of its

decision-making process [while respecting the legal limits imposed by its Articles of Agreement]', emphasis added.

78 V. Bhargava (ed.), *Global Issues for Global Citizens: An Introduction to Key Development Challenges* (World Bank, 2006).

79 Claessens, 'The Search for Stability' in Bhargava (ed.), p. 47.

80 See, e.g. *Gender Justice: A Citizen's Guide to Gender Accountability at International Financial Institutions* (Centre for International Environmental Law and Gender Action, June 2007), www.ciel.org/Publications/ GenderJustice_Jun07.pdf.

81 The Centre for International Environmental Law (US) says, for example: 'Bank-financed projects can involve significant social and environmental costs, such as displacement of local communities, threats to indigenous peoples, and the destruction or degradation of the environment.' It concedes, however: 'In response to NGO and donor country pressure, the Bank eventually established a series of policies and procedures that sought to offset some of the environmental and social risks.' See the World Bank's website, www.ciel.org/Ifi/IFIs_Social_Environmental.html.

82 'Righting The Bank's Agenda', in *Bretton Woods Project: Critical Voices on the World Bank and IMF*, www.brettonwoodsproject.org/art-538514.

83 'Justice or conditionality by another name?' World Bank statement at the Human Rights Council, 5 July 2006, in *Bretton Woods Project*.

84 'Righting The Bank's Agenda', *Ibid*.

85 'Justice or conditionality by another name?' World Bank statement at the Human Rights Council, 5 July 2006.

86 Palacio, 'The Way Forward: Human Rights and the World Bank', in *Development Outreach: Putting Knowledge to Work for Development*, June 2007, www1.worldbank.org/devoutreach/article.asp?id=388.

87 See, e.g. M. Koskenniemi, *From Apology to Utopia: The Structure of International Legal Argument* (Cambridge University Press, Reissue with New Epilogue, 2006), and *The Gentle Civilizer of Nations: The Rise and Fall of International Law 1870–1960* (Cambridge University Press, 2001) for a sceptical view of the ability of international law to regulate the conduct of international affairs, including on grounds of what Koskenniemi believes is international law's inherent indeterminacy.

88 See, e.g. A. Clapham *Human Rights Obligations of Non-State Actors* (Oxford University Press, 2006); and M. Darrow, *Between Light and Shadow: The World Bank, the IMF and International Human Rights Law* (Portland, Oreg.: Hart Publishing, 2003), for arguments that international human rights standards ought to apply to international financial institutions (IFIs).

89 Prof. Hunt, Rapporteur of the UN Committee on Economic, Social and Cultural Rights, 'Relations Between the UN Committee on Economic, Social and Cultural Rights and the International Financial Institutions',

Legal Culture, World Bank, IMF and Human Rights: Conference held at Tilburg University, 11–13 October, 2001, reported in *German Law Journal*, 3(2) (1 February 2002), www.germanlawjournal.com/article. php?id=131.

90 Note in this respect a recent report by the Independent Evaluation Group, an in-house monitor on the Bank's work in the middle-income countries (MICs). As *The Economist* points out, the MICs – 'a group whose GDP per head typically ranges from about $1,000 to $6,000' – tend to repay loans and be successful in reducing poverty. The MICs are also 'the biggest customers of the World Bank – accounting for 63% of its loans and half of its administrative budget'. According to *The Economist*, questions are raised nowadays whether 'pleasant and rewarding as this MIC business may be, is it doing anything useful that could not be done just as well by others? And if not, is there anything else the Bank should be doing?', 'The World Bank: That Empty-Nest Feeling', *The Economist* (8 September 2007), pp. 69–70.

91 G. A. Sarfaty, 'The Marginality of Human Rights at the World Bank', *Paper presented at the International Law and International Relations Seminar*, Harvard University, March 2006, p. 30, permission to cite obtained.

92 Sarfaty, 'The Marginality of Human Rights at the World Bank', p. 30.

93 Sarfaty, 'The Marginality of Human Rights at the World Bank', p. 40.

94 J. D. Wolfensohn, 'Some Reflections on Human Rights and Development', in Alston and Robinson, *Human Rights and Development*, p. 19.

95 'Report of the External Review Committee on Bank-Fund Collaboration', *Final Report February 2007*, www.imf.org/external/np/sec/pr/2007/pr07235.htm.

96 See, e.g. www.imf.org/external/np/exr/facts/glance.htm.

97 www.imf.org/external/np/exr/facts/glance.htm.

98 Under its Poverty Reduction and Growth Facility, the IMF provides concessional loans – loans with an annual interest rate of 0.5 per cent and a maturity of ten years – to its poorest member countries. The majority of the IMF's loans now fall into this category. In 2005, it approved the establishment of the Exogenous Shocks Facility, under which it can give low-income countries that are not receiving funds under the Poverty Reduction and Growth Facility, and that are suffering a balance of payments problem because of a shock beyond their control, quick access to funds on a concessional basis. www.imf.org/external/pubs/ft/exrp/what.htm#created.

99 S. P. Leite, 'Human Rights and the IMF', *Finance Development*, 38(4) (IMF, December 2001), www.imf.org/external/pubs/ft/fandd/2001/12/leite.htm.

100 *Ibid.*
101 *Ibid.*
102 *Ibid.*
103 *Ibid*: 'Data from countries with IMF-supported programs during 1985–1999 show, on average, a small rise in social expenditures despite the difficult economic conditions these countries faced. Moreover, according to the World Bank's World Development Indicators database, these countries, on average, registered some improvement during the period in overall primary school enrolment ..., female primary and secondary school enrolment ..., infant mortality ..., mortality for children under the age of 5 ..., births attended by skilled personnel ..., and contraceptive prevalence ...'. Note also that *Revised Guidelines on Conditionality* were adopted by the Fund's Board in 2002, stressing the importance of strong country ownership of any successful economic policy programs, www.imf.org/external/np/exr/facts/conditio.htm.
104 See Sarfaty, 'The Marginality of Human Rights at the World Bank'.
105 LSE Centre for Human Rights, www.lse.ac.uk/Depts/human-rights/Lectures/Economics_Human_Rights.htm.
106 V. Bhargava and A. Gurkan, 'Global Compacts: Building a Better World for All', in Bhargava (ed.), *Global Issues for Global Citizens.*
107 www.undp.org/poverty/overview.htm.
108 You may remember that the last Goal (Goal 8) on global partnership for development has been the topic of consideration by the Open Ended Working Group on the right to development.
109 See, e.g. Piron, *The Right to Development*: 'the RTD could therefore be construed as a right to having the Millennium Development Goals met, an aspect of which could include a right to having effective poverty eradication policies developed and implemented in a manner respectful of all rights'.
110 Committee on Economic, Social and Cultural Rights (CESCR), *Substantive Issues Arising in The Implementation of the International Covenant on Economic, Social and Cultural Rights: Poverty and the International Covenant on Economic, Social and Cultural Rights*, E/C.12/2001/10, 10 May 2001, para 1, www.unhchr.ch/tbs/doc.nsf/(Symbol)/E. C.12.2001.10.En?Opendocument.
111 CESCR, E/C.12/2001/10, para 8.
112 *Ibid.*, para 9.
113 *General Comment No. 3*, adopted in 1990, quoted in CESCR, para 15.
114 *Ibid.*
115 *Ibid.*, para 17, emphasis added.
116 See Chapter 8.
117 Piron, *The Right to Development.*

118 Bhargava and Gurkan, 'Global Compacts', p. 419.
119 De Schutter, 'Transnational Corporations as Instruments of Human Development', in Alston and Robinson (eds.), *Human Rights and Development*, p. 403.
120 TNCs are corporations that operate in many countries, either directly or through subsidiaries or affiliates.
121 UNCTAD, *World Investment Report 2006*, www.unctad.org/wir.
122 J. G. Ruggie, Special Representative of the UN Secretary-General on Business & Human Rights 2007, *Report to UN Human Rights Council*, 28 March 2007, www.business-humanrights.org/Documents/SRSG-report-Human-Rights-Council-19-Feb-2007.pdf.
123 B. Mongoven, *A Potential Tool for Protecting Human Rights in the Third World* (Forecasting Inc., Stratfor, 16 August 2007), reported on www.business-humanrights.org/Links/Repository/485271.
124 Ruggie, *Report to UN Human Rights Council*.
125 See J. G. Ruggie, *State Responsibilities to Regulate and Adjudicate Corporate Activities under the United Nations' Core Human Rights Treaties: Individual Report on the United Nations Convention on the Elimination of All Forms of Discrimination against Women*, Report No. 4, prepared for the Special Representative of the Secretary-General on Human Rights and Transnational Corporations and Other Business Enterprises, with the support of the Office of the United Nations High Commissioner for Human Rights, September 2007, www.business-humanrights.org/Links/Repository/342796. This report outlines the nature of states parties' obligations vis-à-vis corporate activities under the Convention on the Elimination of All Forms of Discrimination Against Women (as elaborated by the Committee on the Elimination of Discrimination Against Women).
126 Human Rights Committee, General Comment 31, *The Nature of the General Legal Obligation Imposed on States Parties to the Covenant*, CCPR/C/21/ Rev.1/Add.13, 26 May 2004, para 8, www.unhchr.ch/tbs/doc.nsf/(Symbol)/CCPR.C.21.Rev.1.Add.13.En?OpenDocument& Click=.
127 *Ibid.*
128 Ruggie, *Report to UN Human Rights Council*. Ruggie clarifies further that '[e]xtraterritorial jurisdiction must also meet an overall reasonableness test, which includes non-intervention in other states' internal affairs. Debate continues over precisely when the protection of human rights justifies extraterritorial jurisdiction'. *Ibid.*, para 15. If international crimes are committed, the principle of universal jurisdiction (discussed elsewhere in our book) would, of course, apply. It is unclear, however, he says, whether and how universal jurisdiction would apply to juridical persons, including corporations. *Ibid.*

129 Ruggie, *Report to UN Human Rights Council*, refers here to A. Clapham, *Human Rights Obligations of Non-State Actors*, Ch. 9; and, on Africa, to N. Udombana, 'Between Promise and Performance: Revisiting States' Obligations under the African Human Rights Charter', *Stanford Journal of International Law*, 40 (2004), 105.

130 Ruggie, *Report to UN Human Rights Council*, para 17.

131 The distinction between the two is not always clear to us. The soft-law instruments refer normally to government or state projects; however, even voluntary guidelines are often government or state-inspired. Following a number of authors, we will adhere nonetheless to the distinction.

132 Ruggie, *Report to UN Human Rights Council*, para 41.

133 See, e.g. *Business Leaders Initiative on Human Rights (BLIHR)*, www. blihr.org/un_norms.htm.

134 For a view on the norms from a business point of view, see, e.g. www. blihr.org/human.htm.

135 De Schutter, 'Transnational Corporations as Instruments of Human Development' in Alston and Robinson, p. 422.

136 B. Mongoven, *A Potential Tool for Protecting Human Rights in the Third World*, (Strategic Forecasting Inc. August 16, 2007), reported on www.business-humanrights.org/Links/Repository/485271.

137 Working Party on the OECD Guidelines for Multinational Enterprises, *The OECD Guidelines for Multinational Enterprises: Text, Commentary and Clarifications*, General Policies II.2 (OECD, 31 October 2001), DAFFE/IME/WPG (2000) 15/FINAL, www.oecd.org/docu ment/28/0,3343,en_2649_34889_2397532_1_1_1_1,00.html.

138 Commentary 4, *The OECD Guidelines on Multinational Enterprises*.

139 Ruggie, *Report to UN Human Rights Council*, para 50.

140 PS1: Social and Environmental Assessment and Management System; PS2: Labor and Working Conditions; PS3: Pollution Prevention and Abatement; PS4: Community Health, Safety and Security; PS5: Land Acquisition and Involuntary Resettlement; PS6: Biodiversity Conservation and Sustainable Natural Resource Management; PS7: Indigenous Peoples; PS8: Cultural Heritage. See www.ifc.org/ifcext/enviro.nsf/ AttachmentsByTitle/pol_PerformanceStandards2006_PSIntro_HTML/ $FILE/PS_Intro.pdf.

141 www.cao-ombudsman.org/.

142 'IFC Leads Development of a Guide to Human Rights Impact Assessment and Management (HRIA)', www.ifc.org/ifcext/enviro.nsf/ Content/OurStories_SocialResponsibility_HumanRights.

143 *Ibid.*

144 www.angloamerican.co.uk/cr/internationalcommitments/voluntary principles/.

145 www.sa-intl.org/index.cfm?fuseaction=Page.viewPage&pageId=487 &parentID=472&nodeID=1.

146 See, e.g. 'Ceres: Investors and Environmentalists for Sustainable Prosperity', www.ceres.org/ceres/.

147 www.globalreporting.org/AboutGRI/.

148 www.globalreporting.org/AboutGRI/WhoWeAre/.

149 www.globalreporting.org/AboutGRI/WhatWeDo/.

150 www.unglobalcompact.org/AboutTheGC/index.html.

151 *Ibid.*

152 www.unglobalcompact.org/NewsAndEvents/news_archives/2007_ 07_05a.html and www.unglobalcompact.org/summitblog/.

153 www.unglobalcompact.org/COP/Review_Project.html.

154 www.globalpolicy.org/reform/business/2005/0719gcreport.htm.

155 www.unglobalcompact.org/NewsAndEvents/news_archives/2007_ 07_05a.html.

156 Michael Porter, *The Competitive Advantage of Nations*, quoted in J. Braithwaite and P. Drahos, *Global Business Regulation* (Cambridge University Press, 2000), p. 267. Porter advises companies thus: 'Establish norms exceeding the toughest regulatory hurdles or product standards. Some localities (or user industries) will lead in terms of the stringency of product standards, pollution limits, noise guidelines, and the like. Tough regulatory standards are not a hindrance, but an opportunity to move early to upgrade products and processes'. But see R. Reich, *Supercapitalism: The Transformation of Business, and Everyday Life* (Knopf, 2007) for an argument that socially responsible firms are not more profitable; and generally, that CSR (corporate social responsibility) is a 'dangerous diversion that is undermining democracy', reviewed in 'Business and society: In Search of the Good Company', *The Economist*, 8 September 2007, pp. 73–4.

157 A. Newton, *Special Report: Finance and Human Rights, Ethical Corporation* ('an independent publisher and conference organiser, launched in 2001 [in London] to encourage debate and discussion on responsible business reports'), 14 November 2006, www.ethicalcorp.com/content. asp?ContentID=4677.

158 *The Economist*, 7 April 2007, p. 11.

159 Business and Human Rights Resource Centre, www.business-human rights.org/Categories/Companypolicysteps/Policies/Codesofconductcorp orate.

160 See, e.g. recent calls by Amnesty International – when launching its campaign against abuses in China before the Beijing Olympics in 2008 – for British businesses to do more to combat human rights abuses in China. Amnesty International stated: 'UK banks, insurers and other companies are battling to invest or do business in China, the world's

fastest-growing major economy, but they can do more to influence the Chinese government on matters like treatment of workers. To any business or important investor in China we would always say they have influence and a responsibility to use that influence. Human rights law says businesses are organisms of society that have responsibilities. The economies of China and many other economies need these companies and their influence can be used', reported in 'UK urged to act on China rights abuse', *Independent Online*, Sean Farrell, 30 August 2007, http://news.independent.co.uk/business/news/article2909559.ece.

161 *The Economist*, 7 April 2007, p. 11. The article adds: 'Just as Toyota and Samsung eventually obliged western multinationals to rethink how to make cars and consumer electronics, so today's young thrusters threaten the veterans wherever they are complacent'.

162 'Human Rights Policies of Chinese Companies: Results from a Survey, Conducted under the Mandate of the UN Secretary-General's Special Representative for Business and Human Rights, Professor John G. Ruggie', Harvard University, September 2007, www.business-humanrights.org/Documents/Ruggie-China-survey-Sep-2007.pdf. Ruggie points out that '[t]he social branding effects of being major global companies may be responsible for the fact that the Chinese firms in our sample that are listed in the FG500 are more likely to have published human rights policies than non-FG500 companies', *Ibid.*, p. 8.

163 Alston and Robinson, *Human Rights and Development.*

164 De Schutter, 'Transnational Corporations', in Alston and Robinson, *Human Rights and Development*, p. 409.

165 *Ibid.*, p. 402.

166 W. Easterly, 'Why Doesn't Aid Work?' 3 April 2006, www.cato-unbound.org: modified excerpt from *The White Man's Burden: Why the West's Efforts to Aid the Rest have Done so Much Ill and so Little Good* (New York: Penguin Press, 2006); see also P. Collier, *The Bottom Billion: Why the Poorest Countries are Failing and What Can be Done About It* (Oxford University Press, 2007); and, for Easterly's debates with J. Sacks, www.nyn.edu/fas/institute/dri/Easterly/Sacks-debates.htm. One billion is equivalent, according to the American usage, to 1,000 million; and one trillion, to 1,000 billion.

167 World Development Indicators database, World Bank, 1 July 2007, http://siteresources.worldbank.org/DATASTATISTICS/Resources/GDP.pdf. Of course, these figures are far less significant when compared to military expenditure in the world. In 2005, this is estimated to have reached $1 trillion: around 2.5 per cent of world GDP or an average spending of $173 per capita. World military expenditure has risen by 34 per cent since 1996. The US is responsible for about 80 per cent of that increase, and its military expenditure accounts now for almost half

of the world total. Stockholm International Peace Research Institute (SPIRI) 2006 Year Book, quoted in www.globalissues.org/Geopolitics/ ArmsTrade/Spending.asp. But note that in terms of military expenditure as a proportion of GDP by countries other than the US, the figures are not hugely greater than the figure of 0.7 per cent of GDP, which is what the developed countries are asked to contribute to aid. The figure we just gave above for the world military expenditure was 2.5 per cent of world GDP. The figure for the UK defence spending, for example, as a percentage of GDP is similar: 2.2 per cent in 2007, just above the NATO European average, and about the same proportion as France and more than Italy and Germany. See, e.g. www.mod.uk/DefenceInternet/ AboutDefence/Organisation/KeyFactsAboutDefence/DefenceSpending. htm.

168 Ch. Kenny, *What Is Effective Aid? How Would Donors Allocate It?* *World Bank Policy Research Working Paper 4005*, September 2006, www-wds.worldbank.org/external/default/WDSContentServer/IW3P/ IB/2006/09/11/000112742_20060911171427/Rendered/PDF/ wps4005. pdf.

169 http://fpolicy.america.gov/fpolicy/aid/index/timeline.html.

170 National Centre for Policy Analysis, www.ncpa.org/pd/pdint140.html.

171 S. Varma, 'Debt Relief, Debt Sustainability, and Growth in Low-Income Countries', in Bhargava (ed.), *Global Issues for Global Citizens*, p. 93.

172 *Ibid.*, p. 98.

173 'A country reaches the completion point, and is granted irrevocable debt relief, when it has implemented the reforms it had previously agreed to, has satisfactorily implemented a Poverty Reduction Strategy, and has maintained sound macroeconomic policies', *Ibid.* Note that the main objective in cancelling this debt is to provide additional resources to help the Heavily Indebted Poor Countries reach the Millennium Development Goals.

174 *The Millennium Development Goals Report 2007*, www.un.org/millenniumgoals/docs/UNSD_MDG_Report_2007e.pdf.

175 S. Varma, 'Debt Relief, Debt Sustainability, and Growth in Low-Income Countries', in Bhargava (ed.), *Global Issues for Global Citizens*, p. 103.

176 *Ibid.*, p. 102.

177 www.imf.org/external/np/exr/facts/glance.htm.

178 'World Bank Group Directs $34.3 Billion in 2007 to Boost Growth and Overcome Poverty', News Release No. 2008/054/EXC, http:// web.worldbank.org/WBSITE/EXTERNAL/NEWS/0,,contentMDK: 21459793~pagePK:34370~ piPK:34424~theSitePK:4607,00.html. Altogether thus, during fiscal year 2007, ending June 30, the World Bank Group committed US$34.3 billion in loans, grants, equity

investments, and guarantees to its members and to private business in its member countries. This is up $2.7 billion (7.8 per cent) from fiscal year 2006. The Bank says: 'the recipients are using these funds in more than 620 projects designed to overcome poverty and enhance growth – for example, by improving education and health services, promoting private sector development, building infrastructure, and strengthening governance and institutions'. *Ibid.*

179 http://web.worldbank.org/WBSITE/EXTERNAL/EXTABOUTUS/EX TANNREP/EXTANNREP2K6/0,,contentMDK:21046829~menuPK: 2915761~pagePK:64168445~piPK:64168309~theSitePK:2838572, 00.html.

180 P. Chuhan and V. Bhargava, 'Development Aid: Key to Balanced Global Development', in Bhargava (ed.), *Global Issues for Global Citizens*, p. 72. The DAC has twenty-two member countries: Australia, Austria, Belgium, Canada, Denmark, Finland, France, Germany, Greece, Ireland, Italy, Japan, Luxembourg, the Netherlands, New Zealand, Norway, Portugal, Spain, Sweden, Switzerland, the UK and the US. See also *Aid Architecture: An Overview of the Main Trends in ODA Flows*, World Bank publication, February 2007, http://siteresources.worldbank.org/IDA/Resources/ Aidarchitecture-execsummary.pdf.

181 See www.oecd.org/document/17/0,3343,en_2649_201185_38341265 _1_1_1_1,00.html. Note that according to the OECD, the fall was predicted. This is because 'ODA was exceptionally high in 2005 due to large Paris Club debt relief operations (notably for Iraq and Nigeria) which boosted ODA to its highest level ever at USD 106.8 billion'.

182 The World Bank, *Global Monitoring Report 2007: Confronting the Challenges of Gender and Fragile States*, Final Text, March 29, 2007, DC2007–0007/1, Overview, p. 16, www.worldbank.org/reference/.

183 P. Chuhan and V. Bhargava, 'Development Aid: Key to Balanced Global Development', in Bhargava (ed.), *Global Issues for Global Citizens*, p. 73. Similar to the Stockholm International Peace Research Institute quoted in footnote 166, the authors point out that development assistance is a fraction of major donors' military spending, which was $648 billion in 2005, i.e. more than nine times their development assistance. *Ibid.*, p. 73.

184 *Ibid.*, p. 74.

185 The World Bank, *Global Monitoring Report 2007*, p. 16.

186 *Ibid.*

187 P. Chuhan and V. Bhargava, 'Development Aid: Key to Balanced Global Development', in Bhargava (ed.), *Global Issues for Global Citizens*, p. 73.

188 *Ibid.*, p. 74.

189 Note, incidentally, how most of the ODA comes from other sources than the multilateral institutions mentioned above and other multilateral development banks (Millennium Development Goals). The term Multilateral Development Banks (MDBs) refers to the World Bank Group and four Regional Development Banks: the African Development Bank, the Asian Development Bank, the European Bank for Reconstruction and Development, and the Inter-American Development Bank Group. As the World Bank points out: 'if disbursements continue to stagnate while donors scale up bilateral ODA, the MDBs will represent **only about 6 per cent of total ODA** flows by 2010'. *Millennium Development Goals Report 2007*, p. 20, emphasis added. As the Report states, 'This poses important questions for the international community over the implications of declining multilateralism, or of the shifting multilateralism to other agencies, primarily the UN system and the EU'. *Ibid.*

190 P. Chuhan and V. Bhargava, 'Development Aid: Key to Balanced Global Development', in Bhargava (ed.), *Global Issues for Global Citizens*, p 83.

191 *Ibid.*, p. 74.

192 For detailed Millennium Development Goals indicators see *The Official UN Site* http://mdgs.un.org/unsd/mdg/Default.aspx.

193 P. Chuhan, 'Poverty and Inequality', in Bhargava (ed.), *Global Issues for Global Citizens*, p. 31.

194 http://web.worldbank.org/WBSITE/EXTERNAL/TOPICS/EXTPOVE RTY/EXTPA/0,,contentMDK:20153855~menuPK:435040~pagePK: 148956~piPK:216618~theSitePK: 430367,00.html.

195 Bhargava, *Global Issues for Global Citizens*.

196 Note that, after doubling from 3 billion in 1960 to 6 billion in 2000, the world's population is expected to increase to 8 billion by 2030. Most of this growth will occur in developing countries. Bhargava, 'Introduction to Global Issues', in Bhargava (ed.), *Global Issues for Global Citizens*, p. 18.

197 C. Welch, '2007 Millennium Development Goals Report: Progress Being Made, More Must Be Done', 2 July 2007, End Poverty Blog, www.end povertyblog.org/node/949.

198 P. Chuhan, 'Poverty and Inequality', in Bhargava (ed.), *Global Issues for Global Citizens*, p. 37.

199 *World Development Indicators* 2007.

200 www.un.org/millenniumgoals/docs/MDGafrica07.pdf.

201 web.worldbank.org/WBSITE/EXTERNAL/EXTDEC/EXTGLOBAL MONITOR/EXTGLOMONREP2007/0,,menuPK:3413296~page PK: 64218926~piPK:64218953 ~theSitePK:3413261,00.html.

202 The World Bank, *Global Monitoring Report 2007*, Overview, at 14, www.worldbank.org/reference/.

203 The World Bank, *Global Monitoring Report 2007*, p. 5.
204 Bhargava, 'Introduction', in Bhargava (ed.), *Global Issues for Global Citizens*, p. 5.
205 *Ibid.*, p. 4.
206 Chuhan, 'Poverty and Inequality', in Bhargava (ed.), *Global Issues for Global Citizens*, p. 40.
207 *Ibid.*, p. 41
208 web.worldbank.org/WBSITE/EXTERNAL/EXTDEC/EXTGLOBAL MONITOR/EXTGLOMONREP2007/0,,contentMDK:21256872~ menuPK:3413277~pagePK:64218950~piPK:64218883~theSitePK: 3413261,00.html.
209 http://publications.worldbank.org/ecommerce/catalog/product?item_ id=6365770.
210 Bhargava, 'Introduction', in Bhargava (ed.), *Global Issues for Global Citizens*, p. 11.
211 Chuhan, 'Poverty and Inequality', in Bhargava (ed.), *Global Issues for Global Citizens*, p. 35. The UN Development Program uses the Human Development Index to provide an annual ranking of countries on these three dimensions. A value below 0.5 represents low development.
212 In the view of some, this is mainly the developed countries' fault. Carol Wench from the *End Poverty Blog* claims, for example, that developing countries are seen to be 'taking their Millennium Development Goals seriously and ... starting to reap rewards from their efforts'. Developed countries, however, are 'failing to live up to their end of the MDG deal'. C. Welch, '2007 Millennium Development Goals Report: Progress Being Made, More Must Be Done'. In view of developing countries' resistance to 'conditionality', we find this comment somehow unfair.
213 www.un.org/millenniumgoals/pdf/mdg2007.pdf.
214 *Global Monitoring Report 2007*, p. 15. This stop in expansion is mainly due to large debt relief operations for Iraq and Nigeria taking place in 2005, dropping in 2006. This means that, in real terms, official aid dropped by 5.2 per cent, the first decline since 1997. Even excluding debt relief, however, aid still declined by one-eighth per cent from the year before. www.un.org/millenniumgoals/pdf/mdg2007.pdf, p. 16.
215 *Ibid.*, p. 1.
216 *Ibid.*, p. 15.
217 *Ibid.*, p. 15.
218 *Ibid.*, p. 16.
219 *Ibid.*, p. 18.
220 For a number of studies on this question, see, e.g. http://rru.worldbank. org/PapersLinks/Development-Assistance/.

221 http://rru.worldbank.org/PapersLinks/Development-Assistance/.

222 Chuhan and Bhargava, 'Development Aid: Key to Balanced Global Development', in Bhargava (ed.), *Global Issues for Global Citizens*, p. 81.

223 *Ibid.*, p. 84.

224 C. Bremner and S. Duva, 'Fraud Inquiry into Leaders Breaks "Special Protection"', *Times Online*, 21 June 2007, www.timesonline.co.uk/tol/news/world/europe/article1963997.ece.

225 Chuhan and Bhargava, 'Development Aid: Key to Balanced Global Development', in Bhargava (ed.), *Global Issues for Global Citizens*, p. 78.

226 Chuhan, 'Poverty and Inequality', in Bhargava (ed.), *Global Issues for Global Citizens*, p. 45.

227 *Ibid.*, p. 41.

228 National Centre for Policy Analysis, www.ncpa.org/pd/pdint140.html.

229 *Ibid.*

230 'Nigeria: Will Africa ever get it right?', *The Economist Online*, Apr 26 2007, www.economist.com/displayStory.cfm?story_id=9079815.

231 *Global Monitoring Report 2007*, p. 3.

232 *Ibid.*, p. 3. See also the latest reports from the World Bank (November 2007).

233 *Global Monitoring Report 2007*, p. 5.

234 M. Foresti, D. Booth and T. O'Neil, *Aid Effectiveness and Human Rights: Strengthening the Implementation of the Paris Declaration* (Overseas Development Institute, 2006), p. 6, www.odi.org.uk/publications/reports/Aid_effectiveness.pdf.

235 See, e.g. www.oecd.org/document/18/0,2340,en_2649_3236398_354 01554_1_1_1_1,00.html.

236 Foresti, Booth and O'Neil, *Aid Effectiveness and Human Rights*, p. 6.

237 www.oecd.org/document/18/0,2340, en_2649_3236398_35401554_1_1_1_1,00.html.

238 Chuhan and Bhargava, 'Development Aid: Key to Balanced Global Development', in Bhargava (ed.), *Global Issues for Global Citizens*, p. 86.

239 Foresti, Booth and O'Neil, *Aid Effectiveness and Human Rights*, p. 6.

240 Chuhan and Bhargava, 'Development Aid: Key to Balanced Global Development', in Bhargava (ed.), *Global Issues for Global Citizens*, p. 86.

241 web.worldbank.org/WBSITE/EXTERNAL/TOPICS/EXTGOVANTI CORR/0,,contentMDK:21447906~pagePK:210058~ piPK:210062~ theSitePK:3035864,00.html.

242 OECD, *Integrating Human Rights into Development: Donor Approaches, Experiences and Challenges*, (Paris: OECD, 2006).

243 www.odi.org.uk/rights/Publications/humanrights_into_development_ execsumm.pdf.

244 Chuhan, 'Poverty and Inequality', in Bhargava (ed.), *Global Issues for Global Citizens*, p. 45.
245 *Ibid.*
246 *Ibid.*
247 See the beginning of this chapter.
248 B. Mongoven, *The Global Evolution of Intellectual Property Rights*, Stratfor Public Policy Intelligence Report, 20 September 2007, www.stratfor.com/products/premium/ppi.php?utm_source=070920-PPI& utm_medium=email-strat-html&utm_content=070920-PPI-header-read&utm_campaign=PPI.
249 *OHCHR Draft Guidelines*, para 16.
250 *Ibid.*, para 11.

7 Women's international human rights

1 For a history of CEDAW, see, e.g. www.un.org/womenwatch/daw/ce-daw/history.htm. Note that even though the US has still not ratified the Convention, it was instrumental in drafting CEDAW, which President Jimmy Carter signed at a special ceremony at the Copenhagen Conference in 1980 (UN Department of Public Information, 2007).
2 http://hrw.org/campaigns/cedaw/.
3 Note that the US is the only developed nation that has not ratified CEDAW (partly due to fears by some that CEDAW would diminish the rights and benefits American women already enjoy. See, e.g. www.iassw-aiets.org/Assets/docs/CEDAW.pdf). The other countries that have not ratified are Iran, Syria, Somalia and Sudan (UN Division for the Advancement of Women, 2007).
4 http://hrw.org/campaigns/cedaw/#CEDAW%20HISTORY.
5 *Amnesty International*, 2006, www.iassw-aiets.org/Assets/docs/CE DAW.pdf.
6 *Ibid.*
7 www.un.org/womenwatch/daw/cedaw/, emphasis added.
8 For a recent overview of those different 'feminisms' today, see K. Knop (ed.), *Gender and Human Rights* (Oxford University Press, 2005).
9 Vienna Convention on the Law of Treaties, 1969, Articles 2(1)(d) and 19–23.
10 As of November 2007, 185 countries – over 90 per cent of the members of the United Nations – are party to the Convention, www.un.org/womenwatch/daw/cedaw/states.htm.
11 'CEDAW is ... the human rights convention with the largest number of state reservations', R. Coomaraswamy, 'Reinventing International

Law: Women's Rights as Human Rights in the International Community', *Bulletin of Concerned Asian Scholars*, Vol. 28, Issue 2 (1996), 16.

12 www.un.org/womenwatch/daw/cedaw/reservations-country.htm.

13 www.un.org/womenwatch/daw/cedaw/reservations.htm, emphasis added.

14 CEDAW/SP/2006/2, www.un.org/womenwatch/daw/cedaw/reservations.htm.

15 E. Mayer, *Islam and Human Rights* (Boulder, Colo.: Westview Press, 1991), Ch. 6, *passim*. See also S. Sardar Ali, 'Women's rights, CEDAW and International Human Rights Debates: Towards Empowerment?', in J. Parpart, S. Rai and K Staudt (eds.), *Rethinking Empowerment: Gender and Development in a Global/Local World* (London: Routledge, 2002); and S. Sardar Ali, *Gender and Human Rights in Islam and International Law: Equal Before Allah, Unequal Before Man?* (The Hague: Kluwer Law International, 2000). See also the discussion in Chapter 10 of Islam and human rights.

16 Article XIX, Right to Found a Family and Related Matters. For the text of the Declaration as well as critical annotations see, e.g. *No To Political Islam* website, www.ntpi.org/html/uidhr.html.

17 Part V, Articles 17–22.

18 Article 21(1), CEDAW.

19 For domestic cases relying on CEDAW to invalidate discriminatory laws and promote equality, see, e.g. www.globaljusticecenter.net/media/Domestic%20use%20of%20CEDAW%20for%20women's%20rights.pdf.

20 www.un.org/rights/dpi1772e.htm.

21 General Recommendation No. 12 (1989), www.un.org/womenwatch/daw/cedaw/recommendations/recomm.htm.

22 General Recommendation No. 19 (1992), *Ibid*.

23 H. Charlesworth, 'Human Rights as Men's Rights' in J. Peters and A. Wolper (eds.), *Women's Rights, Human Rights: International Feminist Perspectives* (Routledge: New York, 1995), p. 104. We return to Charlesworth and evaluate her criticisms below.

24 www.du.edu/intl/humanrights/violencepkstn.pdf.

25 www.ohchr.org/english/issues/women/rapporteur/.

26 www.amnesty.org/library/Index/ENGAMR010012003?open&of=ENG-2AM.

27 www.un.org/rights/dpi1772e.htm.

28 www.amnesty.org/library/Index/ENGAMR010012003?open&of=ENG-2AM.

29 For details, see www.un.org/womenwatch/daw/beijing/index.html.

30 www.un.org/rights/dpi1772e.htm. Note that the Beijing Platform for Action also calls for equality in decision making and gender balance in international institutions.

Notes to pages 211–215

31 www.un.org/rights/dpi1772e.htm.

32 www.osce.org/documents/mcs/2005/12/17433_en.pdf.

33 'Rape and Gender Violence: From Impunity to Accountability in International Law', *Human Rights Dialogue*, 2(10) (Fall 2003), www.cceia. org/resources/publications/dialogue/2_10/articles/1052.html. As Copelon explains, gender usually refers to the differences between men and women that are socially constructed; and hence not essential or inevitable products of biological sex differences. Gender violence refers to violence targeted at women or men because of their sex and/or their socially constructed gender roles, and affecting the members of one sex disproportionately more than another.

34 S. Balthazar, 'Gender Crimes And The International Criminal Tribunals', *Gonz. J. Int'l L.*, 10 (2006), available at www.gonzagajil.org/.

35 Report, E/CN.4/2003/75/Add.1.

36 For a good discussion of how these two tribunals 'broke new ground' in respect of gender crimes, see, e.g. Balthazar, 'Gender Crimes And The International Criminal Tribunals'.

37 This is the first time that sexual slavery and trafficking have been expressly recognized as crimes against humanity in an international treaty.

38 Article 7(1)(h) forbids persecution against an identifiable group or collectivity on political, racial, national, ethnic, cultural, religious, **gender** or other grounds that are universally recognized as impermissible under international law.

39 Balthazar, 'Gender Crimes And The International Criminal Tribunal'. See also www.globaljusticecenter.net/projects/iraq/ and www.iraq-iht. org/en/orgenal.html for how the (controversial) Iraqi High Tribunal takes seriously gender crimes (partly as a result of hard work on the part of feminist groups such as the Global Justice Centre).

40 Balthazar, 'Gender Crimes And The International Criminal Tribunals'.

41 *Ibid.*

42 See, e.g. www.peacewomen.org/un/sc/1325.html for a full analysis and chronology. See also www.globaljusticecenter.net/ for what is unsatisfactory with the 'soft-law' aspect of the resolution and the problems of implementation (as we say below in the text, SC Resolution 1325 was not passed under Ch. VII of the UN Charter and is hence not binding).

43 *Ibid.*

44 S/2006/770, para 28, available at www.un.org/Docs/sc/sgrep06.htm.

45 See www.peacewomen.org/un/sc/1325_Monitor/countryindex.htm.

46 See www.peacewomen.org/wpsindex.html.

47 *Ibid.* See also, for example, Norwegian Ministry of Foreign Affairs, *The Norwegian Government's Action Plan for the Implementation of UN Security Council Resolution 1325 (2000)*, March 2006, www.regjeringen.

no/upload/kilde/ud/rap/2006/0004/ddd/pdfv/279831-actionplan_resolu tion1325.pd. Recommendations for action at the national level include suggestions that a committee should be established in order to ensure the mainstreaming of gender perspectives into all aspects of work for peace, security and development (by Foreign Affairs, Ministry of Defence, etc); that there should be reports by a research institute (independent of government); that government agencies should be made responsible for implementation, including by publishing annual reports: and that there ought to be an annual public hearing. But see H. Charlesworth, 'Not Waving but Drowning: Gender Mainstreaming and Human Rights in the United Nations', *Harvard Human Rights Journal*, Vol. 18 (2005), 1–18, for a scathing critique of gender 'mainstreaming'.

48 H. Charlesworth, 'What are Women's International Human Rights?' in R. Cook (ed.), *Human Rights of Women: National and International Perspectives* (Philadelphia: University of Pennsylvania, 1994), pp. 68–73; H. Charlesworth and C. Chinkin, *The Boundaries of International Law: A Feminist Analysis* (Manchester University Press, 2000) pp. 30–1, 56–7; C. Romany, 'State Responsibility Goes Private: A Feminist Critique of the Public/Private Distinction in International Human Rights Law' in Cook (ed.), *Human Rights of Women*; C. Pateman, 'Feminist Critiques of the Public/Private Distinction' in S. I. Benn and G. F. Gaus (eds.), *Public and Private in Social Life* (London: Croom Helm, 1983); N. Lacey, 'Feminist Legal Theory and the Rights of Women' in K. Knop (ed.), *Gender and Human Rights* (Oxford University Press, 2004), pp. 21–2.

49 S. Okin, 'Recognizing Women's Rights as Human Rights', *APA Newsletters*, Vol. 97, Number 2 (1998). Available at www.apa.udel.edu/apa/archive/newsletters/v97n2/law/recognizing.asp.

50 Lacey, 'Feminist Legal Theory', pp. 38–41; H. Charlesworth, C. Chinkin and S. Wright, 'Feminist Approaches to International Law', *American Journal of International Law*, 85 (1991), 613, 635–8.

51 Charlesworth and Chinkin, *Boundaries of International Law*.

52 R. Brooks, 'Feminist Justice at Home and Abroad', *Yale Journal of International Law and Feminism*, 14 (2002) Section II; Charlesworth, Chinkin and Wright, 'Feminist Approaches', 635.

53 See our discussion in the previous chapter.

54 Lacey, 'Feminist Legal Theory', p. 27, but see also pp. 25–30.

55 However, we are then owed an account of why women and men should be treated as equals and it is difficult to give such an account without reverting to liberal premises. The inspiration for much difference feminism was originally C. Gilligan in her book *In a Different Voice: Psychological Theory and Women's Development* (Cambridge, Mass:

Harvard University Press, 1983). See also C. Weedon, *Feminism, Theory and the Politics of Difference* (Oxford: Blackwell, 1999).

56 A well-known attempt to construct such a conception is I. M. Young, *Justice and the Politics of Difference* (Princeton University Press, 1990).

8 The implementation of international human rights

1 Art. 55(c).

2 Ch. IV, Art. 13.

3 Ch. X, Art. 62.

4 'UN Commission on Human Rights loses all credibility', July 2003, *Reporters Without Borders*, www.rsf.org/IMG/pdf/Report_ONU_gb.pdf#search=%22commission%20human%20rights%20observers%22

5 The official line was that the Commission had 'no power to take any action in regard to any complaints concerning human rights'. ESC Res.75 (V) (1947) quoted in Hurst Hannum, 'Human Rights' in C. C. Joyner (ed.), *The United Nations and International Law* (Cambridge University Press, 1997), p. 135.

6 In the 13-month period in 1951–2, for example, 25,000 complaints were passed to the Commission in this way for its complete non-action. P. Alston, 'The Commission on Human Rights' in Alston (ed.), *The United Nations*, p. 140.

7 J. Humphrey, 'The UN CHR and its Parent Body' in *Rene Cassin: Amicorum Discipulorumque Liber* (1969) i.110, quoted in P. Alston (ed.), *The United Nations and Human Rights* (Oxford: Clarendon Press, 1992), p. 140.

8 As Steiner and Alston point out: 'In principle, each of these procedures [1235, 1503 or Special Procedures] is relatively distinct from the others in terms of its origins, the nature of its mandate, the steps to be followed and the types of outcome available. In practice, there is considerable overlap. It is conceivable that different aspects of a particular situation would be under review by all three procedures at the same time'. Henry J. Steiner and Philip Alston, *International Human Rights in Context: Law, Politics, Morals*, 2nd edn. (Oxford University Press, 2000), p. 611.

9 P. Alston, 'The Commission on Human Rights' in Alston (ed.), *The United Nations*, p. 173.

10 General Assembly Resolution 60/251 of 15 March 2006 entitled 'Human Rights Council', www.ohchr.org/english/bodies/chr/special/index.htm.

11 www.ohchr.org/english/press/hrc/HRCOutcomesFINAL.pdf.

12 'Statement by Louise Arbour, High Commissioner for Human Rights, on the Human Rights Council, 23 February 2006', www.un.org/reform/hr/ohchr23feb06.shtml.

13 *Ibid.*

14 *Ibid.*

15 'UN: Rights Council Should Tackle Crises Worldwide: Expand Agenda to Address Backlog of Work', September 10, 2007, www.hrw.org/eng lish/docs/2007/09/10/global16830.htm.

16 See, e.g. www.ohchr.org/english/bodies/cescr/.

17 http://huachen.org/english/bodies/treaty/glossary.htm#GC. See also, e.g. the introduction to document CCPR/C/21/Rev.1 (General comments adopted by the Human Rights Committee under Art. 40, para 4, of the International Covenant on Civil and Political Rights; date: 19 May 1989) which explains the purpose of the general comments as follows: 'The purpose of these general comments is to make th[e] … experience [of the Committee having examined several State parties' reports] available for the benefit of all States parties in order to promote their further implementation of the Covenant; to draw their attention to insufficiencies disclosed by a large number of reports; to suggest improvements in the reporting procedure and to stimulate the activities of these States and international organizations in the promotion and protection of human rights. These comments should also be of interest to other States, especially those preparing to become parties to the Covenant and thus to strengthen the cooperation of all States in the universal promotion and protection of human rights.' www1.umn.edu/humanrts/gencomm/intro-hr.htm, see also www.unhchr.ch/tbs/doc.nsf.

18 See Ch. VIII of the UN Charter.

19 In the UK, for example, the courts found that, in relation to asylum seekers, ECHR Art. 3 cases regarding inhuman and degrading treatment may also engage ESC rights such as ICESCR Art. 9 (social security), 11 (standard of living), 12 (physical and mental health). See, e.g. *Limbuela* v. *SSHD* [2005] UKHL 66.

20 The Council of Europe is the continent's oldest European-wide political organization, founded in 1949. It groups together forty-seven countries, and was set up to 'defend human rights, parliamentary democracy and the rule of law; develop continent-wide agreements to standardise member countries' social and legal practices; promote awareness of a European identity based on shared values and cutting across different cultures', www.echr.coe.int.

21 See www.echr.coe.int and www.coe.int/T/E/Human_rights/execution/.

22 www.echr.coe.int/NR/rdonlyres/69564084–9825-430B-9150-A9137D D22737/0/Survey_2006.pdf, para 4. In all, 14 protocols have been adopted since the Convention came into force, adding further rights and liberties to those enumerated in the Convention. See www.echr.coe.int.

23 Art. 63(1) of the American Convention on Human Rights, www.Venice. coe.int/docs/2002/CDL-DI(2002)001-e.pdf, *Draft Opinion on the implementation of the Judgments of the European Court of Human Rights*, European Commission on Democracy through Law (Venice Commission), Opinion 209/2002, 6 December 2002, para 33. See also para 32: 'The Court's judgments are declaratory in character and have no direct effect in the internal law of the States; the Court may not repeal, annul or modify domestic provisions or decisions. It rules on whether or not a Convention provision has been breached in the impugned case, without, normally, saying what needs to be done in order to redress the violation and prevent further similar ones. The judgments are not directly enforceable, not even the operative part concerning just satisfaction, which, although obviously binding for the State concerned, is not directly enforceable by the Court or any organ of the Council of Europe'.

24 'The Commission prefers the term "implementation" as opposed to "execution" of judgements ... in that the first encompasses the obligation for Member States to take into account the possible implications which judgements pronounced in cases to which they are not parties may have for their legal system and practice'. *Ibid.*, footnote 1.

25 Art. 46(2): 'The final judgment of the Court shall be transmitted to the Committee of Ministers, which shall supervise its execution'.

26 Venice Commission, para 16.

27 As of 22 January 2007.

28 *Ibid.*, para 101.

29 'Russia always pays the money it is ordered to pay', Bill Bowring, a professor of international human rights law at the University of London's Birkbeck College, quoted in Claire Bigg, 'Russia: Judicial Reform Under Way, But For The Right Reasons?' *Radio Free Europe*, October 24 2007, www.rferl.org/featuresarticle/2007/10/9ad2e375–39ee-4dec-94ef-71ae 55136493.html.

30 Venice Commission, para 17. For a discussion of margin appreciation, see Ch. 4, pp. 104–9.

31 Ibid., para 18.

32 With respect to Russia, thus, according to Bowring: 'when it comes to further incompliance with enforcement, that is, carrying out an investigation where there's been a failure to investigate, prosecuting people from the government who appear to have committed crimes, and changing the law in practice, Russia is simply not doing it'. Bigg, 'Russia: Judicial Reform', *Radio Free Europe*.

33 Bigg, 'Russia: Judicial Reform', *Radio Free Europe*, para 41.

34 *Ibid.*, para 41.

35 *Ibid.*, para 42. See also the Statute of the Council of Europe, Art. 8, conventions.coe.int/Treaty/en/Treaties/Html/001.htm.

36 Recommendation 1477 (2000), Execution of Judgments of the European Court of Human Rights, Parliamentary Assembly, Council of Europe, http://assembly.coe.int/Main.asp?link=/Documents/AdoptedText/ta00/EREC1477.htm.

37 Vienna Commission, para 82.

38 www.oas.org/key%5Fissues/eng/KeyIssue_Detail.asp?kis_sec=17, emphasis added.

39 See, e.g. Project on International Courts and Tribunals, *IACHR, Inter-American Court of Human Rights*, www.pict-pcti.org/courts/IACHR. html: 'Among the member States of the Council of Europe, military and other authoritarian governments have been rare and short-lived, while in Latin America they were almost the norm until well into the 1980s. The major challenges confronting the European system were issues such as the length of pre-trial detention, insufficient redress against decisions by the State bureaucracy, defense of the right of privacy, and protection of human rights in the private sphere. Cases involving a state of emergency have been relatively few. The European Court and the Commission rarely have to deal with completely unresponsive or even antagonistic governments or national systems.'

40 See, e.g. J. M. Pasqualuci, *The Practice and Procedure of the Inter-American Court of Human Rights* (Cambridge University Press: 2003).

41 *African Union Message on Africa Human Rights Day*, 10 October 2007, www.achpr.org/english/_info/news_en.html.

42 See African Commission on Human Rights website, www.achpr.org/english/_info/court_en.html.

43 www.africancourtcoalition.org/. See also *Pampazuka News online*, 22 June 2006, www.pambazuka.org/en/category/features/35337 and www. interights.org/page.php?dir=About&page=africaprogrammeactivities.php.

44 www.africancourtcoalition.org/.

45 Art. 34(6) and 5(3) of the Protocol, www.achpr.org/english/_info/court_en.html.

46 Art. 3 'Jurisdiction: (1). The jurisdiction of the Court shall extend to all cases and disputes submitted to it concerning the interpretation and application of the Charter, this Protocol and any other relevant Human Rights instrument ratified by the States concerned'.

47 Art. 7 'Sources Of Law: The Court shall apply the provision of the Charter and any other relevant human rights instruments ratified by the States concerned'.

48 Project on International Courts and Tribunals: http://www.pict-pcti.org/courts/ACHPR.html.

49 See, e.g. www.echr.coe.int/eng/Press/2004/June/DecisiononAdvisoryo
    pinion.htm; and hei.unige.ch/~clapham/hrdoc/docs/CIS%20convention.
    doc for the text of the Convention.

50 www.coe.am/docs/pace/resolution_1249.pdf.

51 www.coe.am/docs/pace/resolution_1249.pdf.

52 James Silk, *International Criminal Justice and the Protection of Human
    Rights: The Rule of Law or the Hubris of Law?*, p. 2 http://islandia.law.
    yale.edu/sela/esilk.pdf. In his paper, Silk questions whether this revo-
    lution really will advance human rights.

53 Anthony Dworkin, *The Hague Tribunal after Milosevic*, OpenDemocracy
    (14 March 2006), www.opendemocracy.net/globalization-institutions_
    government/hague_3352.jsp.

54 The International Criminal Tribunal for the Former Yugoslavia's website
    is www.un.org/icty. More information on researching the ICTY can be
    found at *The United Nations Documentation: Research Guide* at www.
    un.org/Depts/dhl/resguide/specil.htm#ity.

55 The ICTY lists five successes on its website it claims it has accomplished:
    1. Spearheading the shift from impunity to accountability; 2. Estab-
    lishing the facts; 3. Bringing justice to thousands of victims and giving
    them a voice; 4. The accomplishment in international law referred to
    above; and 5. Strengthening the Rule of Law.

56 Some trials extend for several years. Supporters of the Tribunal respond
    that many of the defendants are charged with multiple crimes against
    many victims, all of which must be proven beyond reasonable doubt,
    thus requiring long trials. Simultaneous translation also slows trials.

57 The two-year budget for the Tribunal for 2004 and 2005 was
    $271,854,600. The cost is borne by all UN members.

58 See, e.g. a Memorandum issued by Austrian Professor Hans Köchler
    submitted to the President of the Security Council in 1999, http://i-p-o.
    org/yu-tribunal-memo1999.htm.

59 'Credibility and Legitimacy of International Criminal Tribunals in the
    Wake of Milosevic's Death', *Harvard International Review*, May 6 2006,
    http://Harvard.edu/articles/1402/.

60 *Ibid.*

61 Some believe further that the Tribunal procedures violate a number
    of long-established principles of Western jurisprudence. See, e.g.
    E. S. Herman and D. Peterson, *Marlise Simons on the Yugoslavia Tri-
    bunal: A Study in Total Propaganda Service*, http://musictravel.free.fr/
    political/political46.htm.

62 Dworkin, *The Hague Tribunal after Milosevic*.

63 This section is mainly based on www.unhcr.ch and www.humanrights
    first.org.

64 Dworkin, *The Hague Tribunal after Milosevic.* An estimated 800,000
    Tutsis and moderate Hutus (out of a population of eight million) were
    killed during the genocidal campaign, the majority within a three-month
    period in 1994. More than two million fled to neighbouring countries.
    At the time, neither the UN nor any other international coalition
    intervened. After the violence, many of the perpetrators fled Rwanda
    and scattered within the region and around the world. To put the figure
    into perspective: more people were killed, injured, internally displaced,
    and refugeed in 100 days in Rwanda than in the whole eight–nine years
    of the Yugoslavia campaign.

65 International Criminal Tribunal for Rwanda website, Achievements of
    the Tribunal, http://69.94.11.53/default.htm.

66 See e.g. www.humanrightsfirst.org.

67 *Prosecutor* v. *Akayesu*, Case No. ICTR-96–4-T (Trial Chamber), 2
    September 1998 and 2 October 1998.

68 www.humanrightsfirst.org/international_justice/w_context/w_cont_03.
    htm.

69 See, e.g. N. Cantwell, *Starting From Zero: The Promotion and Pro-
    tection of Children's Rights in Post-Genocide Rwanda, July 1994–Dec
    1996* (Florence: UN Children's Fund, 1997), p. 28, for a view that the
    Tribunal was 'originally conceived for display and show ... to indicate
    the International Community really did care about the crimes and would
    not let them go unpunished'.

70 Twenty-nine state parties are African States, thirteen are Asian States,
    sixteen are from Eastern Europe, twenty-two are from Latin America
    and the Caribbean, and twenty-five are from Western Europe and other
    states. www.icc-cpi.int/statesparties.html and http://iccnow.org/?mod=
    home.

71 www.icc-cpi.int/about/ataglance/jurisdiction_admissibility.html.

72 Art. 27.

73 www.icc-cpi.int/about/ataglance/works.html.

74 *Ibid.* This section is also based on S. Hanson, 'Africa and the Inter-
    national Criminal Court', Council on Foreign Relations Report (17
    November 2006), www.cfr.org/publication/12048/.

75 www.icc-cpi.int/about/ataglance/today.html, and Hanson, 'Africa and
    the International Criminal Court'.

76 www.icc-cpi.int/press/pressreleases/114.html.

77 http://iccnow.org/?mod=car.

78 See, e.g. J. L. Washburn and W. Punyasena, 'The Commission of Inquiry
    on Darfur: A United Nations Success Story', *UN Association for the
    USA*, No. 10 (20 July 2005), www.unausa.org/site/apps/s/content.asp?

c=fvKRI8MPJpF&b=369041&ct=1207485: 'For more than two years now, the government of Sudan with the government-supported Arab Janjaweed militia has undertaken a policy of ethnic cleansing toward the local black population in the Western region of Darfur. The attacks were started to quell a violent rebellion in the region but have escalated beyond any justifiable counterinsurgency campaign. In March 2005, Jan Egeland, the UN Under-Secretary-General for Humanitarian Affairs reported that approximately 180,000 persons had been killed, and about two million people had been displaced, with 10,000 people dying each month'.

79 See, e.g. www.reuters.com/article/homepageCrisis/idUSN20403567._ CH_.2400.

80 See, e.g. 'ICC prosecutor presses for arrest of Darfur war crimes suspects', Yahoo News, 20 September 2007, news.yahoo.com/s/afp/20070920/ wl_africa_afp/uniccsudandarfur.

81 O. Bekou and S. Shah, 'Realising the Potential of the International Criminal Court: The African Experience', *Human Rights Law Review* (2006), http://hrlr.oxfordjournals.org/cgi/content/abstract/ngl011v1.

82 ICC Deputy Prosecutor Bensouda, in an interview with *Newsweek World News, November 9 2006*, http://msnbc.msn.com/id/15642006/ site/newsweek/.

83 Lee Feinstein, CFR Senior Fellow, in an interview with CFR.org, October 5 2005, www.cfr.org/publication/8980/.

84 Washburn and Punyasena, 'The Commission of Inquiry on Darfur'.

85 The agreements have been sought by the US since 2002. Under the 2004 Nethercutt Amendment, those countries that have signed on to the ICC but refused to sign the so-called Bilateral Immunity Agreements were penalized with cuts in foreign assistance. As of 11 December 2006, 102 agreements had been signed. Forty-six of these agreements were with ICC state parties, twenty-four of which lost US aid in fiscal year 2005. Fifty-four countries had publicly refused to sign, www.iccnow.org/? mod=bia.

86 See 'Four Years Later, U.S. Sees International Criminal Court in Better Light', *International Herald Tribune*, (27 December 2006), www.iht. com/articles/ap/2006/12/28/america/NA_GEN_US_International_Crimi nal_Court.php.

87 See, e.g. *Prosecutor v. Furundzic*, Case N. IT-95–17/I-T, the ICTY Trial Chamber II, Judgment of 10 December 1998, para 156: 'It has been held that international crimes being universally condemned wherever they occur, every State has the right to prosecute and punish the authors of such crimes.'

88 'The Perils of Universal Jurisdiction', *Republican Policy Committee*, December 18 2006.
89 See, e.g. I. Brownlie, *Principles of Public International Law*, 5th edn. (Oxford University Press, 1999), p. 303–9.
90 See, e.g. M. C. Bassiouni, 'Universal Jurisdiction for International Crimes: Historical Perspectives and Contemporary Practice', *Virginia Journal of International Law*, 42 (2001), 81; A. Cassese, *International Criminal Law* (Oxford University Press, 2003), p. 284; and E. Kontorovich, 'A Positive Theory Of Universal Jurisdiction', bepress Legal Series, Working Paper 211, http://law.bepress.com/expresso/eps/211, p. 3.
91 As we saw, *jus cogens* ('compelling law') refers to a limited number of peremptory norms from which no derogation is ever permitted. There is no universally accepted and recognized list of what these norms are; prohibition of piracy is, however, universally recognized as such a norm.
92 See M. Inazumi, *Universal Jurisdiction in Modern International Law: Expansion of National Jurisdiction for Prosecuting Serious Crimes under International Law* (Antwerpen-Oxford: Intersentia, 2005), School of Human Rights Research Series, Volume 19.
93 The Geneva Conventions of 1949 on the conduct of war, ratified by 189 countries including the United States, require each participating state to 'search for' persons who have committed grave breaches of the conventions and to 'bring such persons, regardless of nationality, before its own courts'. Note also that although the Genocide Convention does not expressly require states parties to exercise universal jurisdiction 'there is overwhelming evidence that ... the drafters of the Genocide Convention did not intend to prevent states parties from exercising such jurisdiction', web.amnesty.org/library/index/engior530012002.
94 The famous *Pinochet* case, for example (which involved the extradition request by Spain to Britain for the prosecution of former Chilean dictator Augusto Pinochet for torture and other international crimes committed during his regime), was decided on the grounds of universal jurisdiction established under the Torture Convention, not under universal jurisdiction derived from customary international law. The Torture Convention contains a universal jurisdiction provision that obligates each state party to establish jurisdiction over the crime of torture when the alleged offender is present in its territory, regardless of whether the offender committed the acts on its territory, is one of its nationals, or victimized one of its nationals. *R v. Bow Street Metropolitan Stipendiary Magistrate, ex parte Pinochet* (No. 3) [1999] 2 All ER 97.
95 M. Dixon, *Textbook on International Law*, 4th edn. (Blackstone Press Limited, London, 2002), p. 139. See also Brownlie, *Principles of Public International Law*, p. 308: 'Hijacking (unlawful seizure of aircraft) and

offences related to traffic in narcotics are probably subject to universal jurisdiction.'

96 R. Higgins, *Problems and Processes: International Law and How to Use It* (Oxford: Clarendon Press, 1994), p 61.

97 For background information on the Nuremberg Tribunal and its Charter, see, e.g. www.yale.edu/lawweb/avalon/imt/proc/imtconst.htm; www.ushmm.org/wlc/article.php?lang=en&ModuleId=10007069; www.un.org/documents/ga/res/1/ares1.htm. The Nuremberg Charter of 1945 was recognized as affirming principles of international law by the United Nations through General Assembly Resolutions 95(I) of 11 December 1946; 177(II) of November 21, 1947; and 488(V), of December 12, 1950. See also G. Mettraux (ed.), *Perspectives on the Nuremberg Trial* (Oxford University Press, 2008).

98 *Republican Policy Committee* p. 7.

99 Note, however, that there is a general limitation on the exercise of universal jurisdiction: a so-called 'heads of state immunity', also extended to other certain high-ranking state ministers. A sitting head of state or high-ranking minister is thus immune from prosecution by another state. See, e.g. the International Court of Justice in 'Arrest Warrant of 11 April 2000 (Democratic Republic of the Congo *v.* Belgium)', Judgment, *I. C. J. Reports* 2002, www.icj-cij.org/.

100 M. Morris, 'Universal Jurisdiction in a Divided World: Conference Remarks', *New England Law Review*, 35(2) (2001), 337–61, www. nesl.edu/lawrev/vol35/2/Morris.PDF.

101 See, e.g. C. Tomuschat, 'Symposium: Issues of Universal Jurisdiction in the Scilingo Case', *Journal of International Criminal Justice*, Vol. 3, No. 5 (2005), 1074–81, jicj.oxfordjournals.org/cgi/content/abstract/3/ 5/1074: 'universal jurisdiction must be seen as *default jurisdiction*, intended to grant extraterritorial jurisdiction whenever the territorial or national state are passive [or where there is no jurisdiction by an international court]', emphasis added.

102 See, e.g. J. Mudingu, 'How Genuine are NGOs?', *New Times (Rwanda)*, 7 August 2006, www.globalpolicy.org/ngos/fund/2006/0807genuine. htm: 'For instance, the Ford Foundation has granted funds to numerous organisations and projects in almost every country in the world that had reached an astronomical figure of $8 billion since its formation in 1936.' See also Michael Lind, 'The Future of US Foreign Policy: a Reply', www. opendemocracy.net/democracy-americanpower/future_reply_4426.jsp (13 March 2007): 'Most NGOs are funded by a small number of wealthy people in north Atlantic nations. Why do they have any more right to meddle in the countries of the global south than did their missionary precursors?'.

103 World Bank, *Working with NGOs A Practical Guide to Operational Collaboration between the World Bank and Non-Governmental Organisations*. Operations Policy Department (World Bank, 1995), p. 7; also www-wds.worldbank.org/external/default/main?pagePK=6419302 78. Other names are often used interchangeably with non-governmental organizations: civil society organizations, private voluntary organizations, charities, non-profits charities/charitable organizations, third sector organizations, and so on. The World Bank, however, for example, considers non-governmental organizations a subset of civil society organizations which thus include: 'community groups, non-governmental organizations ..., labor unions, indigenous groups, charitable organizations, faith-based organizations, professional associations, and foundations', http://web.worldbank.org/WBSITE/EXTERNAL/TOPICS/CSO/0,, pagePK:220469~theSitePK:228717,00.html.
104 World Bank Report, *Working with NGOs*, 1995.
105 web.worldbank.org/
106 See, e.g. R. Robbins, *Global Problems and the Culture of Capitalism*, 2nd edn. (Boston, Mass.: Allyn and Bacon, 2002), for whom the 'neoliberal economic and political agenda' is the main factor responsible for the increasing support of NGOs from governments and official aid agencies trying to limit the role and size of the state. See also S. B. Nefissa, 'NGOs, Governance and Development in the Arab World', MOST Discussion Paper 46, www.unesco.org/most/nefissae.htm.
107 Spokesperson for the Red Cross, www.opendemocracy.net/globali zation-think_tank/civil_society_3413.jsp.
108 NGO Monitor claims thus that 'self-declared "humanitarian NGOs" [including Human Rights Watch, Amnesty International and so forth] ... exploit the label "universal human rights values" to promote politically and ideologically motivated anti-Israel agendas'. According to the Monitor, Israel is almost always guilty of human rights violations, independently of whether it has acted in legitimate self-defence; and the Palestinians are almost always portrayed as victims, independently of their terrorist activities. See www.ngo-monitor.org. See also G. M. Steinberg, 'The Unhelpful Hand: Time to Free the Palestinians from NGOs', *Wall Street Journal Europe*, 10 January 2005, www.globalpolicy.org/ngos/credib/2005/0110unhelpful.htm.
109 M. Macan-Marcar, 'NGOs Can Add to Disasters', quoting from International Federation of Red Cross and Red Crescent Societies' annual 'World Disaster Report' on the international response to the tsunami and other natural disasters during 2004 (5 October 2005). See www.globalpolicy.org/ngos/crdib/2005/1005tsunami.htm.
110 *Ibid.*

111 www.ifrc.org/publicat/conduct/code.asp.

112 www.sphereproject.org.

113 www.hapinternational.org/en/page.php?ID.page=3&Icat=10.

114 www.un.org/documents/ecosoc/res/1996/eres1996–31.htm. Note that Resolution 1296 added that NGOs included: 'organisations which accept members designated by government authorities, provided that such membership does not interfere with the free expression of views of the organisations'.

115 www.un.org.esa/coordination/ngo/.

116 *Report of the Committee on Non-Governmental Organizations on the First and Second Parts of its 2000 Session* (New York, 15–19 May and 12–23 June 2000), Economic and Social Council E/2000/88 (Part II), p. 15, www.un.org/esa/documents/ecosoc/docs/2000/e2000–88part2.pdf.

117 www.un.org/News/Press/docs/2006/ecosoc6202.doc.htm.

118 P. N. Prove, 'Re-commissioning the Commission of Human Rights: UN Reform and the UN Human Rights Architecture', p. 12, on www.lutheranworld.org/What_We_Do/OIahr/Issues_Events/UN_Reform-Human_Rights.pdf.

119 Ibid.

120 *In Larger Freedom: Towards Development, Security and Human Rights for All*, Report of the Secretary-General to the General Assembly, A/59/2005 (21 March 2005), para 181, www2.ohchr.org/english/bodies/hrcouncil/docs/gaA.59.2005.Add.1_En.pdf.

121 www.un.org/largerfreedom/add1.htm, para 16.

122 www.un.org/dpi/ngosection/about-ngo-assoc.html.

123 *Ibid.*

124 *Ibid.*

125 www.opendemocracy.net/globalization-think_tank/civil_society3413.jsp.

126 *Ibid.*

127 R. Mullerson, *Human Rights Diplomacy* (London: Routledge, 1997), p. 21.

128 Thirty-five nations signed the Helsinki Accords. The accords recognized the borders of Europe, as they had been at the end of World War II, thus recognizing Soviet domination of the Baltic States (Estonia, Latvia, and Lithuania). In turn, the Soviets agreed to respect human rights, and acknowledge that the issue of human rights was an international concern. Soon, what became known as Helsinki Watch Groups were established throughout the Soviet Union, becoming 'beacons that kept opposition alive in the Soviet Union', www.historycentral.com/Today/HelsinkiAccords.html.

129 *Charter of Paris for a New Europe* (Paris, 1990), www.osce.org/item/
4047.html, p. 3.

130 Mullerson, *Human Rights*, p. 116. See also our account of the East
Asian values debate in Chapter 10.

131 Mullerson, *Human Rights*, p. 114.

132 J. Donnelly, *Universal Human Rights in Theory and Practice*, 2nd edn.
(Ithaca and London: Cornell University Press, 2003), pp. 171–2.

133 D. Forsythe, *Human Rights in International Relations*, 2nd edn.
(Cambridge University Press, 2006), p. 184.

134 Note that not even the members of Westphalian society saw foreign
policy as limited to national security and economic prosperity. As we
noted in Part I, they saw themselves as possessing a certain substantive
identity. In the seventeenth and eighteenth centuries, this was the idea
of a society of Christian peoples, while in the nineteenth, this conception was transformed into the notion of the European peoples as
having attained a higher degree of civilization – characterized by a
liberal rule of law – than the rest of the world. Nevertheless, it is true
that the nature of the political regime was not an issue in Westphalian
society and that the UN's human rights conventions and Declarations
of international standards go far beyond the concerns of Westphalia.

135 L. H. Gelb and J. A. Rosenthal, 'The Rise of Ethics in Foreign Policy:
Reaching a Values Consensus', *Foreign Affairs* (May/June 2003).

136 See our discussion in Chapter 8 on the Right to Development.

137 R. Wright, 'An American Foreign Policy that Both Realists and Idealists
Should Fall in Love With', *New York Times*, 16 July 2006, part IV.

138 D. B. MacDonald, R. G. Patman and B. Mason-Parker, *The Ethics of
Foreign Policy* (London: Ashgate), p. 12, www.ashgate.com/default.
aspx?page=637&calcTitle=1&title_id=7886&edition_id=8411.

139 We mentioned Saudi Arabia above. See also, Craig Murray, UK's ex-
Ambassador to Uzbekistan (removed from his post in 2004 supposedly
for criticizing the UK for closing its eyes to horrific human rights
abuses in Uzbekistan, America's ally in the 'war on terror'): 'when it
comes to the Karimov regime [ruling regime in Uzbekistan], systematic
torture and rape appear to be treated as peccadilloes, not to affect the
relationship and to be downplayed in the international fora … I hope
that once the present crisis is over we will make plain to the U. S., at
senior level, our serious concern over their policy in Uzbekistan', Letter
2, paras 6 and 7, in *The UK Was Complicit In Torture In Uzbekistan*,
30 December 2005, Scoop Independent News, www.scoop.co.nz/
stories/HL0512/S00297.htm. See also, 'Former British envoy is suspended', *BBC News On-Line* (17 October 2004), news.bbc.co.uk/1/hi/
uk/3750370.stm, and C. Murray, *Murder in Samarkand – A British*

Ambassador's Controversial Defiance of Tyranny in the War on Terror (Mainstream Pub. Project, 2007).

140 'Robin Cook's speech on the government's ethical foreign policy', *Guardian Unlimited* (12 May 1997), www.guardian.co.uk/indonesia/Story/0,2763,190889,00.html.

141 'A prohibited intervention must accordingly be one bearing on matters in which each State is permitted, by the principle of State sovereignty, to decide freely. One of these is the choice of a political, economic, social and cultural system, and the formulation of foreign policy. Intervention is wrongful when it uses methods of coercion in regard to such choices, which must remain free ones. The element of coercion, which defines, and indeed forms the very essence of, prohibited intervention, is particularly obvious in the case of an intervention which uses force, either in the direct form of military action, or in the indirect form of support for subversive or terrorist armed activities within another State'. *Nicaragua Case (Merits)*, I. C. J. Reports 1986, paras 202–5. See also 'Declaration on the Inadmissibility of Intervention in the Domestic Affairs of States and the Protection of their Independence and Sovereignty 1965' in D. J. Harris, *Cases And Materials on International Law* (London: Sweet & Maxwell, 1998), p. 889.

142 Brownlie, *Principles of Public International Law*, p. 602, ft 198.

143 *Case Concerning the Barcelona Traction, Light and Power Company Ltd (Belgium and Spain) (Second Phase)*, I. C. J. Reports 1970 at 32: 'In particular, an essential distinction should be drawn between the obligations of a state towards the international community as a whole, and those arising vis-à-vis another state in the field of diplomatic protection. By their very nature the former are the concern of all states. In view of the importance of the rights involved, all states can be held to have a legal interest in their protection; they are obligations *erga omnes*. Such obligations derive, for example, in contemporary international law, from the outlawing of acts of aggression, and of genocide, as also from the principles and rules concerning the basic rights of the human person, including protection from slavery and racial discrimination.'

144 E. H. Carr, *The Twenty Years' Crisis, 1919–1939* (New York: Perennial, 2001), pp. 79–80.

145 A. Cohen, 'Putin's Middle East Visit: Russia is Back', *The Heritage Foundation website*, 5 March 2007, www.heritage.org/Research/RussiaandEurasia/wm1382.cfm.

146 Indeed, Putin acknowledges as much. For example, he is reported as saying, when paying tribute to Stalin's victims on 31 October 2007, that such tragedies occurred when 'ideas that seem attractive but prove

to be empty are placed above fundamental vales: human life and the rights and liberties of Man'. *The Times*, 31 October 2007, p. 35.

147 J. Pilger, 'Labour claims its actions are lawful while it bombs Iraq, starves its people and sells arms to corrupt states', johnpilger.com, 7 August 2000, www.johnpilger.com/page.asp?partid=308

148 *Ibid.*

149 MacDonald, Patman and Mason-Parker, *The Ethics of Foreign Policy*, p. 17.

150 *Nicaragua Case (Merits)*, I.C.J. Reports 1986, paras 244 and 245.

151 Harris, *Cases and Materials on International Law*, pp. 885 and 890.

152 See also, J.L. Holzgrefe and R.O. Keohane (eds.), *Humanitarian Intervention: Ethical, Legal and Political Dilemmas* (Cambridge University Press, 2003), p. 18: 'Humanitarian intervention refers to the threat or use of force across state borders by a state (or a group of states) aimed at preventing or ending widespread and grave violations of the fundamental human rights of individuals other than its own citizens, without the permission of the state within whose territory force is applied.'

153 This is a huge topic. For a recent bibliography, see, e.g. C.G. Badescu, 'Authorising Humanitarian Intervention: Hard Choices in Saving Strangers', *Canadian Journal of Political Science*, 40(1) (March 2007), 51–78; E.A. Heinze, 'Humanitarian Intervention and the War in Iraq: Norms, Discourse, and State Practice', *Parameters*, Spring 2006, www.carlisle.army.mil/usawc/Parameters/06spring/heinze.htm; J. Stromseth, 'Rethinking Humanitarian Intervention: The Case for Incremental Change' in J.L. Holzgrefe and R.O. Keohane (eds.), *Humanitarian Intervention: Ethical, Legal, and Political Dilemmas* (Cambridge University Press, 2003); T.G. Weiss, forward by B. Urquhart, *Military-civilian Interactions: Humanitarian Crises and the Responsibility to Protect*, 2nd edn., (Rowman & Littlefield, 2004); N. Wheeler, *Saving Strangers: Humanitarian Intervention in International Society* (Oxford University Press, 2000). See also a report by the International Commission on Intervention and State Sovereignty (ICISS), *The Responsibility to Protect* (Ottawa: International Development Research Centre, 2001). The ICISS was established by the Canadian government under UN auspices in the hope of agreeing criteria for humanitarian intervention. The report, which we examine in detail below, is considered an authoritative source on norms of intervention.

154 See, e.g., the 1993 UN World Congress on Human Rights in Vienna.

155 For a good exposition, see, e.g. N. Onuf, 'Humanitarian Intervention: The Early Years', www.cgpacs.uci.edu/research/working_papers/nicholas_onuf_humanitarian_intervention.pdf.

156 Mullerson, *Human Rights*, pp. 148–9.
157 Note that certainly today Britain does not accept that there is a customary international law norm of humanitarian intervention (or at least did not accept until Kosovo).
158 Mullerson, *Human Rights*, p. 156.
159 C. Greenwood, 'Is there a Right of Humanitarian Intervention?', *World Today*, 49(2) (1993), 34.
160 Harris, *Cases and Materials on International Law*, p. 917.
161 Heinze, *Humanitarian Intervention and the War in Iraq*, ft 6. See also, M. Pecny, *Democracy at the Point of Bayonets* (Pennsylvania State University Press, 1999); Louis Henkin, S. Hoffman, J.J. Kirkapatrick, A. Gerson, W.D. Rogers and D.J. Scheffer, forward by J.T. Swing, *Right versus Might: International Law and the Use of Force* (New York: Council on Foreign Relations Press, 1991).
162 See, e.g. T. Farrer, 'Humanitarian Intervention Before and After 9/11: Legality and Legitimacy' in Holzgrefe and Keohane (eds.), *Humanitarian Intervention: Ethical, Legal, and Political Dilemmas*.
163 See, e.g. Stromseth, 'Rethinking Humanitarian Intervention', for arguments that international law allows the emergence of a new rule of customary law on the use of force that can exist alongside the Charter (for example the rescue of nationals). She thinks that, following Kosovo in particular, a norm of customary international law may actually already have started to develop in support of humanitarian intervention in extreme cases. But see, e.g. M. Byers and S. Chesterman, 'Changing the Rules about Rules? Unilateral Humanitarian Intervention and the Future of International Law' in Holzgrefe and Keohane (eds.), *Humanitarian Intervention*, for arguments that the only way humanitarian intervention could be legitimate is if the norm attains the status of a peremptory norm (*jus cogens*), thereby overriding the UN Charter's prohibition on the use of force.
164 www.iciss-ciise.gc.ca.
165 See, e.g. The Responsibility to Protect – Engaging Civil Society, www. responsibilitytoprotect.org; The Genocide Intervention Network, www.genocideintervention.net.
166 UNGA, '2005 Summit Outcome', A/60/L.1 (September 15 2005), www.un.org/summit2005/documents.html.
167 Alex J. Bellamy, 'Preventing Future Kosovos and Future Rwandas: The Responsibility to Protect After the 2005 World Summit', *Policy Brief No.1 of the Initiative Ethics in a Violent World: What Can Institutions Do?* (Carnegy Council, 2006).
168 Letter from the Secretary General to the President of the Security Council, UN Doc. S/2004/567 (July 13 2004).

169 S/RES/1674 (2006), para 4.
170 www.responsibilitytoprotect.org.
171 Non-violent demonstrations began in August 2007 when the military government raised fuel prices, and they intensified when Buddhist monks joined the protesters. The government subsequently arrested thousands of protesters and killed hundreds or thousands of citizens, according to various reports.
172 www.responsibilitytoprotect.org/.
173 'High Commissioner Addresses the 5th Special Session of the Human Rights Council on the Human Rights Situation in Myanmar', 2 October 2007, www.ohchr.org/english/press/hrc/index.htm.
174 www.responsibilitytoprotect.org/.
175 *Ibid.*
176 See e.g., Badescu, 'Authorising Humanitarian Intervention', p. 74: 'Instead of lamenting that interventions can only take place when the Council authorizes them, we should regard regional organizations as legitimate alternatives to UN authorization when the Security Council is at a deadlock'. She concludes, quoting S. Chesterman in M. Byers and S. Chesterman, 'Changing the Rules about Rules' in Holzgrefe and Keohane (eds.), *Humanitarian Intervention*, p. 54: 'Ultimately, the basic problem that transpires is not the legitimacy of humanitarian intervention, but the predisposition towards "inhumanitarian non-intervention" '.
177 T. Dunne and N. J. Wheeler (eds.), *Human Rights in Global Politics* (Cambridge University Press, 1999), pp. 2–3; P. G. Lauren, *The Evolution of International Human Rights* (University of Pennsylvania Press, 2003), p. 303; G. M. Lyons and J. Mayall (eds.), *International Human Rights in the Twenty-first Century* (Lanham: Rowman and Littlefield, 2003), p. 3; P. Evans, *The Politics of Human Rights*, 2nd edn. (London: Pluto Press, 2005), p. 6.
178 The 1975 Helsinki Final Act of the Conference on Security and Co-operation in Europe linked security to human rights. See D. C. Thomas, *The Helsinki Effect: International Norms, Human Rights and the Demise of Communism* (Princeton University Press, 2001).
179 The main proponent of the so-called 'democratic peace' is M. Doyle. See his 'Liberalism and World Politics', *American Political Science Review*, 80 (1986), 1151–70. But see also E. Mansfield and J. Snyder, *Electing to Fight: Why Emerging Democracies go to War* (Cambridge, Mass.: MIT Press, 2005).
180 Cohen, 'Putin's Middle East Visit: Russia is Back', see fn 146.
181 See M. Ignatieff (ed.), *American Exceptionalism and Human Rights* (Princeton University Press, 2005).

182 See our discussion of Herder and nationalism in Chapter 5 above.
183 R. J. Vincent, *Human Rights and International Relations* (Cambridge University Press, 1986), pp. 143–50.
184 Donnelly, *Universal Human Rights*, Ch. 12, *passim*.
185 See, e.g. F. Zakaria, *The Future of Freedom: Illiberal Democracy at Home and Abroad* (New York: W. W. Norton, 2003).
186 See, e.g. T. Courcelle, 'Chechnya: the Parliamentary Assembly of the Council of Europe Shaking off its Apathy', translated by T. Murphy, 18 February 2006, www.caucaz.com/home_eng/breve_contenu.php?id=229: 'On 25 January 2006, after much inaction, the Parliamentary Assembly of the Council of Europe finally passed a resolution condemning the methods employed by Russian security forces in Chechnya and harshly criticised the Committee of Ministers … for its passivity in the face of the continuing human rights abuses in the province'. To our knowledge (as of 2 November 2007), the resolution, accompanied by a recommendation, has yet to be approved by the Council of Ministers. See also A. Gill, Director of Human Rights Watch's representative office in Russia, 'Betraying Human Rights in Russia', 11 June 2007, http://hrw.org/english/docs/2007/06/11/russia16149.htm: 'When he was here [Moscow] last week, Prime Minister Jose Socrates [the present President of the European Union] told Russia's President Vladimir Putin that there would be no more European Union moralizing about Russia's human rights record, saying that "no one should claim to lecture anyone else" … This was a victory for Putin's increasingly authoritarian policies, a terrible blow to Russia's besieged civil society, and a bad omen for Portugal's upcoming presidency of the European Union'.

9 Western critiques of liberal human rights

1 It should be recalled that Bentham was attacking the idea of natural or human rights and not liberalism itself. Nevertheless, this attack has been enormously influential and antagonistic towards rights regimes of the UN type.
2 J. Bentham, 'Anarchical Fallacies' in A. I. Melden (ed.), *Human Rights* (Belmont: Wadsworth, 1970).
3 *Ibid.*, p. 32.
4 This is a point made much of by Rawls in his rejection of utilitarianism. See his *A Theory of Justice*, (Oxford University Press, 1971), pp. 21–4, 163–5.
5 A. MacIntyre, *After Virtue* (London: Duckworth, 1981); M. Sandel, *Liberalism and the Limits of Justice* (Cambridge University Press, 1982);

C. Taylor, *Philosophical Papers, Vol. 1: Human Agency and Language; Vol. 2: Philosophy and the Human Sciences* (Cambridge University Press, 1985) and *Sources of the Self* (Cambridge University Press, 1990); M. Walzer, *Interpretation and Social Criticism* (Cambridge, Mass.: Harvard University Press, 1987) and *Thick and Thin: Moral Argument at Home and Abroad* (University of Notre Dame Press, 1994).

6 R. Nozick, *Anarchy, State and Utopia* (New York: Basic Books, 1974).

7 MacIntyre, *After Virtue*, pp. 55–6, Chs. 10, 15, *passim*.

8 This is above all true of Sandel, *Liberalism and the Limits of Justice*, p. 152. See also his 'The Procedural Republic and the Unencumbered Self', *Political Theory*, 12 (1) (1984), 81–96.

9 A. MacIntyre, *Whose Justice? Which Rationality?* (London: Duckworth, 1988).

10 I. M. Young, *Justice and the Politics of Difference* (Princeton University Press, 1990); W. Kymlicka, *Multicultural Citizenship* (Oxford: Clarendon Press, 1995). For a powerful criticism of various multicultural theories, see B. Barry, *Culture and Equality* (Cambridge: Polity Press, 2001).

11 For a fuller discussion of the feminist claims, see Chapter 7 above.

12 D. McLellan (ed.), 'On the Jewish Question' *Karl Marx: Early Texts* (Oxford: Basil Blackwell, 1971).

13 *Ibid.*, p. 108

14 L. Feuerbach, *The Essence of Christianity*, translated M. Evans (London: J. Chapman, 1854) p. 59.

15 This section has been greatly influenced by S. Holmes, *The Anatomy of Antiliberalism* (Cambridge, Mass.: Harvard University Press, 1993).

16 J. Lively (ed.), *The Works of Joseph de Maistre* (London: George Allen & Unwin, 1968), see especially pp. 93–128.

17 C. Schmitt, *The Concept of the Political* (University of Chicago Press, 1996); *Political Theology* (Cambridge, Mass.: MIT Press, 1985); *The Crisis of Parliamentary Democracy* (Cambridge, Mass.: MIT Press, 1985).

18 M. Mann, *Fascists* (Cambridge University Press, 2004), pp. 13–17.

19 F. Nietzsche, 'The Genealogy of Morals', 'Thus Spake Zarathustra' and 'Beyond Good and Evil' in K. Ansell-Pearson and D. Large (eds.), *The Nietzsche Reader* (Oxford: Blackwell Publishing, 2006).

20 For Strauss's ideas, see S. Drury, *The Political Ideas of Leo Strauss* (New York: St Martin's Press, 1988).

10 Liberalism and non-Western cultures

1 On this subject, see J. Rachels, 'The Challenge of Cultural Relativism' in P. Moser and T. Carson (eds.), *Moral Relativism* (Oxford University

Press, 2001). See also the other essays in this volume as well as J. Donnelly, *Universal Human Rights in Theory and Practice*, 2nd edn. (Ithaca and London: Cornell University Press, 2003), pp. 89–106.

2 www.alhewar.com/ISLAMDECL.html.

3 A. A. Mawdudi, *Human Rights in Islam* (Leicester: The Islamic Foundation, 1976), p. 10.

4 Donnelly, *Universal Human Rights*, pp. 92–4.

5 M. Khadduri, 'Human Rights in Islam', *The Annals*, 243 (January 1946), 79.

6 H. Enayat, *Modern Islamic Political Thought* (London: Macmillan, 1982), pp. 127–8; A. E. Mayer, *Islam and Human Rights* (Boulder, Colo.: Westview Press, 1991), pp. 80–2; K. Dalacoura, *Islam, Liberalism and Human Rights* (London: I. B. Tauris, 1998), p. 44.

7 The Sunna is the authentic record of the sayings and doings of the Prophet Mohammed and is generally taken to have the same sacred status as the Koran.

8 www.iranonline.com/iran/iran-info/Government/Constitution.html.

9 www.religlaw.org/interdocs/docs/cairohrislam1990.htm.

10 See the English translation in the *Arab Law Quarterly*, 8 (1993), 295–331.

11 S. H. Hashmi, 'Islamic Ethics in International Society' in S. H. Hashmi (ed.), *Islamic Political Ethics: Civil Society, Pluralism and Conflict* (Princeton University Press, 2002), pp. 151–2; M. Ruthven, *Islam in the World*, 3rd edn. (London: Granta Books, 2006), pp. 135–44; Z. Sardar, *What do Muslims Believe?* (London: Granta Books, 2006), p. 58.

12 Dalacoura, *Islam, Liberalism and Human Rights*, pp. 46–7.

13 H. Bielefeldt, 'Western vs. Islamic Human Rights Conceptions', *Political Theory*, 28(1) (2000), 106–8.

14 Bielefeldt, 'Western vs Islamic Human Rights', 108–11; C. Kurzman, 'Introduction', in C. Kurzman (ed.), *Liberal Islam: A Source Book* (Oxford University Press, 1998).

15 A. An Na'im, 'Human Rights in the Muslim World', *Harvard Human Rights Journal*, 3 (1990), quoted in Henry J. Steiner and Philip Alston, *International Human Rights in Context: Law, Politics, Morals*, 2nd edn. (Oxford University Press, 2000), pp. 390–5. See also his *Towards an Islamic Reformation: Civil Liberties, Human Rights and International Law* (Syracuse University Press, 1990), pp. 161–87.

16 One such contemporary who is made much of in Europe is Tariq Ramadan. He claims that it is possible for European Muslims to endorse liberal principles of political association without abandoning traditional or conservative Islamic views. He bases this claim on a definition of the Islamic social code in terms of core general principles and values which have to be interpreted appropriately 'in light of every specific era and

environment'. Whether this view can be called traditional or conservative is surely doubtful. See his book _To Be a European Muslim_ (Leicester: Islamic Foundation, 1999), p. 75, _passim_.

17 _The Koran_ at 4:34. translated by N. J. Dawood (London: Penguin Books, 1999): 'Men have authority over women because God has made the one superior to the other, and because they spend their wealth to maintain them. Good women are obedient.'

18 _Koran_, at 5:38. 'As for the man or woman who is guilty of theft, cut off their hands to punish them for their crimes. That is the punishment enjoined by God.'

19 _Koran_, 8:39; 9:5; 9:29.

20 Hashmi, 'Islamic Ethics', pp. 164–5; Dalacoura, _Islam, Liberalism and Human Rights_, p. 47; Mayer, _Islam and Human Rights_, pp. 93–8.

21 _Koran_ at 2:256.

22 Hashmi, 'Islamic Ethics', pp. 150–2; Ruthven, _Islam in the World_, pp. 97–9.

23 A. Abd al-Raziq, 'Message not Government, Religion not State' in Kurzman (ed.), _Liberal Islam_, pp. 29–36.

24 On the East Asian Values debate, see A. J. Langlois, _The Politics of Justice and Human Rights: South East Asia and Universalist Theory_ (Cambridge University Press, 2001), Ch. 1; J. R. Bauer and D. A. Bell (eds.), _The East Asian Challenge for Human Rights_ (Cambridge University Press, 1999); M Jacobsen and O. Bruun (eds.), _Human Rights and Asian Values_ (Richmond, Surrey: Curzon Press, 2000); Theodore de Bary, _Asian Values and Human Rights_ (Cambridge, Mass.: Harvard University Press, 1998).

25 For Lee Kuan Yew's views see F. Zakaria, 'Culture is Destiny: A Conversation with Lee Kuan Yew', _Foreign Affairs_ (March/April 1994), 109–26.

26 Inoue Tatsuo, 'Liberal Democracy and Asian Orientalism', in Bauer and Bell (eds.), _The East Asian Challenge_, Ch. 1.

27 Th. de Bary, 'Introduction' in Th. de Bary and Tu Wei-ming (eds.), _Confucianism and Human Rights_ (New York: Columbia University Press, 1998); J. Paltiel, 'Confucianism Contested: Human Rights and the Chinese Tradition in Contemporary Chinese Political Discourse' in de Bary and Wei-ming (eds.), _Confucianism_, Ch. 15; D. A. Bell and H. Chaiborg, 'Introduction' in D. A. Bell and H. Chaiborg (eds.), _Confucianism for the Modern World_ (Cambridge University Press, 2003).

28 M. Goldman, 'Confucian Influence on Intellectuals in the People's Republic of China', de Bary and Wei-ming (eds.), _Confucianism_, Ch. 14. See also the already cited essays by de Bary and Paltiel in the above volume.

29 Paltiel, 'Confucianism Contested' in de Bary and Wei-ming (eds.), *Confucianism*.

30 This picture is drawn from the following works: A. Waley (ed.), *The Analects of Confucius* (London and New York: Routledge, 2005), first published 1938; J. Chan, 'A Confucian Perspective on Human Rights for Contemporary China' in Bauer and Bell (eds.), *East Asian Challenge*, Ch. 9; Lusina Ho, 'Traditional Confucian Values and Western Legal Frameworks: The Law of Succession' in Bell and Chaiborg (eds.), *Confucianism for the Modern World*; Julia Ching, 'Human Rights: A Valid Chinese Concept?' and Wegen Chang, 'The Confucian Theory of Norms and Human Rights' in de Bary and Wei-ming (eds.), *Confucianism*.

31 Wei-ming, 'Epilogue: Human Rights as a Confucian Moral Discourse' in de Bary and Wei-ming (eds.), *Confucianism*.

32 J. Chan, 'A Confucian Perspective on Human Rights for Contemporary China' in Bauer and Bell (eds.), *East Asia Challenge*. In a personal communication, Po-Chung Chow describes Wei-ming's position as a *strong* compatibilist view of the relation between Confucianism and human rights. On this view, democracy and human rights can be derived or deduced from Confucianism. Chan's position is described as a *moderate* compatibilist view which holds that Confucianism suitably re-interpreted is not incompatible with human rights. This distinction seems right.

33 Sor-hoon Tan, *Confucian Democracy: A Deweyan Reconstruction* (State University of New York, 2005).

34 R. Panikkar, 'Is the Notion of Human Rights a Western Concept?', *Diogenes*, 120 (1982), 75–102.

35 A. Sharma, *Hinduism and Human Rights* (New Delhi: Oxford University Press, 2003), pp. 2–3.

36 Sharma, *Hinduism*, pp. 14–16.

37 C. Taylor, 'Conditions of an Unforced Consensus on Human Rights' in Bauer and Bell, *East Asia Challlenge*, Ch. 5.

38 S. Caney, 'Human Rights, Compatibility and Diverse Cultures' in S. Caney and P. Jones (eds.), *Human Rights and Global Diversity* (London: Frank Cass, 2001).

11 In defence of liberalism

1 Plato, *Republic* (Oxford: Clarendon Press, 1941), p. 311.

Index